DESIGNING CONSTRUCTIONIST FUTURES

DESIGNING CONSTRUCTIONIST FUTURES

The Art, Theory, and Practice
of Learning Designs

edited by Nathan Holbert, Matthew Berland,
and Yasmin B. Kafai

The MIT Press
Cambridge, Massachusetts
London, England

This book was set in Stone Serif by Westchester Publishing Services. Printed and bound in the United States of America.

Library of Congress Cataloging-in-Publication Data
Names: Holbert, Nathan, editor. | Berland, Matthew, editor. |
    Kafai, Yasmin B., editor.
Title: Designing constructionist futures : the art, theory, and practice of learning
    designs / edited by Nathan Holbert, Matthew Berland, and Yasmin B. Kafai.
Description: Cambridge, Massachusetts : The MIT Press, 2020. | Includes
    bibliographical references and index.
Identifiers: LCCN 2020003271 | ISBN 9780262539845 (paperback)
Subjects: LCSH: Constructivism (Education) | Computer science--Study
    and teaching. | Maker movement in education.
Classification: LCC LB1062 .D4856 2020 | DDC 370.15/2--dc23
LC record available at https://lccn.loc.gov/2020003271

10 9 8 7 6 5 4 3 2 1

CONTENTS

▌ INCREASING SCALE

II SUPPORTING EQUITY

V   THE FUTURE OF CONSTRUCTIONISM

FOREWORD: SEYMOUR *IS* A POWERFUL IDEA

Alan Kay

A special kind of genius is one who can look at what most people think they understand and see something very different, larger, and much more important—then can elevate those around them to think in ways they never thought possible. Seymour Papert is one of these, and I was catapulted into a different world when I first met him in 1968 at the first "Logo classroom" that Cynthia Solomon and he had set up.

I vividly remember the shock I felt when I realized that, although I already "understood" much of the math and computing Seymour was using, I <u>hadn't at all understood what was really important</u>! The computer could open the doors for children to real forms of mathematics and science—and powerful approaches to thinking itself—many years before even optimistic people had ever dreamed. In that instant my life's goals changed. I wanted to help with the next steps in inventing and designing computer languages and personal computers whose deep users would include children as first-class citizens.

Many of us will remember having similar life-changing moments catalyzed by Seymour.

I refer to him in the present tense because he remains vividly present in the minds of all of us who were deeply affected by him and his ideas. And he is vividly present for the children and others who have been lifted by his ideas, even though they may not know his name nor be aware that there were important starts to many of the things they enjoy learning and doing.

"Powerful Ideas" create a qualitative change in how we are able to think about things. Seymour carried a very large number of these around, and he was one himself! The ways he went about thinking about thinking and helping and encouraging everyone he met to think about thinking were qualitatively powerful and life changing.

When I first started to write this foreword, I got into the almost infinite regress of trying to explain as many important "Seymour Ideas" as possible. But such a collection would fill a book at the least, not a few pages. The reason Seymour had so many ideas is that he was trying to find the best ways to help others learn and understand "the epistemology of modern thought." This goes beyond "modern maths" or "modern science," even though both are important carriers of the larger ideas. For Seymour, "modern epistemology" was also rooted in how humans can grow and react with very new perspectives to what their senses receive and how their genetic brains and traditional cultures try to "make meanings." The "genetic epistemology" of Piaget greatly influenced Seymour's ideas, but his own approach was more flexible, both in general and especially in ways for children to find and make deep meanings of their own that would be powerful both for them and for their surrounding cultures.

Our brain/minds are set up for remembering and believing, and we treat our memories and beliefs so strongly as reality that *we seem to project them onto the world*. McLuhan's great slogan for this was: *"Until I believe it, I can't see it."* This leads to what has sometimes been called "private universes" (those set up between our ears), and considerable contention between them. Because some of our belief formation is from the social surround, parts of our private universes will be shared as tribal beliefs at different levels of tribe, but these will also be disputed at every level.

And because what's outside us often doesn't agree with our internal "realities," there are constant conflicts, most of which are dealt with by ignoring, denying, or ascribing error or evil to "what's out there?". Still, some of what is remembered and believed has been enough to get today's cultures to their next generations. It's not surprising that it took hundreds of thousands of years for our species to finally invent modern science!

Four hundred years ago Francis Bacon declared[1] that we are "marvelously led astray" in our attempts to think—via our genetics, our internal deductions, the beliefs of our cultures, the forms of our languages, and nature of our schooling—and called for a "new science" that would be a gathering and invention of heuristic methods and tools that could as much as possible get around "what's wrong with our brains."

The "new science" was so successful—partly from trying to remove human subjectivity from its heuristic methods—that it initially *missed the subjectivity that remains* because of who and what we are. In many respects, modern epistemology is the attempt to consider what "knowing" and "knowledge" and "finding out" could mean given our intrinsic difficulties with how our poor-at-thinking brain tries to think, even when trying its best: *to consider knowledge and knowing we must consider the knowers*.

---

1. Bacon, F. (1620). *Novum organum scientia.*

Taking this as a main context for pondering education in general, and of children in particular, gives rise to a rich set of ideas and explorations. We might ask: If we are still going to wind up with stories and beliefs, could we understand that they *are* stories and beliefs rather than raw reality? Could the most important ones be very careful stories? Are there ways to make these careful stories? Could we realize that we not only have to *negotiate meaning* with what's outside of our beliefs, but also with each and every other human being? And much more.

Imagine one night going into a theater with many others to see and hear beautiful people, words, music, settings, ideas, stories.... We are entranced and give ourselves over to it, and so we should: this is one of the deepest ways we have to feel life itself and the larger dimensions of being human and the stories that are us. On the very next night we go to the same building with the same audience to see and hear similar beautiful people, words, music, settings, and more. Should we again give ourselves over to it? The first night was theater, and the second is a political rally for our democracy but presented in theatrical form. The modern answer—and an aim of modern education in a democracy—should be, "No, we mustn't treat democratic politics as stories and theater." Somehow we have to be helped to learn when to open our hundred thousand–year channels for involvement and pleasure and when to close them down as much as possible so we can actually think very differently about what is going on. We can see that this is tricky—getting really good at the latter can dim out much of the pleasure and fantasy of the former. We don't want to be crushingly analytic about art: one of our modern dilemmas is to learn how to choose without dimming either mode of thought.

And before we have the luxury of that dilemma, we have the larger one of helping most of the population to learn to think in the second way at all, and especially to even be aware of the very different approaches to "knowing" and inferring.

Seymour was tireless in his efforts to get the majority of people—especially educators and parents—to see that official approaches to schooling were quite missing most of the *important qualities*. Perhaps most central of the many he carried with him was to "lead with joy": the *joy of finding things out*[2] and the *joy of feeling one's agency in a world of things, ideas, and people*. I think this is the best way to approach a highly developed set of ideas

---

2. There is an excellent essay by Richard Feynman: "The Pleasure of Finding Things Out" in a book of the same name: Feynman, R. P. (1999). *The pleasure of finding things out: The best short works of Richard P. Feynman*. New York, NY: Basic Books.

that have deep art as their base. As with art and music, which also require a lifetime of technique to be developed in all areas, *Technique should be the Servant of Art, not the Master.* The art—the humanness—has to shine through or the result is something highly intricate but dead. This is Goethe's "Gray is all Theory, but Green grows the Golden Tree of Life!"[3]

One of the challenges of the modern era is how to help children "start with their art" and the deep pleasures and feelings brought by "creating and being in the world" and yet also spend the thousands of hours needed to develop modern techniques. If we look to see what most children do spend thousands of voluntary hours doing and hence learning, we find: games and sports, experiencing stories, many kinds of social interactions including dancing, and more. This should not be surprising because these have been the main routes for children's learning since our species appeared. We are biologically disposed to learn our surrounding environment and culture, especially when our goals will be furthered, and we also are born with dispositions for learning language. Still, we sometimes forget that *what* is being talked about takes quite a while to learn, and so does *how* to talk about it. Children spend thousands of hours learning how to talk and what can be talked about.

Also not surprising, we find considerable correlations between what parents do at home and what children will spend thousands of hours learning. This can include less-usual pursuits like playing musical instruments, math and science, and more. Maria Montessori recognized the strong built-in desires of children to learn the environment and culture around them and declared that you *can't learn the 20th century in a classroom.* So she invented/designed her schools to *embody* the powerful ideas of the culture in the culture of the school "as though all the adults already understood and exhibited them." She asserted that the primary goal of early childhood education is epistemological: to have the child grow up immersed in the most powerful ideas of their time (as she said, "the 20th century rather than the 10th") so that their *basic outlook* is through powerful ideas thinking and feeling.

This was picked up very strongly by Seymour in his parallel: "To learn French best, go to France; to learn Maths best, go to MathLand." I think this is the key idea, and is more important than a great children's programming language on their very own personal computer. This is because most of the really powerful ideas of our modern era don't need much in the way of advanced technologies to be learned, but most children do desperately

---

3. Grau ist alle Theorie, und grün des Lebens goldner Baum. von Goethe, J. W. (1837). *Faust.* New York, NY: Verlags-handlung.

need a learning culture around them full of the most powerful perspectives embodied in the human groups they are part of. One of the best uses of technologies is to amplify already positive and enlightened interest and movement. We can sing and dance with our own biological technologies, but musical instruments really do add something to a musically inclined culture. We can make things from what's around us, but tools really do help. We can do science and math without computers—even for children— but we can vastly enlarge the range of things that can be worked on and made relevant in the world of the child.

On the other hand, "the music isn't in the piano," and the "math and science aren't in the computer." We don't want to put children in a state of one hundred thousand years ago surrounded by modern gear. They will use it, but they won't be able to invent enough by themselves (imagine someone twice as smart as Leonardo being born in 10,000 BC: he would not get far).

This is why, for most children, the critical education crises of our time cannot be helped by better technologies. We need better cultures, and we have to start by doing as Montessori did: by creating better artificial cultures in our nurturing and schooling of our young. At the 1972 ACM National Conference in Boston, Seymour gave a talk in the middle of which he spontaneously jumped on a table to show how children could get insights by "playing turtle" with their bodies. The table was shaking back and forth; Seymour would get close to the edges; the crowd full of teachers and computer people was oohing and aahing—the whole thing was brilliant and vividly memorable. Later, having coffee, I asked Seymour whether he was afraid that the table would collapse, and he said, "Oh no, I tested it out ahead of time!"

During that chat I also asked him how he came to write so well. He said that he realized that had to re-teach himself once he understood that much of his reading audience was going to be teachers and others involved with helping children learn—and that it had taken him about two years of conscious work to retool his approach to writing. This made a huge impression on me, to add to all the other huge impressions he had made on me. He was trying from the start to *help the helpers* grow enough to fill the expanded roles that our time requires.

Seymour had many powerful ideas of his own. He explained the powerful ideas of others and got us to find more of them. And he catalyzed many of us to try to find new powerful ideas and to teach others how to as best we could.

Seymour *is* a powerful idea!

INTRODUCTION: FIFTY YEARS OF CONSTRUCTIONISM

Nathan Holbert, Matthew Berland, and Yasmin B. Kafai

> People are both world makers and beings-in-the-world: they at once create their habitats, inhabit their creations, and become "inhabited" by them.
> —Ackermann, 2004, p. 26

More than fifty years ago, a computer language was created specifically to enable children to control what were then the world's most powerful and expensive machines. The goal wasn't to train the children to be mindless operators of these machines by punching in commands dictated by some expert. Nor was the goal to use the programming language to efficiently deliver information to those children. Instead, the language, and computers more generally, would be tools in the hands of children, who would learn that they are all creative, inquisitive, serious, and thoughtful young thinkers. This has been a core goal of constructionists ever since: to respect children as creators, to enable them to engage in making meaning for themselves through construction, and to do this by democratizing access to the world's most creative and powerful tools.

Constructionism, as a concept, was born from that premise. Constructionism is a framework for learning to understand something by making an artifact for and with other people, which, to be built, requires the builders to use that understanding. That said, Seymour Papert, the definer of the term and parent of the field, was somewhat cagey about a precise definition for constructionism, for a good reason: if he believed that constructionism is something worth understanding, the reader would have to construct his or her own understanding of the term rather than only read a definition.

Of course, this is but one possible definition. There are probably numerous similar definitions used throughout the history of constructionism, and each reflects its context. Early definitions of constructionism located it entirely in one brain: a learner learns something by making an artifact.

However, research in the learning sciences has shown that learning does not reside in one individual's brain. Consequently, as the field has integrated distributed, situated, and sociocultural models of learning, so too have our definitions of constructionism evolved.

Similarly, this volume too reflects that diversity. It follows two earlier books of collected works that describe core constructionist projects, ideas, and theories. The first book, simply titled *Constructionism* (Harel & Papert, 1991)—written almost entirely by Papert and his students—laid out this design paradigm's theoretical foundations. The second book, *Constructionism in Practice* (Kafai & Resnick, 1996), extended the constructionist agenda by describing new tools and implementations toward making a reality the vision of the child programming the computer rather than the computer programming the child (Papert, 1980). Constructionist ideas have not been static in the intervening years. In this book, *Designing Constructionist Futures*, we have invited original contributors as well as emerging scholars that have been inspired by and, in many cases, brought up on the tools and ideas discussed in those earlier volumes to articulate models of constructionism that engage deeply with culture, communities, contexts, race, ethnicity, modes of power, and modalities of agency. In other words, the book itself exists as an argument that constructionism can learn and has learned from learning sciences and educational research—from culturally responsive teaching, notions of power, redefinitions of the possibilities of education as resistance, and conversation—and that, in turn, educational research can, we hope, learn from constructionism—how to foster understanding and powerful ideas in humane, collaborative, cooperative, and other ways that deeply respect learners and their innate goodness and creativity.

A VERY BRIEF HISTORY OF CONSTRUCTIONISM

Although the term *constructionism* was officially coined in a chapter of that first volume edited by Harel and Papert (1991), many of the ideas were formed two decades earlier, as recounted by Feurzeig (2010) and Solomon (2016). The different time periods of constructionist activity over the past fifty years can loosely be categorized as the *Logo*, the *Project Headlight*, and the *Scratch* years.

When Papert arrived in 1964 at the Massachusetts Institute of Technology (MIT) after having spent five years at Jean Piaget's Le Centre International d'Épistémologie Génétique in Geneva, he was asked to join the Educational Technology Department, a research group formed by Wally Feurzeig at

Bolt, Beranek, and Newman (BBN), as a consultant. Logo was developed as a dialect of Lisp by Seymour Papert, Daniel Bobrow, Richard Grant, Cynthia Solomon, Wally Feurzeig, and Frank Frazier; the latter also published the first Logo manual in 1967. Together, these visionaries imagined the possibility of putting the most powerful and "protean" tool for knowledge construction—the computer—into the hands of children decades before the existence of the personal computer. The first version of Logo was piloted with students in the Hanscom Field School in Lincoln, Massachusetts, funded by the US Office of Naval Research, whereas later studies in various Boston schools were funded by the National Science Foundation.

Initially, Logo only allowed children to play with words and sentences. In an effort to expand what children could do with Logo, the team at MIT began experimenting with using Logo to drive a physical robot. Because of the domed shape of early robotic prototypes, the Logo robot became known as the "turtle." Eventually, the physical robot migrated to a digital screen and the turtle became a sort of digital cursor. By issuing simple commands to this turtle, the children could use Logo to create computer graphics. The language of Logo resembled play commands children might give to one another in a game of "Simon Says," imagining themselves as the turtle, walking out and drawing squares, circles, spirals, and more. These designs and explorations engaged children in playfully tinkering with complex mathematical concepts, leveraging their intuitive understanding of how their body functions in the world to experiment with and articulate ideas at the heart of geometry, calculus, and computing.

In 1970 Papert founded the Logo Laboratory at MIT and continued the research of educational applications in Logo. A report first published by the MIT Artificial Intelligence (AI) Lab titled "Twenty Things to Do with a Computer" (Papert & Solomon, 1971) captured the various programming activities that had been developed and tested in the previous years with Logo. It also became the foundation of the book *Mindstorms* (Papert, 1980), which introduced the larger public to the idea of how young children could engage and learn with computers. MIT also hosted several Logo conferences that brought together an international group of educators and computer scientists interested in the various applications of programming to not just mathematics but also the arts.

In 1982 three years before the MIT Media Lab launched, Seymour Papert and Nicholas Negroponte decamped to France to open (with support of the French government) the World Center for Computation and Human Resources, which put Logo and computers in classrooms in both Paris and in Dakar, Senegal, with the goal of making computers accessible to children all over the world. When Papert returned to MIT, he launched an initiative called Project Headlight in the Hennigan School, a public elementary school located in Jamaica Plain (an under-resourced neighborhood in Boston). Project Headlight would showcase a future of schools in which computers were readily accessible to all children and teachers and integrated throughout the curriculum. This was part of the MIT Media Lab's overall mission to "invent the future" (Brand, 1987).

In Project Headlight, over 80 computers were set up in one of the wings of the Hennigan School. However, rather than place these computers in a computer lab where students might only encounter them once every week for 45 minutes before returning to their classrooms, the project took advantage of the open architecture of the school, which had pods of classrooms with no walls around large open areas. Four circles with 20 computers each were set up in a way that not only made the computers accessible but also made what the students were working on with the computers visible to all passing through the school wing. Each student from first to fifth grades had access to these computers at least one hour every day, in addition to individual workstations in their classrooms. A team of adventurous teachers and hundreds of elementary students worked with a large group of graduate students from the MIT Media Lab to use these computers to develop new activities, curricula, and educational technologies.

What emerged from *Project Headlight* in the late 1980s and early 1990s were various illustrations of how computers and programming could become part of schooling in meaningful and novel ways. For instance, the Instructional Software Design Project, conceived by Harel (Harel & Papert, 1990), challenged many of the traditional programming approaches by asking students to develop and program software applications that would teach younger students in their school about mathematics. Rather than writing short programs, as was common in schools that introduced students to Logo, Basic, or Pascal, students worked on complex programs over long periods of time. Programming was integrated into the learning of mathematics and promoted by encouraging students to use code to explain and represent their ideas.

This approach was the bedrock for what today has become one of the most popular approaches to introduce programming in schools: rather than learning coding for the sake of coding, learning to code is contextualized as part of developing applications such as games (Kafai, 1995), stories, or animations (Kafai & Burke, 2014). The work in Project Headlight presented a bold vision, but it came to an end as personal computers themselves became less flexible: multimedia CD-ROMs and web browsers no longer required students to learn the language of computers. Programming was removed from schools entirely in the 1990s when high-stakes testing took over.

For those reasons, the *Scratch* years, which continue to the present, did not start in schools like the previous projects. Instead, Scratch was developed as part of the Computer Clubhouse, which was launched in the early 1990s at the then Computer Museum in Boston (Resnick, Rusk, & Cooke, 1998). Eventually the Computer Clubhouse, which offered youth from underserved communities access to creative computing, grew into a network with over 100 clubhouses located in community centers around the globe (Kafai, Peppler, & Chapman, 2009). Computer Clubhouses showcased a rich Photoshop and remix culture, in which members connected to digital media in new ways. In an effort to connect coding with this digital media production culture, Resnick, Kafai, and Maeda submitted a proposal in 2002 to the National Science Foundation that outlined the development of a programming environment and community that would be focused on the manipulation of multimedia; this led to the development of Scratch. In 2007, after several years of prototyping various versions in Los Angeles and Boston clubhouses, Scratch, the programming tool, was released together with the ability to upload and share programs on an MIT server.

Of course, there are many, many other examples of constructionist activities that, because of space constraints, we are unable to detail. There were international efforts to spread Logo to communities in Thailand, Costa Rica, and Brazil; telecommunication technologies and Logo activities that encourage learners to play with language and writing and decades-long cycles of development and iteration of physical computing technologies that included both open-source hardware and the hugely popular Lego brick (Blikstein, 2015; Resnick & Ocko, 1990). Furthermore, the development of parallel programming was captured in programming tools such as StarLogo (Resnick, 1997) and NetLogo (Wilensky, 1999), introducing K-12 students once again to powerful modeling tools.

Today the computer is ubiquitous, Logo-like software can be found on devices of all kinds, and new fabrication tools and technologies that enable anyone to create sophisticated physical artifacts continue to emerge. Though Papert's work and the Logo language were central in the initial formation of constructionism, the past fifty years has seen constructionist thought and design nurtured and extended by teachers, facilitators, parents, practitioners, and scholars around the world. This volume is an effort to capture that work, to reenvision constructionism in this new context, to claim constructionist activity in emerging educational movements, and to offer potential directions for how constructionism can continue to evolve into the future.

RECONSTRUCTING CONSTRUCTIONISM

Papert famously enjoyed offering parables to explain the ideas behind constructionism. One of his most famous was that of Mathland. Mathland wasn't a video game, or a virtual environment; it was a hypothetical community whose culture and language was mathematics. Just as a child who grows up in France easily learns not only the French language but also what it means to *be* French, so too would mathematics become a core part of a Mathland resident's language, identity, and way of being. Logo (and many of the other technologies innovated by constructionists over the years) was not only a tool for teaching coding or even mathematics but also an attempt to build a community, culture, and context.

Constructionism is about playing and creating with powerful ideas in meaningful and authentic contexts. As constructionists, we aim to leverage design and theories of cognition to create spaces, tools, and technologies that empower more learners to do more things. What it means to do that work has changed, just as the world has changed considerably since constructionism first reached widespread awareness in the form of *Mindstorms* in 1980. Technology is not just smaller, faster, and cheaper, it is ubiquitous and has fundamentally transformed how we exist and interact with our environment and one another. Likewise, theories of cognition have begun to recognize that cognition extends beyond the head and into the world, that all knowledge is cultural and that learning is interaction. And so, as constructionism invites us to do, we must take apart our prior conceptions of constructionism to examine its core components, affordances, and relationships; bring in new perspectives and possibilities offered by evolving theory and technology; and then rebuild constructionism to suit this new context in which we find ourselves.

CONSTRUCTIONISM IN A NEW AGE OF TECHNOLOGY

Papert's predictions about the availability of computers have come to fruition. Computational power has become ubiquitous, and few still debate whether technology has a useful role to play in the learning process. Smartphones—which are multiple times more powerful than the classroom computers that first ran Logo—are owned by over a third of the world's population (eMarketer, n.d.). Though it is reasonable to question whether access to these devices, which are often closed to tinkering, has truly democratized access to computational practices, their inclusion of powerful cameras and sensors and their always-networked architecture have enabled users to engage in a variety of creative digital media construction enterprises, including movie making, app development, game making, and more. Smartphones are, of course, powerful in part because of their ability to make the internet mobile. The Internet, which Papert (1993) described in vivid detail in his book *The Children's Machine*, has reached maturity and become a place not only for information retrieval but also for public construction and sharing.

As these technologies proliferate, corporations, government officials, parents, and children across the world have come to agree that coding is not only a useful skill but also an invaluable one. Coding movements in the United States, Europe, and Asia promise to make programming as core to the curriculum as reading, writing, and arithmetic (Obama, 2016). And while educators continue to debate the very important question "to what end," the idea of the child programming the computer (rather than the computer programming the child) is no longer considered revolutionary. And yet, as computation is increasingly embedded in physical spaces such as our homes, schools, parks, transportation, and others, our ability to function in, move through, and be identified in physical spaces is determined and defined by algorithms—algorithms that are not visible to citizens and, with the advent of neural nets, may even be opaque to their designers (Shapiro, Fiebrink, & Norvig, 2018). To meet this demand, new authoring environments, curriculum, and education infrastructure have been developed to lower the floor, raise the ceiling, and widen the walls of participation in computer science. While worldwide efforts to increase access to coding practices are promising, these efforts have come quite late and have yet to diversify the homogenous community of coders that have built the computational world we now live in (National Science Foundation [NSF], 2015).

The extremely low cost of computer hardware and high-tech prototyping equipment has also led to a revolution in making and fabrication. Three-dimensional (3D) objects designed on a computer can now be printed or cut out in a huge variety of materials using machines that fit onto a desk. Computers themselves can be built with few components and a couple dollars and be made of metal and wire, or fabric and thread. Devices that can read data from the world and drive motors, actuators, LEDs, and sensors are not only widely available, they're increasingly understandable, playful, and personal. Further, making is no longer restricted to electrical components. Our understanding of biology itself has reached a level where tinkering with the building blocks of life is no longer science fiction but is becoming accessible in school classrooms (Kafai, Telhan, Hogan, Lui, Anderson, Walker, & Hanna, 2017). Research on and with these tools and practices has provided new insight into constructionist commitments such as the centrality of sharing (Brennan, Monroy-Hernández, & Resnick, 2010), the role of personal choice and play in construction activities (Berland, 2016; Honey & Kanter, 2013; Kafai & Burke, 2016; Weintrop, Holbert, Horn, & Wilensky, 2016), the trade-offs of different representations of code (Kahn, 1999; Weintrop & Wilensky, 2017; Wilkerson-Jerde, Wagh, & Wilensky, 2015), the relationship between materials and practices (Buchholz, Shively, Peppler, & Wohlwend, 2014), and a new appreciation for values in addition to interests (DesPortes, Spells, & DiSalvo, 2016; Holbert, 2016) to name but a few.

While technological innovation has led many to embrace construction activities in coding and making, too often these efforts neglect the social and cultural values at the heart of the constructionist design paradigm.

CONSTRUCTIONISM IN A NEW AGE OF COGNITIVE THEORY

Constructionism's birth from Piaget's constructivism has meant that much of the community's research on learning has focused on the individual. While constructionist designers have always acknowledged the importance of social interaction, tools, representations, and context, learning in constructionist spaces is generally described in terms of changing mental knowledge structures. However, new theories of cognition have gained prominence since the two previous volumes of constructionist writings were published. These new theories don't just suggest that tools, social interaction, the environment, and the body support conceptual change; rather, they propose that cognition is at the intersection of these interactions— that cognition is in fact interaction itself. What, then, is the story of learning in constructionist design in light of these new theories of cognition?

Constructionist design fits neatly into descriptions of learning described by theories of embodied cognition. The earliest constructionist environment, Logo, relied on what Papert called *body syntonicity* (Papert, 1980). Creating with the turtle meant putting oneself inside of this external agent: imagining walking and rotating to draw the shapes and objects that were drawn onto the floor or screen. But as we shift from seeing the body as an external appendage of the brain, and instead define it as part of the cognitive system itself, body syntonicity shifts from being a useful design principle to a fundamental description of learning. This shift raises new questions for how to design and study constructionist environments. For example, what does our understanding of the role of the sensorimotor system in cognition suggest about both how learning happens in perspective taking systems ("playing turtle") as well as how we might observe and measure this learning (Ackermann, 1996; Lindgren, 2012; Wilensky & Reisman, 2006)? How does our understanding of gesture and embodiment explain prior research with Logo, or what does it suggest about the design of new constructionist environments using emerging immersive technologies or motion tracking (Abrahamson, 2009; Enyedy, Danish, Delacruz, & Kumar, 2012; Nemirovsky, Tierney, & Wright, 1998)?

The advent of sociocultural theory both offers theoretical underpinnings for some prior constructionist commitments, such as the importance of sharing or of building with materials and artifacts, and expands how we think about and study what it means to learn in a constructionist system. Rather than define learning as in-the-head conceptual change, sociocultural theory invites us to view all knowledge as cultural and learning as an interaction between a community of learners, the materials and tools, the local environment, the historical context, and more (Cole, 1995; Lave & Wenger, 1991; Rogoff, Paradise, Arauz, Correa-Chávez, & Angelillo, 2003). Learning in a constructionist environment then isn't just a story of mental knowledge structures mirroring the hands-on construction of an artifact, it's a description of a distributed and social activity system evolving and changing in interaction—the construction itself is the learning (Barron, Gomez, Martin, & Pinkard, 2014; Calabrese Barton & Tan, 2018; DiSalvo, Crowley, & Norwood, 2008).

Furthermore, when adopting a sociocultural model of cognition, the methods of capturing and describing learning in a constructionist space must also change. Here the unit of study is not the head of the learner; it is layers upon layers of ecosystems (Bronfenbrenner, 1979). Rather than attempt to isolate particular concepts or skills and measure how these change before and after the use of constructionist tools and interventions, or between a constructionist and nonconstructionist tool, we must instead leverage techniques and technologies that allow us to capture the process itself. We need to document the dialogue between the learner and the materials, the building primitives, the physical space in which they work, other builders, the instructor, the framing of their construction activity, and more. As always, this dialogue is bidirectional with these artifacts, materials, spaces, and communities not only affecting the learner but also being changed, defined, and modified by the learner as well.

THEMES IN DESIGNING CONSTRUCTIONIST FUTURES

These technological and pedagogical innovations have been central to the evolution of constructionism over the past fifty years. A key motivation for the design of this volume was to document that evolution, as well as to lay claim to the ways in which constructionist efforts have defined many of today's most exciting areas of educational research. Constructionism in the last decade has gone far beyond the initial successes of Logo and Mindstorms: the return of coding in school, now an international phenomenon, the growth of the Maker Movement and efforts to bring these into schools, the development of constructionist communities around Scratch, ScratchEd, and Globaloria are but a few of many recent accomplishments. Indeed, the massive numbers of the Scratch community (30+ million projects and 30+ million users) suggest that these ideas are significant, spreading, and growing.

Putting together a volume that captures the breadth and complexity of activities, research, and designs has been a tall order. The chapters in the book are a testament to the many directions constructionist ideas have developed. We intentionally invited an international and diverse group of scholars who situate their work in a variety of traditions and methodologies. We have asked these authors to be brief in their writing and to limit their citations to those most central to their argument; we suggest that readers interested in going deeper on a topic follow up on those cited sources for more information. We hope that by continuing to expand the scope of the community, we can together reconstruct constructionism for our present context and offer perspectives and possibilities for how constructionism might evolve in the future.

This volume is divided into five themes reflecting the wide space of work currently being done in constructionism. In the first section, *Increasing Scale*, we examine how constructionist design can both support large numbers of learners and function within diverse contexts from schools, to the home, to virtual spaces addressing one of the early concerns that only individual classes or small groups could engage in such activities. Perhaps not surprisingly, the many ways in which young people and educators encounter and use Scratch are a dominant theme of this section. But Scratch is by no means the only success story of constructionism increasing in scale. The innovations documented in the creation and expansion of Globaloria, principles behind the design of constructionist toys and technologies for children of all ages, and DIY technologies that support learners in sharing constructions have all been important in the expansion of constructionism to millions of students around the world. Finally, this section also examines how constructionist design might be used to enrich the learning experiences of educators, whether during a few weekends in the summer or over two decades in a small school in Thailand.

Possibly the most critical challenge faced by constructionism is the equitable distribution of and access to resources, facilitators, tools, projects, and activities. Scale must not come at the cost of equity. Making emerging and powerful technologies available to children should not mean many of the projects and ideas are only available to wealthy schools and communities. And empowering learners to pursue ideas of interest, or to take time to explore and experiment, must not be only for those with the means and privilege to elevate personal interests above community values and needs. In the second section, *Supporting Equity,* authors explore how young people use their unique individual and communal perspectives, values, and voices, through constructionist design efforts, to make meaningful change in their environment, communities, and world. The nature of and the culture surrounding the tools and materials matter, as do the ways in which constructionist design communicates what it means to make and why.

While early constructionist writings focused on the individual—effectively ignoring the sociocultural implications and ramifications of their work—by incorporating emerging cognitive theories, constructionists have made important headway in understanding the social dimensions of learning. In the third section, *Expanding the Social*, we see the implications of social practice taken up across multiple contexts in multiple projects. For instance, what is created and learned in the construction process is greatly affected by who we build with, and for whom we build. By moving our analytical lens beyond the individual, we begin to see how ideas, artifacts, and experiences emerge from interactions among bodies, conversations, and the physical space itself. However, creating communities around creativity and technology is hard, and success is not ensured.

In constructionism there has always been a focus on the creative. For example, creative computing in Logo and beyond emphasizes the notion that learning to code can serve to express creativity rather than to simply develop technical skills. In the fourth section, *Developing the Creative*, authors engage deeply with the implications of learning as a creative process of construction. What can constructionists learn from the arts and research on creativity? How can constructionist design expand to incorporate new materials, practices, and epistemologies? And how can these creative enterprises be supported and enacted in the constraints of formal classrooms?

But the process of constructing constructionism is not yet complete. And so, as we look forward to the challenges of the future, we also hope that this volume offers a few critical agendas for the current and next generation of constructionist researchers, educators, and designers to consider. In the fifth and final section, *The Future of Constructionism,* we engage leading constructionist visionaries in a conversation about where constructionism, design, and research might go next. While admitting to the many barriers to expanding constructionism into existing educational systems and spaces, Mitchel Resnick is optimistic that with active efforts to develop new technologies and to engage a broad range of stakeholders and communities into the learning experience, the future of education will be one where kids have the time, opportunity, and support to meaningfully engage with and transform their world. Leah Buechley imagines that this transformation will necessarily require looking beyond science and mathematics disciplines—to being inspired by aesthetics, to experiment with new materials and practices, and to embrace the humanities. Orkan Telhan and Yasmin Kafai examine how innovations in molecular biology will increasingly play a role in transforming our thinking from *building* toward *growing* in the future. Echoing Buechley's recognition that the world's social, political, and environmental challenges are increasingly beyond the scope of STEM domains as they have been traditionally conceived, Telhan and Kafai see biological materials and new molecular engineering techniques as a central tool in humanity's future. And yet, Ben Shapiro points out that in our excitement to engage learners in imagining and creating new systems and technologies, we must take time to encourage designers to consider both the good and evil that might be done with their designs. Finally, in a conversation that occurred shortly before his passing, Michael Eisenberg reminds the constructionist community to continue to elevate children's playful ideas and idiosyncratic passions. Eisenberg also warns that society's corporate-skewed notions of science, and of what it means to be a success, is incommensurate with the constructionist value system.

CLOSING WORDS

In one of his earliest writings, *Teaching Children Thinking,* Papert (1971) outlined a

> grander vision of an educational system in which technology is not used in the form of processing children but as something that the child himself will learn to manipulate, to extend, to apply to projects, thereby gaining a greater and more articulate mastery of the world, a sense of power of applied knowledge and a self-confidently realistic image of himself as an intellectual agent. Stated more simply, I believe with Dewey, Montessori and Piaget, that children learn by doing and by thinking about what they do. And so the fundamental ingredients of educational innovation must be better things to do and better ways to think about oneself doing these things ... (p. 1)

Papert saw clearly that innovative technologies often perpetuate traditional practices rather than providing new, better agencies; these struggles were present then as much as they are today. Nearly fifty years later, we can see powerful realizations of this vision, many of them captured in this volume. But we cannot rest there, because educational innovation should never be just about becoming an intellectual agent but always also about becoming a critical agent (Freire, 1972). The constructionist work of today, and tomorrow, must be dedicated to laying a foundation for learners' critical engagement that allows them to question how the world in which they live is constructed, interrogate and challenge that construction, and to imagine and participate in the construction of an improved, more equitable world.

REFERENCES

Abrahamson, D. (2009). Embodied design: Constructing means for constructing meaning. *Educational Studies in Mathematics, 70*(1), 27–47. https://doi.org/10.1007/s10649 -008-9137-1

Ackermann, E. (1996). Perspective-taking and object construction: Two keys to learning. In Y. B. Kafai & M. Resnick (Eds.), *Constructionism in practice: Designing, thinking, and learning in a digital world* (pp. 25–37). Mahwah, NJ: Lawrence Erlbaum. https:// doi.org/10.4324/9780203053492-8

Ackerman, E. (2004). Constructing knowledge and transforming the world. In M. Tokoro and L.Steels (Eds.), *A learning zone of one's own: Sharing representations and flow in collaborative learning environments* (pp. 15–37). Washington, DC: IOS Press.

Barron, B., Gomez, K., Martin, C. K., & Pinkard, N. (2014). *The digital youth network: Cultivating digital media citizenship in urban communities.* Cambridge, MA: MIT Press.

Berland, M. (2016). Making, tinkering, and computational literacy. In K. Peppler, E. Halverson, & Y. B. Kafai (Eds.), *Makeology: Makers as learners* (Vol. 2, pp. 196–205). New York, NY: Routledge.

Blikstein, P. (2015). Computationally enhanced toolkits for children: Historical review and a framework for future design. *Foundations and Trends Human–Computer Interaction, 9*(1), 1–68.

Brand, S. (1987). *The media lab: Inventing the future at MIT.* New York, NY: Penguin.

Brennan, K., Monroy-Hernández, A., & Resnick, M. (2010). Making projects, making friends: Online community as catalyst for interactive media creation. *New Directions for Youth Development, 2010*(128), 75–83. https://doi.org/10.1002/yd.377

Bronfenbrenner, U. (1979). *The ecology of human development: Experiment by nature and design.* Cambridge, MA: Harvard University Press.

Buchholz, B., Shively, K., Peppler, K., & Wohlwend, K. (2014). Hands on, hands off: Gendered access in crafting and electronics practices. *Mind, Culture, and Activity*, *21*(4), 278–297. https://doi.org/10.1080/10749039.2014.939762

Calabrese Barton, A., & Tan, E. (2018). A longitudinal study of equity-oriented STEM-rich making among youth from historically marginalized communities. *American Educational Research Journal*, *55*(4), 761–800. https://doi.org/10.3102/0002831218758668

Cole, M. (1995). Cultural-historical psychology: A meso-genetic approach. In L. M. W. Martin, K. Nelson, & E. Tobach (Eds.), *Sociocultural psychology: Theory and practice of doing and knowing* (pp. 168–204). Cambridge, UK: Cambridge University Press.

DesPortes, K., Spells, M., & DiSalvo, B. (2016, June). Interdisciplinary computing and the emergence of boundary objects: A case-study of dance and technology. Presented at the 12th International Conference on the Learning Sciences, Singapore, Singapore.

DiSalvo, B. J., Crowley, K., & Norwood, R. (2008). Learning in context digital games and young black men. *Games and Culture*, *3*(2), 131–141. https://doi.org/10.1177/1555412008314130

eMarketer. (n.d.). *Smartphone penetration worldwide 2014–2021*. Retrieved October 26, 2018, from https://www.statista.com/statistics/203734/global-smartphone-penetration-per-capita-since-2005/

Enyedy, N., Danish, J. A., Delacruz, G., & Kumar, M. (2012). Learning physics through play in an augmented reality environment. *International Journal of Computer-Supported Collaborative Learning*, *7*(3), 347–378. https://doi.org/10.1007/s11412-012-9150-3

Feurzeig, W. (2010). Toward a culture of creativity: A personal perspective on Logo's early years and ongoing potential. *International Journal of Computers for Mathematical Learning*, *15*(3), 257–265. https://doi.org/10.1007/s10758-010-9168-4

Freire, P. (1972). *Pedagogy of the oppressed*. New York, NY: Herder and Herder.

Harel, I., & Papert, S. (1990). Software design as a learning environment. *Interactive Learning Environments*, *1*(1), 1–32. https://doi.org/10.1080/1049482900010102

Harel, I., & Papert, S. (Eds.). (1991). *Constructionism*. Westport, CT: Ablex Publishing.

Holbert, N. (2016). Leveraging cultural values and "ways of knowing" to increase diversity in maker activities. *International Journal of Child-Computer Interaction*, *9–10*, 33–39. https://doi.org/10.1016/j.ijcci.2016.10.002

Honey, M., & Kanter, D. E. (2013). *Design, make, play: Growing the next generation of STEM innovators*. New York, NY: Routledge.

Kafai, Y. B. (1995). *Minds in play: Computer game design as a context for children's learning*. Hillsdale, NJ: Lawrence Erlbaum Associates.

Kafai, Y. B., & Burke, Q. (2014). *Connected code: Why children need to learn programming*. Cambridge, MA: MIT Press.

Kafai, Y. B., & Burke, Q. (2016). *Connected gaming: What making video games can teach us about learning and literacy*. Cambridge, MA: MIT Press.

Kafai, Y. B., Peppler, K. A., & Chapman, R. N. (2009). *The Computer Clubhouse: Constructionism and creativity in youth communities. Technology, Education–Connections*. New York, NY: Teachers College Press.

Kafai, Y. B., & Resnick, M. (Eds.). (1996). *Constructionism in practice: Designing, thinking, and learning in a digital world*. New York, NY: Routledge.

Kafai, Y. B., Telhan, O., Hogan, K., Lui, D., Anderson, E., Walker, J., & Hanna, S. (2017). Growing designs with biomakerlab in high school classrooms. In *IDC '17: Proceedings of the 2017 Conference on Interaction Design and Children* (pp. 503–508). New York, NY: ACM. https://doi.org/10.1145/3078072.3084316

Kahn, K. (1999). From prolog to Zelda to ToonTalk. In D. Schreye (Ed.), *Logic Programming: Proceedings of the 1999 International Conference on Logic Programming* (pp. 67–78). Cambridge, MA: MIT Press.

Lave, J., & Wenger, E. (1991). *Situated learning: Legitimate peripheral participation*. London, UK: Cambridge University Press.

Lindgren, R. (2012). Generating a learning stance through perspective-taking in a virtual environment. *Computers in Human Behavior, 28*(4), 1130–1139. https://doi.org/10.1016/j.chb.2012.01.021

National Science Foundation. (2015). *Women, minorities, and persons with disabilities in science and engineering*. Retrieved from http://www.nsf.gov/statistics/wmpd/

Nemirovsky, R., Tierney, C., & Wright, T. (1998). Body motion and graphing. *Cognition and Instruction, 16*, 199–172.

Obama, B. (2016, January 30). *Weekly address: Giving every student an opportunity to learn through computer science for all*. Retrieved November 23, 2016, from https://www.whitehouse.gov/the-press-office/2016/01/30/weekly-address-giving-every-student-opportunity-learn-through-computer

Papers, S. (1971). *Teaching children thinking*. AIM-247. Cambridge, MA: MIT.

Papert, S. (1980). *Mindstorms: Children, computers and powerful ideas*. New York, NY: Basic Books.

Papert, S. (1993). *The children's machine: Rethinking school in the age of the computer*. New York, NY: Basic Books.

Papert, S., & Solomon, C. (1971). Twenty things to do with a computer. Retrieved from http://dspace.mit.edu/handle/1721.1/5836

Resnick, M. (1997). *StarLogo reference manual*. Cambridge, MA: MIT Media Laboratory.

Resnick, M., & Ocko, S. (1990). LEGO/Logo: Learning through and about design. In *Constructionist learning* (pp. 121–128). Cambridge, MA: MIT Media Laboratory.

Resnick, M., Rusk, N., & Cooke, S. (1998). The computer clubhouse: Technological fluency in the inner-city. In *High technology and low income communities* (pp. 266–286). Cambridge, MA: MIT Press.

Rogoff, B., Paradise, R., Arauz, R. M., Correa-Chávez, M., & Angelillo, C. (2003). First-hand learning through intent participation. *Annual Review of Psychology*, *54*(1), 175–203. https://doi.org/10.1146/annurev.psych.54.101601.145118

Shapiro, R. B., Fiebrink, R., & Norvig, P. (2018). How machine learning impacts the undergraduate computing curriculum. *Communications of the ACM*, *61*(11), 27–29. https://doi.org/10.1145/3277567

Solomon, C. (2016, February). *A personal history of kids and computers: Toasting Seymour Papert and Marvin Minsky* [video presentation]. Presented at Constructionism 2016, Bangkok, Thailand. Retrieved from https://www.youtube.com/watch?v=z0A1Nx7EDis&feature=youtu.be

Weintrop, D., Holbert, N., Horn, M. S., & Wilensky, U. (2016). Computational thinking in constructionist video games. *International Journal of Game-Based Learning*, *6*(1), 1–17. https://doi.org/10.4018/IJGBL.2016010101

Weintrop, D., & Wilensky, U. (2017). Comparing block-based and text-based programming in high school computer science classrooms. *ACM Transactions on Computing Education*, *18*(1), 3:1–3:25. https://doi.org/10.1145/3089799

Wilensky, U. (1999). *NetLogo*. Evanston, IL: Center for Connected Learning and Computer-Based Modeling, Northwestern University. http://ccl.northwestern.edu/netlogo/

Wilensky, U., & Reisman, K. (2006). Thinking like a wolf, a sheep, or a firefly: Learning biology through constructing and testing computational theories—An embodied modeling approach. *Cognition and Instruction*, *24*(2), 171–209. https://doi.org/10.1207/s1532690xci2402_1

Wilkerson-Jerde, M., Wagh, A., & Wilensky, U. (2015). Balancing curricular and pedagogical needs in computational construction kits: Lessons from the DeltaTick Project. *Science Education*, *99*(3), 465–499. https://doi.org/10.1002/sce.21157

I   INCREASING SCALE

One of major challenges for constructionism has been to overcome its perception as a boutique theory, one that works well for individual learners and small classrooms but would not scale up to districts and massive communities. The chapters in this section are testament to the contrary: they document how millions of youth flock to Scratch to program and share projects with each other; as thousands of educators organize in learning communities, sharing teaching experiences and learning activities; and whole countries implement constructionist-infused math inquiries—to name but a few examples.

The success story of Scratch, launched in 2007, which moved Logo into visual programming and provided an online community, begins this section. Chapter 1, "Engaging Learners in Constructing Constructionist Environments" by Dasgupta, Hill, and Monroy-Hernández, showcases new programming features, special "community blocks" that not only let Scratch users create projects but also help them understand how participation data are collected, used, and disseminated on the site and within many existing online communities. By giving users the opportunity to creatively play and develop personalized projects with these blocks, students became more cognizant of numerous issues surrounding big data today, whether a realization of the privacy implication of data collection and retention or possible avenues for exclusion through data-driven algorithms. These kinds of creative and exploratory investigations are also open to much younger users, as Bers illustrates in chapter 2, "Playgrounds and Microworlds: Learning to Code in Early Childhood," describing learning experiences with ScratchJr and KIBO robotics designed for children 4 to 7 years old. These widely available coding activities, or "playgrounds" as Bers calls them, support not only cognitive but also personal, social, emotional, and moral development with a playful approach, crucial in early childhood education.

Scratch is populated with millions of users and even more projects. While many young people join the community on their own volition, Scratch is also prominent in schools now that computer science education has become a national priority in countries around the world. In chapter 3, "Making Constructionism Work at Scale: The Story of ScratchMaths," British educators Noss, Hoyles, Saunders, Clark-Wilson, Benton, and Kalas report how the project ScratchMaths was implemented across English schools to promote students' (aged 9–11 years) computational thinking in alignment with their mathematical thinking and reasoning. Casting a wide net in terms of learning outcomes, the project not only examined the impact of ScratchMaths on students' computational thinking and on their scores in the English national test but also sought to understand how different schools and teachers achieved this success. While ScratchMaths was a government-sponsored initiative, the development of Globaloria illustrates how independently developed educational platforms can promote constructionist learning at scale. Chapter 4, "Lessons Learned during Research and Development of Globaloria, 2006–2017" by Reynolds and Harel, illustrates how Globaloria supported teachers and administrators with tools, curricula, and professional development in bringing game design into their school districts. Thousands of students not only enjoyed designing and sharing their games but also learned programming. In chapter 5, "Half-Baked Constructionism," Kynigos reports on various efforts to introduce constructionist ideas in Greece over the last 25 years. Teachers, teacher educators, and students themselves learn geometry and mathematics with new tools and microworlds. Finally, a reprint of "Why School Reform Is Impossible" in chapter 6 illustrates how Papert himself grappled with the challenges of reform in school systems, that powerful ideas alone are not enough to make change.

The last chapters in this section turn to educators who play a central role in successfully implementing constructionist activities inside and outside of schools. The ScratchEd community launched around the same time Scratch was released in 2007, providing a forum for interested educators to share their learning experiences. In chapter 7, "The Scratch Educator Meetup: Useful Learning in a Playful Space," Brennan and Jimenez describe the Scratch Educator Meetup—a participatory approach to teacher learning for K-12 educators who want to support computing education with the Scratch programming environment in their classrooms. Drawing on Papert's description of samba schools in *Mindstorms* as learning communities, the meetups become powerful spaces for learning that are social, personal, collaborative, useful, and reflective. These ideas are also present in chapter 8,

"Applied Constructionism in Thailand: Two Decades of a Constructionist School in Thailand," in which Tutiyaphuengprasert tells the story of the Darunsikkhalai School for Innovative Learning, in which students, parents, facilitators and administrators developed a constructionist primary and secondary school. Finally, in chapter 9, "Connecting Modern Knowledge: Crafting the Next Generation of Constructionists," Stager outlines critical features of a conference for educators that meets every year. Constructing Modern Knowledge, the conference and meetup, is a different type of professional development that puts making rather than talking at its center as educators reinvent their own notions of learning and teaching in the process.

1 ENGAGING LEARNERS IN CONSTRUCTING CONSTRUCTIONIST ENVIRONMENTS

Sayamindu Dasgupta, Benjamin Mako Hill, and Andrés Monroy-Hernández

Individuals make connections and construct knowledge in ways that vary significantly from learner to learner. As we see it, one of constructionism's most important features is a commitment to let learners control and direct their learning experiences. Given that this value is widely shared among constructionists, it surprises us that the design of the most influential constructionist learning environments—from Logo to Scratch—have relied heavily on top-down design processes based on the experience and insight of individuals or small teams of designers.

Most details of constructionist environments are designed by expert designers, nearly always adults, whose role is to create environments with affordances and features that will maximize learners' ability to follow their interests and to learn in their own ways. Of course, these designs are frequently quite effective. Designers often spend large amounts of time in the communities they are designing for and make carefully considered decisions about what goes into a toolkit and what stays out (Papert, 1987; Resnick & Silverman, 2005). They frequently follow a growing body of constructionist design principles to ensure, for example, that their learning environments have "high ceilings," "low floors," and "wide walls." But this approach also relies on the implicit assumption that there should be clear distinctions between environments and learning activities as well as between designers and learners. We believe that some of the most effective constructionist environments are ones that blur the lines between toolkit use and design and—more critically—between the role of designer and learners.

How can we support a *second-order constructionism*, in which learners construct not only knowledge in a self-directed way but also the environments that they use to construct the knowledge? How can designers open up the process of defining learning environments so that learners can play a more active role as designers not just of artifacts but of the environments themselves? How can we design environments that learners can both use and shape? In the remainder of this chapter, we explore these questions while making a case for such a move. Drawing from the broader literature on design, we reflect on how more of the design of constructionist environments can be pushed "down the stack." To do so, we describe three examples from our experience with Scratch that reflect ways in which Scratch has—implicitly and explicitly—attempted to do so. Finally, we reflect on the promises and challenges of the approach we are advocating.

MODELS FOR OPENING UP THE DESIGN OF CONSTRUCTIONIST LEARNING ENVIRONMENTS

Constructionist systems are often described in terms of "toolkits." We use the term "environment" in this essay to describe both the technological tools that might include a programming language or construction kit as well as the designed features of the social context—like the affordances of an online community or the setting and rules of an after-school program. As constructionist designers have focused more on participation and collaboration, they have described the importance of the design of the social context in which learning takes place (Bruckman, 1998; Kafai, 2016). We use the term "environment" to include these types of contextual features in our scope.

Involving users in the design of their tools has a long tradition in design and computing. These approaches can be placed along a spectrum of end-user involvement. On one end is the idea of the enlightened designer, in which little involvement is expected from end-users in the design process. At some distance from this point are a variety of human-centered design approaches advocating for closely studying users and eliciting information from them in passive ways, such as user observation and logging, as well as more active techniques, such as interviews and surveys (Bannon, 2011). Further along this spectrum are participatory design approaches, where end-users are seen not just as informants but as active partners in the design process (Muller & Kuhn, 1993). In participatory design, these partners need not be adults. For example, a significant body of technology design work has shown that young people can be effective partners in designing interactive digital systems for learning, play, and more (Druin, 1999).

Even further along this spectrum are approaches based on "user innovation," which conceive of users as the primary sources of new designs (von Hippel, 2006). In a user innovation framework, a designer's job might only involve monitoring users and integrating and disseminating the systems that they create. For example, prefixing words with a "#" to indicate a topic—now called "hashtags"—was a norm created by users on Twitter that was integrated as a feature by Twitter's engineers after the practice had already become widespread. Although frequently hidden and unrecognized, empirical research suggests that user innovation is the source of many of the most important and widely used innovations (von Hippel, 2006).

User innovation is sometimes structured as an ecosystem distributed among end-users building upon a centrally designed core. For example, although often credited to the language's original author, the success of the Perl programming language in the late 1990s was driven by the Comprehensive Perl Archive Network (CPAN), which contains over a hundred thousand "modules" published by over ten thousand people. Increasingly, add-on or plug-in based systems are a feature of browsers, games, and many other pieces of software and often serve as a primary driver of interest in a system. Design approaches based on user innovation shift the locus of design from dedicated specialists to a group of potential designers that includes every user. Despite the increasingly widespread nature of these approaches, most constructionist environments are designed by small teams in a centralized way.

EXAMPLES FROM SCRATCH

The design of Scratch—built by a small team primarily located at MIT—is not an example of user innovation or participatory design. Scratch was, like most constructionist environments, designed by a small group of thoughtful professional designers. Two of the authors of this piece count themselves as members of that small group over the last decade. That said, our experience as part of the Scratch design team has convinced us that many of Scratch's most exciting advances stem from more "participatory" turns in the Scratch design processes that opened up the design of Scratch in sometimes unanticipated ways—frequently with unanticipated results. To illustrate this point, we describe three examples from our experiences with Scratch: Scratch Cloud Variables, "mods" and "forks," and the Scratch Extension System.

Scratch Cloud Variables

A first example stems from the way that, like Twitter's hashtags, Scratch's design evolved by incorporating features that reflected the existing activities of its online community's members. Before 2013, Scratch had no publicly available built-in affordances to allow for persistent or shared data—an early prototype called NetScratch, which allowed shared variables, was never released publicly (Stern, 2007). As a result, learners could not easily create survey projects that recorded input from multiple viewers or global, persistent high-scores lists in games. Instead, members of the Scratch community systematically repurposed the project comments section of the website to report their game scores, to respond to survey questions posted in the project, and more.

After watching this behavior become widespread, the Scratch team designed and introduced two interrelated programming features to the programming language in 2013 (Dasgupta, 2013). The first, the Scratch Cloud Variables system, allowed Scratch users to store data persistently in a shared data store online. This feature allowed for web application-like projects, such as games with leaderboards (figure 1.1), collaborative digital art canvases, and multiplayer games. The second programming feature was the ability to "sense" the username of the community member accessing the project; a new block would return the username of the person viewing the project. Combined with Cloud Variables, this new feature allowed Scratch users to create projects that introduced new social affordances, such as the ability to respond to surveys. Although designed by the Scratch team and deployed as part of the centrally controlled platform, the innovation behind Cloud Variables was drawn directly from the creative behavior of Scratch users.

FIGURE 1.1
Scratch code for a program that uses a cloud variable to keep track of global, community-wide high scores. This script compares the value of the cloud variable "High Score" to the score from the recently concluded game. If the score is higher, then High Score is set to the score. The cloud icon indicates that the variable High Score is a cloud variable. Cloud variables were inspired by the practice of Scratch users repurposing the comments section of the website to keep track of high scores and survey responses.

Scratch Mods and Forks

Scratch "mods" and "forks" are two closely related phenomena that describe a more extensive shift of control over Scratch, from the system's design team to learners themselves. Mods are a largely unanticipated feature of the fact that the first generation of the Scratch language (in use through 2013) was developed in the Squeak programming language, which was itself designed as a programmable constructionist toolkit. Although it was never a documented feature, an Easter egg hidden in the Scratch user-interface allowed any user to open up the Scratch source code and edit it. Scratch "forks" were attempts to build distinct languages based on Scratch by modifying the Scratch codebase.

To the surprise (and sometimes consternation) of Scratch's designers, a vibrant "modding" culture emerged in Scratch, and a number of forks were published and shared—mostly through messages in the Scratch discussion forum. Developers of mods and forks included young community members of Scratch as well as adult researchers and educators. Mods and forks introduced new functionality and sometimes added new grammatical constructs to the language. For examples, modders added the ability to scrape content from web pages or open local files from within a Scratch program. Several forks enabled and extended the design of blocks that allowed Scratch sprites to be programmatically duplicated or "cloned." These blocks had been disabled by the Scratch team in the official version because they could potentially confuse learners (Maloney, Resnick, Rusk, Silverman, & Eastmond, 2010). In several cases—like the case of cloning—the Scratch team re-added functionality into the main version of Scratch based on experimentation by learners in mods and forks.

Scratch Extension System

A final example is the Scratch Extension System, an attempt by the Scratch team to allow user innovation within the Scratch community in a controlled way. Early on, Scratch provided a mechanism for a communication channel to be established with an external program running on the same computer as Scratch. Among other capabilities, this mechanism was often used for allowing Scratch projects to interact with external hardware. Building on this mechanism, the Scratch Extension System was introduced in 2015 to allow anyone to build new functionality into the Scratch language (Dasgupta, Clements, Idlbi, Willis-Ford, & Resnick, 2015). This system was designed to enable anyone to extend the vocabulary of the Scratch language through custom programming blocks written in JavaScript. One of the stated goals of the Scratch Extension System was to "enable *innovating on* the Scratch programming language itself, in addition to *innovating through* projects" (p. 165).

By its design, the Scratch Extension System tried to prevent extension authors from changing Scratch's grammar. Only new commands, event-handlers, and reporter blocks could be introduced through extensions. In this way, an extension could turn on a light bulb, react to a button press, or report temperature from a sensor but could not define a new type of loop. Through extensions, the Scratch language was opened up to new creative possibilities. For example, an extension allowed speech recognition so that the viewers of a Scratch project could say their response to a prompt out loud rather than typing it into a text box. Using an extension developed by a Scratch community member, a Scratch project could query Twitter for recent tweets with a given hashtag.

BENEFITS

Our three examples of Scratch design extensions illustrate how the benefits of allowing learners to play a more active role in shaping and modifying their constructionist learning environment stem from two core guiding principles of constructionism. First, environments shaped by learners are better able to connect to learners' interests. Second, user-shaped environments are better able to connect to learners' knowledge.

For example, users' ability to create mods allowed them and others to experiment with features such as the ability to clone objects. These experiments helped the Scratch designers gauge learner interest and resolve open design questions. Scratch's designers did not need to guess that Scratch users would be interested in cloning blocks or assume that learners would be able to overcome potential confusion with the feature—they could see both happening through the mods. In that multiple mods supported cloning in different ways, the designers' decisions were informed by the fact that they could compare different design choices in actual use. Designers could also observe that at least some learners wanted the feature enough that they had modified Scratch's code to reenable and extend the feature or had installed a mod with the feature created and shared by someone else. Similarly, Scratch's designers knew that Scratch users had the knowledge to use a system like Cloud Variables, which provided persistent data stores, because thousands of Scratch users had already painfully reappropriated existing features of the environment by turning the website commenting system into a persistent data store to keep track of high scores and survey responses.

CHALLENGES

Despite the many benefits of allowing learners to define their environments, doing so introduces several important challenges. First, allowing learners to alter their learning environments can introduce interoperability challenges. For example, a group of researchers forked Scratch to create *Snap!*, a derivative of Scratch that enabled people to create their own blocks and first-class procedures, lists, and objects (Harvey & Mönig, 2010). Unfortunately, the projects created with Snap!—like any other fork or mod—could not be executed by the Scratch player online nor could they be rendered in the original Scratch authoring environment. This lack of interoperability made it such that Snap! users, or users of any other mods, could not be full participants of the larger Scratch community.

Second, allowing people to alter the online infrastructure for social interactions can disrupt communication, enable harassment, and curtail participation of specific groups. Scratch published the full source code of its website software early in its life to allow users to innovate through the creation of alternate Scratch communities. A small group of Scratch community members took advantage of this by creating their own community devoted to sharing hateful Scratch projects aimed to harass members of the original Scratch community. Since this website ran on a server managed independently, there was little that the Scratch team could do about its content and operations.

Finally, allowing learners to change their environments might mean undoing many of the benefits that come from centralized control by a thoughtful team of designers. In at least some cases, designers do, in fact, know better than their users. A small group of designers can ensure consistency and quality in ways that an open and distributed process will struggle to reproduce. For example, maintaining design cohesiveness between extensions and the "core" Scratch system proved to be a challenge in the Scratch Extension System. Extensions would sometimes act in ways that were contrary to established design conventions on Scratch. For example, they might not provide both a "set" and a "change" block for modifying numerical variables or properties or might include blocks that are complex or that address relatively rare use cases—all problems that would have been avoided in a design created by the Scratch design team.

CONCLUSION

Mitchel Resnick and Brian Silverman (2005) presented ten guiding principles for designing constructionist environments. One of these principles is, "Give people what they want—not what they ask for" (Resnick & Silverman, 2005). In this chapter, we have argued that that there are important gains to be had by enabling people to *make what they want*. We do so with a healthy appreciation of the challenges of striking a balance between empowering users to define their environment and maintaining a healthy and predictable learning environment.

When the Scratch Extension System was released, Scratch's designers made a policy decision to make projects with user-created extensions unshareable on the Scratch community website. This decision was made mostly as a means to avoid confusing members of the community, especially newcomers, with unfamiliar blocks. Additionally, the extension mechanism intentionally limited what could be added to the Scratch block palette. Did these decisions restrict the kinds of changes learners could make to Scratch too much? Did they not restrict it enough? Striking a balance between the benefits and the challenges remains very much an open research question for constructionist designers.

REFERENCES

Bannon, L. (2011). Reimagining HCI: Toward a more human-centered perspective. *Interactions, 18*(4), 50–57.

Bruckman, A. (1998). Community support for constructionist learning. *Computer Supported Cooperative Work (CSCW), 7*(1), 47–86.

Dasgupta, S. (2013). From surveys to collaborative art: Enabling children to program with online data. In *Proceedings of the 12th International Conference on Interaction Design and Children (IDC '13)* (pp. 28–35). New York, NY: ACM.

Dasgupta, S., Clements, S. M., Idlbi, A. Y., Willis-Ford, C., & Resnick, M. (2015). Extending Scratch: New pathways into programming. In *2015 IEEE Symposium on Visual Languages and Human-Centric Computing (VL/HCC)* (pp. 165–169).

Druin, A. (1999). Cooperative inquiry: Developing new technologies for children with children. In *Proceedings of the SIGCHI Conference on Human Factors in Computing Systems* (pp. 592–599). New York, NY: ACM.

Harvey, B., & Mönig, J. (2010). Bringing "no ceiling" to Scratch: Can one language serve kids and computer scientists. In *Proceedings of Constructionism 2010* (pp. 1–10).

Kafai, Y. B. (2016). From computational thinking to computational participation in K–12 education. *Communications of the ACM, 59*(8), 26–27.

Maloney, J., Resnick, M., Rusk, N., Silverman, B., & Eastmond, E. (2010). The Scratch programming language and environment. *ACM Transactions on Computing Education, 10*(4), 16:1–16:15.

Muller, M. J., & Kuhn, S. (1993). Participatory design. *Communications of the ACM, 36*(6), 24–28.

Papert, S. (1980). *Mindstorms: Children, computers, and powerful ideas.* New York, NY: Basic Books, Inc.

Papert, S. (1987). Computer criticism vs. technocentric thinking. *Educational Researcher, 16*(1), 22–30.

Resnick, M., & Silverman, B. (2005). Some reflections on designing construction kits for kids. In *Proceedings of the 2005 Conference on Interaction Design and Children* (pp. 117–122). New York, NY: ACM.

Stern, T. I. (2007). *NetScratch: A networked programming environment for children* (master's thesis). Cambridge, MA: Massachusetts Institute of Technology.

von Hippel, E. (2006). *Democratizing innovation.* Cambridge, MA: MIT Press.

2 PLAYGROUNDS AND MICROWORLDS: LEARNING TO CODE IN EARLY CHILDHOOD

Marina Umaschi Bers

PROGRAMMING THE "HOKEY POKEY"

In my book *Coding as a Playground* (Bers, 2018), I told the story of Maya and Natan, who are in kindergarten. They are working on a joint KIBO robotics project. KIBO is a robot kit developed in my DevTech research group at Tufts University. It belongs to the family of robotic-based constructionist programming environments, inspired by the Logo turtle and the LEGO Mindstorms robotic kit, but it is explicitly designed for children four to seven years old. KIBO has a programming language made of wooden blocks with pegs and holes that can be inserted into each other to form a tangible sequence of commands. No screens, tables, or keyboards are needed. Each block has an icon, as well as text, representing an instruction: forward, shake, wait for clap, light on, beep, and so on. In addition, each block has a unique bar code. These bar codes are read by an embedded scanner in the KIBO robot (see figure 2.1). That is how coding happens.

During class, Maya and Natan's teacher invited students to program their KIBOs to dance the "Hokey Pokey." Maya carefully chooses the blocks to use. She starts by picking the green "begin" block and concludes with the red "end" block but needs other blocks in between. Those are the ones that will tell KIBO how to dance. She forgot the KIBO "Hokey Pokey" song the teacher taught them, so she is at a loss about what blocks to choose. Natan, her teammate, reminds her of the song:

You put your robot in
You put your robot out
You put your robot in
And you shake it all about
You do the Hokey Pokey
and you turn yourself around
That's what it's all about!

FIGURE 2.1
The KIBO robot.

Maya sings along and, as the song progresses, she chooses the blocks and starts putting them together in a sequence. Begin, "You put your robot in" forward, "You put your robot out" backward, "You put your robot in" forward, "And you shake it all about." She suddenly stops and says, "Natan, I can't find the 'do the Hokey Pokey' block!" "There is no block for that, silly," responds Natan. "We need to make it up. Let's have KIBO turn on the blue and red light instead. That will be our 'Hokey Pokey' block." Maya agrees, adds those two blocks to the sequence, and also adds "shake," "spin," and "beep" to represent the "what it's all about" part of the song. Maya and Natan look at their program while singing the song to make sure they have put together all the needed blocks, in the right order. Then they turn on KIBO for testing. The red light of KIBO's scanner (the "mouth," as Maya calls it) is flashing, meaning that the robot is ready to scan each of the bar codes printed on the wooden programming blocks.

Natan takes his turn and scans the blocks one by one. He goes too fast and skips the "red light" block. Maya points that out and he restarts the scanning. The children are excited to see their robot dance the "Hokey Pokey." "When I count to three, you start singing," says Maya to Natan. They know the drill. They have practiced it during technology circle time in class. Natan sings and both KIBO and Maya dance the "Hokey Pokey." It goes too fast. KIBO dances too fast. "Can you sing faster?" asks Maya. Natan tries one more time, but it still doesn't work. "We have a problem," he says. "I can't sing fast enough to keep up with KIBO." Maya has an idea. For each action in the song, she puts two blocks so that KIBO's motions will last longer. For example, for the "you put your robot in" part, instead of just one "forward" block, she puts two forward, and so on, for each of the commands. Natan tries singing again, and this time KIBO dances at the right pace.

Both children start clapping, shaking their bodies, and jumping up and down. Without knowing it, they engaged with many powerful ideas of computer science, such as sequencing, algorithmic thinking, and debugging or problem solving. They also explored math concepts they are learning in kindergarten, such as estimation, prediction, and counting. Furthermore, they engaged in collaboration. "Children already have too much screen time at home. When they are at school, I want them learning new concepts and skills in STEM, but as importantly, I want them learning to socialize and collaborate with others. I want them looking at each other, and not at the screen," explains Marisa, their kindergarten teacher. "KIBO is just perfect for that." During technology circle time, Marisa asks every group of children to give a demo of their dancing KIBOs. Everyone else is invited to stand up and dance alongside. There is laughter and clapping. There is physical activity, socialization and language development, problem solving, and creative play. It is fun. It feels like a playground, not a coding class.

I coined the metaphor "playground vs. playpen" (Bers, 2012) to discuss the role that new technologies can have in young children's lives. Playgrounds are open ended. Playpens are limited. Playgrounds invite fantasy play, imagination and creativity, social interaction, and teamwork; they require conflict resolution and little adult supervision. The story of Maya and Natan provides an illustration of what learning looks like within a coding playground. In my work at Tufts University, my colleagues and I focus on designing experiences and programming environments that support a playground approach. Our work with KIBO and ScratchJr are some examples (Bers, 2018). In this chapter, I further examine the concept of coding playgrounds and explore the similarities and differences between coding playgrounds and the concept of microworlds, as described by Papert.

CODING PLAYGROUNDS AND MICROWORLDS

The "playground vs. playpen" metaphor provides a way to understand the kind of developmentally appropriate experiences that new technologies, such as programming languages, can promote: problem solving, imagination, cognitive challenges, social interactions, motor skills development, emotional exploration, and making different choices. In order to understand playgrounds, and their relationship with microworlds, we first need to understand playpens. In contrast to the open-ended playground, play-pens convey lack of freedom to experiment, lack of autonomy for explo-ration, lack of creative opportunities, and lack of taking risks. Although playpens are safer, playgrounds provide infinite possibilities for growth and learning. Microworlds are closer to playgrounds than to playpens. However, there are some differences.

Papert (1980) described microworlds as:

> A subset of reality or a constructed reality whose structures matches that of a given cognitive mechanism so as to provide an environment where the latter can operate effectively. The concept leads to the project of inventing microworlds so structured as to allow a human learner to exercise particular powerful ideas or intellectual skills (p. 204).

In this definition, a microworld, like a playground, presents a subset of a reality, a subset so carefully chosen that its structures are explicitly designed to encourage children to engage with a particular set of powerful ideas. Programming languages, such as KIBO, ScratchJr, or Logo, are microworlds with structures called programming blocks, scripts, or commands. When these are put together following an orderly sequence (an algorithm), we can observe a range of possible behaviors. While coding, children exercise par-ticular powerful ideas or intellectual skills. Those are associated with what researchers now call computational thinking (Wing, 2006). The cognitive mechanisms that Papert refers to are sequencing, abstraction, modulariza-tion, problem solving, and logical thinking.

A playground can also be seen as a microworld. As such, it is a subset of reality that presents itself with structures carefully chosen to encourage children to encounter a particular set of powerful ideas. For example, climb-ing structures, slides, seesaws, and swings allows children to explore ideas from physics. However, the powerful ideas children encounter when visit-ing the playground go beyond the cognitive domain. At the playground, children also encounter ideas relevant at the personal, social, emotional, and moral domains. Coding playgrounds, in contrast with Papert's micro-worlds, reinforce the notion of a "whole child," not only a thinking child. This child learns about the social world by negotiating for her favorite toys in the sandbox, about her own emotions when she struggles to keep up with others on the monkey bars, about moral choices and consequences when she is faced with the dilemma to wait politely for her turn on the swing or cut the existent line. In the playground, this child is encountering all of the dimensions of human development. However, she is doing it in a safe space, a place where she can make mistakes and learn how to try again.

She has autonomy to discover her own way of doing things and to ask for help when needed. Usually the adults are nearby, sitting on a bench and talking with each other.

When Papert developed the concept of microworlds, he was heavily influenced by his experience working with Piaget. Thus, the emphasis was on the cognitive dimension and the methodological approach of exploratory, hands-on learning. Within this perspective, programming languages such as Logo provided an innovative opportunity to create microworlds to support active learning by creating personally meaningful projects while exploring deep ideas from a particular domain of knowledge. While Logo's central domain was mathematics, children were also learning how to program and, most importantly, how to think in new ways when making their own projects.

Coding playgrounds extend the notion of microworlds by making explicit the connection to playfulness and the multifaceted dimensions of human development. Going beyond the cognitive is important when addressing early childhood (four to seven years old). This is a life stage characterized by genuine curiosity and desire for learning about many things. Children need to learn about the natural world and the artificial world, the world of emotions and the world of ideas, the world by themselves, and the world of others in social contexts. This learning happens not only by thinking but by doing in a developmentally appropriate way (Bredekamp, Copple, & National Association for the Education of Young Children, 1997). Thus, coding playgrounds, or microworlds, must support experiences that engage young children in positive behaviors within the full range of human experience.

POSITIVE TECHNOLOGICAL DEVELOPMENT

Grounding my work in constructionism, I developed a framework called Positive Technological Development (PTD) (Bers, 2012) to highlight how technologies can engage children not only in thinking in new ways but also in behaving in new ways. The PTD framework identifies six positive behaviors that coding playgrounds or microworlds should support: communication, collaboration, community-building, content creation, creativity, and choices of conduct. From a theoretical perspective, these behaviors are associated with personal assets that have been described by decades of research on positive youth development as needed for thriving in life (Lerner, Almerigi, Theokas, & Lerner, 2005).

PTD is a natural extension of constructionism, but it explicitly incorporates psychosocial, civic, and ethical components. The framework examines the developmental tasks of a child growing up in our digital era and provides a model for designing and evaluating technology-rich youth programs (Bers, 2012). In learning experiences designed with a PTD framework, context plays a big role. It is not enough to use a wonderful coding playground or micro-world. Classroom culture, curriculum, logistical, and physical organization of the learning environments, teachers, and more are as important as the technology itself. However, technologies must be designed in such a way as to support the emergence of positive behaviors in a developmentally appropriate way. ScratchJr and KIBO robotics are two examples of those technologies.

COMPUTATIONAL PLAYGROUNDS FOR EARLY CHILDHOOD

Papert described microworlds as being "sufficiently bounded and transparent for constructive exploration and yet sufficiently rich for significant discovery" (p. 208). ScratchJr and KIBO provide both the bounds, grounded on developmental theory, and the richness of programming environments so that young children can create their own projects to communicate ideas and express who they are.

Most importantly, within both of these playgrounds, coding—or the manipulation of the symbol system—is a major component of the experience, but not the only one. Just like at the playground, children have many options for things to do. At the playground, children can go to the sandbox, the swing, the slide, or just run around. They can play with sticks, ride their bikes, or create fantasy worlds. Similarly, while using KIBO or ScratchJr, children can engage in all kinds of activities beyond coding. For example, in ScratchJr they can create and modify characters in the paint editor, record their own voices and sounds, and even insert photos of themselves that they take in the paint editor using the camera option.

ScratchJr is a free introductory programming environment for young children ages five to seven. Inspired by Scratch (Resnick et al., 2009), ScratchJr was first launched as a freely downloadable app on iPads in July 2014 and has since been released for multiple platforms (Bers & Resnick, 2015). Used in classrooms and homes worldwide, ScratchJr enables children to create interactive stories and games by snapping together graphical programming blocks to make characters move, jump, dance, and sing, without the need of knowing how to read or write.

ScratchJr has a small basic set of graphics compared to the hundreds available in Scratch. Just as playgrounds for younger children offer limited play structures when compared to those for older children, this design decision was motivated by our overarching theme that "less is more" to ease children's difficulty in navigating vast arrays of options. However, it provides tools for children to create their own new graphics.

Whereas ScratchJr provides a screen-based coding playground, KIBO robotics offers a tangible experience (Bers, 2018). Children can build their own robot, program it to do what they want, and decorate it with art supplies. KIBO gives children the chance to make their ideas physical and tangible—without requiring screen time from PCs, tablets, or smartphones. As a playground, KIBO offers motors, lights, sensors, and art platforms as well as wooden blocks to sequence commands for the robot to follow once it is programmed.

The aesthetic features of KIBO, with an "unfinished" look, invites children to complete the robot using their own imaginative creations. Much like a blank canvas or unsculpted clay, KIBO inspires children to add to it. This supports a variety of sensory and aesthetic experiences. KIBO supports children in making almost anything: a character from a story, a carousel, a dancer, a dog sled. The possibilities are endless, as wide as children's own imaginations. The physicality of KIBO invites children to use their bodies, like in the playground, and engage in motor activities, while also collaborating with others.

Both KIBO and ScratchJr are coding playgrounds that support different dimensions of the multifaceted process of learning. Although we could claim that they are also microworlds, in Papert's sense, the term *coding playgrounds* makes explicit the emphasis on playfulness and the developmental needs of young children.

CONCLUSION

We do not always take children to the playground. There are other places to visit and other skills to develop. But when we do go to the playground, we want it to be a developmentally appropriate space. The same applies to programming environments for young children. There are other kinds of technological environments to explore, games and apps, simulations, and social media. But when young children are exposed to coding, playgrounds, and not only microworlds, provide a powerful metaphor for the best kind of learning experiences for young children. These playgrounds go beyond the cognitive dimension to encompass the social, emotional, personal, and moral dimensions.

ACKNOWLEDGMENTS

This work is possible through generous funding from the National Science Foundation (NSF) and the Scratch Foundation. Any opinions, findings, conclusions, or recommendations expressed in this paper are those of the author and do not necessarily reflect the views of neither NSF nor Tufts University. ScratchJr was developed as a collaboration between the DevTech research group at Tufts University, the MIT Lifelong Kindergarten Group, and the Playful Invention Company, with funding from the NSF and the Scratch Foundation. KIBO was developed by the DevTech research group in 2011 through generous funding from the NSF and is being commercialized worldwide by KinderLab Robotics.

REFERENCES

Bers, M. U. (2012). *Designing digital experiences for positive youth development: From playpen to playground.* Oxford, UK: Oxford University Press.

Bers, M. U. (2018). *Coding as a playground: Computational thinking and programming in early childhood. London, UK:* Routledge.

Bers, M. U., & Resnick, M. (2015). *The official ScratchJr book.* San Francisco, CA: No Starch Press.

Bredekamp, S., Copple, C., & National Association for the Education of Young Children. (1997). *Developmentally appropriate practice in early childhood programs.* Washington, DC: National Association for the Education of Young Children.

Lerner, R. M., Almerigi, J. B., Theokas, C., & Lerner, J. V. (2005). Positive youth development: A view of the issues. *The Journal of Early Adolescence, 25*(1), 10–16.

Papert, S. (1980). Computer-based microworlds as incubators for powerful ideas. In R. Taylor (Ed.), *The computer in the school: Tutor, tool, tutee* (pp. 203–210). New York, NY: Teacher's College Press.

Papert, S. (1980). *Mindstorms: Children, computers, and powerful ideas.* New York, NY: Basic Books, Inc.

Resnick, M., Maloney, J., Monroy-Hernández, A., Rusk, N., Eastmond, E., Brennan, K., Millner, A., Rosenbaum, E., Silver, J., Silverman, B., & Kafai, Y. (2009). Scratch: Programming for all. *Communications of the ACM, 52*(11), 60–67.

Wing, J. (2006). Computational thinking. *Communications of the ACM, 49*(3), 33–36.

3 MAKING CONSTRUCTIONISM WORK AT SCALE: THE STORY OF SCRATCHMATHS

Richard Noss, Celia Hoyles, Piers Saunders, Alison Clark-Wilson, Laura Benton, and Ivan Kalas

Papert (1980) proposed that a powerful way for students to build knowledge structures in their minds is to build with external representations, to construct physical or virtual entities that can be reflected on, edited, and shared. In our view of constructionism this makes the case for programming embedded in a learning environment where students can not only construct and explore powerful ideas guided by feedback but also, in doing so, retain some ownership of the construction process (Noss & Hoyles, 2017).

The *ScratchMaths* (SM) project, through the mobilization of computational thinking for mathematics learning, represents one example of how this might be achieved by building on prior research into the impact of programming on students' mathematical thinking (Hoyles & Noss, 1992). It provides a comprehensive set of materials designed to support a computing curriculum that "connects" with students and addresses the core concepts of computing necessary to support implementation (at least in its early stages), along with documentation of the teacher's role. Specification of how "computing across the curriculum" might be realized is critical but largely under-researched. Moreover, curriculum specification is only the first step toward exploiting computing across the curriculum. What can fluency in programming bring to learning? What can teachers do to make this happen in their classrooms? In this chapter, we set out to address these questions in the context of SM.

AIMS AND STRUCTURE OF THE RESEARCH

In England, a statutory national curriculum for computing was introduced in 2013 with the intention that "pupils are taught the principles of information and computation, how digital systems work, and how to put this knowledge to use through programming" (Department for Education, 2013). The case for computer science in schools is made in Peyton Jones's polemical piece, "Code to Joy" (Peyton Jones, 2015). In this work, Peyton Jones welcomed the computing curriculum but, at the same time, called for digital technology to support teaching and learning in every subject. It is only in this way, he argued, that the national computing initiative could be transformational. SM was designed to develop the computational thinking and mathematical knowledge of students ages nine through eleven years through programming. Research undertaken during the 1980s and 1990s explored the potential beneficial impact and the challenges of learning to program and noted the need to master the programming syntax as well as the semantics of the code (Lewis, 2010). In this respect, blocks-based programming languages such as Scratch, with visual cues including color, shape, and constrained nesting to indicate usage, flow, and scope, do seem to render some complex concepts more accessible (Resnick, 2012).

Through a process of design research, SM developed a two-year curriculum for this age group (years five [Y5] and six [Y6] in England), which was aligned to the national computing and mathematics primary curricula and required approximately forty hours of teaching time. The SM curriculum promoted the teaching of carefully selected core ideas of computer programming alongside specific fundamental mathematical concepts. SM devised materials for teachers as well as students and for professional development to be delivered face-to-face over two days per year. All the activities and approaches were iteratively designed and trialed in four "design schools."

The SM content was divided into six modules, three modules per year. In the first year for nine- to ten-year-old students, computational concepts were preceded by mathematical ideas more implicit in modules titled *Tiling Patterns*, *Beetle Geometry*, and *Collaborating Sprites*. In the second year, the same students, now ten to eleven years old, were introduced to mathematical concepts and mathematical reasoning explicitly through a programming approach along with a set of new computational concepts[1] in modules titled *Building with Numbers*, *Exploring Mathematical Relationships*, and *Coordinates and Geometry*.

Given the challenge of implementing a brand-new curriculum, the SM teachers were provided with detailed guidance for navigation through the materials, which were themselves carefully structured and progressive.[2] However, the SM team recognized the tension arising from their quest to provide comprehensive support and the need for teacher appropriation and autonomy, whereby teachers had space to customize the materials to suit their own goals and their students' needs. This is often referred to as the tension, or gap, between *fidelity*[3] and *adaptation*. At the very least, the

Module	Investigation	Computing concepts (+ Scratch terms)	Mathematics concepts
Module 1: Tiling Patterns	*1.1 Moving, Turning and Stamping*	Sprite and its attributes Command, command with input (stamp, move, turn) Program, sequence of commands	• (Y2) Patterns • (Y2) Rotation • (Y3) Angles • (Y4) Coordinates • (Y4) Symmetry • (Y4) Multiplication • (Y5) Translation • (Y5) Transformation • (Y5) Sequences • (Y5) Positive and negative numbers
	1.2 Repeating and Alternating Patterns	Control structures, repetition (repeat) Designing, building and debugging programs (costume)	
	1.3 Circular Rose Patterns	Algorithms Logical reasoning	
	1.4 Defining your own Pattern Blocks	Defining new commands (make a new block)	

FIGURE 3.1
Module 1 overview.

challenge is to reduce this gap and crucially, to avoid "lethal mutations" (Brown & Campione, 1996), where the aims of the intervention are lost in its implementation.

The SM approach was first to specify each activity in terms of both the computing curriculum and the mathematics curriculum. For example, figure 3.1 shows the overview of Module 1.

Second, the SM team made explicit within the materials, and in the professional development, the pedagogical framework through which the SM curriculum was designed to be operationalized in the classroom, the *"5Es framework"* (Benton, Hoyles, Kalas, & Noss, 2017). This provided guidance for teachers as to how they might support their students to appropriate the core ideas of computational thinking, to reason on the basis of their programs and, later, to express key mathematical ideas in Scratch.[4]

The five (unordered) constructs underpinning the framework are as follows:

Explore: Students should have opportunities to explore different ways of engaging with and developing computational and mathematical concepts and be encouraged to take control of their own learning as they express these concepts in their programs.

Explain: Students should have opportunities to explain their own ideas, articulate their own learning and the reasoning behind choices of approach, as well as answer and discuss reflective questions from the teacher and peers. Students should be encouraged to use the programming language as a "tool to think with" and support their explanations.

Envisage: Students should predict outcomes of their own and others' programs *prior* to testing out on the computer.

Exchange: Students should have opportunities to share and build on others' ideas and be encouraged to justify their own solutions and understand or debug others' perspectives.

Bridge: Students should be supported to make links between the Scratch environment and the mathematics domain through explicit recontextualization and reconstruction.

EVALUATION OF THE SM PROJECT

In the first phase of SM, the team engaged in design research with four schools where learning goals, curriculum materials, and pedagogic strategies were refined in the process of trialing. At the same time, SM was subject to an independent evaluation, conducted by a team of researchers from another university (Boylan, Demack, Wolstenholme, Reidy, & Reaney-Wood, 2018), who adopted a randomized controlled trial (RCT) methodology involving 6,232 students[5] in 110 schools. 2,986 student scores in fifty-five treatment schools and 3,246 student scores in fifty-five control schools were compared on a specially designed test of CT administered after one year of the project (students age nine to ten years), and on the national tests in mathematics (Key Stage 2 Standard Assessment Tests) after two years, at the age of eleven years. The schools were matched at the unit of the school according to two standard measures: socioeconomic status (using a proxy measure of eligibility for free school meals, FSM) and prior attainment, as measured by the national standardized mathematics assessment at age eight years.[6]

Professional development was undertaken in seven "hubs" across England and led by the SM team with support from local coordinators. Inferences were made about SM implementation from survey data. All schools participating in the trial were asked to complete online surveys at the end of the first year following the teaching of the nine- to ten-year-olds (S1) and again after the second year following the teaching of the same students, now ten to eleven years old (S2). In terms of survey participation, thirty-eight schools responded to S1, thirty-one responded to S2, and twenty-eight schools responded to both.

These survey results, along with data triangulation with follow-up communications with schools and selected school visits, were used by the SM team to classify the schools according to their fidelity, that is, how far the innovation was implemented according to its aims and objectives. The team developed five criteria to be used as proxy measures of fidelity: engagement in professional development (PD), technology access, curriculum coverage, time, and curriculum progression (Dane & Schneider, 1998).

FIDELITY OF IMPLEMENTATION IN THE FIRST YEAR AND OUTCOMES IN COMPUTATIONAL THINKING

The fidelity measures were applied to each school in the trial and the results for the first year were as follows.

Professional development: Fifty-four out of our fifty-five schools attended some SM PD involving a total of 105 teachers. Forty-eight schools were judged as high fidelity on this measure (87 percent of the sample), six medium, and one low.

Technology access: Only one school was unable to provide a pupil-to-computer ratio of at least 2:1, which accords with Organisation for Economic Cooperation and Development (OECD) data on the high levels of computer access in UK schools (OECD, 2015).

Coverage: We used S1 survey data from thirty-six out of fifty-five respondents to assess the fidelity of SM coverage in Y5. These data indicated that twenty-six schools implemented SM with high fidelity; that is, they covered all three SM modules, and nine with medium fidelity, covering two modules, together representing 97 percent of the sample. In only one school was SM coverage judged to exhibit low fidelity.

Curriculum time: Similarly, we used S1 survey data from thirty-six out of fifty-five respondents to assess the fidelity of teaching time devoted to SM in Y5. These data indicated that nineteen schools implemented SM with high fidelity, that is teaching SM for twenty or more hours, and sixteen with medium fidelity, that is teaching SM for between twelve and twenty hours, together representing 97 percent of the sample. In only one school was SM curriculum time judged to exhibit low fidelity.

Curriculum progression: For the thirty-six schools who responded, thirty-five reported that they followed the progression as set out in the materials. These data suggest that in the first year of implementation, schools were highly engaged with SM and the implementation, at least in terms of these measures, was aligned with the intentions of SM.

The results of the quantitative analysis of the scores on the CT test by the independent evaluator revealed that after one year of the ScratchMaths intervention there was a statistically significant and positive impact on computational thinking for Y5 students aged nine to ten years with an effect size of +0.15 standard deviations and an estimated statistical power of 60 percent. In addition, when the data were controlled for students who had been eligible for free school meals, the impact of the SM intervention was greater with an effect size of +0.25 standard deviations. This positive result runs contrary to that of other recent coding initiatives in England.[7] In addition, there was no evidence of any interaction between the impact of SM on CT test scores and gender. This again is important and worthy of further investigation, given that girls tend not to engage with computing in comparison with boys (see, for example, Zagami et al., 2015).

There are two reasons why the SM team regards this finding as particularly encouraging. First, it must be recalled that *all* schools are *required* to implement the English National Computing curriculum, so control school students would have engaged in computing according to the national curriculum specifications and not, as is sometimes the case, in RCTs where control groups undertake an activity not designed for the same learning goals. Second, the intervention and control school baseline samples, although matched on maths and FSM measures, did not show a good balance in their classifications of school effectiveness,[8] as measured by the English Office for Standards in Education (Ofsted, 2018). Eighteen of the control schools (35 percent) were classed as "outstanding" compared to only nine of the intervention schools (17 percent). In addition, two of the control schools (4 percent) were deemed likely to be classed as "requires improvement" compared with nine (17 percent) of the intervention schools. This suggests that the intervention schools were likely to find it more challenging to introduce an innovation (like SM) than their matched control schools. Yet this was not the case: the results were in fact better in the treatment schools.

FIDELITY OF IMPLEMENTATION IN THE SECOND YEAR AND OUTCOMES IN MATHEMATICS NATIONAL TESTS

As in the first-year analysis, the outcomes for each of the fidelity measures are reported separately with the interpretation of coverage and curriculum time as in the first year. We found that technology access remained high fidelity for all schools, forty-two out of fifty-five schools attended any SM PD, a total of sixty-five teachers. Thirty-four schools were judged as high fidelity on this measure (62 percent of the sample), a drop from fifty-four recorded in the first year, eight were medium and thirteen were low, up from only one rated low in the first year.

Coverage: While twenty-seven of thirty-one responding schools reported that they followed the progression, only eleven schools implemented SM curriculum with high fidelity and six medium, together representing 63 per-cent of the sample, a sharp drop from the previous year (although nine fewer schools responded to the Y6 survey). Furthermore, only four schools were high fidelity and sixteen medium fidelity, together 74 percent of the sample, again a considerable drop from the previous year.

The independent evaluators reported no impact on mathematical attain-ment as measured by the Key Stage 2 tests for eleven-year-olds at the end of Y6. This is a disappointing result; although, given the circumstances and the reduction in fidelity as indicated above, it is not altogether surprising. We also note the acknowledged differences in the control and interven-tion school contexts as evidenced by their Ofsted judgments, which might partially explain this result: Mathematics is such a high-stakes subject, it is likely that only more confident schools would follow through with a new approach to mathematics in the year leading up the tests. In fact, the SM team learned from survey data that at least twenty-five schools had stopped teaching SM as early as January of the second year rather than continuing until the KS2 tests took place in May to give space for mathematics revi-sion. In addition, because PD was measured at the school level, it is possible that in a high-fidelity school an individual teacher teaching the Y6 SM curriculum may not have participated in any SM training nor received any school-based professional support due to changes in staffing,[9] as illustrated in the case study below.

A HIGH-FIDELITY SCHOOL: EMERALD PRIMARY

The following example highlights that fidelity of implementation is a com-plex construct potentially oversimplified by the survey data reported above. Consider the case of Emerald Primary,[10] a larger-than-average two-form entry North London primary school with approximately 8 percent of stu-dents speaking English as their first language. After the school was rated as "requires improvement" by Ofsted, the head teacher enrolled the school in SM as a means of developing computing across the school.

Two Emerald Primary Y5 teachers attended the SM professional develop-ment, which focused on using the 5E's framework and the core underly-ing computational ideas from the first three modules. These two teachers taught the majority of the activities from the first three modules, but at the end of Y5, only one teacher, Rina, continued to teach SM in Y6.

In the second year a new teacher, Sally, was appointed to teach the Y6 SM curriculum and to serve as the computing lead for the school. She did not attend any SM professional development before joining the school. An early observation of Sally's teaching revealed that she was unaware of the SM teacher materials designed to support teachers in implementing SM. In one observed session, Sally did not understand a core idea of *turn* from the module (the onscreen beetle turns through the exterior angle when drawing shapes), and in another she had clearly misunderstood how broadcasting was implemented in Scratch.[11] In both cases, she pieced together her lesson from the small knowledge fragments that she did understand. Her pedagogic approach was to explain the code step by step, without using the computer, and then to show the correct solution script, which the students copied. Sally reflected on her practice, saying, "If someone was dragging you through the grass and you don't want to be dragged, you try to grab bits of grass to stop you from being pulled! So, I'm trying to remember the content with the pedagogy that I don't have yet.... I was trying to grab any blades of grass that would stop me."

By contrast, Rina had attended all of the SM professional development and taught the Y5 SM modules. She enacted the planned sequence of activities from the teaching materials consistently using the 5E pedagogical approach. For example, in one teaching sequence, the students built a script shown to the class in a PowerPoint slide, then *Explored* the script by running it and then tried to *Explain* what was happening. Finally, the students were brought together for demonstration and *Exchanging* of results. Rina's lessons were videorecorded and then viewed by both teachers as an object for stimulated recall during post-lesson discussion. Sally cites this as an important turning point in the development of her pedagogic approach and her own learning. Sally's later lessons included adaptations and additions to the SM materials using multimodal representations, such as moving a cutout beetle on the whiteboard to illustrate beetle turns. In terms of her own learning, there appeared to be two main developments. First, she saw CT as a legitimate and complex curricular challenge, rather than a prescribed set of targets, and second, she was beginning to appreciate its complexity, recognizing that "there aren't enough people who really know enough about CT and the very delicate elements of it." Critically, she had begun to appreciate the importance of seeing how each block worked individually or together in a program:

> Scratch in many ways has become an app which kids go on to make games ... they play on it, they can move the sprite. **But the relationships between the blocks, how they link, how they work, and how they are manipulated to get an outcome, they don't have a true understanding of that.**

Sally's case is significant in capturing the change in teacher knowledge as much as change in pedagogy. Sally was coming to see the central elements of computing as a sophisticated network of far-from-arbitrary rules and procedures, while taking on a pedagogic approach that allowed students time to explore, reflect, and explain.

DISCUSSION

We begin by returning to the significant positive effect of the SM intervention on CT scores as measured by the test used at the end of the first year of the trial. As far as we know, this is the first reported effect of its kind; for example, an effect was not found in a similar study in England (Straw, Bamford, & Styles, 2017). A still more significant outcome was the greater increase in CT score for educationally disadvantaged students, as measured by the standard FSM proxy. Briefly, disadvantaged students stood to gain most from SM, raising attainment in CT beyond that of the control group. The samples of schools were matched only on test scores and FSM and, as reported above, the control schools had much higher Ofsted ratings than the treatment schools, which makes the effect even more striking. What could account for this?

We speculate SM provided a systematic, progressive research-based curriculum to address computing, whereas the control schools were likely to have experienced a less-structured and possibly incomplete approach. The PD curricula and the teacher materials were developed following extensive design research, which revealed fundamental pedagogical challenges, such as student appreciation of algorithms (Benton, Kalas, Saunders, Hoyles, & Noss, 2018). SM was also popular; the independent evaluators remarked, "Teachers who sustained participation were, in general, positive about the quality of the professional development and materials, particularly in Y" (Boylan, Demack, Wolstenhome, Reidy, & Noss, 2018). Anecdotally, our school visits suggest that students typically labeled "less able" thrived in SM. In one such incident, a young girl labeled by the teacher as "not very good" became one of the most inventive students in her SM class, showing outstanding creativity, and was desperate to share her work with the two researchers.

We now turn to the outcome of finding no impact of SM on mathematics attainment as measured by the KS2 test results. It does seem clear that SM implementation was impeded, particularly in Y6, by two factors outside of the control of the innovation and more or less independent of it: high-stakes testing in mathematics, and teachers teaching SM with little or no professional development. Related to the first point, the survey data showed that the fidelity of the implementation in the second year dropped dramatically as evidenced by curriculum coverage and time, and the limited engagement in professional development. The notion of fidelity is admittedly a rather crude measure, and here it was self-reported.[12] Observations from school visits made it clear that SM time was negatively impacted by a focus on high-stakes testing in mathematics at the end of the school year, with more and more time given to revision and practice. We also surmise that teachers felt more able to adopt novel curricula and techniques for a "new" subject, computing, rather than to change their practice in an established and higher-stakes subject, mathematics.

As to the second point, forty-two of the 110 SM Y6 classes, approximately 1,050 students, were in the trial but may not been taught SM, or may have been taught by teachers with neither experience of Y5 SM nor exposure to SM professional development. There were two reasons for this. First, there is considerable teacher "churn" in England (teachers move to teach different year groups, move schools, and even move out of the profession). Second, the design only allowed for the attendance of two teachers per year group available at PD events. So when the schools were larger (up to four-form entry), it was inevitable that "untrained" teachers would teach SM. This situation was exacerbated in that, even in high-fidelity schools, teachers within the same school did not always support each other, as illustrated in the case study.

The SM evaluation was undertaken almost concurrently with the first implementation of SM, so most, if not all, of the teachers were new to programming. Thus, the importance of the PD cannot be overestimated. Where PD was taken seriously by schools, as in the first year of the innovation, implementation tended to be successful. However, by contrast, many teachers sent by schools to the second-year SM PD sessions were newcomers, and as shown in the fidelity data, many schools sent no Y6 teachers to PD. It is likely that these "SM novice" teachers would not be familiar with the computational concepts from the first year themselves, nor know how to build on what the students had experienced the year before. Thus, without considerable time on PD in or out of school, it is hard to see how this group of teachers could implement SM effectively.

CONCLUSIONS

We recognize that there is a need for more intensive and systematic classroom research to explore SM classroom implementation in more detail, to document how it evolves over time as it becomes embedded in practice, and to track the engagement of different groups of students (for example, girls, "low attainment"). It is clear that adopting an SM approach to mathematics teaching is challenging. SM provided detailed lesson plans with a thoroughly designed strategy of gradually building the need for new computational constructs to explore mathematical ideas and a program of professional training through the 5Es strategy. We wanted teachers to encourage student thinking about their programs and thinking with the programs in mathematical and computational activities. Asking teachers to learn programming and new ways to think about and teach (Peyton Jones, 2015) is clearly an enormous task. But we would argue that this must be addressed seriously if constructionism is to "work."

So, we end with one of the many positive stories of student engagement with SM that reassures us of the enduring value of the constructionist vision. One girl, delighted in the dynamic display following an activity involving angles and polygons, exclaimed, "What we really like … is when you press that start button and you see your script come into life, it's like magic in front of your eyes!"

ACKNOWLEDGMENTS

We thank the Education Endowment Foundation for funding this work as well as our SM colleagues Dave Pratt and Johanna Carvajal for their invaluable contributions to the intervention design. We also acknowledge the invaluable insights provided by the ScratchMaths independent evaluation report, undertaken by Sheffield Hallam University. We are also extremely grateful to the teachers and pupils at all of the SM project schools for their continued engagement, hard work, and enthusiasm in trialing our intervention and participating in our research.

NOTES

1. For example, events, animation, control structures, variable, operators, and expressions.

2. All SM materials are available at https://www.ucl.ac.uk/scratchmaths

3. Fidelity of implementation within an education context has been defined as "the determination of how well an intervention is implemented in comparison with the original program design during an efficacy and/or effectiveness study" (O'Donnell, 2008).

4. The framework was introduced in the professional development days: for example, in the first year around the computational concepts, *direct drive, scripts, making new blocks, randomness,* and *broadcasting.*

5. Following randomization, data on the mathematics outcome was obtained from 5,818 students.

6. The statistical protocol for the project evaluation is published at: https://educationendowmentfoundation.org.uk/projects-and-evaluation/projects/scratch-programming/

7. For example, no effect on computational thinking was found in the evaluation of the Code Clubs in England (Straw, Bamford, & Styles, 2017).

8. Ofsted judges schools on a four-point scale: outstanding, good, requires improvement, and inadequate. For details of Ofsted inspections and their data methods, see https://www.gov.uk/government/organisations/ofsted. All schools are required to make their latest Ofsted report available via their website.

9. In addition to teacher movement, some treatment schools had more than a two-form entry, so, inevitably, given only two teachers could be trained per school, some teachers would not have engaged in the PD.

10. All school and teacher names have been changed.

11. Broadcasting is a Scratch metaphor for understanding how sprites can communicate.

12. The SM team estimate that there was less coverage in Y6 than reported, as teachers were clearly concerned to put a positive gloss on their school's engagement.

REFERENCES

Benton, L., Hoyles, C., Kalas, I., & Noss, R. (2017). Bridging primary programming and mathematics: Some findings of design research in England. *Digital Experiences in Mathematics Education*, 1–24. https://doi.org/10.1007/s40751-017-0028-x

Benton, L., Kalas, I., Saunders, P., Hoyles, C., & Noss, R. (2018). Beyond jam sandwiches and cups of tea: An exploration of primary pupils' algorithm-evaluation strategies. *Journal of Computer Assisted Learning, 34*(5), 590–601. https://doi.org/10.1111/jcal.12266

Boylan, M., Demack, S., Wolstenholme, C., Reidy, J., & Reaney-Wood, S. (2018). *ScratchMaths Evaluation Report*. Retrieved from https://pdfs.semanticscholar.org/0f19/e996f06f087b259e30e260fce6999c672f90.pdf

Brown, A. L., & Campione, J. C. (1996). *Psychological theory and the design of innovative learning environments: On procedures, principles, and systems*. Hillsdale, NJ: Lawrence Erlbaum Associates, Inc.

Dane, A. V., & Schneider, B. H. (1998). Program integrity in primary and early secondary prevention: are implementation effects out of control? *Clinical Psychology Review, 18*(1), 23–45.

Department for Education (2013). *Primary National Curriculum until 2014—English: Key Stage 2*.

Hoyles, C., & Noss, R. (1992). *Learning mathematics and logo.* Cambridge, MA: MIT Press.

Lewis, C. M. (2010). *How programming environment shapes perception, learning and goals: Logo vs. Scratch.* Paper presented at the Proceedings of the 41st ACM Technical Symposium on Computer Science Education. Milwaukee, Wisconsin.

Noss, R., & Hoyles, C. (2017). Constructionism and microworlds. In E. Duval, M. Sharples, & R. Sutherland (Eds.), *Technology enhanced learning* (pp. 29–35). Cham, Switzerland: Springer.

O'Donnell, C. L. (2008). Defining, conceptualizing, and measuring fidelity of implementation and its relationship to outcomes in K–12 curriculum intervention research. *Review of Educational Research, 78*(1), 33–84. https://doi.org/10.3102/0034654307313793

Office for Standards in Education, Children's Services and Skills (Ofsted). (2018). *School inspection handbook: Handbook for inspecting schools in England under section 5 of the Education Act 2005.* Retrieved from https://assets.publishing.service.gov.uk /government/uploads/system/uploads/attachment_data/file/730127/School_inspec tion_handbook_section_5_270718.pdf

Organisation for Economic Cooperation and Development (OECD). (2015). Students, computers and learning. In *OECD Factbook 2015–2016: Economic, Environmental and Social Statistics.* Paris, France: OECD Publishing. Retrieved from http://dx.doi .org/10.1787/factbook-2015-en

Papert, S. (1980). *Mindstorms: Children, computers, and powerful ideas.* New York, NY: Basic Books.

Peyton Jones, S. (2015). Code to joy. *Times Educational Supplement.* Retrieved from https://www.tes.com/news/code-joy

Resnick, M. (2012). Reviving Papert's dream. *Educational Technology, 52*(4), 42–46.

Straw, S., Bamford, S., & Styles, B. (2017). *Randomised controlled trial and process evaluation of code clubs.* Slough, UK: NFER. Retrieved from https://www.nfer.ac.uk/randomised -controlled-trial-and-process-evaluation-of-code-clubs

Zagami, J., Boden, M., Keane, T., Moreton, B., & Schulz, K. (2015). Girls and computing: Female participation in computing in schools. *Australian Educational Computing, 30*(2).

4 LESSONS LEARNED DURING RESEARCH AND DEVELOPMENT OF GLOBALORIA, 2006–2017

Rebecca Reynolds and Idit Harel

Questions of how to spread constructionist education in the US school system have been discussed for decades, dating back to investigations done by Papert, Harel, and colleagues into children learning mathematics with Logo in Boston city schools in the mid-1980s. Anticipating that computer science (CS) education would be a national economic and educational priority, Harel's team incorporated strategies upfront for scaling constructionist learning in the design and development of Globaloria from 2006 to 2017. Globaloria's development, implementation, and research involved close collaboration with districts, administrators, and teachers to provide a system to be flexible, customizable, and responsive to local needs such as participants' barriers to technology acceptance, prior computing, school technology integration, and students' language status.

In this short summary brief, we discuss instructional design affordances that have contributed to the development of Globaloria and its successes, awards, and ultimate acquisition. We propose that as a constructionist e-learning platform for CS education in the US school system, Globaloria's path may offer both technological and conceptual innovations for designers and inventors whose projects are also inspired by constructionism and who may be considering the importance of expansion, replication, and scale in their next steps.

GLOBALORIA DESIGN

The Globaloria e-learning solution was designed based on the premise that the US K-12 education system's growing CS educational priorities cannot be met only with short-term, infrequent interventions or a simple *Hour of Code*. From 2006 to 2017 Globaloria (now integrated into Carnegie Learning's Zulama suite) developed and offered design and coding courses for daily semester- or year-long integration in partnering middle schools and high schools. In many of these settings, the courses were credit bearing and offered for a grade.

By 2017 Globaloria had developed 14 different CS education courses designed to fit into the school curriculum or as after-school/summer programs. The courses are customizable for a variety of integration models and learning levels, including as stand-alone courses in CS, game design, or digital skills; for integration into core curriculum classes such as math or English; as subject enrichment classes; or in combination with electives. The curriculum was articulated in formal alignment with several national and state standards frameworks. By 2017 courses were available for younger learners in elementary and intermediate schools, as well as more advanced learners in high school. Courses for younger and novice learners are sequenced as "100-level" and include titles such as "101: Essentials of Coding." Courses for middle and early high school students include titles such as "201a: Intro to Computer Science, Web Design," "202a: Game Design and Coding: Action Game," and "203: Mobile App Design and Coding." More advanced middle and high school students take classes such as "301: Teamwork CS: Game Development in Teams," "302: 3D Game Design and Coding: Adventure Game," and "303: Game Design for Computer Science and Design Thinking." Learning progressions are scaffolded and supported in developmentally aligned curriculum pathways. In many of the courses, students are able to personalize their game and simulation projects as well as focus on social issues.

To deliver these learning experiences at increasing levels of scale, the Globaloria organization developed an innovative blended e-learning platform approach to course curriculum distribution, comprising multiple components outlined in table 4.1, including online learning affordances for students, which encompass project-based curriculum activities, instructional materials, and social collaboration affordances; professional development resources for teachers; content and systems for network administrators; a repository and judging system for the annual game design competition called the Globeys; and an online mentor network of student and teacher alumni "Help Center Coding Coaches" to help launch and manage school implementations.

Overall, the online platform infrastructure for blended e-learning enables replication, customization, and tracking of course experiences for teachers, students, and administrators. These features were designed in part to address CS teacher shortages and training challenges at the K-12 level nationwide. The platform shoulders some of the burden of curriculum design and class management of introductory CS experiences tailored especially to the

Table 4.1 Globaloria Network of School Learning Platforms

	School Learning Platform (SLP)	Professional Development Platform (PDP)	Learning Management Platform (LMP)	Network Administration Platform (NAP)	Globey Competition Platform (GCP)
User group	Students, educators, experts, support staff	Educators, experts, support staff	Educators, support staff	Support staff	Support staff, judges
Selected tools	Project-based digital text-books and workbooks; help center; coding coach-ers; progress tracker and social tools; gamified badges, levels, points; portfolio-building tracker	Professional development courses; on-demand virtual and in-person support and co-teaching; classroom management dashboard (individual/teams); grading and evaluation rubrics	Proprietary license management platform; user data tracking and backend dashboards; customized Salesforce platform; robust reporting features	Fully hosted and secured; account management tools; classroom and student account creation tools	Competition management system, submission management, and judging tools

middle school and high school level. The design of the system was informed by learning sciences and design-based research literatures, in areas includ-ing collaborative learning and teamwork in CS; use of worked examples and programming problem sets; homegrown video tutorials tailored to the cur-riculum at task and activity levels; use of an integrated development envi-ronment (IDE) for student practice and experimentation with code; student online documentation, sharing, and peer feedback around in-progress and completed CS project artifacts; use of recordable web conferencing for online teacher professional development and mentoring; the collecting, packaging, and reporting of learning analytics site use metrics in the aggre-gate to participating schools, enabling productivity comparison within and across sites (see Reynolds & Leeder, 2017); cultural responsiveness features such as multiple language supports; and more. These affordances and more are described in greater detail in Reynolds (2016a, 2016b) and in Harel's articles featured in the URL at chapter's end.

GLOBALORIA USERS

To develop Globaloria, the organization worked in situ in schools composed almost entirely of groups under-represented in the computing disciplines, including students in very low–income rural school communities in the states of West Virginia, Wyoming, and Oklahoma, as well as predominantly African-American, Hispanic, and Asian, recent immigrant, and English language learner (ELL) student populations in Austin, Texas; Houston, Texas; San Jose, California; Queens; and the Bronx. School partnerships such as our work with Hispanic teachers and students in Texas led to a host of design-based research findings on situated local context needs and contingencies, for instance, around language and instruction. These findings sparked innovation of new features such as a specialized bilingual CS education curriculum for Spanish-speaking learners, which were then implemented in several Texas schools from 2015 to 2017. Table 4.2 provides a framework of principles guiding a responsive CS learning culture, which Harel developed based on her in situ observations on cultural responsiveness. The principles in table 4.2 are shared with all partner schools as well as Globaloria staff to guide ongoing program development and implementation.

SUMMARY OF KEY RESEARCH FINDINGS

Scholarly and evaluative research on Globaloria has been conducted by a network of approximately 15 academic research partner collaborators since

Table 4.2 Globaloria Principles Guiding a Responsive and Successful "Computer Science Learning Culture"

1.	Facilitate learning the *actual* concepts and practices of computer science.
2.	Encourage everybody's participation, equity, and diversity.
3.	Focus on creating computational artifacts (i.e., software, websites, animated characters, games, simulations, mobile apps).
4.	Support the study of computational thinking and algorithmic processes, as well as understanding their design, implementation, and impact on society.
5.	Emphasize how computing influences culture and culture shapes how people engage with computing.
6.	Facilitate computational thinking (CT) as central to the practices and concepts of computer science.
7.	Practice how to communicate about computing.
8.	Provide multiple pathways supporting a learning progression covering many CS concepts and principles.

2006. Findings have shown overall positive effects of learner participation on student interest, engagement, and motivation in six digital learning domains, as well as measured game design and CS knowledge outcomes, and attenuation of digital divide effects (e.g., Reynolds & Harel Caperton, 2011; Reynolds & Chiu, 2012, 2013, 2015; Reynolds, 2016a). Results with matched-case control groups in earlier years of the curriculum development also showed significant increases in standardized test scores in science, social studies, and English and language arts as a result of student participation (e.g., Chadwick & Gore 2010, 2011; Ho, Gore, & Chadwick, 2012).

While these early evaluative research results were encouraging, Globaloria's ongoing design-based research also led to iterative advances in the system's design. As one example, we note that Globaloria's early instructional design modeled constructionist and "discovery-based" learning philosophies supporting student choice, openness, play, fun, and self-structuring of work processes, encouraging learners' uses of online informational resources such as text- and video-based instructions and tutorials (Reynolds & Harel Caperton 2011). This early approach facilitated students' use of diverse and tailored online informational resources, but which were not necessarily matched with or adjacent to the given task in the user interface, requiring students to search, navigate, and locate resources to address their own personal information need at any given moment of their project's creation, in situ.

Video observations of students' in-class interactions with each other, teachers, and platform resources in earlier years indicated that students associated particular inquiry strategies with particular project tasks, showing some acumen in tailoring resource-seeking by task. For example, for simpler and more creative graphic design tasks, students more often engaged peer input with in-class neighbors, whereas for more challenging programming tasks, students engaged formal sources of expertise such as Globaloria video tutorials, the teacher, or the small handful of expert peer programmers in the class (which helped the seekers but occasionally sidetracked the experts) (Reynolds, 2016b; Reynolds & Chiu, 2012). And while students evidenced discernment regarding relevance of expertise sources for given tasks, some students struggled to identify more specifically the precise informational resource text that was meant to help them complete more challenging tasks. These results support past research on novice users, task difficulty, cognitive load, and need for structure in instructional design (discussed in 2016b).

Based on these results, alongside observations and conversations with principals, teachers, and CS education leaders, Globaloria established a more structured, "coursified approach" from 2013 to 2017, each year designing more modular learning sequences and activities with explicit topics and exercises supporting students' understanding of introductory programming and design fundamentals. This removed much of the self-structuring and information resource library searching/navigation, offering targeted resources in situ and adjacent to the given task in the scoped activity sequences. Educators requested and received more training on the new resources, curriculum sequences, and their own programming skills. A more clearly designed and labeled library of additional resources was offered for learners ready to move beyond the baseline exercises. Further, the novice learner GIDE (Globaloria integrated development environment) and its structured programming exercises offered students worked examples they could practice and experiment with. Assessment rubrics and badges provided added learning benchmarks.

These instructional design affordances were designed to maintain playfulness and student choice per constructionism (e.g., their game topics, graphic design and animations, and conveyance of meaningful personal expressions in design), while more closely structuring "guided discovery" toward delimited programming tasks in specific sequence. These changes may be seen by some to diverge somewhat from constructionist tenets of discovery: they were driven by the pragmatism of the project and the realities of implementing the curriculum, in a diverse and growing range of schools, while responding to school leaders' accountability imperatives for establishing clear learning goals and objectives they could speak to and demonstrable and reportable student learning outcomes.

LESSONS LEARNED

Since 2006 Globaloria has offered an engaging constructionist and structured sequence of programming experiences using a school-friendly e-learning platform whose features provide an integrated CS curriculum for students, teachers, and administrators. It is exciting for the authors to see the development of this innovation being continued by Carnegie Learning in Zulama. Constructionism has always had "disruptive" qualities vis-à-vis its implementation in school settings. In line with this, Globaloria has also demonstrated a pragmatic form of disruption, stretching and challenging developers, school partners, and teachers. Here we summarize a few of its particular categorical design innovations: (a) Globaloria's in situ school-based research and development, based in research and development work with a diverse set of school partners almost entirely reflective of populations under-represented in computing; (b) the employment of a homegrown blended e-learning platform for the curriculum delivery and replication; (c) development of a browser-based IDE that can be opened in adjacent browser tab with worked coding examples aligning with specific course activities. Our research reports and articles further outline additional instructional innovations.

Future research directions are recommended in these areas: (1) identifying the best method(s) for an organization to centrally manage further scale up of the now-commercialized "product," while maintaining effective customization for site-specific needs and close partnership with schools; (2) further articulating design-based research at finer levels of analysis *through continued in situ work with school partners* to identify and target improvements; (3) considering how to further integrate critical pedagogies, especially given the challenges of "workforce development" imperatives of US CS education goals and occasional nonreceptivity of school cultures to critical frames of reference; and (4) discovering means to deploy feasible upgrade models for future launch releases that do not over-tax participating schools with continuous platform change.

We hope that others may build upon this case study brief on our research and development of an e-learning platform for CS education in the US school system—to continue expanding beneficial constructionist learning opportunities to today's young people—balancing targeted responsive focus in local contexts, with growth and achieving greater levels of scale.

ACKNOWLEDGMENTS

The research studies summarized in this document authored by Professor Rebecca Reynolds and her collaborators were conducted with generous support from the Institute of Museum and Library Services, grant #RE-04-12-0048-12. The views, findings, conclusions, or recommendations expressed in this chapter do not necessarily represent those of the Institute of Museum and Library Services. At the time this book goes to print, Dr. Idit Harel has merged the Globaloria organization with Carnegie Learning, and under its new name *Zulama*, it continues to grow and develop in US schools and abroad.

NOTE: Additional resources and publications, including Dr. Idit Harel's popular press and public scholarship articles on Globaloria and CS Education, are available at: http://www.iditharel.com/publications/

REFERENCES

Chadwick, K., & Gore, J. (2010). *The relationship of Globaloria participation and student achievement.* Charleston, WV: Edvantia.

Chadwick, K., & Gore, J. (2011). *Globaloria replication study: Examining the robustness of relationships between Globaloria participation and student achievement.* Charleston, WV: Edvantia.

Ho, H., Gore, J., & Chadwick, K. (2012). *Globaloria replication study: An examination of the relationships between Globaloria participation and student achievement in year 4 of the West Virginia pilot implementation.* Charleston, WV: Edvantia.

Reynolds, R. (2016a). Defining, designing for, and measuring "digital literacy" development in learners: A proposed framework. *Educational Technology Research & Development, 64*(4), 735–762.

Reynolds, R. (2016b). Relationships among tasks, collaborative inquiry processes, inquiry resolutions, and knowledge outcomes in adolescents during guided discovery-based game design in school. *Journal of Information Science: Special Issue on Searching as Learning, 42,* 35–58.

Reynolds, R., & Chiu, M. (2012). Contribution of motivational orientations to student outcomes in a discovery-based program of game design learning. *Proceedings of the July 2012 International Conference of the Learning Sciences* (ICLS), Sydney, Australia.

Reynolds, R., & Chiu, M. (2013). Formal and informal context factors as contributors to student engagement in a guided discovery-based program of game design learning. *Journal of Learning, Media & Technology, 38*(4), 429–462.

Reynolds, R., & Chiu, M. (2015). Reducing digital divide effects through student engagement in coordinated game design, online resource uses, and social computing activities in school. *Journal of the Association for Information Science and Technology (JASIST), 67*(8), 1822–1835.

Reynolds, R., & Harel Caperton, I. (2011). Contrasts in student engagement, meaning-making, dislikes, and challenges in a discovery-based program of game design learning. *Journal of Educational Technology Research and Development, 59*(2), 267–289.

Reynolds, R., & Leeder, C. (2017, Jan). Information uses and learning outcomes during guided discovery in a blended e-learning game design program for secondary computer science education. *Proceedings of the Hawaii International Conference on System Sciences (HICSS),* Waikoloa, HI.

5 HALF-BAKED CONSTRUCTIONISM: A STRATEGY TO ADDRESS THE CHALLENGE OF INFUSING CONSTRUCTIONISM IN EDUCATION IN GREECE

Chronis Kynigos

Constructionist-minded attempts to intervene in educational systems on a large scale have always been met with the challenge of addressing epistemology and pedagogy as a priority in educational reform followed by the disillusionment of it turning out to be a much more complex and contentious enterprise. They have thus been perceived by many as an unsubstantiated promise, perturbing established institutionalized mindsets, practices, and organizational structures (Hoyles, 1993). Consider initiatives showcasing constructionist meaning-making communities, tools, productions, and exchanges as encapsulating a *silo approach* to spreading such individual and collective practices. Typically, they embody a purist mindset, primarily addressing learners at large outside the educational system, tacitly or explicitly expecting the system to notice and somehow modulate or transform accordingly. Even attempts to intervene within the system may be thought to perceive constructionism as a distinct module or paradigm to plug and play alongside everything else (Benton, Hoyles, Kalas, & Noss, 2017). In this chapter, I argue that it is time to seriously address an alternative strategy that may very well co-exist with silo-minded approaches: the strategy of slowly and messily infusing constructionist thinking in the system, letting it spread from within. I call this the *integrated approach* and, in this chapter, discuss some like-minded tools and strategies longitudinally developed and spread within a challenging education system in Greece.

THE CASE OF GREECE

I take the example of Greece and its local educational paradigm because the obstacles and, at the same time, the potential are distinct enough to perhaps be interesting for a more general discussion on constructionism on a large scale. The Greek education paradigm contains characteristics that seem to stand fundamentally opposed to constructionism. Historically, education in Greece has focused on transmitting and acquiring both fixed knowledge and national cultural heritage. The prevailing paradigm has characteristics of "humanism" with elements of "encyclopaedism" with a moral-revelatory approach, which has influenced the epistemological view of knowledge production and education. This orientation has inevitably favored factual rote learning and formal instruction, with little opportunity for class discussion or self-regulated independent work. Teachers are appointed and controlled by the state, while students are primarily being prepared for the examination that gives entry to university yielding an academic school (Kontogiannopoulou-Polydorides, Georgakakos, & Zavoudakis, 1996). What are the chances of a constructionist movement in this context, to inspire, to generate alternative mindsets, and to instigate practices that may have a chance of preservation and development over the years?

The discussion in this chapter is based on a 25-year longitudinal collaboration between a university-based Educational Technology Lab at the School of Philosophy, National and Kapodistrian University of Athens, and CTI-Diophantus, an institute belonging to the Ministry of Education, employed to implement initiatives and policy for the use of digital media in the education system. Despite the overarching paradigm, constructionist ideas were well received and agreed to be a non-antagonistic distinct element of a longitudinal reform strategy involving the use of digital media in primary and secondary education. The collaboration was in the context of two long-term initiatives:

1. In-service teacher education, which has generated 600 teacher educators and reached 30% of teachers in the country so far

2. Digital infrastructures involving portals, pedagogically principled social media services, and teacher resource and practice forums

My role in these initiatives was as a member of the steering committee in each respective case; I was responsible for mathematics education. The strategy for intervention, which originated at the lab but was agreed upon and developed by both institutions, adopted an integrated context-sensitive approach.

This had two main aspects:

1. A focus on substance, that is, on epistemology, learning theory, and frameworks for action mediated explicitly and employed to give a central role to the understanding and supporting of teachers through their professional development (Kynigos, 2007). The theoretical approach for the

use of digital media for learning was based on connections between constructionism and semiotic mediation, activity theory, situated abstractions, and instrumentalization (references and discussion can be found in Kynigos, 2015a). With respect to teachers, the approach connected theoretical constructs such as Documentational Genesis (for resource design, production, and versioning) with boundary crossings as a way to think of communication among teachers over digital artifacts in design. There was thus a central emphasis on their function and role as resource and activity designers (diSessa, 1997), encouraging collaborative designs and supporting the generation of sociotechnical environments (respectively, see Kynigos, 2015b, 2007).

2. The design and mediation of a suite of resources based on an integration-minded design approach. The process centrally focused on three otherwise diverse constructs in conjunction: conceptual fields for the design of problem situations for students (Vergnaud, 2009), restructurations to express out-of-the-box search for powerful ideas for meaning making (Wilensky & Papert, 2010), and black-and-white architectures for digital media providing pedagogically engineered transparency so that students could tinker with more complex building blocks and create more interesting artifacts and simulations than silo constructionist tools (Kynigos, 2004).

The design of these resources and their mediation and sustained adoption on a large scale was the focus with emphasis given to substance, to recognizing and empowering the role of educational professionals, and to providing students with a context to engage and generate meanings. The resources were thus designed with the principle of *engineered* transparency, that is, providing ideas, tools, and resources for all to shape and to build with, but respectively with diverse entry points and building block granularity (Kynigos, 2004, 2016).

ENGINEERED TRANSPARENCY: BLACK AND WHITE DESIGNS

Constructionism is about learning through tinkering and thus designing artifacts inviting this kind of malleability. Transparency and a low threshold have been key elements of purist constructionist designs so that learners can start early in life. Artifacts allow building things from scratch, based on some generic primitives and affordances and a powerful language to express and create models, games, and simulations (Resnick, Berg, & Eisenberg, 2000). This has excited many youngsters and generated a large community of tinkerers. However, the downside of a low threshold and pure transparency has been that users can only create relatively simple things and always have to start from the beginning. An integrated approach maintains a constructionist language but relies on a pedagogically engineered level of transparency, affording, for instance, the functionality to build on a complex model, or work with black-box building blocks, which embed a technical complexity (Kynigos, 2004).

MESHING EXPRESSIVITIES

Collaboration between the lab and a research group at CTI-Diophantus led to the co-design and development of *E-slate*, a component-based authoring environment, in which the primitives are pieces of software sometimes quite complex, such as a database, a Geographical Information System (GIS), a Logo language, or a scene for graphical output.[1] Connectivity primitives exist but can also be defined via the Logo language. Like many Java-based pieces of software, E-slate is now obsolete, but in recent years at the lab, we have engaged in re-designing and developing the best ideas generated with E-slate. So far, we have developed two such authorable pieces of software, based on the principle of black-and-white design, and have been operationally including artifacts designed with these in the Ministry's portal and the teacher education curriculum. We call them "MaLT2" (machinelab turtleworlds) and "ChoiCo" (choices with consequences).[2] Both of these integrate hitherto diverse functionalities, moving some distance from totally transparent constructionist tools with an agenda to be employed by a large number of users not necessarily into or aware of the constructionist community.

ELUSIVE CONCEPTS AND MODELS MADE AVAILABLE

MaLT2 is a Logo-based, three-dimensional turtle graphics tool including camera perusal and uniquely integrated with affordances for the dynamic manipulation of variable values to procedures (Kynigos & Grizioti, 2018). Through both large-scale CTI initiatives, it is particularly enjoyed by mathematics teachers and students and provides potential for the creation of some models hardly possible with tangible materials, embedding mathematical concepts that could not be available to students otherwise, at least at school age. For instance, imagine the perimeter of a cylinder produced by bending the opposite sides of a square to form circular arcs until they

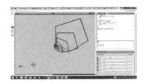

FIGURE 5.1
MaLT2—Logo programming, 3D, Dynamic Manipulation, ChoiCo-Blockly programming, GIS, DB.

create circles, or a rectangle in which one side is twisted on a perpendicular plane. Imagine a di-angle, a polygon with just two angles only possible on a sphere. Now visualize these figures dynamically manipulated to form unexpected behaviors, especially when placed in complicated structures in the role of a building block (figure 5.1).

Even on one plane, concepts are shaped by means of the integrated affordances of programmability and dynamic manipulation of variable values. A rectangle is a mathematical object only when it is defined so that it remains so when any parameter value is manipulated. Alternatively, it is just an instance of a rectangle, not a mathematical object. Proportionality can be expressed when figures shrink and expand without losing their form. Segments can dynamically change into constant and then exponential curves. Sorting out and debugging figures with faulty behavior necessarily involves using mathematical/programming formalism to get at the figures' properties (Kynigos, 2016).

So, students are not asked to build things from scratch as would be the case in a silo approach; nor are they only given the most rudimentary set of primitives to work with. They are instead asked to start from tinkering with an artifact already designed by a teacher as a higher-order primitive and are given functionalities enabling the "tangible" dynamic manipulation of variable values to visualize the behavior of an artifact. MaLT2 is becoming popular among teachers and students through the digital school and teacher education initiatives precisely because of the integrated affordance to manipulate the products of explicit mathematical formalism.

CONTEXTUALIZING MATHEMATICS IN COMPLEX VALUE-LADEN ISSUES

ChoiCo is an authoring tool for creating "choices with consequences" games. The player makes choices: for instance, "visit the bakery," and each choice has consequences on a variety of values such as pleasure, cost, nutrition, environmental ethos, and weight gain. There is no choice with only positive or only negative values. The object of the game is to stay on as long as possible before a value goes over a "red line." The author can use a GIS affordance to define or change the game map and insert geo-located (not necessarily geographical) choices, giving a name to each. They can use a database to define values and insert the consequences of each choice. They can then use Blockly to provide game rules, aggregate consequences, insert little cautionary texts and define the red lines.

ChoiCo is designed to embed powerful ideas in wider socioscientific real-life issues rather than mathematical or simulation behavior-driven models. Students and teachers of diverse domains have been designing a surprising variety of games involving issues such as sustainability, compost heap, dietary habits, work ethics, and supermarket shopping and making decisions while aspiring to become an MP in ancient Athens and avoiding trouble in the classroom (by seventh-year students). Using ChoiCo involves alternating roles from player to designer, modding a game and talking intensely in groups about the issues involved with respect to the consequences and the choice of choices (Kynigos & Yiannoutsou, 2018). Therefore, there is integration at two levels. One is that of very diverse affordances, including a wider idea of constructionism with these (e.g., building a geo-located database). The other is the alternative role of a powerful idea in the spirit of restructuration. Rather than being a vehicle to provide a solution or an explanation, such an idea becomes a tool toward gaining sensitivity to a complex socioscientific issue that may not have a solution as of yet.

HALF-BAKED MICROWORLDS AND MICRO-EXPERIMENTS

Over the years, the lab engaged in pedagogical design with the use of E-slate, MaLT2, ChoiCo, and other systems such as Geometry Sketchpad, Cabri Geometry, and recently GeoGebra. Maintaining the black-and-white box design principle led to two main kinds of artifacts as key elements of resources for student work. We called them "Half-baked microworlds" (Kynigos, 2007) and the relatively recently coined "Micro-experiments" (Kynigos, 2016). The former type of resource involves the pedagogically principled placing of bugs in an artifact or the creation of wanting artifacts. We provide students with these and a story engaging them in the role of "de-buggers." Then, after they mod, improve, or correct such an artifact, we encourage them to build their own complex structures with their corrected version as a building block. Half-baked microworlds have permeated the way we think and design in the lab. In our research with teacher and student users, we have appreciated how they work as frames to focus on powerful ideas more succinctly, as organizers and context providers for meaning making through discussion, exchange, and rich versioning. Ownership is still there; it comes from the way a half-baked artifact is changed and from the structures subsequently built, the ways in which it is being put to use. We have also studied the craft of designing half-baked microworlds as a means for teachers to engage in professional development contexts, including communities of practice and diverse communities of interest, yielding creative ideas for the development of constructionist resources for students. A buggy, fallible artifact here is the primitive, rather than just the pure state-changing and object primitives in Logo, Scratch, or NetLogo.

Micro-experiments are designed to be readily used on a large scale. They are resources involving a half-baked artifact but containing some closed questions readily matching equivalent questions from traditional curriculum exercises. Only here, there is one or two open-ended, constructionist or exploratory questions at the end. A wonderful group of teacher designers worked at the lab and developed 1,800 original micro-experiments spanning from year 3 to 11, dynamically connected to the respective curriculum books and made available through the Ministry of Education's "Digital School" infrastructure. Out of these, 240 are developed with MaLT2 and around 1,200 with GeoGebra, including simulations of physical phenomena but with a lesser constructionist element. Constructionism here has a distinct but not exclusive role and presence; it has been placed among affordances allowing for other paradigms (such as show and explain) to co-exist.

SCENARIOS

Finally, the term "scenario" originated in the large-scale in-service initiative, started in 1996 and then re-initiated and maintained from 2003 to today. The initiative is truly large scale, involving a 96-hour course providing a central role to constructionist ideas, methods, and tools. It has reached 30% of teachers in the whole of Greece so far (2,500/7,000 mathematics teachers) and has resulted in ninety-eight mathematics teacher educators providing the ninety-six-hour course who subsequently completed a 380-hour training course at the university. Scenarios have developed into a key element in this enterprise. In effect, they constitute structured activity plans written by teachers for teachers, focusing on pedagogy and substance and allowing for their readers to shape their own teaching practice based on the content of the scenario. They necessarily contain detail on aspired student activity with digital media and explain how meaning making may be encouraged; they also detail suggested social orchestration and time-topology parameters. Widespread scenario production from the teachers joining the Ministry's initiative has given credence to the construct, which is also used as a main element of learning and assessment in our post-graduate courses at the university. Naturally, there is no request for a purist constructionist character to the activities described in a scenario, but at least in mathematics, teachers are gently encouraged to consider this element in at least part of the activities they design for their students.

DISCUSSION

The suite of resource templates described here originated from a constructionist research lab but gained wide recognition and systemic value by a gradual process of being put to use by many. I argue that the adopted integrated, context-sensitive approach in their design and mediation through the teacher education and digital school initiatives were key in their adoption by one-third of teachers in the country so far, in this case, regarding the domain of mathematics primarily but not exclusively. Constructionism has a recognized place here. Activity plans may well involve a primarily constructionist activity, including half-baked microworlds. A micro-experiment may have a constructionist element including a half-baked artifact. Most of the MaLT2 micro-experiments in the digital school portal, for instance, are about fixing a buggy program and discussing the process. ChoiCo, finally, is our spearhead to approach other domains, such as computational thinking, informatics, environmental education, ethics, and nutrition education. The mediation strategy was also principled, enhancing a sense of role empowerment for everyone, including teachers and students who felt of course the value of ownership and intellectual discursive exchange. The strategy also focused on giving value to personal satisfaction, agency, a sense of participation in something big, the addressing of pedagogical substance, the progressive professional recognition, and the flexibility for realistic take-up within regular professional life. This is a messy process, and it is impossible to predict where it will go in the next 25 years. But it leaves open questions, such as how can we study meaning-making cultures and their growth in large-scale, integrated situations? How can we communicate the value of meaning-making, constructionism, and creativity in the context of diverse educational paradigms and in an era of administration, accountability, and information inflation? How can we generate resilience in these ideas in a context which focuses on innovation changes? Now, at least in Europe, focus is on "twenty-first-century skills," on socioscientific paradigms, on the inclusion of social media and computational thinking, on digital citizenship. How do we make constructionist ideas visible and recognizable in this era of innovation and in those to come? I suggest that these questions can only be asked and investigated in the context of situations emerging from integrated approaches.

Here I discussed how emphasizing substance via an integrated approach and providing tools affording pedagogically engineered transparency were the two elements of infusing constructionism in a revelatory paradigm. I am sure there are other strategies out there and even more to be conceived and implemented as integrated approaches become included in constructionist agendas worldwide.

ACKNOWLEDGMENTS

I would like to thank the professional development and the digital school intiatives of the Greek National Operational Programme "Education and Lifelong Learning" of the Greek National Strategic Reference Framework (NSRF), co-financed by the European Union (ESF) and National funds implemented by CTI-Diophantus.

I would also like to thank the Educational Technology Lab PhD students, Post Doc researchers and teacher collaborators for their engagement and wanderful work at http://etl.eds.uoa.gr.

NOTES

1. http://e-slate.cti.gr/

2. http://etl.ppp.uoa.gr/MaLT2 and http://etl.ppp.uoa.gr/choico

REFERENCES

Artigue, M., & Mariotti, M. A. (2014). Networking theoretical frames: The ReMath enterprise, in digital representations in mathematics education: Conceptualizing the role of context and networking theories. [Special issue]. *Educational Studies in Mathematics, 85*(3), 329–355.

Benton, L., Hoyles, C., Kalas, I., & Noss, R. (2017). Bridging primary programming and mathematics: Some findings of design research in England. *Digital Experiences in Mathematics Education,* 1–24.

diSessa, A. (1997). Open toolsets: New ends and new means in learning mathematics and science with computers. In E. Pehkonen (Ed.), *Proceedings of the 21st Conference of the International Group for the Psychology of Mathematics Education, 1,* 47–62, Lahti, Finland.

Hoyles, C. (1993). Microworlds/schoolworlds: The transformation of an innovation. In C. Keitel & K. Ruthven (Eds.), *Learning from computers: Mathematics education and technology* (pp. 10–17). Berlin, Germany: Springer.

Kontogiannopoulou-Polydorides, G., Georgakakos, S., & Zavoudakis, A. (1996). Greek schools and computer education: Sociocultural interpretations. In R. Anderson, G. Kontogiannopoulou-Polydorides, & T. J. Plomp (Eds.), *Cross national policies and practices on computers in education* (pp. 223–247). Dordrecht, The Netherlands: Kluwer Academic Publishers.

Kynigos, C. (2004). A "black-and-white box" approach to user empowerment with component computing. *Interactive Learning Environments, 12*(1–2), 27–71. https://doi.org/10.1080/1049482042000300896

Kynigos, C. (2007). Half-baked microworlds in use in challenging teacher educators' knowing. *International Journal of Computers for Mathematical Learning. 12*(2), 87–111.

Kynigos, C. (2015a). Constructionism: Theory of learning or theory of design? In Sung Je Cho (Ed.), *Selected Regular Lectures from the 12th International Congress on Mathematical Education* 417–438, https://doi.org/10.1007/978-3-319-17187-6

Kynigos, C. (2015b). Designing constructionist e-books: New mediations for creative mathematical thinking? *Constructivist Foundations 10*(3), 305–313.

Kynigos, C. (2016). Constructionist mathematics with institutionalized infrastructures: the case of Dimitris and his students. In A. Montone & E. Faggiano (Eds.), *Innovation and technology. Perspectives on mathematics education in the digital era,* 197–214. New York, NY: Springer International Publishing.

Kynigos, C., & Grizioti, M. (2018). Programming approaches to computational thinking: Integrating turtle geometry, dynamic manipulation and 3D space. In *Informatics in Education, 17.2* (pp. 321–340). Vilnius, Lithuania: Vilnius University.

Kynigos, C. & Yiannoutsou, N. (2018). Children challenging the design of half-baked games: Expressing values through the process of game modding. *International Journal of Child-Computer Interaction.* Retrieved from https://doi.org/10.1016/j.ijcci.2018.04.001

Resnick, M., Berg, R., & Eisenberg, M. (2000). Beyond black boxes: Bringing transparency and aesthetics back to scientific investigation. *Journal of the Learning Sciences, 9*(1), 7–30.

Vergnaud, G. (2009). The theory of conceptual fields. *Human Development, 52,* 83–94. https://doi.org/10.1159/000202727

Wilensky, U., & Papert, S. (2010). Restructurations: Reformulations of knowledge disciplines through new representational forms. In J. Clayson & I. Kalas (Eds.), Constructionist approaches to creative learning, thinking and education: Lessons for the 21st century. *Proceedings of the Constructionism 2010 Conference Paris: American University of Paris,* 97–105, Paris, France.

6 WHY SCHOOL REFORM IS IMPOSSIBLE

Seymour Papert

Reviewed Work: David Tyack and Larry Cuban. *Tinkering Towards Utopia: A Century of Public School Reform.* Cambridge, MA: Harvard University Press, 1995, 184pp., ISBN No. 0-674-89282-8.

With commentary on O'Shea's and Koschmann's reviews of *The Children's Machine*.

The common theme of *Tinkering towards Utopia* (Tyack & Cuban, 1995) and the two reviews of *The Children's Machine* (Papert, 1993) is the failure of educational reform to change School.[1] O'Shea and Koschmann each tell aspects of a story in which the failed reform is the "Logo movement." Tyack and Cuban present a story of larger scope whose plot starts with the birth of the generic twentieth-century American education reform movement, develops through its interaction with School, and ends leaving School essentially unchanged. The following pages are the outcome of my attempt to understand all three texts by situating them in an even larger story about change in education.

REFORM VERSUS REVOLUTION

My first reaction to *Tinkering towards Utopia* (Tyack & Cuban, 1995) was adversarial. I am convinced that education will undergo the kind of mega-change that came in the wake of technological and scientific develop-ments in areas such as medicine. Yet as Koschmann pointed out in the introduction to this section, although Tyack and Cuban present their work as analysis of the past, "the implication is plain that the prospects for *any* technology, ... leading to radical change in our educational institutions appear quite bleak" (Koschmann & Kolodner, this issue, p. 399). One of us, it seemed at first sight, has to be wrong.

Only at first sight. Working on this review brought me the intellectual bonus of a better understanding of my own position by making explicit a simple distinction that has long lurked unformulated in the shadows of my intuitions: "Reform" and "change" are not synonymous. Tyack and Cuban clinched my belief that the prospects really are indeed bleak for deep change coming from deliberate attempts to impose a specific new form on education. However, some changes, arguably the most important ones in sociocultural spheres, come about by evolution rather than by deliberate design—by what I am inspired by Dan Dennett (1994) to call "Darwinian design."[2] For example, the concept of learning disability entered School in a manner more akin to the way that memes invade cultures than to the conduct of an education reform movement; institutionalization from above followed the cultural movement.

Examples closer to my focus here are to be found in the unintended effects on the classroom of the presence of computers in homes. The title of an article by Cuban (1992), "Computers Meet Classroom: Classroom Wins," refers to School's defense mechanisms against reform being brought into the classroom by computers. School exerts less influence on what children do with home computers, and as the number of these reaches significant levels, we are beginning to observe changes in the relationship between teachers and students brought about not by a reform, but by the fact that the students have acquired a new kind of sophistication—not only about computers but also about ways to learn and methods of research (Papert, 1996a).

With the evolution-reform distinction in mind, I found myself reading *Tinkering towards Utopia* more sympathetically. I could now appreciate the elucidation of mechanisms by which the system systematically frustrates reform without feeling obliged to defend my own intellectual commitments. In fact, I could learn from it—the shift from a stance of reform to a stance of evolution does not exclude active intervention, but the role of the change agent becomes less like the architect or builder and more like the plant- or animal breeder whose interventions take the form of influencing processes that have their own dynamic. *Tinkering towards Utopia* is a gold mine of insights into the dynamic of School's defense mechanisms.

Nevertheless, a sense of residual discomfort lasted until I managed to formulate yet another respect in which *Tinkering towards Utopia* says less than I first thought: The mechanisms described in it are *concomitants* rather than *causes* of the stability of School. Making this distinction will lead me to suggest that Tyack and Cuban are blinded to a deeper layer of explanation by a theoretical stance that looks deeply into the sociological processes at play in education while treating as a black box the actual content of what is being taught and (supposedly) learned.

COGNITIVE SCIENCE VERSUS SOCIOLOGY OF INSTITUTIONS

The contrast between the sociological stance of *Tinkering towards Utopia* and the cognitive stance of the two reviews of *The Children's Machine* is characteristic of large subcommunities in education research and innovation: At a typical conference on educational technology virtually all the talk is in the style represented by O'Shea and Koschmann; at a conference on restructuring schools virtually all is in the style represented by Tyack and Cuban. In the hope of bridging this separation by showing complementary strengths and weaknesses of the two sides, I take a quick look at two ways of thinking about why Logo, and in fact, the computer presence in general, has not had a bigger effect on School. The need for bridging may be seen by reflecting on the sense in which Tyack and Cuban are overly sociological and O'Shea overly cognitive.

Discourse in the educational technology culture tends to have an aura of "scientific method": Logo is based on a theory of learning; experiments were mounted to test predictions made from this theory; the predictions were or were not verified. I shall comment later on the interpretation of the experiments, but what is relevant for the moment is the contrast with another way of thinking that gives little importance to the truth or falsity of cognitive theories in influencing, one way or another, the fate of education reforms. In *The Children's Machine*, I tell a story in terms of institutional and cultural dynamics rather than of cognitive science along the lines of the following brief outline: The first microcomputers in schools were in the classrooms of visionary teachers who used them (often with Logo) in very personal ways to cut across deeply rooted features of School (what Tyack and Cuban neatly call "the grammar of school"), such as a bureaucratically imposed linear curriculum, separation of subjects, and depersonalization of work. School responded to this foreign body by an "immune reaction" that blocked these subversive features: The control of computers was shifted from the classrooms of subversive teachers into "computer labs" isolated from the mainstream of learning, a computer curriculum was developed ... in short, before the computer could change School, School changed the computer.

Unless I am missing Tyack and Cuban's point, this account is in the spirit of *Tinkering towards Utopia* and, in fact, exemplifies one of the major principles in its presentation of the generic life cycle of reforms: The reform sets out to change School, but in the end School changes the reform. One may at first blush see a tautology in using this proposition to explain failures of reform. But to say that School changes the reform is very different from simply saying that School resists or rejects the reform. It resists the reform in a particular way—by appropriating or assimilating it to its own structures. By doing so, it defuses the reformers and sometimes manages to take in something of what they are proposing.

A PIAGETIAN MODEL OF EDUCATIONAL DEVELOPMENT

The word *assimilation* in the previous paragraph is a first step in an assimilation of the Tyack-Cuban analysis to a Piagetian view (generalized from a theory of the child to apply to institutions such as School) in which development advances through a series of temporarily stable states of equilibrium.[3] Transferring Piaget's language to this context, I see Tyack and Cuban as discussing what happens within a stage of development, while my perception of imminent change in education is more like the transition to a new stage.

The difference between intra-stage and inter-stage phenomena is categorical: The former has to do with how a system in equilibrium functions, whereas the latter has to do with breakdown of existing states of equilibrium and the emergence of new ones. I see School as a system in which major components have developed harmonious and mutually supportive— mutually matched—forms. There is a match of curriculum content, of epistemological framework, of organizational structure, and—here comes the trickiest point for Tyack and Cuban—of knowledge technology. A typical failed education reform is like tweaking one component of a well-equilibrated dynamic system: When you let go, it is pulled back by all the other components. *Tinkering towards Utopia* describes the processes by which the tweaked component springs back into its equilibrium position but says nothing about the nature or the source of the equilibrium and, most seriously, is blind to the forces most likely to break it.

In *Mindstorms* (Papert, 1980), I asked (choosing one out of a vast number of possible examples) why the quadratic equation of the parabola is included in the mathematical knowledge every educated citizen is expected to know. Saying that it is "good math" is not enough reason: The curriculum includes only a minute sliver of the total body of good mathematics. The real reason is that it matches the technology of pencil and paper: It is easy for a student to draw the curve on squared paper and for a teacher to verify that the assignment has been done correctly.

I have noted elsewhere (Papert, 1996b), that School's math can be characterized by the fact that its typical act is making marks on paper. "Explorations in the Space of Mathematics Education" develops this idea by imagining an alternative mathematical education in which the typical activity begins with and consists of creating, modifying, or controlling dynamic computational objects. In this context the parabola may be first encountered by a child creating a videogame as the trajectory of an animal's leap or a missile's flight; here, the natural first formalism for the parabola is an expression in a child-appropriate computational language of something like "the path followed when horizontal speed and vertical acceleration are both constant."

Many readers will say that is too abstract for children. This is because they have in mind children who grew up using the static medium of pencil and paper as the primary medium for representing mathematical ideas. Attempts to inject this treatment of the parabola as an isolated innovation into an otherwise unchanged School will confirm their negative view. For children who have acquired true computational fluency by growing up with the dynamic medium as a primary representation for mathematical thinking, I argue that it would plausibly be more concrete, more intuitive, and far more motivating than quadratic equations. My experiments support this expectation by showing that the dynamic definition is indeed accessible even to elementary school children who are given the opportunity to acquire a degree of computational fluency that is still very limited though considerably more extensive than a few students develop in what are misleadingly called "computer labs" in contemporary schools.

ASSIMILATION BLINDNESS

I am grateful to Tyack and Cuban for their concept of a "grammar of school." The structure of School is so deeply rooted that one reacts to deviations from it as one would to a grammatically deviant utterance: Both feel wrong on a level deeper than one's ability to formulate reasons. This phenomenon is related to "assimilation blindness" insofar as it refers to a mechanism of mental closure to foreign ideas. I would make the relation even closer by noting that when one is not paying careful attention, one often actually hears the deviant utterance as the "nearest" grammatical utterance a transformation that might bring drastic change in meaning.

I see an example of this in Tyack and Cuban's assimilation of the computer to a concept of "electronic pedagogy"—a "teaching machine"—that puts it in the same category as radio, movies, tape recorders, and the like. The superficial physical resemblance cannot be a sufficient reason for lumping these diverse things together: nobody puts textbooks and comic strips in the same category just because they are made of paper. The real reason is that the constructionist use of the computer has no place in the grammar of school, which casts everything in the role of teaching device and thus creates an assimilation blindness to the use of computers to support noninstructionist forms of learning. The point can be seen most simply by borrowing from experimental psycholinguists a standard test for assimilation. If you ask, "Which is not like the other two?" in the list "educational movie, textbook, computer," it is pretty obvious from my perspective that the answer must be "computer." The choice of "textbook" that is implicit in *Tinkering towards Utopia's* use of language appears to me to be a clear example of assimilating the new technology to the old grammar of School—as is the fact that, although Tyack and Cuban do not consider constructionist uses of the computer to be worth mentioning, they give prominent mention to Edison's prediction that the motion picture would displace the textbook.[4]

I see two prima facie objections to this analysis. The simplest is to shift the responsibility for the assimilation from the minds of the theoretical observer to the practices of schools: Instructionist uses in conformity with the grammar of school constitute the reality that the theorist is trying to interpret. However, in the context of explaining why schools don't change, this begs the question, for surely School's assimilation (even if it were universal, which it is not) is part of what has to be explained and, in my view, the essential part. The more substantial objection appeals to a widely held belief that research has shown that the noninstructionist uses of the computer are mere chimera based on romantic, unfulfilled claims. It is therefore appropriate to take a look at the kinds of discourse from which these beliefs have developed. I do this by focusing on one case in which I have been centrally involved.

BUT DIDN'T ROY PEA REFUTE THIS "LOGO VISION"?

In his review of *The Children's Machine,* O'Shea at least partly endorses the belief that Roy Pea (and others) demonstrated that "Logo did not live up to Papert's predictions" (Koschmann, this issue; Noss & Hoyles, 1996; Papert, 1987; Pea & Kurland, 1984). In the spirit of elucidating the logic of the belief, I use a review of some history to make two related points. First, Pea's experiment (Pea & Kurland, 1984) and some of O'Shea's comments reflect an assimilation of my thesis to the grammar of school by reading it as a statement about improving rather than radically changing School. Second, although I and many others (including Koschmann, this issue) have pointed to specific flaws of experimental method in the procedures adopted by Pea and Kurland, a more fundamental flaw lies in the fact that no experiment on the paradigm of school psychology could refute my thesis. Indeed, one may be more justified in leveling at me the Popperian criticism that my thesis is not amenable to refutation at all. Perhaps so, but that is a horse of a different color.

The intention of *Mindstorms* (Papert, 1980) was really to deconstruct the necessity of School by showing that something very different—far more different than the reforms discussed by Tyack and Cuban—could at least be imagined. In the first chapter, I explicitly cast my goal in terms that fit the Tyack and Cuban perspective: "Conservatism in the world of education has become a self-perpetuating *social* [italics added] phenomenon." The vicious circle would be broken when "people with good ideas, different ideas, exciting ideas will no longer be faced with a dilemma where they have either to 'sell' their ideas to a conservative bureaucracy or shelve them." (p. 37). I saw the social penetration of computers as eventually providing individuals or communities with the instruments to develop and to implement new educational ideas. It takes the next 150 pages of the book for me to develop a rather complex example of such an idea that I call a "LOGO environment." I suggest that the penetration of computers into everyday life and dissatisfaction with traditional school can (not will) come together in the construction of educationally powerful environments and then say:

> I do not present LOGO environments as my proposal for doing this. They are too primitive, too limited. The role I hope they fill is ... an object-to-think-with, that will contribute to the essentially social process of constructing the education of the future, ... there will be more tries, and more and more. And eventually, somewhere, all the pieces will come together and it will "catch." (p. 182)

I describe in *The Children's Machine* (Papert, 1993) how surprised I was to find that many thousands of people—mainly visionary teachers—found in this book an articulation of their desire for something different from School. Many of them tried ... and tried. Many burned out. Many were defeated by the bureaucracy of School. Many are still trying. The most insightful of those who are teachers working in conventional schools who understand what they are doing today in the same spirit as my remark about my early Logo environments not being the ideal they wish for, or even an approximation to it. As ideas multiply and as the ubiquitous computer presence solidifies, the prospect of deep change becomes more real. Their day-to-day work with computers will be the seeds from which it will grow.

I feel honored and flattered by the good things Tim O'Shea writes about me in his review of *The Children's Machine*, but I am all the more surprised by his falling for the belief that Roy Pea could be held to have "evaluated" the vision presented in *Mindstorms*. The strongest negative conclusion that could in principle be drawn from one experiment that has children "doing

Logo" for a few hours a week in their otherwise unchanged school culture is that a particular implementation of a very primitive early form of the Logo idea failed to "work" according to a particular measure of success (and, in Pea's case, one that I would have regarded as a measure of failure had it, in fact, shown significant change).

Tim Koschmann's review of my book suggests two more optimistic reactions to Pea. One he makes explicitly: Learn from the failure and try again. The other is implicit in his comparison of Logo with Latin.

TWO SENSES OF "LATIN"

Koschmann's comparison of Logo with Latin focuses on the issue of transfer of cognitive skills from programming to other areas of intellectual activity. I agree completely with the soundness and importance of his conclusion that what is needed here is richer study of the cultural context of transfer. On that issue I would just add one observation. Psychologists have studied transfer as if it were something that happens to you; I look at it as something you do and am especially interested in the development of cultures that give transfer the status of a deliberate act.

I also like Koschmann's title for its suggestion of a connection between Logo and an altogether different erstwhile function of Latin. In recent times, Latin was taught in schools because it was supposed to be good for the development of general cognitive skills. Further back, it was taught because it was the language in which all scholarly knowledge was expressed, and I have suggested that computational language could come to play a similar role in relation to quite extensive areas of knowledge.

The shift in the treatment of the parabola mentioned earlier is typical of examples developed in *Mindstorms* and in *Explorations in the Space of Mathematics Educations* of how knowledge can become far more accessible and far more learnable when couched in computational language. I am sure that in the course of time this greater ease will result in a Darwinian evolution of mathematics education. Similar to biological evolution it will take time, and it is worth the risk of a little repetition to review some of the factors that militate against quick change.

THE CONTENT OF CHANGE AND THE CHANGE OF CONTENT

The key point is that many components of the system have to change and in a matched way. Introducing the suggested new treatment of the parabola into a school without computers would quickly prove that it is hopelessly bad. Even putting in a lot of computers would be insufficient unless the conditions were present for the students to acquire fluency in a suitable computational language. This would require time. Again, time would not be sufficient. To learn French you certainly need time, but you would not learn it well unless you had the opportunity for engaging talk or reading in French. In the case of the parabola, if this were all that was available to the students of the new language, they would be no more likely to show success in learning than students of French who had access to one short passage in that language. For success, there would have to have developed the analog of a diverse collection of books written in French and access to French-speaking people.

The central issue is analogous to one that has played a central role in theories of biological evolution: How do features of the system whose functions are mutually dependent come into being without a guiding designer? Attempts to change the medium and leave the content (e.g., use computers to teach the same math) or change the content but keep the medium (e.g., National Council of Teachers of Mathematics standards or "The New Math" performed in the old medium) do not create a new equilibrium—in fact they make a "camel" in the sense of "a horse designed by a committee." Nobody is satisfied with the camel, and the system snaps back to the old equilibrium, manifesting as it does so the mechanisms so brilliantly described by Tyack and Cuban.

In his review, O'Shea puts his finger on one strategy to deal with this problem when he refers to the need to develop content that embodies the Logo vision and yet can be used within School curriculum. I have to agree with him: Although I, and a few others, have done some work on this "Trojan Horse" strategy, much more is needed. I hope he will be pleased to note that my recent work (Papert, 1996b) marks an intensification of this effort as does a publication in preparation that gives a more curriculum-like and more substantive development of the material in the chapter on cybernetics in *The Children's Machine*.[5]

Reformulating knowledge in the "new Latin" while at the same time developing the language and creating conditions for children to learn is formidable enough as a research program, but I believe that even this would not be enough to create a new equilibrated system. Changes would be needed in other components in addition to content and medium. One that is nicely picked up by Koschmann and, I am afraid, seems to be entirely missed by O'Shea is epistemological style. The style I call bricolage (following Lévi-Strauss, Robert Lawler, and my own work with Sherry Turkle) fits the learning styles of many or most children but is powerfully at odds with School's style. The point missed by O'Shea's comments is that the chapter of *The Children's Machine* on cybernetics is really about how to introduce into a curriculum for children an area of knowledge that allows work in a bricolage style to support an entry into rigorous mathematics and science. The deeper point is to offer an example showing a different content, different style of learning, different epistemology, and a different medium all matched to one another and to a form of school structured without curriculum or age segregation.

My apparent failure to make the intention of that chapter clear enough lies behind another of O'Shea's comments with which I agree completely in principle. He writes, "We now need an account of how, for example, the innovative work of Mitchel Resnick on computational construction kits may relate to and support school learning" (p. 405). But the intention of the chapter on cybernetics was to sketch informally some aspects of one way to do exactly that. Work on what my colleague Mitchel Resnick calls computational construction kits is an integral part of the further development by the team we jointly lead at the Massachusetts Institute of Technology Media Laboratory of the vision that began with the early work on Logo. We are busy doing what O'Shea recommends. Readers who are interested in following this ongoing development should keep in touch with the publication list of the Epistemology and Learning group at the Media Lab via its website (see note 5).

DARWIN VERSUS THE GOSPLAN

In conclusion, I use a political metaphor to express my most profound points of agreement and of disagreement with Tyack and Cuban. Designing an alternative education is a Soviet-Gosplan-like enterprise whose ultimate fatal flaw is what made the Soviet system impossible. Tyack and Cuban spell out in the case of School reform how centralized social engineering inexorably goes wrong. Complex systems are not made. They evolve. Where I part company from Tyack and Cuban is when they turn from the book's historical theme of showing that reform will not work to give advice to reformers about how to do it better. My own view is that education activists can be effective in fostering radical change by rejecting the concept of a planned reform and concentrating on creating the obvious conditions for Darwinian evolution: Allow rich diversity to play itself out. Of course, neither of us can prove the other is wrong. That's what I mean by diversity.

NOTES

From "Why School Reform Is Impossible," by Seymour Papert, 1997, *Journal of the Learning Sciences*, *6*(4), pp. 417–427. Copyright 2007 by Lawrence Erlbaum Associates, Inc. Reprinted with permission.

1. The capitalized word "School" refers to an idealized theoretical entity of which actual schools are more or less approximate representatives. In using it, I am asserting (a) that despite a real degree of individual difference, it is useful to treat schools on the whole as essentially the same, and (b) that despite a real degree of autonomy, the dynamic of how schools responds is best seen as the response of a system or an institution that transcends the individual school.

2. Dennett (1994) agrees with creationists that life and the Universe, must have been designed by developing a naturalized version of the concept of design as an algorithmic process with no need of a designer.

3. Accounts of Piaget often forget that the motivation for the stage theory is a recognition of the need for development to stand still long enough for new structures to consolidate.

4. I see the treatment of Edison's remark as the low point of the book. In the literal sense, in which it seems to be used here, the remark is just silly. Devoting space to it ridicules people who believe in educational technology. But in a deeper sense Edison is surely right—the printed textbook is being displaced by electronic publications.

5. The interested reader can track this activity on the World Wide Web at www .media.mit.edu

REFERENCES

Cuban, L. (1992, November 11). Computers meet classroom: Classroom wins. *Education Week*, *27*, 36.

Dennett, D. (1994). *Darwin's dangerous idea*. New York, NY: Simon & Schuster.

Koschmann, T. (1997). Logo-as-Latin redux. *The Journal of the Learning Sciences, 6*, 409–415.

Koschmann, T., & Kolodner, J. L. (1997). Technology and educational reform. *Journal of the Learning Sciences*, *6*(4), 397–400. https://doi.org/10.1207/s15327809jls0604_3

Noss, R., & Hoyles, C. (1996). *Windows on mathematical meaning*. Amsterdam, The Netherlands: Kluwer.

O'Shea, T., & Koschmann, T. (1997). Mindstorms 2. *Journal of the Learning Sciences*, *6*(4), 401–415. https://doi.org/10.1207/s15327809jls0604_4

Papert, S. (1980). *Mindstorms: Children, computers, and powerful ideas.* New York, NY: Basic Books.

Papert, S. (1987). Computer criticism vs. technocentric thinking. *Educational Researcher, 16*(1), 22–30.

Papert, S. (1993). *The children's machine.* New York, NY: Basic Books.

Papert, S. (1996a). *The connected family: bridging the digital generation gap.* Atlanta, GA: Longstreet.

Papert, S. (1996b). Explorations in the space of mathematics educations. *International Journal of Computers in Mathematics Learning, 1,* 95–123.

Pea, R., & Kurland, D. M. (1984). On the cognitive effects of learning computer programming. *New Ideas in Psychology, 2,* 137–168.

Tyack, D., and Cuban, L. (1995). *Tinkering towards utopia: A century of public school reform.* Cambridge, MA: Harvard University Press.

7 THE SCRATCH EDUCATOR MEETUP: USEFUL LEARNING IN A PLAYFUL SPACE

Karen Brennan and Raquel Jimenez

THE EXPERIENCE OF THE SCRATCH EDUCATOR MEETUP

If you visit the technology lab on an ordinary school day, you might find a jungle of tangled cords spilling from computer workstations like invasive electronic flora, threatening to take over the space. However, on this Saturday morning, the space has been playfully repurposed. Colorful beanbag chairs are set out adjacent to a table with coffee and other refreshments, three dozen chairs are arranged in a circle in the middle of the room, and tables are grouped together in pods on the periphery, helping to create a more inviting, social atmosphere. The lab's computers remain tucked away, quietly idling in sleep mode.

Once a month, teachers in the area converge on the space to make new connections, share experiences, and learn from one another about new resources they can use in their classrooms. In contrast to many professional development experiences that target specific grade levels and content areas, there's astonishing diversity in the room. The teachers come from public schools, charter schools, dual-language immersion schools, and after-school clubs. They teach in early elementary, upper elementary, middle school, and high school classrooms. They specialize in a range of disciplines, such as math, science, ELA, and art. They teach students with special needs, advanced learners, and English language learners. Some are veteran teachers, others fresh out of teacher preparation programs, and a few have taken up teaching as a second career. This diverse group gathers in the school's technology lab to learn more about integrating computer science learning in their classrooms with Scratch, a programming language used by millions of young people to design, build, and share creative computational projects with one another.

A few minutes before 10 a.m., teachers begin arriving at the school, where they find hallway signs adorned with a large orange cat, the Scratch programming language's mascot, pointing the way to the lab. The sounds of Justin Timberlake's unmistakable tenor voice waft in the background, adding an unexpected musical dimension to the space, and several teachers begin trickling into the room. As they wait to sign in, they greet one another with hugs and chat about morning commutes and weekend plans to catch a parade. One of the event's facilitators greets them with a hearty, "Welcome!" and directs them to the breakfast table, which contains an impressive spread of croissants, scones, bagels, fruit, yogurt, and cheese.

Efforts are underway in cities throughout the United States and across the globe to expand access to computer science education throughout K-12 public schools. Like other reform initiatives, teachers play a key role in enacting this ambitious vision and, consequently, supporting teachers' professional learning is especially important. Unlike professional development experiences that are led by an outside expert for the purpose of "training" teachers, the educators at today's gathering are here for something different. As participants in a Scratch Educator Meetup, teachers are here to "meet up" in a literal sense; the event is centered around meeting and forging connections with other teachers. But perhaps less obvious is the fact that teachers are here for a more participatory learning experience—one that encourages them to define and pursue their own learning goals based on their unique needs, and one that enables them to take advantage of the company and expertise of their colleagues.

Although meetups are participatory, they are not without structure. Meetups are typically three hours in length and are structured into three parts. Part one involves networking and introductions, in which people get to know each other—or, given the number of repeat attendees—to reconnect and get reacquainted. Part two, the heart of the meetup, consists of a collaborative schedule-building process and self-organized breakout sessions. This is where participants define learning goals that suit their interests and break out into smaller groups to pursue those interests. Part three involves sharing breakout group experiences, general group updates, and an opportunity to engage in reflection.

As teachers congregate around the breakfast table, participants are encouraged to get to know one another. Accompanying the food are nametags and an icebreaker activity. The activity invites the teachers to make profiles of themselves using a paper template. Frederic takes a copy of the activity template and grabs a marker. He starts to fill in information about himself—his name, where he works, what he hopes to learn today, a favorite book, and, if he were a superhero, a desired superpower. He completes his form with an illustration of himself. He carefully adds tape to the back of his page and then walks to the wall where others have posted their profile pages. Frederic notices that others have made connections between profiles with pieces of string. He affixes his page to the wall and then adds string connections to two other people: a fellow dual-language elementary school teacher and someone he notes has recently read the same book. While conventional approaches to professional learning follow pre-planned agendas, today's meetup agenda will be co-constructed by the participants themselves and will follow an emergent structure informed by the ideas and questions participants bring to the event. In this context, casual networking lays crucial groundwork for the group's agenda-building process.

After a few minutes, one of several facilitators reluctantly interrupts the lively conversations that are underway. This facilitator, who has hosted numerous meetups, easily launches into a standard introduction to the format, greeting the group, "Happy Saturday! It's so wonderful to see all of you here—lots of familiar faces and a few new friends. For those of you who are new, let me tell you a little about what's going to happen today." Though the sound of her voice competes with the many conversations that are happening simultaneously, she continues. She walks over to a blank grid that's been drawn on the board, as the group settles down. She says,

> As you can see, we don't have a schedule. Meetups are co-designed learning experiences. We've been getting to know each other through conversation. We're going to transition now—figuring out what people want to learn about and building our schedule for the day, filling in this blank grid. On your table, you'll find sticky notes. With a partner, think about one or two things you'd like to learn today. Maybe you came in with a question, maybe somebody sparked an idea over breakfast, or maybe there's something you'd like to share. Maybe you're totally new and are just getting started with Scratch, or maybe you want to focus specifically on elementary education. Write an idea for a session on a sticky note and bring it up to the blank schedule. Once we've collected all of our ideas, we'll look for recurring themes, and we'll refine our many ideas into five different sessions. This schedule building is a messy process, but I promise that we'll get through it.

With this basic overview, participants begin brainstorming possible breakout sessions, talking through their ideas. "There are so many good websites for learning how to program, but there's so much available online. It's too much! If you're just beginning, it's hard to get over the hump," says Candice, a woman in her late twenties with a background in literacy instruction, who has just landed a job teaching in a computer lab. She's recently begun trying to teach herself the basics of computer science so that she can help her students, but she is overwhelmed by the massive volume of resources online. "Oh, it's taken me many years to figure out where to go," says Michael, an experienced teacher nearing retirement, "Maybe we can start with a tutorial?" Jeraul, a third person sitting nearby, chimes in, "That would be great!" Jeraul is a technology coordinator for the district, and his most pressing concern, as he explains, is figuring out how to help teachers begin. "I've spoken to many teachers, and they say, 'How do we get started?' The biggest thing is structure. Teachers don't just throw kids into it; they want structure and ideas for curriculum. Especially at the K-8 level, there's a desire to bring CS in the classroom, but it's not easy for teachers to research curriculum when there's so much already to do!" The trio comes to enthusiastic agreement on this topic, and Candice scribbles "getting started with Scratch" on a lime green sticky note and hands it to a facilitator.

At the same time, over a dozen conversations like this play out in the room, and facilitators receive a pile of sticky notes to sort through. Based on these ideas, at the end of the schedule-building process, a facilitator announces the sessions that will be the focus of the day's meetup: Introduction to Scratch, Best Practices, Curriculum Integration, Helpful Resources, Extensions and Advanced Applications, and an additional session called Coffee Talk, where anyone can go for more informal, ad hoc conversations. The facilitator gives a quick overview of what each session might entail.

For the next 90 minutes, teachers participate in the sessions they find most interesting. Some take in the day like a buffet, sampling as many sessions as they can, while others engage in a deep dive, sticking with one group for the entire time. The room is quickly filled with the lively buzz of activity. For the Introduction to Scratch session, a more experienced teacher joins to help the newcomers make their very first Scratch project, getting them started with a playful and collaborative programming prompt. At the Helpful Resources breakout, a teacher suggests that everyone share one favorite resource. After a few minutes of selection and curation, everyone in the group takes a turn sharing their resource; the exclamations of excitement and delight in response to the helpful discoveries are easily overheard by the other breakout groups. A group of people who are gathered at the Extensions and Advanced Applications session decide to further subdivide their group: one subgroup focuses on programming languages for high school students to try after Scratch, and the other on Scratch-compatible hardware extensions. In the Best Practices group, one teacher offers to share a lesson plan he wants to improve, which leads to a passionate conversation, with group members debating the merits of their respective strategies for designing learning environments: how much structure to provide, what roles students and teachers play in the environment, and which resources to make available.

As the end of the breakout sessions approaches, one of the facilitators moves from group to group, encouraging people to wrap up their session and to help themselves to lunch, which has appeared amid the bustling backdrop of the morning's activities. Although reluctant to leave their groups, the focused effort and energy have made everyone eager for food. With plates piled high with sandwiches, salads, chips, and cookies, the group reassembles. Someone from each breakout session provides a recap of their group's activities, while a facilitator transcribes important ideas and helpful resources into an online document that participants can access. Next, there are group announcements. One teacher shares that the city's educational technology interest group is meeting next Thursday and everyone is invited to join. Another teacher shares a project that her students created in collaboration with students from a classroom in Japan. And, finally, a teacher asks the group if anyone would like to collaborate on a proposal for a session about Scratch at a local teacher professional development day.

Before the meetup concludes for the day, the facilitator who welcomed everyone stands up, thanking everyone for joining in and reminding people when the next Scratch Educator Meetup will be. "Before you go," she says, as a final activity, "let's take a few minutes for reflection. Think back to three hours ago. What brought you here? Think about yourself now. What did you do today? How did it advance your thinking? Your practice?" After a few minutes of quiet reflection, people turn to a neighbor and share their thoughts, followed by whole-group sharing. Teachers talk about things that they learned and ideas that they plan to try with their students, either the following week or further out. Rick, who is new to the group, has a twinkle in his eye as he speaks about his experience. "I wasn't sure what to expect," he says. "But I learned so much and I met such great people! I definitely want to bring some of my colleagues next time." Isabel, a longtime Scratch Educator Meetup participant, smiles, "What will you tell them meetups are?" Rick pauses, then grins, "That's easy: 'useful learning in a playful space.'"

THE ORIGINS OF THE SCRATCH EDUCATOR MEETUP

For several years, from 2007 to 2010, we regularly hosted introductory, single-session workshops for educators interested in working with the Scratch programming environment. To our surprise, some educators became regular attendees. They weren't returning because they wanted to revisit the fundamentals of Scratch, but because they enjoyed learning and creating with their colleagues. This prompted us to think about other ways of supporting educators in their next steps with Scratch. What types of experiences—what culture of learning—would be of greatest value? As Borko, Jacobs, and Koellner (2010) recommended, "high-quality PD incorporates processes such as modeling preferred instructional strategies, engaging teachers in active learning, and building a professional learning community," an approach that "is particularly important in times of reform, when teachers frequently are being asked to teach in ways that are substantially different from how they were taught or how they learned to teach" (p. 550).

This questioning led us to experiment with introducing an additional format for face-to-face gatherings: the Scratch Educator Meetup, described in detail in the ethnographic vignette of the previous section. Our primary aim for the meetup was that it would be an opportunity for educators to engage in the kinds of constructionist learning experiences that would ideally be made available to their students—learning experiences that teachers may not have experienced themselves. We hosted our first meetup in Boston at the MIT Media Lab in 2010, which developed into a regularly occurring monthly event. Interest in attending meetups steadily increased after that first gathering, demonstrated by increasing numbers of teachers participating in the monthly events and teachers traveling great distances to attend the Boston-area meetups.

This interest encouraged us to find ways of spreading the model to other locations, leading to the development in 2016 of a set of resources for people to host their own events. These resources included a Getting Started guide for hosts and online infrastructure for connecting with people—both with local meetup participants and with other meetups around the world. In the first two years of this effort, we have grown the network of meetups from one site in Boston, with approximately one hundred members, to more than forty-five sites in twelve countries, with more than 3,500 members. The opening vignette offers a peek into one of these sites, an example of how some of the most productive meetups unfold based on our experiences as participant observers.

The design of the Scratch Educator Meetup has been informed by prior theoretical and empirical scholarship about teacher professional learning. In particular, we were drawn to conceptualizations of teacher learning that emphasize supporting teacher agency—placing teacher thinking, ambitions, and actions at the center of the learning—as a necessary strategy for transforming teacher practice, rather than teacher training, which often frames the teacher-learner as passive in relation to their learning (Butler, Schnellert, & MacNeil, 2015; Vescio & Adams, 2008; Voogt et al., 2015). We also drew on the extensive scholarship about communities of practice, which frame learning as a process that depends on relationships with others who possess varying degrees of prior knowledge and expertise, in the service of pursuing a shared purpose (Grossman, Wineburg, & Woolworth, 2001; Lave & Wenger, 1991; Putnam & Borko, 2000; Rogoff, 1994).

We have described meetups and our related research in detail in other contexts (Brennan, 2012; Brennan, 2015). As this book is about constructionism, we will highlight one source of inspiration in particular: Papert's description of samba school culture in Brazil. In the culminating chapter of his 1980 book, *Mindstorms*, Papert described a longing for a new culture of learning, an alternative to the bureaucratic, purposeless, and joyless learning he argued dominated the school experiences of most young people. He offered samba schools—settings in which community members gather to prepare performances for the annual Carnival—as an example of what this new culture could be like. The samba school, Papert argued, "represents a set of attributes a learning environment should and could have" (p. 179).

THE ATTRIBUTES OF THE SCRATCH EDUCATOR MEETUP

Reflecting on Papert's description of the samba school, we observed congruence between Papert's conception of environments for powerful learning and our experiences of meetups. Five attributes, in particular, recur in the description of the samba school in *Mindstorms* and align with the design of meetups—both in the theoretical and empirical motivation of meetups, and in how attendees and organizers have described their experiences spontaneously at events and more formally in interviews. Samba schools and Scratch Educator Meetups are (1) social, (2) personal, (3) collaborative, (4) useful, and (5) reflective.

People experience meetups initially as *social* spaces. As evidenced throughout the initial vignette, meetups are characterized by convivial interactions, accompanied by food and music. This parallels Papert's description of the samba school as a "social club," where members go "to dance, to drink, to meet their friends," and his description of the strong "social cohesion, the sense of belonging" in the service of "a sense of common purpose" (p. 178). While these opportunities for people to informally connect could be dismissed as superfluous to some more formal notion of learning, the connections formed among participants are a necessary precursor to the pursuit of shared goals and responsibilities. Meetup participants and organizers often describe the friendships they have formed through their meetup participation, friendships that have offered necessary psychological support for the vulnerability and risk-taking required when thinking about one's teaching practice in new ways, both at meetups and when returning to the classroom.

People experience meetups as *personal* spaces. Another word for this attribute might be *participatory*—in either case, it communicates a vision of the individual teacher in relation to the learning experience. A meetup is done *by* you and *with* you, not *to* you. This is an unexpected shift for many participants, who have had abundant professional learning experiences in which they were the object, rather than the agent, of the experience. From the very first moments of a meetup, the individual's role and value are communicated: from sharing history and experiences informally via networking, to bringing individuals' interests and priorities to the schedule-building process. There is an expectation that what one learns at a meetup will be meaningfully connected to one's individual needs, not delivered in an abstract fashion that is inattentive to individual context.

People experience meetups as *collaborative* spaces. This is the most common word that meetups organizers from around the world use to describe the meetup format; they talk about how traditional educational hierarchies are dissolved, notions of expertise feel more fluid, and responsibilities for learning are shared by everyone in the room. From our perspective, this is one of the most powerful outcomes of the meetup, in terms of how the teacher's learning experience might then be translated into the daily practices of the classroom. Many participants have described their uncertainty and anxiety about introducing creative approaches to computing education. They share how the meetup enables them to experience those approaches, helping them build their confidence about what might be possible in their classrooms. They describe the power of peer learning, contrasted with experiences of being supervised by an "expert," and a desire to create the same opportunities for their learners. They describe the value of distributed and differentiated expertise, inspiring multiple ways of perceiving and approaching problems of practice, whether related to pedagogy or to programming. This reconfiguration of the relationship among teachers and learners is a constant refrain in *Mindstorms* and its presentation of the samba school as well. "Novice is not separated from expert," Papert wrote, "and the experts are also learning" (p. 179). It leads to an environment where "the line between learners and teachers can fade," an environment that "enriches and facilitates the interaction between all participants and offers opportunities for more articulate, effective, and honest teaching relationships" (p. 180).

People experience meetups as *useful* spaces. Papert described samba schools as *purposeful* (i.e., "Learning is not separate from reality. The samba school has a purpose, and learning is integrated in the school for this purpose" [p. 179]), with activity being organized in a *deliberate* fashion (i.e., "For five or for twenty minutes a specific learning group comes into existence. Its learning is deliberate and focused. Then it dissolves into the crowd" [p. 178–179]). Although *useful* is the most commonly invoked word, organizers and participants use a broad set of words to describe this attribute of a meetup: *meaningful, authentic, engaging, informative, inspiring, energizing,* and *practical*. Many participants contrast this, again, with their typical professional learning experiences; overwhelmingly, participants are drawn to meetups because they are tired of professional development that is not responsive, helpful, or useful to them, with those experiences feeling like a rehash of ideas and practices they are already familiar with or feel is beyond their present capability or need.

Meetup organizers describe the "usefulness" of meetups primarily in two ways. In one sense, they hope that participants will experience the meetup as tactically worthwhile in the short term, by offering an activity or pedagogical strategy that could be used the following week. Simultaneously, "useful" is invoked in a broader, longer-term fashion, with organizers hoping that meetups are inspiring, a model of what learning could be possibly or eventually—not necessarily achieved immediately upon returning to the classroom.

This broader, aspirational framing of a meetup's usefulness connects to our fifth and final attribute: people experience meetups as *reflective* spaces. The structure of a meetup depends on participants adopting a reflective stance; to participate fully in a meetup means expressing desires for oneself as a learner, which demands an evolving self-awareness before, during, and after the meetup experience. This awareness, in the words of one meetup participant, creates opportunities for "Aha!" moments, instances in which one encounters and then negotiates new ideas and experiences. Not only is this awareness the foundation of participants learning about Scratch or about playful pedagogy or about creative computing but also it contributes to a broader culture of learning, one that "helps us not only to learn but to learn about learning" (p. 177).

To be so inspired by Papert's vision of the learning society and of the samba school as an instance thereof invites careful attention also to the cautions he set out in the text about how to make sense of the samba school as design aspiration.

> ... the school samba was not designed by researchers, funded by grants, nor implemented by government action. It was not made. It happened. This must be true too of any new successful forms of associations for learning. ... Powerful new social forms must have their roots in the culture, not be the creatures of bureaucrats. (p. 181)

While the ultimate broader impact and sustained longevity of Scratch Educator Meetups cannot be known in these early days of the network, we are acutely aware that meetups will not be the panacea for uninspired teacher professional learning experiences. But we are cautiously optimistic about the individual and in-network impacts of the learning that has been taking place, about the role of meetups as an instance of support for teachers who desire to experience new types of learning, knowing, and interacting. We hope that by sharing the Scratch Educator Meetups story and attributes here, we can inspire others—as Papert's samba schools story inspired us—to create new models of learning for teachers and the young learners they serve, contributing to the evolving and complicated portrait of life-wide and lifelong learning for all.

ACKNOWLEDGMENTS

This material is based upon work supported by the Scratch Foundation. Any opinions, findings, and conclusions or recommendations expressed in this material are those of the authors and do not necessarily reflect the views of the Foundation.

REFERENCES

Borko, H., Jacobs, J., & Koellner, K. (2010). Contemporary approaches to teacher professional development. In P. Peterson, E. Baker, & B. McGaw (Eds.), *International Encyclopedia of Education* (3rd ed., pp. 548–556). Oxford, UK: Elsevier.

Brennan, K. (2012). ScratchEd: Developing support for educators as designers. In E. Reilly & I. Literat (Eds.), *Designing with teachers: Participatory professional development in education*. Retrieved from http://dmlcentral.net/sites/dmlcentral/files/resource_files/pdworkinggroup-v6-reduced.pdf

Brennan, K. (2015). Beyond technocentrism: Supporting constructionism in the classroom. *Constructivist Foundations, 10*(3), 289–296.

Butler, D. L., Schnellert, L., & MacNeil, K. (2015). Collaborative inquiry and distributed agency in educational change: A case study of a multi-level community of inquiry. *Journal of Educational Change, 16*(1), 1–26.

Grossman, P., Wineburg, S., & Woolworth, S. (2001). Toward a theory of teacher community. *Teachers College Record, 103*(6), 942–1012.

Lave, J., & Wenger, E. (1991). *Situated learning: Legitimate peripheral participation.* New York, NY: Cambridge University Press.

Papert, S. (1980). *Mindstorms: Children, computers, and powerful ideas.* New York, NY: Basic Books.

Putnam, R. T., & Borko, H. (2000). What do new views of knowledge and thinking have to say about research on teacher learning? *Educational Researcher, 29*(1), 4–15.

Rogoff, B. (1994). Developing understanding of the idea of communities of learners. *Mind, Culture and Activity, 1*(4), 209–229.

Vescio, V., Ross, D., & Adams, A. (2008). A review of research on the impact of professional learning communities on teaching practice and student learning. *Teaching and Teacher Education, 24*(1), 80–91.

Voogt, J., Laferrière, T., Breuleux, A., Itow, R. C., Hickey, D., & McKenney, S. (2015). Collaborative design as a form of professional development. *Instructional Science, 43*(2), 259–282.

8 APPLIED CONSTRUCTIONISM IN THAILAND: TWO DECADES OF A CONSTRUCTIONIST SCHOOL IN THAILAND

Nalin Tutiyaphuengprasert

ORIGINS OF CONSTRUCTIONISM IN THAILAND

In 1997 the Suksapattana Foundation invited Seymour Papert to visit Thailand. Following that visit, Papert partnered with Paron Israsena to start the "Lighthouse Project" to promote and support constructionist learning in Thailand. Constructionism was introduced to Thai educators using Logo to convey the new type of learning environment. Teachers were excited and motivated by their learning experience in the workshops; however, they struggled to apply that experience when they returned to their schools. Consequently, the idea of creating a school that fully supported constructionism was conceived and, in 2000, the project was initiated. In 2001 Darunsikkhalai School for Innovative Learning (DSIL) was established as a practice school for constructionism in collaboration with King Mongkut's University of Technology Thonburi and Suksapattana Foundation (figure 8.1).

THE FIRST CONSTRUCTIONIST SCHOOL IN THAILAND

DSIL is located on the campus of King Mongkut's University of Technology Thonburi (KMUTT). In 1997, when Thailand went through an economic crisis, the Suksapattana Foundation realized that for Thailand to survive in a changing world, it needed to change its education system. KMUTT and the Suksapattana Foundation planned to start an educational project, DSIL, to develop the learning capacity of Thai citizens. Constructionism was the guiding pedagogy for DSIL from day one. DSIL's first vision statement was to provide a constructionist experience to learners to develop students into global citizens who can learn and adjust in a changing world. The national curriculum was suspended during the first few years to clear all constraints and provide an open creative space for teachers to develop classroom practice where learning would be the first priority.

FIGURE 8.1
Students at DSIL construct extensive and complex projects throughout the
year and frequently share this work with parents, educators, and others
from the school community.

GROWING THROUGH RESISTANCE AND NONBELIEVERS

Despite this optimism, there was limited public understanding about progressive education in Thailand and, in the school's first five years, the number of students fluctuated. In 2004 Mr. Paron Israsena, the school's founder
and director, made a public statement of commitment saying that "Thailand can't waste any more time to move our education from where it was.
Please continue. I will still support this project even if we have five students" (Paron, personal communication, 2003). This determined statement
encouraged DSIL to continue their efforts.

In 2008 DSIL students started to show their unique character by their ability to think creatively and manage projects distinguishing DSIL from other
schools. In the same year, the national curriculum was made more flexible
and changed to push schools to focus on developing analytical thinking skills
and support student centered learning. DSIL was suddenly on the national
stage and became a showcase of constructionist education in Thailand.

PROFESSIONAL DEVELOPMENT

Rather than use the word "teacher," DSIL began referring to educators as "facilitators" to differentiate the concept of constructionist learning from instructionist teaching. To promote experiential learning, DSIL hired professionals from a variety of careers. For example, I came from a cinematography background and started my career as a facilitator by first relearning how to learn and experiencing constructionist culture firsthand through a Logo workshop with other facilitators.

To promote experimentation with project-based learning, DSIL suspended the use of the national curriculum for the first few years of the school. Constructionism was being applied not only through the use of Logo but also through the emphasis on building a constructionist learning atmosphere. In project classes, facilitators learned to build soap-sculpture learning environments, one of Papert's initial inspiration for constructionism (Papert & Harel, 1991). Reflection was held every day after classes as on-the-job training for facilitators:

> I graduated in Biology. I had no idea what learning was. Education was just trying to pass the exam with good grades. Becoming a facilitator at DSIL allowed me to understand what learning really is. I realized that the most important task of teaching is being able to understand and motivate students to learn. I learned that spiritual development is important as a teacher. Once you understand yourself, how you learn and grow, you will be able to guide students on the same path. (personal communication with a senior facilitator, March 2018)

DSIL also brought in experts to give feedback and guidelines. Carol Sperry, a teacher educator, was invited to observe classrooms and provide coaching to facilitators. Reflecting on her visit in 2003, Sperry noted:

> Introducing constructionist ideas into a traditional culture requires a delicate balance of knowledge, understanding, and respect. The founding administrators of DSIL had the foresight to allow our teacher workshops to model the freedom, self-reflection, choice of project, opportunities to collaborate, and exploration that would inspire them to bring organic and authentic activities to their own classrooms. I believe that allowing these teachers to experience for themselves the power of constructing their own knowledge, instead of simply "telling" them ... accelerated their ability to experience and understand the power of the ideas that support constructionist teaching and learning. (personal communication, 2018)

LEARNING MODEL OF DSIL

DSIL's first priority is to fully support constructionism in the classroom. For the school's management, organizational learning (Senge, 1991) was chosen in order to promote a culture of co-creation and resilience and to replace rigid top-down management. In addition, mindfulness practice (Yeganeh & Kolb, 2009) was a core principle used to nurture an environment of constructive collaboration and enhance experiential learning.

DSIL maximized hours for project time and minimized time for compulsory classes. Projects allowed students to explore their interests and to learn how to acquire knowledge and manage projects. However, hours of project time and compulsory classes created a tension within the school. Over the years, DSIL has oscillated between two extremes: a conservative one and a liberal multidisciplinary one. The school continues to work to find a balance between these two extremes to meet the needs of the dynamically changing circumstances and needs such as changes in leadership, facilitator turnover, and pressure from parents. However, DSIL has set new standards for project time in school (see table 8.1) and influenced many schools to follow and provide time for students to do independent study.

Constructionism is applied in classrooms in different ways. Some classes integrate Logo culture, in which students and facilitators co-create

Table 8.1 Time Structure of DSIL Classroom Management in 2018

Class	Minutes per week (Primary School 1st–6th grade)	Minutes per week (Secondary School 7th–9th Grade)	Minutes per week (High school 10th–12th Grade)
Student's Project Class	500	510	510
Compulsory Classes	540	810	900
Arts, Music, Scouts, and PE	420	330	330
Lunch serving and cleaning up	510	60	60
Team Building and Inspirational Talk	—	180	180
Spiritual Development	60	60	60
Digital Fabrication Class (FabLab)	70 (G.2–6)	90	—
College Planning	—	—	60
Break and others	250	150	150

student-chosen projects. Show and share (show and tell) and reflection are used to promote learning by getting feedback and ideas. Compulsory classes are perceived of as tools to help students better create their projects. Likewise, homework is selected to be meaningful for projects rather than work that just focuses on mundane drilling. Classrooms look like small communities or workplaces. Some students have even suggested that coming to school is like going to work, not to class.

> When I was a student at other schools, my role in classrooms was just to listen, take notes, and pass the exams. I wasn't a front row student until I moved to DSIL and my attitude about studying has been changed. I found my passion in engineering when I worked on projects. DSIL gives me time to use my creativity and allow me to think of my future career. (personal communication with an eleventh-grade student, 2018)

In secondary school, since 2015, project classes are called "Houses," which represent a community of students and teachers with similar interests. There are three houses: Engineering House, Multimedia Art and Design House, and Science House. In each house, students can pursue projects of their interest in depth. Students have quality time and resources to create portfolios for their college preparation, a feature which makes DSIL a unique educational program in Thailand.

LEARNING OUTCOMES

On national standardized examinations, DSIL students have consistently performed in the middle range over the past 10 years. In the past 3 years, the average high score was a 3.2 and low score was at 1.8 (in a four-grade points system). Meanwhile, 100% of DSIL students have been accepted to college using portfolios.

> I got to try and make projects of interest while I was at DSIL. It helped me to realize my passion and it gave me ideas for my future study. Even though this school may not have a reputation of academic strength, DSIL taught us to be able to think and able to execute our ideas. Especially now that we can use portfolios to apply for colleges, DSIL experience became our advantage for college applications. (personal communication with a former student, March 2018)

Self-learning and self-management skills became unique characteristics of DSIL students. Students enjoy their time at school and show a high level of hands on and practical skills.

> When my children attend DSIL, they get to learn from real world experiences. My children have very good development. They are happy about learning. They are

confident to speak up ideas and present themselves in public. They are also self-responsible kids. (personal communication with a parent of third-grade student and a former student, 2018)

Parents and students reflected that the ability to understand one's own passion and interests is a unique advantage of attending DSIL. DSIL students occasionally receive scholarships from colleges and sponsorships from outside organizations to scale up their projects and conduct research. Such recognition gives us confidence that it is beneficial to forgo some mandatory classes in order to provide students space to explore their passions and interests.

REFLECTIONS ON DSIL

Facilitators interpreted their learning experiences from initial Logo workshops and created their own style of project-based learning. Students learn to identify their interests and make plans of action for their projects. They learn to follow up and adjust their plans according to changes or challenges they encounter. This design exposes students to computational thinking in a real-world classroom with or without computers.

> DSIL taught me how to learn by myself and learn how to acquire data and learn how to select relevant and valid information for projects. We learned from practical problems and these problems have useful answers unlike problems from textbooks. Nowadays, students can access content easily. I think students need skills to be able to choose information for each situation. You may forget some content while you grow up, but teaching students how to think and learn can be a great foundation for future learning. (personal communication with a former student, 2018)

Logo culture became the core of learning culture at DSIL. As Nussarin, a project facilitator, said, "As a facilitator, it's important to *not* steal opportunities to learn from students. This means opportunities to think, to make mistakes, and learn from them. However, learning may not take place without reflection and appropriate guiding questions" (personal communication, 2018). Students and facilitators together become "collaborative researchers" (Solomon, 2018) who learn from "bugs" and work together to fix them.

Facilitators reflected that to understand this learning environment, facilitators need to have some knowledge of child psychology, the learning sciences, and positive psychology (Seligman, Ernst, Gillham, Reivich, & Linkins, 2009) to be able to understand and respond to a variety of educational situations appropriately. Watchara, a project facilitator, said "trust" and "confidence" in students are essential to the process (personal communication, 2018). Students need to feel safe to learn from mistakes in this environment. This creates honest relationships between facilitators and students at DSIL.

CONCLUSIONS

Through years of experience, DSIL came to realize the purpose of education at a deeper level. Facilitators shifted their paradigm of education to take on a different perspective. As Ittichai, a project facilitator, said, "Certificate is just a part of the journey. Getting to know who they are helps students to have clear goals for their life and create passion in learning. They will become lifelong learners which is essential in the changing world" (personal communication, 2018).

Constructionism for DSIL became a life-changing project. School became a place to nurture a passion for learning, not just for schooling. In 2018 DSIL invited parents, students, and facilitators to co-create a plan of DSIL's future direction. I have been fortunate to be part of this 18-year story since the beginning and am thankful for the efforts of all who have been part of the DSIL—especially Paron and Papert, who lit the torch of constructionism in Thailand. I am confident that DSIL will continue to be courageous as new educational journeys await!

REFERENCES

Papert, S., & Harel, I. (1991). Situating constructionism. *Constructionism, 36*(2), 1–11.

Seligman, M. E., Ernst, R. M., Gillham, J., Reivich, K., & Linkins, M. (2009). Positive education: Positive psychology and classroom interventions. *Oxford Review of Education, 35*(3), 293–311.

Senge, P. M. (1991). *The fifth discipline, the art and practice of the learning organization. Performance+ Instruction, 30*(5), 37–37.

Solomon, C. (2018). When Computers Were New Logo A Computer Created for Children. A collection of papers from 1970–1976. [Unpublished Manuscript]

Yeganeh, B., & Kolb, D. (2009). Mindfulness and experiential learning. In OD Network, J. Vogelsange, M. Townsend, M. Minahan, D. Jamieson, J. Vogel, A. Viet, C. Royal, & L. Valek (Eds.), *Handbook for Strategic HR*. New York, NY: AMACOM.

9 CONNECTING MODERN KNOWLEDGE: CRAFTING THE NEXT GENERATION OF CONSTRUCTIONISTS

Gary S. Stager

During the late 1990s, Seymour Papert and I engaged in many conversations about why, when our allies in the progressive education community were asked about "technology" in schools, their responses were often naive, reactionary, or dystopian. This may have reflected misplaced nostalgia for a bygone era but was more likely a rejection of the dominant instructionist paradigm of technology use in schools, such as computer-based testing and drill-and-practice software.

At the same time, it was becoming clear that the mainstream educational technology field was giving too little thought to learning and ignorant of the contributions of progressive educators. An event was needed to build a bridge between both communities. Our hope was that progressive educators would learn the potential of constructive computing, while technology-focused educators would come in contact with powerful ideas about learning, teaching, and school reform. Since Papert was not able to create such a summit, I decided that it was my responsibility to do so.

In 2008 without grant funding, institutional support, or corporate sponsorship, I created the Constructing Modern Knowledge (CMK) Institute. For the past twelve years, educators from around the world have assembled in Manchester, New Hampshire, for a four-day learning adventure unlike any other. CMK is uncompromising in its commitment to constructionism and the competence of learners, with the overt goal of crafting the next generation of constructionist educators.

THE FORMAT

The format of CMK has remained unchanged since its inception. The model has proven successful even when the number of participants went from 25 to 250 while absorbing the advances in computational technology of the past decade. It is based on lessons I learned from Dan and Molly

Watt in the 1980s, my work with Papert in creating an alternative learning environment inside a troubled prison for teens (Cavallo, Papert, & Stager, 2004; Stager, 2006), the subtle complexity of the Reggio Emilia approach (Edwards, Gandini, & Forman, 2011), and the primacy of the project as an educator's smallest unit of concern. While some may see CMK as educators just "playing around," CMK's seeming lack of structure has been carefully designed.

CMK begins by asking participants to take off their teacher hat and put on their learner hat. Papert favored that plea as a way to suggest that educators be selfish with the experience in order to enjoy maximum benefit. The project planning ritual begins with the question, "What do you want to make?" This minimizes skill-based ideas such as, "I want to learn to use Photoshop."

No idea is too crazy and no idea is rejected. Some projects are incredibly practical, others whimsical, like an Internet for chickens, and many are beautiful, like a robotics installation called "The Poetry of Wind." Members of our faculty write each idea on large Post-it Notes surrounding our meeting space.

After all of the ideas are shared, participants write their names under all project ideas in which they are interested. Next, those who are determined to begin a particular project are asked to stand in a common area as a beacon (not a leader), where others who share their desire can join them. This seemingly casual act shows that the groups are not made of leaders and followers, but of equal collaborators. Once most people "bunch up," groups begin to work on their projects, uninterrupted for the next four days.

Before the planning ritual, I prepare CMK participants for a predictable emotional arc. By the end of the first day, they will be exhausted and might even feel frustrated or worse. If they are patient and trust the process, on the afternoon of the second day everything clicks and they speed toward the finish line. The third night, the learning space is open until after midnight for groups anxious to put finishing touches on their masterpieces. That late-night session has a lovely celebratory feeling, leading into the last day's pride in their accomplishments. Year after year, educators confirm that is exactly what happens. Projects proceed from impossible to demonstrable in just four days. Participants often comment that this causes them to think deeply about the emotional arc of the students in their classrooms.

On the final afternoon, projects are exhibited informally. While the resulting projects are often extraordinary, there is no need for formal presentations. Participants have been looking around and collaborating for days. Project development is the most nutritious part of CMK.

In addition to a few planned social events and guest speakers, each day ends with reflection circles led by faculty members. Faculty members rotate through the reflection circle locations so that participants benefit from interacting with different leaders without having to stray far from their projects. These circles offer a form of pastoral care and encouragement to participants while focusing on learning, not teaching.

NOT A CONFERENCE

Although featuring remarkable speakers, CMK is not a conference. There are a few guest speakers at each year's institute spread out across four days so as to distract as little as possible from project development. We invite speakers to spend as much time as possible at CMK interacting informally with participants, in addition to their presentations.

Our speakers fall into three essential categories: visionary educators, technological innovators, and experts in fields your guidance counselor never imagined. We have featured National Endowment for the Arts Jazz Masters, treehouse designers, scientists, historians, inventors, and accomplished teens. The CMK guest speakers are carefully chosen in an attempt to acquaint educators with what greatness sounds, feels, and tastes like across an unexpected spectrum. This expands their community of practice, expands vistas, and elevates their self-concept.

As hoped, CMK impacts our guest speakers as well. Alfie Kohn took his kids to a Scratch workshop. Deborah Meier remarked that she never thought before of using computers in a way consistent with her progressive ideals. Reggio Emilia educators cherished the beauty of the projects and recognized "the miracle." CMK aspires to be the "samba school" Papert describes in *Mindstorms*, where everyone dances together. Constructionist learning is reciprocal among all members of a community (figure 9.1).

NOT A WORKSHOP

Several years ago, a faculty member was frustrated by the wide variety of microcontrollers available at CMK and asked, "Why can't we just standardize on one model of Arduino?" My response was, "Then this would be an Arduino workshop." CMK is focused on the unique centrality of each learner and epistemological pluralism (Turkle & Papert, 1992). Each year, we purchase all sorts of new technology that might be useful, even if none of us knows a thing about it. Every year a teacher or group of educators, regardless of their prior knowledge, uses that "bleeding edge" item to propel a successful project.

Legendary civil rights activist Jonathan Kozol explores a project

Young Aussie teachers collaborate with Reggio's Carla Rinaldi

4-person dragon attacks the castle defended by robots

Space and lots of stuff

The "living" Marie Antoinette wig

Pneumatic trumpet

FIGURE 9.1
The project, speakers, and structure of CMK.

Workshops are intended to teach you something discrete to perform your job better. Some educators have attended CMK as many as six times. Educators who attend multiple times are not coming to learn a tool or skill, but as a gift to themselves and a commitment to personal growth.

COERCION-FREE

CMK offers multiple reminders that coercion is the enemy of learning. Nothing is mandatory and time is flexible. One of the benefits of the setting is that there are dozens of restaurants within walking distance of the institute. This not only reduces catering costs but also invites participants to make friends and break bread together. Early morning or late-night diner runs, meals with guest speakers, illicit coffee expeditions, and lunches of indeterminate length are a tacit, yet powerful model of a noncoercive learning environment. The free choice of projects, collaborators, materials, processes, and even where you eat embodies the commitment to noncoercion.

THE ENVIRONMENT

One participant remarked that, overnight, CMK turns an empty hotel ballroom into a utopian school. None of the artifice of classroom instruction is found; there are no rules, plans, flowcharts, or rubrics. There are wacky signs, snacks, an inflatable moose, and a presentation screen made of Post-it Notes. This denotes a different sort of learning environment with an emphasis on self-reliance, whimsy, and ingenuity.

STUFF

CMK stretches the idea of objects-to-think-with to the maximum. It is our goal to have anything a learner might need or be inspired by within arm's reach. CMK requires sixty cases of materials, including toys, tools, microcontrollers, fabric, Raspberry Pis, a sewing machine, 3D printers, art supplies, green screens, cameras, MIDI keyboards, electronics, and a library of five hundred books. A plastic chicken that poops gumballs inspired countless projects. A stuffed Eeyore toy traveled to CMK for several years, largely ignored. Then one year, pieces of Eeyore found their way into three different projects and were then lovingly stitched back together for many more years of service. CMK shares Thomas Edison's goal of a storeroom that includes "everything from an elephant hide to the eyeball of a United States senator."

AN ABSENCE OF INSTRUCTION

With the exception of brief impromptu tutorials and on-demand project assistance, CMK is accomplished without instruction. Faculty share expertise, assist in thinking through a challenge, or help with debugging when called upon to do so. CMK embraces Mitra's concept of minimally invasive education (Mitra, 2000) and Papert's adage, "Every time you teach something you deprive a child of the pleasure and benefit of discovery" (1996).

CMK PROJECTS

Across twelve years, CMK projects show evidence of how educators develop when they are treated as creative, competent learners. While hundreds of projects have been developed at CMK, one example may serve to demonstrate how cutting-edge technology, timeless craft traditions, programming, and whimsy combine to demonstrate the powerful ideas of constructionism and progressive education.

CMK 2018 generated a project idea to build a "living" Marie Antoinette wig. The idea sprung from a participant attending for the third time who understood that great projects need not be practical. Lo and behold, she and a group of new colleagues created a giant wearable paper wig, complete with birds that circled above, bees that shot out of flowers, and other behaviors instigated by a microcontroller-based accelerometer. The animation was accompanied by a monochromatic garden of meticulous paper curls. The STEM skills demonstrated in this project are only rivaled by its creativity, beauty, and whimsy.

Consistent with CMK's emphasis on self-reliance and learner agency, projects—both processes and artifacts—are memorialized via social media, blogs, and a shared Vimeo account. No elaborate system or teacher labor is required. Readers may explore project videos and participant reflections at constructingmodernknowledge.com/?p=2382.

UNCOMPROMISING CONSTRUCTIONISM

CMK is uncompromising in its adherence to the constructionist principles outlined in Papert's Eight Big Ideas (Martinez & Stager, 2017) while reanimating progressive education for a new generation of educators. As a learning theory, constructionism needs the productive context of progressive education to ensure that educators realize the possible. CMK values the competence of educators at a time when curricula is made "teacher-proof" and professional development offerings are too often limited to Google training.

One hopes that educators reacquainted with their own power as learners use the experience of a noncoercive constructionist setting as a catalyst for constructing similar experiences for the students they serve. Through the experience of personal invention, educators reinvent themselves, and only then can they invent the future of education.

REFERENCES

Cavallo, D., Papert, S., & Stager, G. (2004, June). Climbing to understanding: Lessons from an experimental learning environment for adjudicated youth. In *Proceedings of the 6th International Conference on Learning Sciences* (pp. 113–120). International Society of the Learning Sciences, Los Angeles, CA.

Edwards, C., Gandini, L., & Forman, G. (Eds.). (2011). *The Hundred Languages of Children: The Reggio Emilia Experience in Transformation: The Reggio Emilia Experience in Transformation*. (3rd ed.). Santa Barbara, CA: Praeger.

Martinez, S., & Stager, G. (2017, March 16). *Around the World with the 8 Big Ideas of the Constructionist Learning Lab*. Retrieved from http://inventtolearn.com/around-the -world-with-the-8-big-ideas-of-the-constructionist-learning-lab/

Mitra, S. (2000, June). Minimally invasive education for mass computer literacy. In *Conference on Research in Distance and Adult Learning in Asia* (pp. 21–25). Hong Kong, China.

Papert, S. (1980). *Mindstorms: Computers, children, and powerful ideas*. New York, NY: Basic Books.

Papert, S. (1996). *The connected family: bridging the digital generation gap*. Atlanta, GA: Longstreet.

Stager, G. S. (2006). *An investigation of constructionism in the Maine Youth Center*. Doctoral dissertation, University of Melbourne, Department of Education, Melbourne, Australia.

Turkle, S., & Papert, S. (1992). Epistemological pluralism and the revaluation of the concrete. *Journal of Mathematical Behavior, 11*(1), 3–33.

II   SUPPORTING EQUITY

In supporting learners' construction of knowledge, a critical question is learning toward what end? Schools are often tasked with providing work skills to promote economic agency in students, whereas others see supporting personal expression to promote creative agency as equally important endeavors. Still others promote critical agency—inviting students to interrogate power structures and question what is learned and how it should take place. This section puts these tensions around equity front and center, asking who gets access to knowledge, what are the topics of learning, and how should it be learned?

Although people have been engaged in making for centuries, the recent growth of the maker movement has revitalized an interest in hands-on activities that often use traditional crafts and tools in combination with now more affordable and accessible electronics. The maker movement has become a popular model for constructionist learning environments in community centers, public libraries, and school classrooms around the globe. However, many constructionist scholars have noted the popularized version of "making" promoted by corporate influences can lead to problematic assumptions about the critical values of making.

In chapter 10, "Cheesemaking Emancipation: A Critical Theory of Cultural Making," Blikstein examines important issues of equity in the maker movement. Reviewing examples of maker activities around the world, Blikstein challenges the community to consider the context, culture, and history when determining whether maker activities are truly critical and emancipatory. Peppler, Keune, and Thompson in chapter 11, "Reclaiming Traditionally Feminine Practices and Materials for STEM Learning Through the Modern Maker Movement," continue this examination with a focus on female craft activities that are often seen in contrast to the more male engineering and computing activities. Taking the examples of weaving, crocheting, and other textile crafts, they explore the relationship between the practices of the fiber crafts and mathematical and computational concepts. Reflecting on the implications of the truly student-centered goals of constructionism, in chapter 12, "Constructionism as a Pedagogy of Disrespect," Holbert argues that maker experiences must be responsive to the broader sociopolitical context beyond the maker space and create room for young people to be antsy, frustrated, and even angry. In chapter 13, "Cultivating Community Change While Creating Construction Kits: Launching Scratch, Modkit, and L2TT2L," Millner, Baafi, and Klimczak provide examples such as the Truth Chair and Rainbow Glove, motivated by social injustices, that push the development and use of construction kits as tools for youth empowerment.

What do equitable and constructionist learning communities look like? In chapter 14, "Jeitismo Construcionismo in Brasilian Learning Communities," Cavallo describes constructionist work deeply embedded in Brasilian culture. By creating learning environments in which students had voice to determine their own projects and express their own ideas through these projects, they could connect contextually and personally with underlying scientific, mathematical, and computational knowledge. Cavallo proposes ways to build upon culture and create environments and ecosystems to support this type of learning environment. Likewise, in chapter 15, "The Role of Critical Identity Science Artifacts in Youth Claiming a Rightful Presence in STEM," Barton and Tan propose that youth develop critical science identity artifacts that let them connect maker activities with personally relevant projects drawn from their community. Developed over a four-year period, these kinds of projects work toward establishing a youth's rightful presence in STEM. In chapter 16, "Indigenous Youth Making Community Tours," Searle, Litts, Brayboy, Kafai, Casort, Benson, and Dance examine how broader community making practices influence and inform the digital local making practices of indigenous youth. Describing how youth created community tours about a series of metal sculptures made by a local artist, this chapter demonstrates the importance of the "why" behind making, how tools afford and constrain the purpose of making, and the identities making affords in designing for learning in community settings. Finally, in chapter 17, "Computational Making with Children in Intercultural Computer Club," Weibert, Aal, Krüger, Ahmadi, Stevens, and Wulf provide a comparative study of two collaborative maker projects in an intercultural neighborhood in Germany. Computational making in the computer club setting fostered understanding of the cross-cultural and neighborhood level.

10 CHEESEMAKING EMANCIPATION: A CRITICAL THEORY OF CULTURAL MAKING

Paulo Blikstein

The explosive growth of the maker movement and fab labs in education might appear sudden, but the pillars upon which these movements rest—constructivism, constructionism, project-based learning, critical pedagogy—have been slowly engendered for decades. Critical pedagogy theorists emphasized learners' empowerment, emancipation, and culture (D'Ambrosio, 1986; Freire, 2000). Constructionism brought visibility to the role of media, tools, "objects to think with" and powerful ideas. As a much-cited Papert quote states:

> Construction that takes place "in the head" often happens especially felicitously when it is supported by construction of a more public sort "in the world"—a sand castle, a Lego house, a computer program ... Part of what I mean by "in the world" is that the product can be shown, discussed, examined, probed, and admired. (Papert, 1991, p. 142)

Edith Ackermann, creatively combining Piaget and Papert, contributed with the idea of a cognitive dance—"diving in," or being immersed in the activity and being one with the medium, and then "stepping out," or emerging from the embeddedness. She reminds us that the attention to "hands-on" learning is just half of the story, and that the full cycle of building and reflecting, closeness and distance is what makes constructionist-inspired learning so powerful (Ackermann, 2001). Finally, Turkle and Papert completed the puzzle by reminding us that this process could take many forms and shapes and that children might want to program a computer or build robots in ways that might violate the canonical rules of professional coding and engineering—productively and creatively going against the grain of well-established practices in these technical fields (epistemological pluralism, Turkle & Papert, 1991).

Even though this primordial soup has been around for decades, it was not until the advent of the suitable social and technological infrastructure that the maker movement was able to take flight in schools at scale. It was a perfect storm: in the early 2000s, these theories and early experiences were met with cheaper and better technology (e.g., low-cost microcontroller boards, 3D printers), social acceptance of the tenets of progressive education (the rise of "twenty-first-century skills"), abundant funding for STEM education, user-friendly software (block-based programming, web-based software), and a critical mass of like-minded researchers and practitioners (Blikstein, 2018). Unfortunately, instead of celebrating and honoring the intellectual roots of maker education, many of its advocates are reinventing the same ideas and repackaging them into discourses that embrace the agendas of corporations and national bureaucracies, leaving youth empowerment and agency as an afterthought.

But the worldwide growth of the maker movement has been so fast—compared to the customary pace of educational reform—that we have not been able to reflect on fundamental questions about making in education. *Chief among those questions is how to think about equity, culture, power, and context.* In the Logo days, this question was somewhat less explicit since computers were new and unfamiliar, so there were no "indigenous" or familiar ways to deal with programming. But making is a more general type of practice, enacted on basic or advanced materials, with no or high technology: we have been programming for just a few decades, but people have been "making" for millennia. The fact that the term "making" can encompass such a wide range of activities makes its relationship with learners' culture and previous knowledge more intricate.

This poses a challenge that critical theorists and historians of science have already struggled with when considering the relationship between Western science and the local knowledge of indigenous peoples about nature and biology (Morrow, 2008). This scholarship, more recently framed in the context of Decoloniality (Quijano, 2000), has increasingly influenced science and mathematics education research (Carter, 2004). But we are still in the midst of this turbulent debate between cultural totality, respect for others and their epistemologies (Carter, 2004), and romanticization of the *beau-sauvage* (Semali & Kincheloe, 1999).

WHO ARE WE TO IMPOSE OUR PRACTICES AND EPISTEMOLOGIES ONTO OTHERS?

This question, which has concerned Freire, D'Ambrosio, and many other scholars (emancipatory postfoundationalism, Morrow, 2008) for decades, is as vivid and timely now as it was then: who are we to impose practices and epistemologies on others, de-historicize science and technology, and deem some types of knowledge as superior? Ethnomathematics (D'Ambrosio, 1986) was the first well-developed attempt to find curricular and theoretical combinations of so-called normative and alternative knowledge in the field of mathematics—but it has nevertheless been controversial. Some scholars condemn attempts to equalize Western and indigenous or local knowledge, claiming that such attempts overromanticize oppressed populations and uncritically accept their knowledge as intrinsically superior or unquestionable. On the other side of the spectrum, researchers claim that conventional science or mathematics, as well as its methods and goals, cannot be taken separately from the historical context that generated them. Therefore, claims to its superiority would also be biased toward the dominant culture—perpetuating existing oppressive schemes and historical injustices. Freire, a man of praxis who was often confronted with the challenge of bringing these ideas to real school systems, tried to find compromises:

> Low-income boys and girls have the right to know the same mathematics, the same physics, the same biology as affluent boys and girls, but we should not accept the teaching of any content that does not include a critical analysis of how society functions. (Freire, 2000, p. 44)

Freire's position makes it clear that even after decades of work on critical pedagogy and ethnomathematics, the devil is in the details: how exactly can we balance conventional and indigenous knowledge in real classrooms, in the complex balancing act between building cultural capital, fostering inclusive learning environments, and connecting students' lived experiences to their education? For mathematics, Adam, Alangui, & Barton (2003) hypothesized these possible scenarios: Ethnomathematics as (1) a full replacement for conventional mathematics, (2) a supplement so that students see mathematics as a response to human needs found in nearly every culture, (3) a springboard for academic mathematics, (4) a progression in which ethnomathematics is a stage in a process that starts from the mathematical world of the child and then moves into other cultures, (5) a support for preparing rich learning situations and activities, and (6) an approach that looks at the classroom itself as a situated cultural context and mathematical learning as part of this context.

Even after decades of work and debates on mathematics, there seems to be a vast space of possibilities, which points to the complexity of the challenge for the much younger field of maker education. But can these previous debates shed light into the role that culture might play in maker education? Could there be Ethnomaking? Would it be a mere transposition of the six categories?

ETHNOMAKING: CONVENTIONAL VERSUS LOCAL KNOWLEDGE IN MATHEMATICS, SCIENCE, AND MAKING

One difficulty in examining scientific versus local knowledge in mathematics and science is that in modern societies they have become vast, specialized professional practices, rarely performed by ordinary citizens. But making is intrinsically less of a specialized profession and more connected to everyday life, so the comparison between conventional and other types of making might be more apt. Second, everyday practices and devices across cultures, although diverse, have a lot of commonalities. Most societies need to farm, build houses, prepare food, shape materials, or automate or offload repetitive chores—which embed micro-tasks that relate to making. In that context, what would culturally aware making look like? To examine that question, we first need to establish the "maker equivalent" to conventional mathematics or science. The activities in most makerspaces in the United States and Europe revolve around working with robotics, electronics, and microcontrollers; programming computers; generating objects using 3D printers or laser cutters; and working with e-textiles and other enhanced craft materials. Ethnomaking, or cultural making, would then comprise activities, materials, practices, and themes that are attuned to a more specific group, culture, or region (such as basket making, pottery, electronics upcycling, woodworking, or costume making).

One way to envision the possibilities of cultural making is to hypothesize an analogy with ethnomathematics, thus as (1) a replacement for conventional making, in which indigenous or local making techniques would take the centerstage, (2) a supplement to conventional making classes so that students can appreciate human ingenuity, materials, and techniques in other cultures, (3) a springboard or motivation for learning about conventional making, (4) a progression in which ethnomaking is a stage in a process that starts from the maker world of the child and then moves into other cultures, (5) a support for preparing more rich and diverse learning activities in makerspaces, or (6) a framework to structure the maker classroom itself as a situated cultural context. Not all of these possible frameworks have been enacted in maker education, but there are three common designs. The first is to let children choose personally or community-meaningful projects to make. The second is to create materials and kits that connect existing cultural practices to emerging technologies (e.g., Buechley & Perner-Wilson, 2012), and the third is to choose themes or project prompts that align with students' cultures and lived experiences (e.g., Blikstein, 2008). Even though these have resulted in rich learning experiences and significant advances in how we think about maker education, it is clear that there is a wide space for new research and design in cultural making. But the main goal of this chapter is to take a step back and examine one possibly overlooked aspect: the fundamental rationales and justifications for maker education, and their own cultural bias.

Even within progressive educators, the predominant rationales for making are dominated by European or US-centric perspectives, with little regard for international or nontraditional contexts. These rationales can be summarized as follows:

- *Making as a job market skill:* Helping children learn engineering and programming
- *Making as a tool for deconstruction of industrial products:* Repairing/reusing, and as resistance to mass standardization and industrialization
- *Making as a way to have control of what you eat/use:* Rejecting industrialized products and making your own food (e.g., to have control of the ingredients), furniture, lamps, or other products (e.g., to make sure they are sustainable)
- *Making as understanding technology around you:* Understanding how everyday technology works, such as social media, computers, cell phones, household appliances
- *Making as personal expression and creativity:* Creating artistic or creative inventions

Although some of these components might seem hard to argue against, they came about in the context of the richer parts of the globe. Perhaps progressive educators in developed countries are unaware that goals such as "rejecting industrialized products" or resisting against technology massification are concerns germane to the developed world. Thus, counterintuitively, despite seemingly harmless, some of these rationales might become obstacles for designing truly inclusive experiences, especially in the Global South and other developing areas. To further examine this issue, I will resort to two vignettes of observations collected as part of a series of interviews with artisans from different countries.

MAKERS AROUND THE WORLD?

Vignette 1: Fatma in the Bedouin Village
In a remote Bedouin village in the Middle East, Fatma shows a spherical and dense piece of goat cheese and talks about how much work it was to make

it. She is a very special member of the village, being one of the few women who were interested in studying and getting a degree. In the village, Fatma says, women spend copious amounts of time making many of the products needed for daily life from scratch, such as food and clothes. I asked her if she felt proud of the cheese she made, and if it was different from buying it ready-made from the supermarket. She looked at me puzzled and replied that being able to go to a grocery store and buy ready-made goods was a true liberation. She liked her goat cheese, but there was nothing magical about it. For her, saving hours a day by going to the supermarket was empowering and useful since she was able to redirect her time to other endeavors, such as studying and reading.

Vignette 2: Somsak in the Rural Village

Somsak is an artisan who lives in a small rural village in Southeast Asia. He makes wooden horses that are sold as souvenirs for tourists. He uses a soft, easy-to-carve wood and a set of metal tools that he proudly claims to be the only carving instruments he has ever used. As I talk to Somsak, he keeps working, undisturbed, as if the sculpting was completely automatic. I was initially impressed: not only was he using native materials and tools, but he was being artistic and doing what he loved for a living. But in the course of the interview I realized that I was mistaken. I learned that Somsak makes many identical horses a day—sometimes twenty in just a few hours. He sells them for one US dollar each to a middleman, who also tells him the exact horse poses to make, based on what sells well. The horses are then taken to a different facility to be attached to a base and receive a coat of varnish. Somsak was just a small piece in a large distributed industrial complex.

I asked him if he ever thinks of doing his own designs and horse poses. He looked at me perplexed, and said, "No, why would I?" He had no say on the poses or even the animals to be sculpted, and he did not miss it. I then asked if he would feel differently about his craft if he had a machine to make the horses. He welcomed the idea wholeheartedly and said that he would not miss making horse sculptures, telling me that if I was to create such a machine, "I will be your first customer!" I also asked Somsak if he was proud of his horses, and if he had any at his home for decoration, to which he replied, "Why would I have such ugly things at home?"

FATMA AND SOMSAK: MAKING IN CONTEXT

Fatma's vignette shows that the idea of makers as deconstructors of industrial products and producers of their own "stuff" found no echo in her life, despite being a progressive, valuable goal in a developed country. For Fatma, it was empowering to be able to stop making some of her own food and instead buy it at the supermarket. Resisting against industrial foods or mass-produced household items made no sense and would not have improved her life.

Somsak's story shows the breakdown of another component of the conventional, US-centric definition of making. An external observer could see in Somsak the prototypical indigenous maker: a naïve artist in a remote rural village, using native materials to make beautiful wooden sculptures. He had the "maker mindset." He was using his hands. He was being artistic. But in reality, he was just a small peg in a geographically distributed system for the production of souvenirs, more a factory worker than an artist. Somsak's horses would be worth nothing if they were not "made by hand": no tourist would want to take home a sculpture made by machine. Somsak could look like a maker, but he was just a factory worker producing objects with no personal connection or meaning. Ironically, making by hand was a prison for him: because of the attribution of value that affluent tourists make to "hand made," any automation or improvement to the process would immediately annul the value of the product he had to offer.

IMPLICATIONS FOR DESIGN: HANDS-ON OPPRESSION AND CHEESEMAKING EMANCIPATION

The US-centric definitions of making that prevail in most makerspaces would be at odds with the lived experiences of Fatma and Somsak, for whom producing objects by hand was a symbol of oppression, alienation, and poverty. Sculpting wooden horses, or generating physical objects from organic materials, although romantic from the outside, was a proxy for repetitive and meaningless work. However, the exact same activity could well be a sign of liberation for an engineer in Palo Alto, United States, who might crave craft activities with organic materials, instead of dealing with computers. The process of making homemade cheese in the Bedouin tribe reminds Fatma of her long hours at home and of the college classes she could be taking instead. But cheesemaking might be emancipatory and life changing for a child of an affluent family in New York City, United States, who has never been to a farm or made his or her own food. Conversely, in Somsak's own words, a horse-making industrial machine would be liberating, and he would be happy to never touch his "maker" tools again. Fatma would rather just go to the supermarket and acquire her industrialized food.

In reality, for most of the world's population, not having to make your own food or furniture from scratch would hardly be considered a problem, and soapmaking, glass blowing, or woodcarving still represent exploitative practices or unhealthy work. As making celebrates the customized, the anti-industrial, the artistic, and the inefficiency of giving up industrial production, it often ignores that those might not make sense outside of affluent regions of the world. Glorifying the "handmade" is a profound demonstration of power.

But this does not mean that a *soapmaking epiphany* in Palo Alto is not real nor that we should not pay attention to *cheesemaking emancipation*. A misguided response would be to conclude that cheese and soapmaking are not worth studying or promoting and that technology only emancipates the less affluent. But it is of concern that most of the makerspaces, materials, curricula, machines, and theoretical frameworks are coming from prosperous nations and communities. What would Fatma's or Somsak's children think or feel when attending a maker workshop that celebrates practices that oppress their own parents? Definitions of making and makers such as "everyone is a maker" or "every child is a maker" reinforce the assumption that all forms of making "things" are voluntary and empowering. Perhaps some adults and children around the world would rather not make anything with their own hands?

CULTURAL MAKING

Researchers have responded to these challenges by creating new sets of materials or adapting themes of maker activities to different populations. But in Freirean pedagogy, the fundamental question is not only about respecting the local culture and context, but fundamentally about the compromise between what is already there—the culture, the practices, the materials—and the new elements that teachers or designers want to bring. And there lies perhaps the most important element of culturally aware making, since there are so many pre-existing making practices in any given community, as well as culturally specific values attached to those practices.

Whereas much of the academic debate in mathematics or science education is about epistemologies and bodies of knowledge often at odds with one another given the convergent nature of traditional science, *the divergent nature of engineering and making might offer opportunities for more creative, democratic, and inclusive combinations.* Conventional science seeks to find one single law to explain a wide range of phenomena, so different worldviews and epistemologies are not easily combined. But the divergent nature of engineering—per which multiple solutions to the same problem are accepted and encouraged—might offer a more fertile ground for different perspectives. For example, Cavallo's work in Thailand (Cavallo, 2000) identified deep local expertise in repurposing internal combustion engines for a variety of purposes, and my work in Brazil showed the same type of expertise in repurposing electronics (Blikstein, 2008). Both the Thai engines and the Brazilian repurposed tape decks are rich examples of spaces in which different epistemologies and knowledge systems co-exist productively, so the pre-existing and the new might not necessarily compete but complement one another. Internal combustion engines could be considered, for Western scholars, a symbol of economic exploitation, environmental damage, and pollution. But those same engines, in the context of rural Thai communities, became instruments of community development and emancipation, as self-taught local engineers managed to adapt engines for their boats, rice mills, and water pumps. Similarly, in the hands of the creative minds of Heliópolis, Brazil, consumer electronics were repurposed into all sorts of machines and contraptions that improved the livelihood of entire communities. These cases counter the "beau-sauvage" assumption, in which Thai farmers would only care about their traditional agricultural appliances, or that Heliópolis dwellers would not want to approach "foreign" technology.

These hybridizations should not be only about tools and materials but also about emancipation. Cultural making or ethnomaking should be about engaging with different populations, cultures, and contexts to identify and leverage the most emancipatory components of a given process, since we know that ultimately the mere existence of physical built artifacts—a wooden sculpture, blinking LEDs, or a 3D-printed keychain—is not an assurance of learner empowerment.

This goes against the common assumption that technology or science is necessarily oppressive for nondominant populations. In fact, it begs the question: who are we to impose our own academic views of what emancipation looks like to others, using stereotypical templates of what others want and need? What if local populations do not want to reject science or technology, but rather reshape and repurpose them to their own ways? The work of Paulo Freire is a good example—Freire did bring an element from the outside (normative written language) to disenfranchised populations but did so in a way that empowered individuals against an oppressive system.

Cultural making, thus, should go beyond specific materials, machines, themes, or spaces that exist in schools. It should be about finding mutual space for the enhancement and enrichment of old and new individual and social practices that could be at the same time locally relevant and intrinsically valuable. And even though the determination of what is "intrinsically valuable" could be controversial, I would like to suggest three possible criteria:

1. *The Principle of Emancipatory Making.* The first is the Freirean assumption that humans have an ontological vocation to change and improve one's own reality. Freire eloquently states that humans have the latent potential to go from the "consciousness of the real" to the "consciousness of the possible" by understanding "viable new alternatives." Thus, an intrinsically valuable goal of culturally aware maker education would be to take students from the acceptance of one's given reality to the possibility of changing it, *latu sensu*—which could apply to all cultures, countries, and contexts—even if "change," for many communities, might mean to resist external pressures to abandon their culture and habitat or, conversely, creatively appropriate external tools to enhance their own livelihood.

2. *The Principle of Powerful Expressiveness in Making.* A second intrinsically valuable goal for maker education derives from the first. To create new solutions, one needs exposure to diverse ways of connecting intention and implementation—it is the mediation of powerful tools and ideas. An idea that stays in the head and cannot be realized is not very useful. In many makerspaces, tools such as 3D printers and laser cutters are the ones that help students connect idea and realization and express themselves, but there could be many others (including traditional and indigenous tools and ways of making). Thus, maker education should be constantly concerned with the design of high *and* low technologies that ease the path between imagination and the world. In some contexts, laser cutters will the best tools to make this connection; in others, it might be a powerful technique for shaping clay. But there could be, also, many indigenous or high-technology tools that do not enable children to express their ideas—therefore, the value of tools and practices should be proportional to their expressive power rather than where they come from.

3. *The Principle of Learnability in Making.* A final intrinsically valuable element in culturally aware maker education is that there should be some measure of sophistication and complexity for products and processes so that *learning* can take place. Even within a given culture or context, there should be ways to determine if a given artifact is interesting, sophisticated, or clever. We should resist the all-too-Western custom of falling for the *beau-sauvage* fallacy: the fact that Somkat's horses were created locally with traditional tools does not mean that they are remarkable

artifacts. Hence, even within a given culture and context we should understand the criteria by which quality, sophistication, and complexity are judged—there should be such a thing as an uninteresting wooden horse or an unremarkable clay sculpture, in the same way that there could be a dull LEGO robot. Having culturally aware ways of assessing the quality of artifacts also guarantees the existence of a trajectory of learning—students should be able to get more skilled at expressing their ideas. In the absence of a learning pathway and rubrics of quality, maker education becomes merely "making."

Thus, in dialogue with different populations we can understand what they want to achieve, if the tools and practices of making can help, and how to ascertain quality to students' productions. Even new or foreign procedures and technologies can give novel meaning to everyday routines and objects, improving them along community-relevant metrics: either more sustainable, aesthetically pleasing, elegant, or efficient. In this process we should focus on empowering people to change their world and on supporting social and cognitive processes that would enable this transformation (D'Ambrosio, personal communication, October 4, 2019).

We should not de-historicize science and technology nor uncritically accept local knowledge. We should also not make assumptions about what oppressed populations want based on armchair views of those populations, forcing US- and European-centric academic frameworks onto complex, historically constructed realities.

Cultural making should not be about romanticization of the *local* or simplistic incorporation of cultural elements into the production of objects. Cultural making should not be about uncritically importing academic agendas that do not fully understand learning and education, or ignoring that youth culture around the world does not always follow the calcified, same-old views of US-centric "revolutionary" researchers. It should be about powerfully engaging youth with the political, human, and social challenges of subverting and transforming one's reality through powerful tools and representations. No culture is good if it does not allow its children to rebel against the powers that be.

REFERENCES

Ackermann, E. (2001). *Piaget's Constructivism, Papert's Constructionism: What's the difference?* Paper presented at the Constructivism: Uses and Perspectives in Education, Geneva, Switzerland.

Adam, S., Alangui, W., & Barton, B. (2003). A Comment on: Rowlands & Carson "Where would formal, academic mathematics stand in a curriculum informed by ethnomathematics? A critical review." *Educational Studies in Mathematics, 52*(3), 327–335.

Blikstein, P. (2008). Travels in Troy with Freire: Technology as an agent for emancipation. In P. Noguera & C. A. Torres (Eds.), *Social justice education for teachers: Paulo Freire and the possible dream* (pp. 205–244). Rotterdam, The Netherlands: Sense.

Blikstein, P. (2018). Maker movement in education: History and prospects. In M. J. de Vries (Ed.), *Handbook of technology education* (pp. 419–437). Cham, Switzerland: Springer International Publishing.

Buechley, L., & Perner-Wilson, H. (2012). Crafting technology: Reimagining the processes, materials, and cultures of electronics. *ACM Transactions on Computer-Human Interaction (TOCHI), 19*(3), 21.

Carter, L. (2004). Thinking differently about cultural diversity: Using postcolonial theory to (re)read science education. *Science Education, 88*(6), 819–836. https://doi.org/10.1002/sce.20000

Cavallo, D. (2000). *Technological fluency and the art of motorcycle maintenance: Emergent design of learning environments* (Doctoral dissertation). Media Lab, Massachusetts Institute of Technology, Cambridge, MA.

D'Ambrosio, U. (1986). Socio-cultural bases for mathematical education. In M. Carss (Ed.), *Proceedings of the Fifth International Congress on Mathematical Education* (pp. 1–6). Boston, MA: Birkhäuser Boston.

Freire, P. (2000). *A educação na cidade (Education in the city)* (4th ed.). São Paulo, Brazil: Cortez.

Morrow, R. A. (2008). Paulo Freire, indigenous knowledge and Eurocentric critiques of development: Three perspectives. In P. Noguera & C. A. Torres (Eds.), *Social justice education for teachers: Paulo Freire and the possible dream* (pp. 81–100). Rotterdam, The Netherlands: Sense.

Papert, S. (1991). Situating constructionism. In S. Papert & I. Harel (Eds.), *Constructionism*. Cambridge, MA: MIT Press.

Quijano, A. (2000). Coloniality of power, knowledge, and Latin America. *Nepantla: Views from South, 1*(3).

Semali, L. M., & Kincheloe, J. L. (1999). Introduction: What is indigenous knowledge and why should we study it? In L. M. Semali & J. L. Kincheloe (Eds.), *What is indigenous knowledge?: Voices from the Academy* (pp. 3–58). New York, NY: Taylor & Francis.

Turkle, S., & Papert, S. (1991). Epistemological pluralism and revaluation of the concrete. In I. H. A. S. Papert (Ed.), *Constructionism* (pp. 161–192). Norwood, NJ: Ablex Publishing Co.

11 RECLAIMING TRADITIONALLY FEMININE PRACTICES AND MATERIALS FOR STEM LEARNING THROUGH THE MODERN MAKER MOVEMENT

Kylie Peppler, Anna Keune, and Naomi Thompson

Making, an educational reform movement that celebrates hands-on creative practices and technological inventiveness, is expanding in K-16 settings (Peppler, Halverson, & Kafai, 2016). The practice of making is conceptually inclusive of a range of tools and materials. From creating cardboard castles to laser cutting nature-inspired models, making provides youth the space to design personally meaningful artifacts. In our view, this aligns with constructionist approaches to learning (Papert, 1980) and promises a particularly impactful entry point for traditionally underrepresented youth to science, technology, engineering, and mathematics (STEM) fields.

Despite these promises, critiques have been raised from inside the maker educational movement that making is all too often associated with high-technology practices, including robotics, which may traditionally be more appealing to male audiences (Buechley, 2013). Although other material practices, such as fiber crafts, are also featured at world Maker Faires, flagship events showcase the state-of-the-art projects, while other practices are often relegated to the sidelines. Today, textile crafts have seen a resurgence of interest both within the maker movement and beyond, prompting us to re-examine the connections between crafting, mathematics, and computing. History demonstrates repeated patterns of innovation that have stemmed from traditionally feminine practices and materials. One prominent example arcs back to the history of computing, which is rooted in weaving, crocheting, and other textile crafts. Central to this examination is the role of embodied forms of learning, inherent in this view of constructionist theory in the form of body syntonicity.

This chapter examines contemporary cases of traditionally feminine crafts through the lens of constructionist theory to uncover how embodied forms of learning can disrupt—and ultimately benefit—STEM learning through the integration of new materials and practices. The data presented here draw heavily on our interventionist work in school and out-of-school settings with middle-school-aged youth to test how and to what extent fiber crafts can be used in to teach and learn STEM concepts. These interventions included the exploration of computational aspects of sewing (i.e., fabric manipulation or fabric origami) and rigid heddle loom weaving and mathematical aspects of handloom weaving. We analyzed youth engagement with fiber crafts in relation to emergent mathematical and computational concepts and further examined their body movements in relation to the computational and mathematical concepts we identified in their crafting. Collectively, this work offers a way to reclaim historically marginalized practices in ways that disrupt stagnant practices and spur innovation in STEM fields.

OBJECTS-TO-THINK-WITH, EPISTEMOLOGICAL PLURALISM, AND BODY SYNTONICITY

Papert (1980) theorized materials as "objects-to-think-with" that allow learners to discover formal systems as they explore inherent properties of materials while designing personally meaningful projects. Objects-to-think-with have two leading characteristics: They support epistemological pluralism and body syntonicity (Papert, 1980; Turkle & Papert, 1992).

Epistemological pluralism honors the existence of multiple productive approaches to engaging with a given subject and asserts that it is important to legitimize undervalued ways of engagement to diversify the learning culture of a particular domain (Turkle & Papert, 1992). Concerned with cognitive styles in the context of computing, Turkle and Papert observed people's practices and sense-making processes in relation to computational concepts. They found that expressive and relationship-forming engagement with computational materials was a legitimate approach to learning about computational concepts that, if devalued, led people to turn away from computing. Furthermore, they identified that technological innovations of computational materials made expressive approaches to computing possible. Thus, introducing new materials may change who engages with a subject and how.

Body syntonicity suggests that learning emerges as learners draw on experiences of imagining their own bodies in place of or in relation to the object they are manipulating. Papert (1980) developed the idea of body syntonicity in the context of computation when children manipulated digital representations and robotic materials by applying computational instructions. Certain computational materials supported children to imagine themselves as a computational representation that they were manipulating. Thus, the way in which materials are designed can support or obstruct learners to draw on their bodily understanding.

Together, the notions of body syntonicity and epistemological plural-ism present a conceptual starting point for strategically designing STEM learning contexts that broaden participation by considering how materials shape the learning process for diverse learners. However, it remains unclear how exactly certain materials that are historically connected with under-represented groups may support formal engagement in STEM in ways that can be equally recognized.

MATERIAL FEMINISMS

The learning theory of material feminisms extends this prior understanding to consider the body as one of many objects that shape a learner's under-standing. At its core, material feminism takes into consideration that the actual physical body of the learner plays an active role in the shaping of possible experiences (Alaimo & Hekman, 2008). This extends the idea of body syntonicity. Papert argued that body syntonicity relates to the learn-ers' imagination of the body in place of the objects they manipulate. The material feminist tradition recenters the actual body as source that opens up opportunities to learn. Although the body plays a role across feminist approaches, the focus on the physical body extends postmodern feminism that has focused on the discursive role of materials and their production through discourse (Alaimo & Hekman, 2008). Rather than considering the role of the body as a product of material-discursive practices and represen-tations thereof, Barad (2003) suggests that the physiology of the body is also a force of production and to understand what it produces, the relation-ship among the material-discursive and its production must be illuminated.

Related to STEM learning, de Freitas and Sinclair (2013) have taken up Barad's materialist approaches for understanding the "materiality in/of mathematics" to advance the understanding of how the material nature of mathematics can radically shift the way mathematics is taught and learned. Instead of considering a learner's body as something that needs to be sup-plied with fixed, abstract concepts, de Freitas and Sinclair found that math-ematical concepts, the materials of learning, as well as the learners doing mathematics, emerge in context as they physically come together. This view of seeing what else mathematics may become, in terms of continually developing concepts and practices, invites creativity and inventiveness into learning settings in ways that foster the kinds of learning that construction-ist scholars aim to support.

The idea of how the personal, disciplinary, and material have come together over time—and the cultural assumptions that may have formed around their interaction—lead us to take a historical look at patterned trends of materials of STEM innovations and material-discursive notions of these materials in society (e.g., who uses what) to reveal which materials represent an ontological cut within disciplines. Material traces of exclusion can reveal possibilities for reintroducing historically relevant materials and the ways of knowing and producing they support. This presents possibilities for a renewed look at how we theorize, capture, and design constructionist learning environments that help broaden how legitimate participation in disciplinary learning happens.

STEM AND TEXTILES

Despite recent efforts of educational reform movements to foster inclusive STEM cultures, most STEM fields remain predominantly masculine domains with an incorrigible gender gap, especially in the United States (Sax et al., 2017). The underrepresentation of women is particularly problematic as diverse workplace environments have been linked to national economic security and productivity (Sax et al., 2017). While there continues to be a significant discrepancy in women's representation in STEM careers, researchers have observed that there is generally no gender difference in girls' and boys' mathematical achievement (Hyde, Lindberg, Linn, Ellis, & Williams, 2008). Still, there has been a steady decline in women's representation in the STEM workforce and higher education (Landivar, 2013). Nuanced studies of girls' and women's mathematical participation suggests that these differences stem from perceptions of the discipline of mathematics and the extent to which the cultures surrounding mathematics are welcoming to women (Alper, 1993). Mathematics as taught is frequently removed from the contexts in which the ideas make sense; leveraging design is useful as a pedagogical tool; allowing students to experience the mathematical ideas they are working with as an "object-to-think-with" (Papert, 1980) is likely to change the very nature of what they understand about mathematics.

A noteworthy "object-to-think-with" in STEM is electronic textiles (Buechley, 2006), which consistently present a cogent context and notable exception for introducing youth—especially girls—to circuitry learning (Buchholz, Shively, Peppler, & Wohlwend, 2014; Kafai, Fields, & Searle, 2014). Throughout history, fiber crafts have held an intimate relationship with technology innovation (Plant, 1995). For example, the earliest computers that women operated through punch cards for storing and accessing information were based on the Jacquard loom, which used punch cards to program fabric patterns (e.g., Plant, 1995). Such pivotal fiber craft-based innovations in STEM fields are not outliers. In mathematics, Taimina and Handerson (2005), proofed the possibilities to model smooth hyperbolic planes using crochet techniques, which had previously been considered impossible to construct. Using these models in teaching can support learning of mathematics (Taimina & Henderson, 2005). Fiber crafts offer opportunities for profound engagement in complex STEM concepts. However, despite this intimate relationship, we know little about how fiber crafts could be a context for STEM learning and for diversifying participation in STEM.

CONTEXT

Although part of a larger initiative related to fiber crafts and STEM learning, the data presented here draw heavily on our interventionist work in school and out-of-school settings. We facilitated interventions in school and out-of-school settings with middle-school-aged youth to test how and to what extent fiber crafts can be used in teaching and learning STEM concepts. These interventions included a week-long fiber crafts camp at the Indiana University School of Education's maker space to explore computational aspects of sewing (i.e., fabric manipulation or fabric origami) and rigid heddle loom weaving, as well as mathematical aspects of handloom weaving. We also conducted extended fiber crafts courses at a Midwestern public school to study the inherent computational concepts, practices, and products of heddle loom weaving and fabric manipulation. Across school and out-of-school settings, each session lasted between sixty and ninety minutes and was joined by eight to ten middle-school-aged youth.

During the interventions, we videorecorded youth crafting and conducted five- to ten-minute–long semi-structured interviews with the youth as they worked on personally meaningful projects. The interviews asked youth to explain their design process and any surprises they encountered while crafting. The interviews were also videorecorded using mobile cameras to capture the embodied meaning making of the youth around the construction of the fiber artifacts. Last, we captured project dimensionality and complexity through videorecordings of youth projects to support a detailed view of materialized STEM concepts.

We analyzed the youth engagement with the fiber crafts in relation to emergent mathematical and computational concepts by iteratively coding the video based on the K12CS framework for computer science education (e.g., functions and loops) and the Common Core (CC) state standards for mathematical proficiency (e.g., algebraic reasoning). Then, we coded the interviews for markers of artifact formation and how youth described their body movements in relation to the computational and mathematical concepts we identified in their crafting. As case studies, we selected three youth who performed the craft activities in ways that made the facilitated craft technique and pattern recognizable in their artifact. As most youth accomplished that, the youth we selected serve as typical examples of the movements of tools and materials that brought about deep engagement with STEM learning.

ALGEBRAIC REASONING: WEAVING PATTERNS

Two CC math practice standards that span across grades ask students to seek out structures and to express patterns. Both practices are visible as one young weaver, Kade, attempted to incorporate a recursive sequence pattern into his weaving design. Just over halfway through a weaving introduction workshop, participants were handed paper with blank one-inch-by-one-inch grid squares to help them continue to design their weaving patterns. A facilitator—one of the authors of this chapter—sat down with Kade to help him see how his grid paper could be used. Looking at the few rows he had already woven, the facilitator began reading his project, "Sort of looks like, like over over over, under under, over over over over, under under under." Together, Kade (K) and the facilitator (F) started to translate the weaving into a number pattern and to continue it forward. The weaver had a vision that the facilitator couldn't see at first:

K: *Three, two, four, three*

F: *Three*

F: *Two // K: Five (overlapping speech)*

K: *Four*

F: *Ohh*

K: *And then six. And then that's supposed to be five.*

F: *Ok cool.*

K: *And then it would go on to seven, six, and eight, seven, and nine, eight, and then ten, nine. I don't know.*

F: *Oh, I see what you're doing.*

Kade was developing a recursive sequence (3, 2, 4, 3, 5, 4, 6, 5, 7, 6, 8, 7, 9, 8, 10, 9) that could be described as following the pattern: "minus one, plus two." Mathematical proficiency, as described by CC standards 7 & 8 includes "discern[ing] a pattern or structure" and "notice[ing] if calculations are repeated" (National Governors Association Center for Best Practices & Council of Chief State School Officers, 2010). Not only does the work with pattern and sequence in this episode align with these descriptions of proficiency but also this weaver went a step further than noticing and discerning by inventing a structure with repeated calculations. Thinking about patterns in this way may also have implications for more advanced and pure mathematics. He was not asked or instructed to invent such a sequence but was prompted to do so by the weaving activity itself. Additionally, the grid planning sheet (figure 11.1) helped him imagine the sequence further and to determine how his plan would play out in the physical world with the weaving materials.

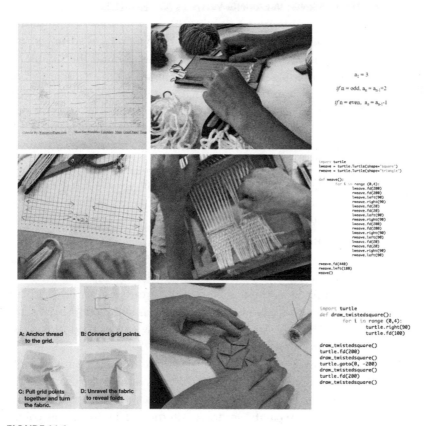

FIGURE 11.1

Top: Kade weaving (left), Kade's project plan (center), Recursive function for Kade's pattern (right). *Center:* Jasmine's project plan (left), her weaving project (middle), parallel process translated into Python (right). *Bottom:* Twisted square technique (left); Emma's project (center); Python code of stitch pattern (right).

Kade's engagement with the loom led to the creation of a unique and beautiful woven tapestry as well as the invention of a recursive sequence that exceeded some measures of mathematical proficiency. The materiality of weaving, composed of Kade's hands and his threaded shuttle moving "over over over, under under" the vertically warped thread, produced a grid pattern that shifted form through movement and invited playful recursive number sequences. The mathematical concept spilled across rows, transformed, and became form in the world that could be further manipulated.

PARALLEL PROCESSING: WEAVING WITH TWO SHUTTLES

Parallel process while developing a computer program is an advanced and challenging mental exercise that requires keeping in mind the simultaneous progression of multiple moving parts. At the same time, middle-school-aged weavers, such as Jasmine, who participated in a weaving course, seem to grasp this idea immediately as they created beginner lace patterns. Jasmine intended to weave an opening into her tapestry and explained her graphical project plan (figure 11.1, *center left*):

> So this is the hole right here. And [the yarn] goes one way, then [the yarn] goes the other way. And then [the yarn] goes this way and then you skip these strings, where the hole is going to be, and then you go the same way and then you go this way and do the same as you did.

In her explanation of the first three lines in her project plan, which include the first lace weft, Jasmine's use of "skip these strings" suggests that she plans to use one color of yarn on only one shuttle to produce the lace design. This is mirrored by the direction of the arrows on her project plan, where the arrow on line three points into the same direction before and after the "hole." This seems to continue the row, rather than build both sides of the fabric in parallel.

However, after seven rows into her weave, Jasmine arrived at a place in her tapestry where she decided to introduce her simple lace pattern, the "hole." Here, she started to engage two yarn colors, teal and rose, that she wrapped around two separate shuttles. Alternating between the colors, she moved the teal yarn from left to right and the rose yarn from right to left, before turning the handle of the loom to shift the warp positions. On the graph paper, this would have been represented as two arrows pointing toward one another rather than in the same direction as was present in Jasmine's plan, a conceptually more complex task. Figure 11.1 (*center*) shows Jasmine's tapestry with five rows into the lace pattern. Compared to the non-lace weave (rose), the lace pattern shows inconsistencies. This suggests that the added complexity of alternating colors and directions before changing the warp thread positions requires additional practice. However, it is also evident that the teal and rose side of the tapestry are advancing in parallel. This means that the conceptual articulation, rather than the craftsmanship, was foregrounded for Jasmine.

Epistemological pluralism allows us to recognize and value broader definitions of disciplinary engagement than would otherwise be possible. Thus, Jasmine's two weaving shuttles are identifiable as complex programming processes, no less authentic or important than programming that occurs in more traditional or standardized ways. Material feminisms focuses in on the new kind of material instantiation that is being produced as Jasmine, the loom, and the shuttled yarn come together to tangibly reformulate a computational unit that would otherwise not exist. In this example, Jasmine is performing the computation that would typically be delegated to the computer, making the process transparent and possible to ask questions about.

LOOPS AND FUNCTIONS: SEWING

To produce effective code that can be reused in other projects, programmers need to recognize and abstract repetitions. Functions are powerful computational concepts that can do just that. Programmers use functions to define and describe a procedure of steps that can be recalled in the body of a computer program. Functions are challenging to learn even for undergraduate students, yet their use is inherent to fiber crafts. A compelling example emerged when a participant, Emma, recalled and modified a 2D grid pattern while sewing a 3D texture. Emma used the *twisted square* expression (see figure 11.1, *bottom left*): From the point of origin, where her thread was anchored to the fabric, Emma connected four corners of a square by sewing one grid point to the left, one down, one right, and back up where she pulled all points together. Emma repeated this loop three more times and then unfolded her ruffled fabric into four twisted squares (see figure 11.1, *bottom center*). She explained, "I had to separate each little thing to make it square. I had to push it down. It looked like a mess when I finished sewing." Each expression enclosed a particular amount of fabric that, when pulled together, ruffled the surrounding fabric, distorted the grid, and challenged Emma's orientation to the fabric.

The process of exploring the effects of a combination of steps on the resulting texture foregrounded the use of functions. This becomes apparent when translating the 2D grid pattern into Python code (see figure 11.1, *bottom right*) that defines a function at the start of the script and then recalls it in the body of the code. The computation was inherent to the performance of the craft and seemed to present an intimate approach to practicing abstractions that are typically performed by the computer.

Emma's tucking and folding brings loops and functions into the physical world, transforming how abstracted repetitions can be understood and advanced. It is not in spite of, but because of, Emma's engagement with "every little thing" of her fabric, needle, and thread that she was able to create such complex computational expressions. It is her physical hands and her orientation to the material that brings about the computation rather than imagining herself in place of the material and then translating this cognitive capacity into a computer program.

DISCUSSION

The examples broaden ideas of what math and computation can look like and demonstrate high-level engagement with existing and authentic STEM concepts through fiber crafts. Although it may be expected that fiber crafts involve basic, low-level actions such as counting and measuring, the learners in these examples go far beyond. This is one of the promises of intersections between crafts and STEM crafting; the union seems to invite deep engagement with concepts by presenting them in ways that necessitate repetition and "big picture" aesthetic coherence. The artifacts that emerge from these crafting experiences are personally meaningful and relevant. As such, learners' aesthetic desires lead to mathematical and computational complexity, deeply entangling craft and STEM. Where our constructionist perspective on learning provides a productive lens through which to view the work being done in these crafting interactions, the material feminist framing allows us to identify aspects of material-disciplinary workings that would otherwise go unnoticed.

Body syntonicity allows us to understand how interactions in space with materials signal deep learning about traditionally abstract concepts. Beyond the children imagining themselves crawling between warp thread, what produced the computation and mathematical engagement was the way the children's bodies, the looms, the yarn, and the over-and-under came together to form an entity that enclosed the mathematics in ways that did not exist before and that could be further manipulated. The physical form of the children's bodies was a material that came together with other materials at the craft table and produced the crafting activity as well as the new STEM form. Following a material feminist approach to learning, we begin to articulate this as a novel observation. This kind of syntonicity with the material makes it possible to recognize a child's body as a component part rather than the intentional driver of the STEM instantiation. It expands the idea of body syntonicity into the physical realm. The computational and mathematical nature of fiber crafts is a promising context through which to further investigate what this may mean for learning processes for a range of learners.

Epistemological pluralism allows us to see the sewing and weaving activities as compelling and alternative ways for children to get to know complex disciplinary concepts in their own ways and on their own terms. Material feminist perspectives of learning allow us to recognize the coming together of component parts as significantly changing how we can conceive of the nature of STEM, for instance, a computer. In both Jasmine's and Emma's case, the children performed actions that would usually be delegated to the computer. They became part of the physical form of the computer, extending its form to the human. This has the potential to transparently show underlying workings of computers, with which repeated human movements could be freed through automation. This allows researchers to speculate new forms of computers and the children to transparently become part of blurred software and hardware relationships. For example, when the warp threads on the loom, despite their physical form, are perceived as software, the way in which Jasmine weaves two shuttles through top and bottom warp threads to create the lace becomes an artistic way of manipulating a program, similar to ASCII art. At the same time, the shuttles could also be considered the central processing unit of the computational machine that controls its input/output mechanisms. These dual hardware/software roles of material aspects of fiber crafts expand epistemological pluralism. It is no longer just ways of knowing the world but also ways of being in the world that productively enable us to theorize about the role of the youth in the STEM performance.

The examples given here showcase the immense potential in reclaiming traditionally feminine craft techniques for STEM learning. Threading, tucking, weaving, and folding need not be separated from their feminine histories to be valued as intellectually and materially innovative. Our ongoing work, beginning with e-textiles, continues to show the intrinsic and disciplinary value for all types of learners to engage with textile crafts, as well as threads on how to advance theoretical concepts of constructionism.

ACKNOWLEDGMENTS

This work was supported by a collaborative grant from the National Science Foundation (DRL #1420303) and a grant from the Center of Craft, Creativity, and Design awarded to Kylie Peppler. Any opinions, findings, and conclusions or recommendations expressed in this article are not those of National Science Foundation, Indiana University, or the University of California. Portions of this chapter are derived from the dissertation work of Anna Keune and Naomi Thompson. We also thank teachers at the Project School and Indiana Kids as well as Creativity Labs members Janis Watson, Joey Huang, and Suraj Uttamchandani, without whom the work would not have been possible.

REFERENCES

Alaimo, S., & Hekman, S. J. (Eds.). (2008). *Material feminisms*. Bloomington, IN: Indiana University Press.

Alper, J. (1993). The pipeline is leaking women all the way along. *Science, 260,* 409–411.

Barad, K. (2003). Posthumanist performativity: Toward an understanding of how matter comes to matter. *Signs: Journal of Women in Culture and Society, 28*(3), 801–831.

Buchholz, B., Shively, K., Peppler, K., & Wohlwend, K. (2014). Hands on, hands off: Gendered access in crafting and electronics practices. *Mind, Culture, and Activity, 21*(4), 278–297.

Buechley, L. (2006, October). A construction kit for electronic textiles. In *Wearable Computers, 2006 10th IEEE International Symposium* (pp. 83–90). Montreux, Switzerland: IEEE.

Buechley, L. (2013, October). Closing address. *FabLearn Conference,* Stanford University, Palo Alto, CA. Retrieved from http://edstream.stanford.edu/Video/Play/883b61 dd951d4d3f90abeec65eead2911d

de Freitas, E., & Sinclair, N. (2013). New materialist ontologies in mathematics education: The body in/of mathematics. *Educational Studies in Mathematics, 83*(3), 453–470.

Hyde, J. S., Lindberg, S. M., Linn, M. C., Ellis, A. B., & Williams, C. C. (2008). Gender similarities characterize math performance. *Science, 321,* 494–495.

Kafai, Y., Fields, D., & Searle, K. (2014). Electronic textiles as disruptive designs: Supporting and challenging maker activities in schools. *Harvard Educational Review, 84*(4), 532–556.

Landivar, L. C. (2013). Disparities in STEM employment by sex, race, and Hispanic origin. *American Community Survey Reports*, ACS-24, U.S. Census Bureau, Washington, DC.

National Governors Association Center for Best Practices, Council of Chief State School Officers. (2010). *Common Core Mathematics State Standards*. Washington D.C.: National Governors Association Center for Best Practices, Council of Chief State School Officers.

Papert, S. (1980). *Mindstorms: Children, computers, and powerful ideas*. New York, NY: Basic Books.

Peppler, K., Halverson, E., & Kafai, Y. B. (Eds.). (2016). *Makeology: Makerspaces as learning environments* (Vol. 1&2). New York, NY: Routledge.

Plant, S. (1995). The future looms: Weaving women and cybernetics. *Body & Society, 1*(3–4), 45–64.

Sax, L. J., Lehman, K. J., Jacobs, J. A., Kanny, M. A., Lim, G., Monje-Paulson, L., & Zimmerman, H. B. (2017). Anatomy of an enduring gender gap: The evolution of women's participation in computer science. *The Journal of Higher Education, 88*(2), 258–293.

Taimina, D., & Henderson, D. W. (2005). How to use history to clarify common confusions in geometry. *MAA NOTES*, 68, 57.

Turkle, S., & Papert, S. (1992). Epistemological pluralism and the revaluation of the concrete. *Journal of Mathematical Behavior, 11*(1), 3–33.

12 CONSTRUCTIONISM AS A PEDAGOGY OF DISRESPECT

Nathan Holbert

Sociocultural models of learning propose that the body, context, culture, and social environment do more than just influence our thinking. Rather, they are fundamentally components of cognition itself (Greeno & Engeström, 2014). Constructionism is well suited to address the sociocultural complexity of learning. Here, learning isn't an invisible mental act, it's interaction. It isn't represented by a final product or mental state, it's in the process—the conversation between the learner, the tool (Peppler & Glosson, 2013), other learners (Tissenbaum, Berland, & Lyons, 2017), the expectations and culture of the space (Calabrese Barton & Tan, 2018), and the broader history and story of the people and places surrounding the constructionist activity (Searle et al., 2018). These interactions can be messy—full of contradictions and chaos—but capture the complexities of constructionist learning.

Good constructionist design is aware of and open to this messiness and intentionally listens for learning beyond the mental space. However, acknowledging the world beyond the four walls of the classroom also means accepting that the coding assignment, the 3D model, or the e-fashion planned for the constructionist experience may not be the most important thing for the learner. Rather than push back against the encroaching concerns of learner's social, cultural, and political reality, constructionist design is responsive—opening up room to incorporate these concerns in the construction process and supporting learners as they take agency in addressing them.

In constructionist spaces, where learners are invited to take on big challenges and encouraged to make meaningful change in their world, learning takes many forms and can look and sound a variety of ways. A myth of constructionist design is that it "only works in the best schools with the most successful kids." This challenge to constructionism's legitimacy, heard by every constructionist a thousand times, is rooted in a white middle-class expectation of behavior and learning (Vossoughi, Hooper, & Escudé, 2016). Behavior outside of these "norms" are assumed to be without educational value and are labeled unruly and disrespectful.

However, we constructionists love to live in this space of disrespect—to push on the narrow boundaries of insular communities and challenge assumptions about what has value, what's worth learning, and what counts as "correct." As a design paradigm that was originally framed in opposition to "instructionist" pedagogies that privilege hierarchies and hold tight to outdated assumptions about knowledge as a transferable thing, constructionism has always been a bit subversive. We count with our teeth and tongue when the teacher tells us to stop using our fingers (Papert, 1980). Constructionism respects the learner above and beyond any curriculum, institution, or system. And valuing the learner—their experiences, perspectives, and needs—also means valuing their frustration, their anxiety, and their anger. Constructionist design must create space for students to be unhappy, disruptive, and disrespectful.

LISTENING FOR LEARNING

Being open to and supportive of the diverse ways in which learning occurs is the absolute minimum educators can do to respect learners. While the mechanics of learning may not involve a variety of "styles" or personalized cognitive processes, observations of learning suggest that powerful educational experiences come in a variety of activities and forms, and observable markers are likely to vary along a multitude of dimensions. Productive learning may involve high levels of activity, but it also happens in quiet observation occurring in the periphery. Sometimes learning is all smiles and positive feelings, while other times it includes bouts of frustration and anxiety. Learning involves thoughtful attention but may also require reflection and seemingly off-task diversions.

When designing and facilitating constructionist learning environments, one must be aware of and sensitive to modes of meaning making and collaboration that don't fit the "normative" exemplars, honestly reflective about expectations and biases, and creative in how one modifies and adjusts a learning environment to adapt to the dynamic needs of the learner. These goals can cause tensions in contexts structured around a narrow definition of learning (Nasir & Vakil, 2017).

Consider a maker implementation in which my team and I worked with fourth grade students during an afterschool club to make toys for younger kids in their school. Students often came to the club full of energy, ready to chat and talk with their friends. This enthusiasm was reasonable after being expected to sit quietly throughout the day at this traditional school. However, these conversations frequently conflicted with the facilitators' desire to provide instructions or engage the group in discussions, leading to a loud classroom as facilitators tried to out-volume chatty students. During one particularly noisy session when students were being asked to brainstorm project ideas, the school librarian, who had observed throughout the project, took it upon herself to intercede, loudly telling students they were being "disrespectful and rude" and that if they don't "value anything," they shouldn't come to the maker club.

To this librarian, who assumed learning requires quiet listening and still bodies, the students were to blame for the seemingly chaotic space. And though we strongly disagreed with the librarian's overreaction, even the project team initially focused on the students. Maybe they weren't interested in making?

Constructionists' passion for innovative student-centered learning also makes us susceptible to assuming constructionist design is foolproof. The community's close association with the capitalist interests of educational technology, Silicon Valley, and commercial brands such as Make, encourage glossy images of constructionist activity. We *sell* our work by providing positive descriptions of smiling children actively engaged in the production of clean and creative technological marvels. When making doesn't look like a magazine cover, or when learners half-heartedly engage in a construction experience, we may be tempted to look to the students for the problem.

Certainly "disrespectful" behavior can occur in any educational setting, constructionist or otherwise, but disrespect isn't always a bad thing! Educators (constructionist and non-constructionists alike) can be too quick to label behaviors disrespectful, simply because they don't fit norms defined by a narrow and privileged population. Rather than see students' socializing and moving around the learning space as indicative of a need being unfulfilled, constructs such as "grit" are invented and students are blamed for their failure to have self-control. But these are excuses, and when we use "grit" to explain away the tensions between our idea of what a constructionist learning environment can be and what students experience it as, "we forfeit the opportunity to interpret these moments as an indication of what needs pedagogical attention or curricular change" (Vossoughi, Hooper, & Escudé, 2016, p. 217).

As for our maker implementation, rather than assume the constructionist experience had been a failure, or look to the students for the problem, I invited my team to reflect on *our* design and consider what *we* were doing during these moments of conflicting needs? How were we creating space for learners to express and meet their needs? What were we demanding of students and how were those demands supporting, or failing to support, them as they worked toward constructing meaningful artifacts?

In this reflection we realized that our efforts to communicate a design process to students involved too much talking on our part. While we may have provided interesting objects and instruments for learners to explore, the rules of the environment, and the ways in which we distributed power in this setting—away from the students and toward the facilitators—conflicted with students' particular needs and desires in this moment. As we wanted to support collaboratively discussing and sharing ideas, and encourage the socializing that the students felt they needed, we sought to rearrange the activity system (Engeström, 2001) to accommodate both the needs of the learners and the goals of the educational experience.

In response, the project team experimented with ways to replace moments in which only one person talked and the rest remained silent with a set of maker activities that situated the exposure to useful design practices in student-driven and active construction experiences. For example, rather than have students brainstorm project ideas in a discussion format, we invited them to create a brainstorm collage. Rather than require organized turn taking, this revised experience invited students to collaboratively brainstorm in a freeform and casual fashion. Instead of asking ourselves, "Why are the students uninterested?," we reflected on the nature of the constructionist activities and whether they were truly "compelling and meaningful" to students. Instead of, "Why won't they listen?" we asked, "Why are we the ones talking?"

RESPECTING DISRESPECT

Providing learners with consequential choices in constructionist spaces requires allowing for meaningful dialogue between learners, designers, and facilitators—a co-construction that is constantly being negotiated and redefined (DiSalvo & DiSalvo, 2014). This design dialogue exists in a particular context, culture, and history. Constructionist designers must not only create opportunities for students to drive the day-to-day learning and construction process but also configure and reconfigure the context, social arrangements, material choices, and activities to allow for the free flow of the social and cultural experiences of the learners between and across the various spaces in which they move (Bronfenbrenner, 1979; Gutiérrez, Rymes, & Larson, 1995). A constructionist environment that listens must be responsive to the broader sociopolitical environment beyond the walls (virtual or physical) of the learning environment.

Blikstein's work in the Heliópolis shantytown of São Paulo, Brazil, serves as a potent example of how even the most thoughtful constructionist design can fail to consider how the sociopolitical reality is felt by the learner. Blikstein (2008) recounts how the project team initially planned to invite students to design tools to help families monitor their energy consumption to meet the new stringent limits the government had placed on homes because of an energy crisis. However, the students in this workshop informed the team that few households in this poor community could afford to have legal connections to the energy grid. Rather, families often rigged up illegal and dangerous connections to nearby transformers. Blikstein quickly adapted and invited students to create new artifacts—artifacts for which the project team had not planned or prepared—that addressed this community's very real need for creating "safe, yet illegal, energy connections" (Blikstein, 2008, p. 9).

Blikstein's work highlights the need not only to be aware of the local context but also to do so from the particular perspectives and experiences of the learners. Furthermore, constructionist designers must be willing to acknowledge when they've gotten it wrong. Rather than assume the young people don't understand the *real* issues or decide that since the electric connections are illegal, they shouldn't be discussed, Blikstein listened to the learners and empowered them to address the concerns in their lives.

The sociopolitical reality in which our work occurs is tied up in complex histories and power dynamics that constantly modulate the interactions at the heart of the constructionist experience. Empowering students in constructionist activities *requires* that we are also conscious of and sensitive to historical inequities and oppression that may impact relationships between students, the project team, the school, and/or the community, and that we create room for the anger and frustration that comes with that awareness (Gutiérrez & Jurow, 2016). Constructionist experiences that fail to be aware of and responsive to these run the risk of further marginalizing learners and reinforcing problematic power relationships.

In my own work, building toys with kids from a storied Black community during the 2016 US presidential election, this history of racial inequality emerged as central in questions of what, how, and why we make. In this research project, my team and I were interested in studying how learners differently engaged with making when they were invited to create objects for others. In previous implementations, we had found that most participants—and particularly young girls—enjoyed building for the younger children in their school (Holbert, 2016). Consequently, as part of our research design we recruited fourth-grade participants from a racially diverse school in a historically Black community to build toys for younger children in their school. However, whom participants would create for was decided not by the students but by the project team.

Unfortunately, in this implementation, participants were initially uninterested in building toys for the preschool students selected by the project team. After fourth-grade builders interviewed their assigned clients—the younger children—the builders expressed disappointment in the requested toys, suggesting they were "babyish." Although the project team recognized the builders' frustrations, we initially resisted allowing them to decide for whom they would make, instead choosing to preserve the research design. However, when Donald Trump, the candidate whose popularity was based on the explicit vilification of people of color, was elected as the forty-fifth US President, it was clear that our decision to elevate our own needs above those of the students fit a pattern of disempowerment with which these young people were likely too familiar. Although our project had nothing to do with the election, this political event outside of the maker club was part of the context in which students were constructing.

When students arrived to our maker session the day following the election, they were agitated. On entering the library students began talking about the previous night's events, possibly repeating statements they had heard at home from parents or caretakers. One student yelled in disgust, "Donald Trump is our new president!" Another responded, "I'm going to move to Canada for four years." When I asked all the students how they were feeling, a few automatically responded, "Good" before one stopped and yelled, "Wait! No, bad!" Another said he was "mad because Donald Trump sucks!" One student then looked at me and pointedly asked, "Who did you vote for?" Before I could answer, another student, assuming my response said, "Probably Donald Trump."

It would be tempting to assume the students' reactions to the election are completely separate from their experience in the maker project and to label their accusations about my vote as disrespectful. Yet, it was in this moment of being associated with a racist movement that it became clear that my presence, a researcher from a university that had a long history of taking advantage of this community, was a political act. For the fourth-grade builders, the project team's unwillingness to share power in the decision of whom they could build for was not an isolated instance. Rather, it was one of many examples in which their voices were silenced and their power restricted (Vossoughi et al., 2016). For the Black girl and boy asking me, a white man, "Who did you vote for?" this unbalanced power dynamic fit a pattern they may have seen on television, overheard their parents and teachers discussing, and likely experienced too many times already in their young lives. In short, this disrespect was warranted.

As constructionists, the project team and I wanted this maker experience to be an opportunity for these young learners to voice their values and perspectives and to support them as they used their skills and interests to impact their community. And when the world around them tells them their community doesn't matter, constructionist design should invite and amplify voices of disrespect. But it shouldn't stop there. This disrespect should be transformed into action. So, after assuring the students that I had not voted for Trump, I invited the builders to think about our construction work together as a way to respond to our frustration and anxiety about the election. For example, there might be others, besides the preschool children, "People in your life or at school or at home that you really like and want to show your appreciation for?" Builders then began shouting out names of people they cared about, which included family members, friends, their fellow builders, and even "myself"! Builders then took this opportunity to rethink their toy design to be an artifact that expressed empathy.

Students felt anger and anxiety caused by a national election, and those feelings impacted why and how students made. By acknowledging this anxiety, and reflecting on how our identity fit into the racial history that made this moment possible, the project team and I were able to expose and leverage these sociopolitical factors that were implicitly part of the power dynamic of the maker club and create space for students to express frustration and anger. Constructionist design must not be afraid to acknowledge the world beyond the walls of the designed learning environment and to respect the emotions that are part of caring about that world. As the episodes above highlight, concerns, experiences, and events, both immediate and historical, are part of the system in which we do our work. Inviting learners to reflect on the state of their world as part of their construction activity can transform these maker experiences from simply "hands-on" exercises to opportunities to critically evaluate, and potentially change, the educational, social, and political systems in which we live.

CONCLUSION

Our constructionist designs must consider that knowledge construction is deeply tied up in interactions across people, places, objects, cultures, and histories and that this broad ecological system is not just a variable to be managed or a contributing factor in learning, but a building primitive itself. The construction of personally meaningful artifacts includes not just bits and atoms, but also experiences, values, cultures, and histories. The way in which these components come together will take many forms. Constructionist design should not only listen for the diverse ways in which learners make meaning but also be flexible and self-reflective in creating spaces where learners' voices are respected and amplified. And just as constructionist designers must be thoughtful about the generative materials and tools used in construction experiences, so too must we be conscious of, and responsive to, the dynamic sociopolitical climate in which activity occurs. Changing the world isn't always a happy endeavor. Constructionist design that invites learners to critique the social and political systems that make up their world must also be respectful of the anger, sadness, and frustration that comes with recognizing injustice.

REFERENCES

Blikstein, P. (2008). Travels in Troy with Freire: Technology as an agent of emancipation. In *Freire and the possible dream* (pp. 205–244). Rotterdam, The Netherlands: Sense Publishers.

Bronfenbrenner, U. (1979). *The ecology of human development: Experiment by nature and design.* Cambridge, MA: Harvard University Press.

Calabrese Barton, A., & Tan, E. (2018). *STEM-rich maker learning: Designing for equity with youth of color.* New York, NY: Teachers College Press.

DiSalvo, B., & DiSalvo, C. (2014). Designing for democracy in education: Participatory design and the learning sciences. *Proceedings of the Eleventh International Conference of the Learning Sciences (ICLS 2014).* International Society of the Learning Sciences, Boulder, CO.

Engeström, Y. (2001). Expansive Learning at Work: Toward an activity theoretical reconceptualization. *Journal of Education and Work, 14*(1), 133–156. https://doi.org/10.1080/13639080020028747

Greeno, J. G., & Engeström, Y. (2014). Learning in activity. In R. K. Sawyer (Ed.), *The Cambridge handbook of the learning sciences* (pp. 128–147). Cambridge, UK: Cambridge University Press.

Gutiérrez, K., & Jurow, A. S. (2016). Social design experiments: Toward equity by design. *Journal of the Learning Sciences, 25*(4), 565–598. https://doi.org/10.1080/10508406.2016.1204548

Gutiérrez, K., Rymes, B., & Larson, J. (1995). Script, counterscript, and underlife in the classroom: James Brown versus Brown v. Board of Education. *Harvard Educational Review, 65*(3), 445–472. https://doi.org/10.17763/haer.65.3.r16146n25h4mh384

Holbert, N. (2016). Leveraging cultural values and "ways of knowing" to increase diversity in maker activities. *International Journal of Child-Computer Interaction, 9–10*, 33–39. https://doi.org/10.1016/j.ijcci.2016.10.002

Nasir, N. S., & Vakil, S. (2017). STEM-Focused academies in urban schools: Tensions and possibilities. *Journal of the Learning Sciences, 26*(3), 376–406. https://doi.org/10.1080/10508406.2017.1314215

Papert, S. (1980). *Mindstorms: Children, computers and powerful ideas.* New York, NY: Basic Books.

Peppler, K., & Glosson, D. (2013). Stitching circuits: Learning about circuitry through E-textile materials. *Journal of Science Education and Technology, 22*(5), 751–763. https://doi.org/10.1007/s10956-012-9428-2

Searle, K. A., Casort, T., Litts, B. K., Brayboy, B. M. J., Dance, S. L., & Kafai, Y. (2018). Cultural repertoires: Indigenous youth creating with place and story. In J. Kay & R. Luckin (Eds.), *Rethinking learning in the digital age: Making the learning sciences count.* Retrieved from https://repository.isls.org//handle/1/485

Tissenbaum, M., Berland, M., & Lyons, L. (2017). DCLM framework: Understanding collaboration in open-ended tabletop learning environments. *International Journal of Computer-Supported Collaborative Learning*, 1–30. https://doi.org/10.1007/s11412-017-9249-7

Vossoughi, S., Hooper, P. K., & Escudé, M. (2016). Making through the lens of culture and power: Toward transformative visions for educational equity. *Harvard Educational Review, 86*(2), 206–232. https://doi.org/10.17763/0017-8055.86.2.206

13 CULTIVATING COMMUNITY CHANGE WHILE CREATING CONSTRUCTION KITS: LAUNCHING SCRATCH, MODKIT, AND L2TT2L

Amon D. Millner, Edward Baafi, and Susan Klimczak

In 1967 Papert co-invented the Logo programming language that engaged children in creating with construction kits and spawned what came to be known as the constructionist approach to learning. Guided by the constructionist vision, kit developers introduced variants of the Logo language that each took different approaches to supporting children's programming and enabling them to bring ideas in their head into the world via computer screens or robots (or what are now called smart devices). Each of these leaves on the Logo family tree emerged with similar pedagogical underpinnings but enjoyed vastly different technological landscapes that were influenced by the social transformation of the time in education systems, the STEM field, and the experiences of marginalized populations.

In late 1960s Boston, while the first version of Logo ran on computers that took up entire rooms, outside, peaceful protests and riots alike were breaking out in major US cities as the African-American fight for civil rights reached a fever pitch. People from all over the country organized around social injustices using a variety of methods: teens shared strategies for leading desegregation sit-ins at "whites-only" lunch counters in the South, and hundreds of thousands marched in the nation's capital. The dominant media of the time, radio and television, showed the realities of public servants unleashing fire hoses on young African-Americans and also covered coordinated public acts designed to amplify the collective voice of those calling for change.

As Logo turned 50 years old in 2017, the technological landscape looked very different than it did in 1967, but parts of the social climate were uncomfortably similar. At the inaugural Data 4 Black Lives conference (held in 2017 within walking distance of Logo's birthplace), one of this chapter's authors, Amon Millner, joined a panel of speakers to react to the prompt, "Where are the black scientists?" Sitting next to Bob Moses, one of the prominent organizers during the 1960s civil rights movement, Amon paused to think about how the current social climate had played a role in shaping two of the Logo-inspired construction kits that he co-invented: Scratch (with Mitchel Resnick and the MIT Media Lab's Lifelong Kindergarten Group) and Modkit.

Quality public education has been part of what activists have been fighting for since the 1960s; however, barriers still exist for young children of color seeking to shape science, technology, engineering, and math (STEM) fields. In *Radical Equations* (Moses & Cobb, 2002), Bob Moses outlined ways that organizing for civil and voting rights in 1960s Mississippi connected to his work on the Algebra Project into the 2000s. He stressed that economic access and full citizenship in the twenty-first century require STEM literacy. The Young People's Project (an Algebra Project spin-off) emerged to operate in informal settings and incorporate Scratch programming. Influenced by the work of Jean Piaget, Papert was aware that children develop intellectually in and outside of school. The construction kits that followed Logo were built with out-of-school time in mind, where the grounds for invention were fertile even in times of social unrest. Grace Lee Boggs led informal efforts in Detroit, where she championed treating young learners like change makers, capable of infusing experiences (such as persevering through injustices) from their daily lives into their education as they shape new realities for themselves. Boggs argued that this framing of how young people could operate within formal learning system could be the basis of a paradigm shift in all forms of education.

The start of hip-hop culture exemplifies youth shaping new realities amid times of social unrest. A DJ named Grandmaster Flash sourced materials to invent a low-cost cross-fader capable of giving DJs the ability to mix and scratch: seamlessly blending media to keep dance energy flowing smoothly from one song into another. Some emcees used these beat backdrops to develop a voice for rapping stories related to issues that still affect their communities today, such as police brutality. The Scratch Team named the programming language in the spirit of mixing media—except the mixing was controlled by putting together computer code instead of manipulating a cross-fader. Influenced by advances in computing technology and a social climate where imagery of public servants injuring (and killing) young African-Americans was circulating across social and news networks at alarming rates, we sought to create a space of invention for young people to create their own stories, programs, games, and more. Learn 2 Teach, Teach 2 Learn (L2TT2L), a youth empowerment effort, was key to shaping Scratch and Modkit in a way that supported youth who had few outside venues to process injustices around them as they developed their voices. These construction kits and programs dovetail to make learning for all personally meaningful and powerful—changing urban living communities and STEM communities of practice along the way.

LEARN 2 TEACH, TEACH 2 LEARN

Since 2003, L2TT2L has been a multilayered mentoring model for STEM empowerment. L2TT2L's charge is to create a critical mass of Boston youth capable of catalyzing change in their communities using emerging STEM practices. One of the program's goals is to increase the number of underrepresented students who not only pursue STEM studies and careers but also understand how it connects to everyday problem solving.

L2TT2L staff, led by Mel King and another author of this chapter, Susan Klimczak, raised funds to hire thirty-five teenage students, who learn how to program computers, give physical objects behaviors, design digital artifacts, use fabrication machines, and consider alternative energy sources. Participants then incorporate multiple making techniques into projects of their choosing to be displayed at an end-of-summer expo event. Visitors to the expo see L2TT2L participants demonstrating critical making abilities, such as holding conversations about ways that projects they created play a role in their survival (and similar serious topics) and were still created with a playful and fun spirit. Additional critical making skills are on display when L2TT2L participants amplify their voices through technological processes in ways that give them political platforms and an audience when they otherwise would have neither.

While participants build their projects at Boston's South End Technology and/or the MIT Media Lab and/or Olin College's Mobile Maker Trailer, they develop hands-on STEM curricula to teach kids aged six through thirteen in housing developments, community centers, churches, camps, and youth agencies. Teens who return for subsequent years working with L2TT2L become either Returning Youth Teachers or College Mentors—and are enlisted to play a more active role in running L2TT2L. Youth Teachers progress through the upper rungs of Roger Hart's Ladder of Participation, starting with adult-initiated shared decision making, and arriving at teen-initiated. In our work, an ongoing participatory design practice keeps teens in positions to govern much of the program, including shaping decisions related to the design of the construction kits used in L2TT2L.

Near-peer teaching and mentoring has been especially effective; as one participant said, "In L2TT2L, you learn it from someone your age and it's helpful, because they probably experienced the same problems as you.

When you learn in school, the teachers teach you one way and sometimes it doesn't always work."

The adult Program Coordinators are often people who have studied Engineering and/or Education and often mirror the demographic of the participants. A key role that Program Coordinators play is empowering youth participants to (appropriately) share responsibilities of selecting technologies to use, setting up learning workshops, and holding the space for participants to discuss issues affecting their communities. L2TT2L began with early participants learning to program and control electronics using a text-based Logo environment called MicroWorlds. Scratch was in development at L2TT2L's inception as one of the first media-rich environments to offer a graphical-building-blocks way to provide instructions for a computer program to follow. Scratch removed the need to have children remember a catalog of text commands in favor of providing categories of blocks that they could always see, and snap code blocks together with a graphical syntax that prevented errors (e.g., diamond-shaped slots in blocks indicate that diamond-shaped blocks can be dragged and dropped there and most blocks have puzzle-piece notches to show where they connect to other blocks). L2TT2L participants sharing which features worked well for their purposes and which ones didn't led L2TT2L to incorporate Scratch version 1.4, which changed in part due to Youth Teacher feedback, for programming workshops, teaching, and projects.

One of the features of Scratch that L2TT2L made a case for supporting was the sound-recording function. To extend Scratch's built-in media library, users could produce personally meaningful projects that featured their own voices. It was important for L2TT2L participants to feel like they could include their own images and voices into projects because many of them had grown up without seeing a significant amount of people like them (young, female, black or brown-skinned, from less-resourced neighborhoods) represented in STEM contexts. One L2TT2L alumnus of color published an article in an online magazine explaining how she had to overcome barriers to STEM participation. She wrote about her father's response to her asking permission to join L2TT2L, he said, "You can't work in technology; you're not a male, White, or Asian. They're the only people who can get rich off of that." Fortunately, she knew that was false and studied computer science in college while starting her career as a writer, frequently covering race, technology, and gender.

One project, called the Truth Chair, provides an example of how L2TT2L participants used Scratch's capabilities and their own experiences to create artifacts aimed at increasing awareness of societal problems. The Truth

Chair was built from wood and included a custom backrest shaped like a tombstone. The seat included a switch (button) that would trigger a Scratch program that played a voice recording when sat upon. The recordings included details about shootings and victims to make the user aware of how many lives had been lost that summer and to ensure these lives would not be forgotten. The designers finished off the chair by putting a laser-etched "Truth Chair" label on the tombstone made of reflective plastic so that people reading the label would be looking into a mirror as a reminder that they could be affected by gun violence. The experience was designed to change their community, increasing the urgency with which people would address gun violence. The project helped the youth cope during a summer when Boston saw a record number of fatal shootings.

The Truth Chair creators wanted to add LED lights to the chair to make the backrest glow. They used an on/off switch to control the lights, but they wanted to make the lights work with their Scratch program. At the time, Scratch did not support programming LED lights and motors. To bring Scratch-like building-block programming to motors, speakers, and embedded electronics devices, this chapter's authors (led by Ed Baafi) started a project called Modkit. We developed the project at the South End Technology Center, as a way to expose L2TT2L participants to all that was involved with releasing a construction kit. Like Scratch, we offered the Modkit programming environment as a free-to-use tool. We built the tool to work with a variety of devices, especially those common in the L2TT2L context—such as Arduino-compatible microcontrollers. We provided a graphical language for programming such microcontrollers and an ability to represent the code as text as well, to give users a route to understanding multiple ways to modify programs and benefit from examples built in either setting. We built in support for microcontrollers designed to be embedded in clothing, which was a popular backdrop for L2TT2L projects such as the Rainbow Glove.

The Rainbow Glove was a project created by a group of three L2TT2L participants. The glove helped them explore STEM content while also creatively expressing frustration with how others prejudged them before meeting them. They followed their interest in learning how to solder electronics and exploring programming wearable computing devices by buying and building an adafruit kit: the Piano Glove (https://www.adafruit.com). The project came with parts, materials, and a tutorial for making a glove that used a fingertip color sensor to control musical tones it played through a connected speaker. They were able to develop the skills required to complete the Piano Glove but did not feel satisfied until they added their personalities to the project. Each creator wanted to have the project convey a message of acceptance and understanding, because they had grown tired of being treated poorly because of their skin color. One member of the team wanted to show that "it was OK for people to be different" and that "things are better with many colors." Another creator related to the physics of the creation, she explained:

> To see color, you have to have light. When light shines on an object some colors bounce off the object and others are absorbed by it. Our eyes only see the colors that are bounced off or reflected. Racism works that way too. People only see what's reflected back, not what is absorbed. In my own life, I absorb people's criticism of me, I absorb the negative feelings when they don't see who I really am and when they don't believe I'm capable or smart.

The team extended the Piano Glove by covering a multicolor LED attached to the glove's index finger with a 3D-printed plastic light diffuser that they designed. They made different diffusers that could alter the colors that the fingertip light would emit as it played sounds, in a way that suggested that it is unavoidable that color shapes how users experience the world. The trio sewed a rainbow patch onto the glove to represent the colors of everyone.

CONCLUSIONS

We can expect that fifty years from the time of this book's publication, the technological landscape will be vastly different, influenced by unforeseeable social climates, evolved education ecosystems, and experiences affecting marginalized populations. We are encouraged that future Logo descendent construction kits will grow, as Scratch and Modkit have, through youth experimenting with developing their voices around social justice matters that are meaningful to them. It is likely that in the 2060s, it will be important to have spaces and programs set up for artifact-mediated conversations about injustices that affect young creators of all backgrounds. The tools and programs described in this chapter have taken steps toward creating blueprints for young learners and adult facilitators to expand access to platforms for exploring the kind of STEM knowledge that will be required for full participation in tomorrow's communities, while addressing social justice issues that are meaningful to the learners along the way.

ACKNOWLEDGMENTS

We would like to thank the extended MIT Scratch Team and all of the project's supporters; the Modkit team and partners; and the Learn 2 Teach, Teach 2 Learn community and backers.

REFERENCES

Boggs, G. L., & Kurashige, S. (2012). *The next American revolution: Sustainable activism for the twenty-first century.* Berkeley, CA: University of California Press.

Hart, R. A. (2008). Stepping back from "The Ladder": Reflections on a model of participatory work with children. In A. Reid, B. B. Jensen, J. Nikel, & V. Simovska (Eds.), *Participation and learning.* Dordrecht, The Netherlands: Springer.

Moses, R. P., & Cobb, C. E. (2002). *Radical equations: Civil rights from Mississippi to the Algebra Project.* Boston, MA: Beacon Press.

Williams, A., & Tanenbaum, J. (2012). Palettes, punchards and politics. In G. Hertz (Ed.), *Critical Making* (pp. 62–69). Hollywood, CA: Telharmonium Press.

14 JEITISMO CONSTRUCIONISMO IN BRASILIAN LEARNING COMMUNITIES

David Cavallo

Brasilians typically refer to *jeitinho brasileiro* proudly as a defining cultural characteristic, deeply embedded throughout all levels of society and among all Brasilians, that exemplifies a creative spirit to find a way to make things work regardless of the obstacles. The Brasilian historian Sérgio Buarque de Holanda (1936) noted its influence in his landmark work *Raizes do Brasil*.[1] Jeitinho is expressed through the ingenious ways people devise and construct artifacts to overcome a lack of the proper materials. It is expressed through creatively making ways to get through unjust, opaque, or dysfunctional processes.

Some of the most compelling, positive expressions of jeitinho brasileiro occur in creative constructions to accomplish an objective when one may not have the proper devices, materials, or components. It can be considered a kind of bricolage, where people use what is at hand to make what is in one's head (Cavallo, 2000; Lévi-Strauss, 1962; Papert, 1980).

Jeitinho exemplifies some of the fundamental qualities of twenty-first-century skills such as creativity, innovation, and problem solving considered critical for modern learning and development. Being able to make a system function when lacking the proper components requires a depth of understanding and level of creativity that is ripe for being built upon in order to extend the understanding in deeper, more effective, and more complete ways.

What is most germane here is that a constructionist approach, that is, learning through mindful making, potentially facilitates building upon jeitinho in ways that are resonant with the culture and that build upon creativity, problem solving, and technological fluency. Applying computation to the problem solving provides a bridge from ad hoc approaches to more formal, systematic approaches.

We designed and created the project "A Cidade que a Gente Quer," in which students would think about their communities, what they like, what they do not like, what they would like to see improved, and what they dream could become reality (Cavallo et al., 2004). They then design and construct functional computational models expressing their ideas. Through this project, the students had the opportunity to change their agency in regard to society. Rather than feeling powerless, they had the opportunity to think of themselves as actors and not objects.

At the university level we introduced learning by mindful making on projects of local interest as a more effective means for learning. All students, regardless of area of concentration, had to learn to program and learn basic mathematics. Rather than follow the typical path of taking lecture-based courses on the subject areas in isolation, constructionist projects integrated the subject areas to focus on the problems or creative applications. This approach not only better connected the knowledge to the context but also better connected the students and the university to the host communities.

CREATIVITY AND LEARNING IN A CIDADE QUE A GENTE QUER: BUILDING UPON JEITINHO

In one project, students began by investigating the use of water in their school. They creatively designed a gauge that could measure water flow inside pipes so that they could determine which function used what quantity of water. The components of this project in itself led to interesting discoveries, such as optimal geometries for homemade sensors to measure water flow. The students decided they could determine the volume of water used, and understood why it was volume and which unit was most appropriate, by using the diameter of the pipe through which the water flowed and counting the number of rotations of the sensor paddle over time.

As we did not have sufficient resources to provide materials for every student, and because our students from families with very low incomes were somewhat intimidated by working with expensive equipment out of the fear of repercussions if they broke something, one of our graduate students at the time, Paulo Blikstein, asked the students and teachers to bring in any broken or unused devices and materials (Blikstein & Cavallo, 2002). We intended to work with *sucata* (found materials, trash) to help overcome our lack of budget. However, it provided other, much more important benefits. Even though the devices were familiar, the mechanisms that made them function were not. When they wanted to repurpose the mechanisms, they needed to understand them. When they began to take the devices apart, they needed to do so in a way that preserved the mechanisms. Not only did taking them apart lead to understanding the mechanical principles but also repurposing them for the students' creations deepened the scientific and technical understanding.

This activity fit the culture of the students from families with limited resources and fit with the familiar culture of jeitinho, reappropriation, tinkering, and bricolage. Rather than being considered something of low esteem, this talent was highly valued in the ways it contributed to the learning and subsequently the communities. They came to believe in themselves as intelligent agents who could and should be full contributors to creating a more just, equitable society.

Among excluded and disadvantaged populations the development of collective efficacy is often neglected and inhibited, resulting in social damage to their communities (Sampson et al., 1997). Through design critique of colleague's projects, students develop the capacity to assess, think critically, suggest ideas and alternatives, and try to find ways to provide positive feedback. Not only does this practice help develop capacity in critical thinking, problem solving, and creativity but also it helps develop collective efficacy.

One group of male students in a São Paulo public school decided that the biggest problem facing São Paulo was violence. When questioned about what to do to circumvent the violence, the boys came up with a surprising answer. They said that transportation was a major contributor to increased violence. They said that since they live on the periphery of São Paulo, their parents ride several buses to and from work for two to three hours every day. The buses are hot, overcrowded, often in poor condition, and drive over roads in need of repair. The parents, after working many hours and traveling many more in uncomfortable conditions, arrive home tired and agitated, and this leads to violence.

Their idea to diminish violence was to make the ônibus inteligente, an intelligent bus. What would make the bus intelligent? When people arrive at the bus stop, they would tell the system their destination. This would enable optimization of routes to improve efficiency and rider satisfaction and reduce pollution and fuel consumption. The students proposed this project years before the widespread adoption of cell phones and ridesharing applications. The creativity of these students was such that they could have invented these apps if they had the opportunity, access, and resources!

Their intelligent bus would be air conditioned and have music to make the ride more enjoyable. They also decided that the bus would be able to inform potential passengers that the bus was already full and would not stop. When they were asked how the bus would "know" it was full, they replied that someone would occupy every seat. When they were asked

how, they did not have an immediate response. When prompted to consider what other devices functioned that way, one immediately excitedly
responded, "A keyboard!"

They took a keyboard apart. They noticed that when each key was
pressed, the materials conducted electricity and formed a contact that completed a circuit. They observed how a computer could "know" not just that
a key was pressed, but also *which* key was pressed. They noted how the
contacts were arranged on a 2D grid, and thus the exact position of what
was pressed would inform the system exactly which key was pressed. It was
at this point that we introduced the idea of Cartesian coordinates. While
this idea had been previously presented to them in school, it was never
connected to anything that the students wanted to do, and thus they did
not assimilate it.

The organizing principle of the project, chosen by the students, gave
way to intermediate and incrementally more fine-grained problems so that
when personal and in-context issues arose, important ideas like Cartesian
coordinates, a way to represent space so as to exactly define position, were
immediately useful and meaningful.

By creating a learning environment with freedom for students, the behavior of the students changed. The boys of the intelligent bus project were
among the most disruptive students in the school. They did not like school,
and school did not like them. They were seen and treated as problems to
be solved, not as assets for the community. The change in learning environment transformed not only their academic achievement but also their
comportment.

Notable and creative projects in Brasil included systems for water purifi-
cation in an ecologically sensitive region; a variety of projects that improve
environmental conditions in urban areas by automating collection and
recycling, or generating clean energy from street activity, or more equita-
bly and efficiently cooling classrooms. Some projects were more whimsical,
such as a "robô da cidadania" (citizen robot) that, when presented with
questions about problems in the community, would respond with the best
ideas democratically selected from all the students at the school; a varied
series of balances to weigh different types of wasted food at school in order
to extrapolate how many hungry people could be fed with all the food
wasted by all the schools; or a "tele-novela" (soap opera) by young girls
that expresses the difficulties they face in going to the bathrooms in public
schools. This was the first project to actually have impact in the community, as the deputy mayor for the region was sufficiently moved by their

creative work that he committed to improving conditions in the schools of the region.

JEITINHO AT UNIVERSITY: LEARNING, COMPUTATION, AND MEANINGFUL CONSTRUCTION AT UFSB

The Federal University of the South of Bahia (*Universidade Federal do Sul da Bahia*, UFSB) was created as a new public university and opened in 2015 to serve a population and region previously excluded from access to the highest quality tertiary education, the south of the state of Bahia. While there is not space to describe UFSB properly here, UFSB innovated in a variety of ways to achieve its social justice mission.

Perhaps the most important innovations were in the pedagogical approach. Courses were to be project and problem based, focusing on local issues. UFSB set up three campuses in different cities in the region plus a series of *colégio universitarias* (CUNIs, satellite campuses) throughout the region. The goal was to place a CUNI in a public high school of every municipality in the region that had at least 20,000 inhabitants. UFSB did not merely want to transmit lectures; their project-based approach was designed to allow students to remain active in their local projects while receiving support and contextualized teaching.

Each student received a laptop and learned to program, regardless of field of study. Typically, when students are introduced to programming, the approach is to introduce the syntax and constructs of the language first and then to work on exercises. Using the music video of *"Felicidade"* (happiness) by Seu Jorge, which was a simple animation, I took a reverse engineering approach for the introduction. I led them through the process of making the animation, stopping to discuss options. The programming constructs were introduced in the context of a specific project and not in the abstract. The thinking about the choices and their rationales was made explicit. That is, they would see constructs and concepts as they were used in real projects.

After a few small projects, each student made a larger project of their own choosing. Many students took on difficult and socially meaningful projects. One group used App Inventor to make a system for a local public health clinic notorious for making patients wait for hours since there were not enough clinicians to serve the need. Other students made a decision support system to assist ambulance drivers who were undertrained. Another made an app specific for the elderly in the community, to provide them support and comfort.

CONCLUSION

Creativity and innovation are deeply rooted throughout Brasilian culture. Just as *engine culture* in Thailand provided a powerful basis for applying tacit knowledge and mindset in a constructionist way onto new areas when provided with opportunity, resources, and support, so too does *jeitinho culture* provide the same basis in Brasil (Cavallo, 2000). A constructionist approach with a focus on mindful making enables building upon local culture to facilitate learning. Particularly important with more excluded populations, having the experience of making complex projects that serve a social good provides a concrete means not only to help develop a stronger and more positive sense of individual and collective efficacy but also to change how the learner views oneself in relation to society, from one who is marginalized to one who has positive agency.

We only described a few examples but there are many more that exemplified the jeitinho spirit, of creatively addressing a felt necessity by making something to solve the problem. However, when our work in Brasil is combined with our work in the United States, Thailand, Costa Rica, Senegal, Rwanda, Colombia, and others, what is constant is that there are deep, specific, creative cultures in each community that provide a basis for construction for social good and deep learning.

When computational technology and connectivity are available in sufficient mass, Brasilian students and others both appropriate the new materials and continue to innovate and create as well as encounter and engage with important ideas in mathematics, the sciences, engineering, and computation. The availability of flexible computational materials extends the range of areas of investigation, exploration, and creation for students, while also extending the diversity of styles of thinking and expression among students, enabling more students to investigate and explore more areas. These materials used in combination with the computational constructionist approach described here become a way of *mindful making* that is both *hands-on* and *heads-in*.

It is clear that if there is an overall lack of achievement, creativity, and innovation in basic education, particularly among excluded populations, the deficit lies not in the students, teachers, innovators, or culture, but rather in a lack of vision, will, and sustained application that builds upon the strengths of the population. These projects help demonstrate the potential when learning environments attempt to build upon what is strong in the culture as opposed to trying to stifle it in order to conform to the *grammar of school* (Tyack & Cuban, 1995).

ACKNOWLEDGMENTS

The author wishes to gratefully acknowledge the support of the Universidade Federal so Sul da Bahia, the Fab Foundation and its sponsors Chevron and General Electric, Fundação Bradesco, the municipality of São Paulo, and Rodrigo Lara Mesquita for supporting various projects described in this work.

NOTE

1. Raizes do Brasil means Roots of Brasil.

REFERENCES

Blikstein, P. & Cavallo, D. (2002). Technology as a Trojan horse in school environments: The emergence of the learning atmosphere (II). *Proceedings of the Interactive Computer Aided Learning International Workshop*, Carinthia Technology Institute, Villach, Austria.

Buarque de Holanda, S. (1936). *Raizes do Brasil*. Sao Paulo, Brasil: Companhia das Letras.

Cavallo, D. (2000). Emergent design and learning environments: Building upon indigenous knowledge. *IBM Systems Journal, 39*(3–4).

Cavallo, D., Blikstein, P., Sipitakiat, A., Basu, A., Camargo, A., de Deus Lopes, R. & Cavallo, A. (2004). The city that we want: Generative themes, constructionist technologies and school/social change. *Proceedings of the IEEE International Conference on Advanced Learning Technologies*, pp. 1034–1038, Joensuu, Finland.

Lévi-Strauss, C. (1962). *The savage mind*. London, UK: Weidenfeld and Nicolson.

Papert, S. (1980). *Mindstorms: Children, computers, and powerful ideas*. New York, NY: Basic Books.

Sampson, R.J., Raudenbush, S., & Earls, F. (1997). Neighborhoods and violent crime: A multilevel study of collective efficacy. *Science, 277*(5328), 918–924.

Tyack, D. & Cuban, L (1995). *Tinkering towards utopia: A century of public school reform*. Cambridge, MA: Harvard University Press.

15 THE ROLE OF CRITICAL SCIENCE IDENTITY ARTIFACTS IN YOUTH CLAIMING A RIGHTFUL PRESENCE IN STEM

Angela Calabrese Barton and Edna Tan

Consider Maken. He wears his grandfather's sunhat year-round. Peers love his hat, often asking if they can wear it too. The hat holds a repository of stories—of Maken's life with his grandfather in the south, and how his grandfather taught him to use a hammer, a screwdriver, and other tools. When Maken wears his hat, he says he brings a bit of his grandfather with him. At the community center where Maken hangs out, he became involved in the maker club. With friends and mentors, he worked for over six months designing, building and refining a heated, light-up work boot, to help keep feet warm in the winter. When peers left the maker club mid-session to play basketball in the gym, Maken joined their games. When the games ended, he would put his hat back on, and manage to bring a few peers back to the maker club to continue his work. His initial prototyped boot is still proudly exhibited on the display shelf by the room's entrance, two years after completion.

Maken's hat brought his past to his present life, reminding others what he learned from his grandfather. When he put his hat back on after basketball, it symbolically noted it was time to work on the boot. Maken's hat and its enduring, visible presence is a powerful identity artifact. It reflects his funds of knowledge for building, acquired from his original home state where he no longer lives, and represents a connection he has with his peers that allows them to easily transition between basketball and making. His boot, too, symbolically reflects these connections Maken has with his peers, how his funds of knowledge matter in doing powerful things, and it is a visible reminder of what he and his friends were able to accomplish together. Both the hat and the boot act as identity artifacts.

In this chapter we build an argument for the importance of "identity artifacts" in supporting youth in engaging in both equitable and consequential identity work in science, technology, engineering, and math (STEM).

Identity artifacts are powerful material and/or symbolic tools, embodied spaces, texts, or discourses that mediate identity-shaping activity (Leander, 2002). Sometimes these artifacts are created by youth themselves as they engage in social activity, such as the boot that Maken made. Other times, they are artifacts that are granted particular significance through new social meanings accrued through purposeful actions and interactions, such as the hat that Maken wore. Maken did not create the hat his grandfather gave him, but he did use the hat toward positioning himself—his past, present, and future—toward engaging in social activity in particular ways. In this example, we see how the hat, as an identity artifact, helped to mediate his and his friends' collaborative activity to create another identity artifact, this time the boot, which is anchored in both science and community.

From a social practice theory perspective, identities reflect one's ongoing social existence in the world. Identity is a powerful construct for understanding student learning because identities are constructed through practice—practice that requires knowledge, skills, and ways of thinking that characterize the discipline in which one is engaging. However, we find it productive to focus on *identity work* rather than identities themselves because this situates youth with agency toward developing their identities in ways that matter to them (Calabrese Barton, Kang, Tan, O'Neill, & Brecklin, 2012).

By identity work we refer to the actions that individuals take and the relationships they form at any given moment as constrained by the historically, culturally, and socially legitimized norms, rules, and expectations that operate within the spaces in which such work takes place. Such acts of identity work are complex and uncertain, for how one is recognized within new communities is an artifact of the power dynamics that operate there (Nasir, 2011) and which reflect the cultural norms of "local practice" and "historically institutionalized struggles" (Holland, Lachicotte, Skinner, & Cain, 2001).

Identity work within science involves three interrelated dimensions. First, it involves developing knowledge and practice in the discipline but also how such knowledge and practice map onto other forms of knowledge and practice. Second, identity work involves the agency's use of one's knowledge in practice toward doing things that matter to oneself and one's communities. Third, it involves recognition for what one knows and can do.

We are interested in "Critical Science Identity Artifacts" (CSIAs), or identity artifacts that support shifts in youth's science identities trajectories. While identity artifacts can take many forms and play many roles, we are concerned with those that play a critical role in terms of power and positioning. In other words, they helped to open up new forms of identity work that push back against oppressive normative power hierarchies. In addition to desettling power norms, these identity artifacts are also critical in the sense that they are instrumental to youths' subsequent science engagement in empowering ways. Identity artifacts play a role in how identities are stabilized in relation to time scale and to the spatial distribution of resources across these time scales. Identity artifacts can also destabilize how identities are recognized in both positive and negative ways, as artifacts get taken up toward new identity formations.

In the following sections, we present a case of critical science identity artifacts. This case comes from a set of cases in a longitudinal study in which we followed dozens of youths throughout school and community settings, where they engaged in science between four to nine years, in which our foci were on youths' developing identity work across space and time (Tan & Calabrese Barton, 2020).

MAKING SENSE OF IDENTITY WORK: "I WANT TO BE AN ENGINEER"

In what follows we offer Janis' narrative during her four-year participation in an informal science Green Club to flesh out the different forms CSIAs take and how they impact identity work over time and across settings.

Janis is an African-American girl who lives with her mom. While they have little in the way of material resources—"we don't even have Internet"—Janis notes that her mom always pulls enough money together to get Janis the materials that she needs for school. Despite limited and uncertain income, Janis' mother consistently made an effort to supply her with a sketchpad and charcoal pencils.

In fifth grade, science was Janis' least favorite class. She noted, "We do the same routine, every year, over and over, and I can't take that because it's boring." However, she was pleased that her school had an arts focus, "I'll admit, school is a drag … but I am happy to be attending a school that expands my appeal for the arts." A gifted artist, Janis spent hours sketching images from pictures in magazines. As she told us, "I have been drawing since I was one. It's my passion."

During the middle grades, Janis shifted from not being interested in science to wanting to become an engineer who would invent energy-efficient appliances to help families save money while also helping the earth. She points to three key events, with associated CSIAs, which helped her to see that becoming an engineer could be grounded in her love of the arts and the natural world.

STRAWBERRY POSTER

Janis is a quiet girl but always eager to work on projects. When tasked with presenting her work in front of an audience, she would demur, sometimes hiding under her desk. However, when she helped produce an elaborately drawn poster illustrating what happens to a strawberry as it moves from farm to table in a "local" versus a "far away" food system, a different interaction pattern emerged. The poster explored the big ideas of food production, packaging, transportation, and waste in the local farm-to-table system. Janis was grouped with four other youth and, as they discussed, Janis took over creating the actual map (see figure 15.1). Her peers praised and admired her work.

When it was time to share their work, Janis held her poster and her peers explained the six steps in the local system versus the eleven steps in the far away system. Another friend shared a rap she made to explain the poster. While Janis did not speak verbally, her poster became a focal point in the whole group discussion because of its clarity, and many peers complimented Janis for her artistic abilities.

FIGURE 15.1
Strawberry poster.

In an interview, Janis said it was "one of [her] favorite science assignments ever" because "I was happy because people kept complimenting my picture for local strawberries, and [saying] that the pictures were really good. They said that I'm a really good artist. I wrote the steps down, and they said that the steps were nice." She noted her friend wrote a rap that went with her artwork, and this rap helped to show others how important the ideas in her artwork were.

The strawberry poster (figure 15.1), a powerful CSIA, hung on the wall of Janis' after-school Green Club for 2 years. Janis had other drawings hanging at her after-school club at this time too—portraits of family and friends, and abstract drawings. She was awarded Club member of the month for her dedication to her art studies.

THE LIGHTBULB RAP

Leveraging art in science became a theme for Janis. She felt that she could use her expertise in art, as she had with the strawberry poster, to "get the science word out." When studying energy efficiency in the sixth grade at Green Club, Janis made a video documentary explaining energy efficiency. She created some images and wrote a rap. She recruited two peers to sing it with her and to create an original soundtrack using the Apple application GarageBand. Her rap was so well received by her peers they decided to use it as an engaging educative tool in a workshop they conducted at their school. Her teacher at the workshop described the rap as a perfect example of the school's mission—to use the arts to teach and learn school subjects. Janis acknowledged these comments by standing up and taking credit. A local electric company representative, who had been in attendance at the workshop, was so moved by the youths' efforts that she arranged for her company to donate one thousand CFLs for the youth to distribute in their community. This led Janis and her peers to conduct workshops at their churches, where they sent copies of the rap lyrics (figure 15.2) home and required participants to sign pledges to care for their environment before providing them with free bulbs. This is an example of a powerful CSIA moving from one setting (after-school club) into other settings (school and community), shifting how the youth was viewed in these other spaces.

Janis described her work on the rap, and how it was used in the workshop, as an example of her being a "make a difference expert," a term—indeed, a name for her identity work—she coined that year in reference to how she and her peers use science to solve local problems. According to Janis, being a "make a difference expert" involved "doing things that are

The Light Bulb Rap
        by Jayla, Dennis, & Daryl

Verse 1
Just sit down and take a seat
Open your ears and listen to me
I gotta tell something that you won't like
Somethin' you didn't know 'bout your lights
Incandescent light bulbs help global warming
A solution to pollution in this bulb is forming
Fluorescent light bulbs they do last longer
Fluorescent bulbs are brighter and are stronger
So give CFLs a try ....
And wave those ugly bulbs goodbye
Take aim ... at climate change
Cut down your bills, it ain't so strange

Chorus:
Do as I do
Take and unscrew
Throw out the old
And put in the new
One simple thing you all can do
Is change to CFLs, & don't be a fool

Verse 2
Now incandescent bulbs got more watts
Don't last longer, cost more, too hot
Bad bulbs out ... put CFLs in,
If you want lots more change to spend,
Switch your light bulbs, save lots of cash
Go green ... to make energy last
Take aim ... at climate change
Cut down your bills ... it ain't so strange

Chorus

Verse 3
We use lights, computers and gas
We flip on the switch and accelerate to blast
Expending energy is what animals do
They call us humans but we're animals too
Global warmin' comin' down on all of us
Change's what we need for us to discuss
Take aim ... at climate change
Cut down your bills, it ain't so strange

Together:
So if your lights blow out, don't say I didn't warn you
You should've put CFLs in like I told you

FIGURE 15.2
Lightbulb rap.

good for the community because of what we know. We know a lot of science and we also know a lot about our community. Who else can put these ideas together?" The idea of a "make a difference expert" captures a way of being in the world and in science that positions youth with agency to know, do, and be in ways that value who they are and their cultural repertoires of practice. Here, a youth's community knowledge and practice are elemental to accomplishing her science work and transformative to what is recognized as legitimate participation.

GREEN TEEN CENTER

Janis stayed in the Green Club sketching up ideas for new projects her peers could work on, including designing a "green teen center" and "green additions to her club" (e.g., Calabrese Barton & Tan, 2010). In each case, she leveraged her love of art to find a way into science while foregrounding using science to "make a difference." These artifacts played a critical role for her.

Around the time she turned thirteen, she visited a "green resource center" as part of her after-school club. Janis was enamored by the center. In her words, "This is exactly what we need in [our] city." She described the building as "cool and artsy," the layout as "friendly" and "easy." Janis sketched out what a green resource center might look like at her community center. She said the resource center was one way that the youth could really be "make a difference experts." Janis wanted her community to have access to resources that would help them to save "the earth" and "their pocketbook." She also wanted the resource center to be open to her whole community:

> The resource center could be at the Club, but we could bring it over to different schools. It would show people what they can do to make their homes more energy efficient and save money. I could draw pictures of different things people could do so that they could really see how they could do things. It would not just have the information, but real things and pictures, so that people could really see how to do it. We could have energy smart ideas [and] materials that people could come and use.

In the months that followed, Janis shared her pictures with her after-school teachers, who used Janis' sketches to initiate dialogue with the after-school club on steps they could take to make a resource center a reality. During this time, Janis and some friends were all turning thirteen, which meant that they were required to spend their free time in the teen room. This was a challenging transition to make, especially for the quieter youth like Janis, who found the loud and socially vibrant teen space intimidating.

Through dialogue about the resource center, the teens in the group suggested building a "green teen center" instead. Janis sketched ideas for this new center. When younger peers in the club organized a Green Carnival, Janis and her teen peers had a platform for sharing their ideas for the teen center. They spent several months mocking up the sketches into 3D models. (After the Green Carnival, the model sat in the center director's office for 3 years, often spurring reflection by the center leader about "what to do about the teens," "they need more space," and "we could do better." She made it her goal to raise money to build a new teen space for the teens, which was built in winter/spring of 2017.)

CONCLUSIONS

The CSIAs described above were transformative for Janis. Each CSIA carried and transformed meaning over time and space. With the strawberry poster, Janis found an authentic way of leveraging her identity as an "artist" to engage with the science content of local farming. The impact of this CSIA reverberated to the future work she would do at Green Club and, over time, enabled her to re-craft her identity from being an "artist" to a "science artist." This identity shift took place over the course of multiple events and through multiple CSIAs. Janis moved from being an artist outside of science to a "make a difference expert" who can use art to present science to her community so that they can "really see" the importance of making green choices such as selecting low-energy lightbulbs and buying local foods. Her facility for merging art with science through creating different CSIAs became a tool by which Janis not only strengthened her own connections with and understanding of science content but also became a means for teaching others and advocating her stance on particular community science issues. Janis positioned herself with the authority to teach community members "how to make the changes." This transformation in understanding what science is (or can be), her relationship to science, and her growing sense of epistemic authority had significant impact on Janis' science identity trajectory (i.e., initially not identifying with science to "wanting to be an engineer").

Second, within and via the CSIAs, Janis' artwork, as it was recognized by others as a powerful resource in science learning, repositioned her with new forms of epistemic authority that she did not previously have. This authority took the form of wider recognition for her scientific expertise, as well as legitimization of new forms of and reasons for participation among Janis and her peers. Her poster not only became central to the class discussion of the food transportation system but also served as the inspiration for her friend to write and report a rap about strawberry provenance from farm to store. The poster also became a touchstone for others who saw Janis' artwork legitimizing new forms of participation in her science club while also opening up new entry points for Janis' further participation in science. That Janis' sketch-up of a new resource center that then led to a 3D model for a new green teen center served as impetus for dialogue among club leaders for the need for a new teen space shows the expanding boundaries of her authority.

Third, allies play crucial roles in supporting both youths' authoring of CSIAs and the positive impact these CSIAs have on youths' science identity work. Janis needed the collective support of friends and adult mentors/teachers across space and time to engage in productive, CSIA-mediated identity work.

Fourth, CSIAs open up pathways toward establishing a rightful presence in STEM. By rightful presence in STEM education we mean legitimate membership in a science learning community because of who one is (not because of who one should be), where the practices of that community work toward and support restructuring power dynamics toward more just ends, such as by opening up new legitimate ways of being in STEM (Squire & Darling, 2013). Janis articulated a rightful presence in STEM as she talked about herself as being both a "science-artist" and a "make a difference expert," referencing the powerful roles her art played not only in her own identity work in science but also in contributing to her community.

CSIAs serve as useful tools to figure out the unknown worlds youth may be working within and to work toward reconfiguring these worlds toward establishing a rightful presence. CSIAs help to break down marginalizing binaries that define what it means to be a rightful participant or not, such as that of novice/expert, insider/outsider, and successful/unsuccessful. However, the continued support of allies is critical for CSIAs to facilitate youths' continued positive identity work in science, as these nodes of identity work build on one another toward youth establishing a rightful presence.

ACKNOWLEDGMENTS

This work was funded by the National Science Foundation HRD #0936692.

REFERENCES

Calabrese Barton, A., Kang, H., Tan, E., O'Neill, T., & Brecklin, C. (2012). Crafting a future in science: Tracing middle school girls' identity work over time and space. *American Education Research Journal, 50*(1), 37–75.

Calabrese Barton, A., Tan, E., & Rivet, A. (2008). Creating hybrid spaces for engaging school science among urban middle school girls. *American Educational Research Journal, 45*(1), 68–103.

Calabrese Barton, A., & Tan, E. (2010). "It changed our lives": Activism, science, and greening the community. *Canadian Journal of Science, Mathematics and Technology Education. 10*(3), 207–222.

Holland, D., Lachicotte, W., Skinner, D., & Cain, C. (2001). Figured worlds. *Identity and agency in cultural worlds.* Cambridge, MA: Harvard University Press.

Holland, D., & Lave, J. (2009). Social practice theory and the historical production of persons. *Actio: An International Journal of Human Activity Theory, 2,* 1–15.

Leander, K. M. (2002). Locating Latanya: "The situated production of identity artifacts in classroom interaction." *Research in the Teaching of English, 37*(2), 198–250.

Nasir, N. I. (2011). *Racialized identities: Race and achievement among African American youth.* Stanford, CA: Stanford University Press.

Squire, V., & Darling, J. (2013). The "minor" politics of rightful presence: Justice and relationality in City of Sanctuary. *International Political Sociology, 7*(1), 59–74.

Tan, E., & Calabrese Barton, A. (2020, Early View). *Hacking a path in and through STEM: Exploring how youth build connecting pathways between STEM-related landscapes.* Teachers College Record. Retrieved from https://www.tcrecord.org/Content.asp ?ContentId=23204

Wortham, S. (2006). *Learning identity: The joint emergence of social identification and academic learning.* Cambridge, UK: Cambridge University Press.

16 INDIGENOUS YOUTH MAKING COMMUNITY TOURS

Kristin A. Searle, Breanne K. Litts,
Bryan McKinley Jones Brayboy,
Yasmin B. Kafai, Teresa Casort,
Stephanie Benson, and Sequoia L. Dance

It is a hot, sunny day in June in the Sonoran Desert as youth from one of the local Indigenous communities set out in two white school vans to document a series of metal sculptures created by a community artist. The tribe's community relations department asked youth to help them by designing and building digital tours of the sculptures that could be shared to teach visitors about the artist and his sculptures. In particular, each sculpture is accompanied by a story and community relations would like visitors to be aware of these stories. Working in groups of two or three, youth visit seven sculptures throughout the community. Equipped with iPads and paper "investigation checklists," youth document what they see and record the stories the artist, Jerry, shares as he guides them throughout the day (figure 16.1). They take photos and videos and write down important ideas they want to remember to help them accurately (re)tell these stories for a larger audience through their digital tours.

One of the locations the youths visit with Jerry is a place they have been many times before: the tribal government complex. A number of young people notice for the first time that there are large, metal basket sculptures on the wall above their heads. Jerry tells the group:

> When deciding how to make these baskets, I mean the design. I just didn't pick the designs. I went to a group of basket makers here in the community and some of them were from [sister community] but they worked here in the community and they ... I just went to them and told them what I wanted. I wanted four basket designs that they think were important to the people of way back, before all this technology and before life was good. What were the things they think people needed the most? So, a few days later they gave me designs (Audio recording, June 9, 2017).

Jerry goes on to describe why each basket was important and discusses how the basket designs are connected to the community's creation story.

FIGURE 16.1
Youth using an iPad to document Jerry talking about one of his sculptures.

Then, he tells the collected youth, "These baskets, I really wanted you guys to see it because it will mention one of the stories of the people here and I don't think enough of that is told to you guys, you youngsters" (Audio recording, June 9, 2017). In this portion of the tour, Jerry stresses several key aspects of Indigenous Knowledges; they are place based, embodied by people, and often transmitted through story (Basso, 1996; Burkhart, 2003). Further, such knowledge comes with responsibility (Brayboy, 2005). Back in the classroom, youth begin to digitize Jerry's sculpture tour using notes and photos from their field tours. As they constructed their digital tours, they began to ask questions about whether and how their retelling of Jerry's stories were accurate. In this chapter, we focus on how these young people grappled with the digitizing of their cultural narratives through an inter-generational making process with Jerry.

Across groups, young people were concerned with creating representa-tions of community culture that resonated with what they learned on their tours and with the knowledge shared by their larger communities. Here, we examine how group 4, which consisted of two girls and one boy, Veronica, Grace, and Adam, collected stories and (re)presented these stories in their own digital tour in a way that honored Jerry, his making practice, and their larger community.

CAPTURING STORIES ABOUT MAKERS, MATERIALS, AND CULTURAL MEANINGS

As highlighted in the opening vignette, the documentation process (e.g., photographs and note taking) focused youths' attention on things they often passed by without seeing or understanding, reminding us of the ways in which place calls our attention to culturally organized ways of knowing, being, and valuing. As Veronica, a member of group 4, reflected on the cul-tural knowledge she learned from Jerry:

> When he started telling me all the facts about [the sculptures], I kinda thought it was pretty cool … I kind of just figured, that's cool, maybe I should put this into something where it would be useful to other people to learn about our tradition and our tribe and stuff (Interview, June 15, 2017).

In this reflection, Veronica clarified that the cultural knowledge shared by Jerry and embodied by his sculptures played a critical role in her desire to create a vehicle for sharing that knowledge with others. Likewise, dur-ing the sculpture tour, Jerry spoke to youth about how his sculptures rep-resent "the things most important to the people a long time ago" (Audio recording, June 6, 2017) and the stories represented by each of the sculptures they visited. Interestingly, Jerry's process of crafting a representation of community stories mirrored the process young people engaged in to create their digital tours. Jerry shared how intentional he was with each design element of his sculptures, even down to what materials he used and how he sourced them. Group 4 was so enchanted by this piece of the story that they included this element (collecting specific materials) as a mechanic in their game to help show the player how important the materials are in the construction and narrative of the sculpture.

Jerry also spoke at length about his creative processes in representing community stories, including explicit details about the construction and materials for each sculpture. Group 4 documented the information Jerry shared and the sculptures themselves by taking notes on their "investigation checklists," a documentation tool we provided young people, and taking about forty-five photographs with their iPads. Veronica later noted that she committed a lot of the information Jerry shared about the process of making the sculptures and the stories behind them to memory, what she called "the facts" (Interview, June 15, 2017).

(RE)PRESENTING COMMUNITY STORIES THROUGH DIGITAL MAKING

Following the sculpture tour with Jerry, members of group 4 used the Augmented Reality and Interactive Storytelling (ARIS) platform, a narrative-based programming tool for non-programmers, to create digital tours located in these places that could be played on a mobile device (Holden, Gagnon, Litts, & Smith, 2014). The first step was to create a paper and pencil storyboard of key events in the game. As the group created their storyboard, they relied heavily on "the information and notes that [we] took from the tour" to guide their process (Audio recording, June 12, 2017). They took a "treasure hunt" style approach to their digital tour with Jerry serving as the guide. Each time the player visits a new sculpture, "Jerry will already be there" and "he's gonna give them an item … the images of the sculpture" (Audio recording, June 12, 2017). For example, the introductory conversation in ARIS for group 4's game reads, "Hello, we are the creators of this game. You will be going on a scavenger hunt with Jerry. You will be looking for items and collecting them." These game mechanics mirrored their own tour experience, where Jerry served as their guide and told them both how each sculpture was made and the story behind it. As Grace explained, "Our project is a treasure hunt, because we went on a tour with Jerry to look at all the sculptures he made" (Interview, June 15, 2017).

Veronica and Grace both noted that they chose to highlight the "important" sculptures in their tour. Veronica further elaborated that they chose sculptures with more cultural significance that other people might not know about. For instance, in referencing a sculpture of a plant, Veronica noted that most people "just think it hurts you" and don't know that it is used in basket making. She noted, however, that she was aware of how the plant was used because, "My grandma uses it" (Interview, June 15, 2017). In this way, Veronica emphasized the responsibility she and her group members felt at sharing information about community stories and making practices with others in their community, as well as the significance of intergenerational knowledge transmission. Veronica knew about the significance of the plant because it was something her grandmother used.

At group 4's request, Jerry returned on the fifth day of camp to provide feedback, or "check the facts," and address additional questions that arose as the groups worked on constructing their digital tours. Veronica reflected that this meeting was "more helpful" in some ways than the original tour, because "He gave me more facts about it, some stuff I didn't have" (Interview, June 15, 2016). For instance, group members remembered some of the materials used to make one of Jerry's sculptures, but not all of them, and they wanted to know what kind of metal he had used to make one of the sculptures. He provided additional information about the materials used to create the sculpture (Audio recording, June 13, 2017). As Jerry explained to the members of group 4:

> This one's a Corten steel. C-O-R-T-E-N. Corten. And the reason why Corten steel is because … the regular steel rusts a lot faster than Corten steel. Corten steel is harder and it rusts less, and it's kind of between stainless and steel, you know. It still rusts, it still bleeds, but the regular steel will bleed a lot more when it rains and gets wet, and will rust faster and deteriorate faster. So Corten steel is the best—well a lot better for outside.

In this passage, we see Jerry educating the group members more specifically about not just the kind of steel he used for the sculpture but also why that kind of steel was more appropriate. In other words, Jerry educated young people about the affordances and constraints of a particular material used in making. He also answered questions about where the lava rocks and glass pieces used in some of his sculptures could be purchased.

Moreover, the group collectively expressed excitement and pride to have the opportunity to educate others, especially those outside the community, about their culture. They explained that their game would be relevant to those outside their community, because "they can find new facts about the Native American culture, and they can, like, for the sculptures, they can find out who made them and where they're located in case they want to visit them" (Group 4 member, audio recording, June 12, 2017). Furthermore, Veronica reflected, "It's cool to teach people that don't know a lot" and noted, "This stuff," referring to cultural knowledge, "is going dead" (Interview, June 15, 2017). In these comments, we see groups members' awareness of the responsibility that comes with making community tours and the significance of cultural knowledge transmission from Jerry to their groups and from their groups to other community members and visitors.

CONCLUSION

Making is a multilayered process. In Jerry's case, he made sculptures to document community stories. Youth then created digital tours that incorporated the stories and materials behind the sculptures. In both instances, making is an intentional activity directed by a larger community goal. Further, documenting Jerry's making processes through the creation of digital tours provided opportunities for the intergenerational transmission of knowledge. Young people not only relied on Jerry's expertise about his own work but also connected knowledge to their families, such as Veronica's discussion of the plant used in basket making that she learned about from her grandmother.

Within the digital tour activity, expertise was also distributed between young people, who were more expert in the tour design activity, and Jerry, who was an expert in the creation of his sculptures and the stories behind them. Young people took seriously their roles as documenters and sharers of community making practices and the meanings behind them. As Veronica emphasized in her interview, "the facts" were crucial, so Jerry's follow-up visit to camp was particularly helpful for making sure they were sharing correct information through their games. Jerry's sculptures brought community stories and making practices to life for youth. In the process of locating Jerry's sculptures on the map in ARIS, learning about the materials and making processes used, and retelling the stories associated with his sculptures, students also located themselves in community and cultural context. The responsibility they felt to tell the stories further conveys the importance of attending to why making occurs, the affordances and constraints of the tools, what relationships its supports, and the kinds of identities it affords in the learning design.

ACKNOWLEDGMENTS

This work was funded by the National Science Foundation (#1623404 and #1623453).

REFERENCES

Basso, K. H. (1996). *Wisdom sits in places: Landscape and language among the Western Apache*. Albuquerque, NM: University of New Mexico Press.

Brayboy, B. M. (2005). Toward a tribal critical race theory in education. *The Urban Review, 37*(5), 425–446.

Burkhart, B. Y. (2003). What Coyote and Thales can teach us: An outline of American Indian epistemology. In A. Waters (Ed.), *American Indian thought: Philosophical essays* (pp. 15–26). Malden, MA: Blackwell Publishing.

Holden, C. L., Gagnon, D. J., Litts, B. K., & Smith, G. (2014). Reality experimentation. In *Technology platform innovations and forthcoming trends in ubiquitous learning* (pp. 19–34). Hershey, PA: IGI Global.

17 COMPUTATIONAL MAKING WITH CHILDREN IN INTERCULTURAL COMPUTER CLUBS

Anne Weibert, Konstantin Aal, Maximilian Krüger, Michael Ahmadi, Gunnar Stevens, and Volker Wulf

The come_IN computer clubs build upon the US initiative of computer clubhouses. Relying on principles of situated, collaborative learning, and constructionist thinking, the US clubhouses explicitly address inner city youth with educationally and socially deprived backgrounds, aiming to open up chances for disadvantaged local communities in the cities. Their success is well documented (e.g., Kafai, Peppler, & Chapman, 2009; Resnick & Rusk, 1996). Developing this philosophy further, the structure of the intercultural computer clubs in Germany (Stevens, Veith, & Wulf, 2005; Weibert, Randall, & Wulf, 2017) reflects their aim: the fostering of community dynamics and the strengthening of social ties within the family, school, and neighborhood. Also, the collaborative project work in the clubs contribute to the development of individual skills. The computer club at the focus of our study is part of a network of clubs that has developed in socially and culturally diverse neighborhoods in various cities in Germany as well as Palestine over the past 15 years (Aal et al., 2014; Stevens, Veith, & Wulf, 2005; Weibert, Randall, & Wulf, 2017). Contributing to bridging the digital divide—the unequal access of immigrant communities, as compared to mainstream society, to computer infrastructure (e.g., Wagner, Pischner, & Haisken-DeNew, 2002)—the clubs provide open yet guided access to modern information and computer technology for children and adults (Stevens, Veith, & Wulf, 2005; Weibert, Randall, & Wulf, 2017).

They are set up in intercultural neighborhoods as an open space to (1) acquire and deepen computational skills and (2) explore information and communication technology (ICT) as a productive and creative means to support cross-cultural understanding and respect. Collaborative, computer-related project work in the clubs fosters identity building (Stevens, Veith, & Wulf, 2005) and strengthens social ties—within the local family, as well as the school and neighborhood. To achieve this, project work in the computer club relies on three elements. First, the clubhouse is open to individual ideas and questions that youth and adult participants bring with them. Second, links between digital learning and traditional crafts are encouraged (Rode et al., 2015). Finally, the neighborhood itself is a factor in the club work: topical links to local everyday life are fostered, thus supporting identity building in the intercultural setting.

Interlinking the digital and the physical, crafting has been discussed as an act of manipulating materials into physical artifacts in previous research (e.g., Bardzell, Rosner, & Bardzell, 2012). Leisurely constructions of creative, craft-based endeavors rely on craft as a cognitive method for sense making, for example, through play (e.g., Do and Gross, 2007). Learning in this context is closely related to an unlocking of creativity (Tanenbaum, Williams, Desjardins, & Tanenbaum, 2013), a "pleasurable form of interaction, connected in meaningful ways to self-expression, livelihoods and leisure, creativity and innovation, heritage, and sustainability" (Bardzell, Rosner, & Bardzell, 2012, p. 11). In the project works in the come_IN clubs, this speaks to meaningful aspects of identity and everyday life, thus fostering active and creative learning in the intercultural setting.

Primary schools in intercultural neighborhoods in Germany have been chosen as the clubs' locations. In such neighborhoods, the schools are a locus for interaction between people of different backgrounds (e.g., economical, educational, migration). Thus, the school as the clubs' location can be a starting point for regular social interactions that draw on familiar, shared experiences. Nevertheless, the computer clubs aim at being distinct from the school regime. They offer the chance to get acquainted with modern technology and software but do not follow a preset schedule in doing so; they put children and adults in relatively equal positions as learners; they are predicated on tutors and a teacher offering guidance instead of providing directions that are to be followed. Appropriation of computer technology in the club results from constant negotiation among its young and adult participants—tutors and teachers among them.

COMPUTATIONAL MAKING: TWO COLLABORATIVE MAKER PROJECTS WITH CHILDREN

Formal and informal learning and their role in the building of a local community formed a focus for our examination of the constructionist projects. It was our goal to understand how, through the projects, the building of a local community could be fostered. *Identity Building, A Sense of Space and Place,* and *Competitive Collaboration* were key themes emerging.

Identity Building

The geocaching world travels activity developed as a craft-based activity in the club: computer club participants followed the idea to relate the real-world treasure hunt of geocaching (e.g., Neustaedter, Tang, & Judge, 2013) to their own lives by crafting little, individualized objects that would then be sent as so-called trackables on a world tour. The idea was to connect ICT with a topic that reached out in the direction of the neighborhood as well as to the cultural backgrounds present in the computer club. The children decided on building dragonflies as trackables, because the mascot of their school is a dragonfly. They collaborated in teams of two to build their dragonfly; they formed a piece of wire into the shape of a dragonfly and decorated it with beads. For the finalizing of the trackable design, each team would sit down at a computer in the club, writing a text about themselves, the club, their dragonfly, and the destination they had jointly envisioned for it. This text was translated into English and (1) printed on paper with a picture of the computer club and (2) put online on the geocaching website where the club had created an account. With the help of a map and the geocaching website, a nearby cache was spotted and identified by means of GPS devices. Equipped with the devices, the children acted as leaders and directed the adult club members to the place, so all club teams could "set their dragonflies free" for travels (figure 17.1). In the following weeks, children and adults followed the route of their trackables closely.

We saw the geocaching project work speak to the children's identity building (Stevens, Veith, & Wulf, 2005), by allowing what Tanenbaum, Williams, Desjardins, & Tanenbaum have described to be "pleasurable, useful, and expressive engagement with technology" (2013, p. 2611). When they designed their dragonfly trackables and equipped them with a name, character and travel destination, the project made the children think about their own person: Where do I come from? What is special about me and my personal situation? One boy wanted his dragonfly to travel to Albania, his family's country of origin, and found a way to express this by choosing "Albanian" colors for his design. Another wanted his dragonfly to meet "happy people and friends," thus expressing a difficult family situation at home in his digital travel description.

A Sense of Space and Place

A sense for space and place and a close link to the diversity of the neighborhood was apparent when the children chose names or destinations for their trackables that, for example, matched with their own cultural backgrounds or family situations. This awareness for individual characteristics

FIGURE 17.1
Children use a GPS-device to choose a location to set free their crafted dragonflies.

and cultural background unfolded on the informal level of learning, and children were able to explore how these could playfully find an expression, and how they could make use of the IT involved to tell their story. By following their trackables on maps online, awareness of space and place was deepened. Most club participants lived near the school and had already previously spent time showing other club participants their homes via Google Earth; they were now able to take these experiences further and discover new places.

Competitive Collaboration

With an international game box project, the computer club participated in a "day of play" in the neighborhood, where all residents were invited to get together for sport or leisurely activities of play. Reflecting on the diversity of their group, children and adults decided that they would develop and put together an international game box containing the ingredients for their favorite games from the countries of origin present in the club. Children and adults came to think about origin and play as an element of their respective cultures, when working on their games for the game box. All games were of the kind to be played with universally available ingredients: sand, sticks, rocks, or marbles.

Children in the club learned how to use the computer to find information online, and Internet research was conducted to find information about the games, their instructions, ingredients, and backgrounds. Computer club participants teamed up to build these games, and to design the instructions at the computer. All games were assembled in a large box.

At the "day of play," the computer club invited everyone to join them in the club for a round of play of these games. Especially among the women joining the club, there was lively chat and exchange of memories about playing games as children in their countries of origin.

A strong sense of collaboration and community among the participants developed over the course of both projects. This was closely linked to shared acts of making, creating value not of a material kind but "through the act of shared construction, joint conversation, and reflection" (Ratto, 2011, p. 253). During the project work, children would readily offer their specific skills to others in the club, thus helping the overall activity move along. At the same time, they displayed a strong sense of competition, of having their skills and expertise be visible and acknowledged, *"See? I did this,"* and *"I'm done with mine already!"* With this, the projects supported the development of a reputation as a skilled maker among children and adults.

CONCLUSION

Our study of the two projects shows how computational making fosters individual and collaborative development of a sense for space and place and motivates children's active and creative learning within. Prominent among the formal and informal learning stages involved are the support for language acquisition that was promoted through the writing and reading involved in both projects, the use of geocaching data as a spur to math, and the promotion of collaboration among club participants when conducting the projects. We saw the geocaching game motivate traditional school lesson contents and also trigger self-organization among the computer club participants. The international game box project prompted lively participation that reached out into the neighborhood, thus creating personal connections beyond the computer club itself. Overall, the success of both projects showed how the interplay of formal and informal learning in an afterschool setting and the shared acts of making (Ratto, 2011) of culturally relevant, craft-based and IT-relevant projects like these foster both child and adult motivation to engage in them. Computational making with children in come_IN contributes to closing the "gap between the technological 'haves' and 'have-nots'" (Resnick & Rusk, 1996), at the same time supporting the formation of cross-cultural understanding and respect within the children's identity formation.

REFERENCES

Aal, K., Yerousis, G., Schubert, K., Hornung, D., Stickel, O., & Wulf, V. (2014, August). Come_in@ palestine: adapting a German computer club concept to a Palestinian refugee camp. In *Proceedings of the 5th ACM international conference on Collaboration across boundaries: culture, distance & technology* (pp. 111–120). Retrieved from https://doi.org/10.1145/2631488.2631498

Bardzell, S., Rosner, D. K., & Bardzell, J. (2012, June). Crafting quality in design: integrity, creativity, and public sensibility. In *Proceedings of the Designing Interactive Systems Conference,* Newcastle, UK (pp. 11–20).

Do, E. Y. L., & Gross, M. D. (2007, June). Environments for creativity: a lab for making things. In *Proceedings of the 6th ACM SIGCHI Conference on Creativity & Cognition,* Washington, DC (pp. 27–36).

Kafai, Y. B., Peppler, K. A., & Chapman, R. N. (Eds.) (2009). *The computer clubhouse. Constructionism and creativity in youth communities.* New York, NY: Teachers College Press.

Neustaedter, C., Tang, A., & Judge, T. K. (2013). Creating scalable location-based games: Lessons from geocaching. *Personal and Ubiquitous Computing, 17*(2), 335–349.

Ratto, M. (2011). Critical making: Conceptual and material studies in technology and social life. *The Information Society, 27*(4), 252–260.

Resnick, M., & Rusk, N. (1996). The computer clubhouse: Preparing for life in a digital world. *IBM Systems Journal, 35*(3.4), 431–439.

Rode, J. A., Weibert, A., Marshall, A., Aal, K., von Rekowski, T., El Mimouni, H., & Booker, J. (2015, September). From computational thinking to computational making. In *Proceedings of the 2015 ACM International Joint Conference on Pervasive and Ubiquitous Computing*, Osaka, Japan, (pp. 239–250).

Stevens, G., Veith, M., & Wulf, V. (2005). Bridging among ethnic communities by cross-cultural communities of practice. In *Communities and Technologies 2005* (pp. 377–396). Milan, Italy: Springer.

Tanenbaum, J. G., Williams, A. M., Desjardins, A., & Tanenbaum, K. (2013). Democratizing technology: Pleasure, utility and expressiveness in DIY and maker practice. In *Proceedings of the SIGCHI Conference on Human Factors in Computing Systems*, Paris, France (pp. 2603–2612).

Wagner, G., Pischner, R., & Haisken-DeNew, J. (2002). The changing digital divide in Germany. In B. Wellman, C. Haythornthwaite (Eds.), *The Internet in Everyday Life*, pp. 164–185. Oxford, UK: Blackwell.

Weibert, A., Randall, D., & Wulf, V. (2017). Extending value sensitive design to off-the-shelf technology: Lessons learned from a local intercultural computer club. *Interacting with Computers, 29*(5), 715–736.

III EXPANDING THE SOCIAL

This section leans on the notion of the "social" in constructionism: constructionism has been a collaborative framework for learning since its inception, but some models of sociality have tended toward reductive theories of individualist cognition. In this section, the chapters grapple with constructionist praxis from multiple angles: *Who is constructing? For whom are learners constructing? With whom are learners constructing? What is the social language of construction?* and *How do people interpret constructionist product and process?* In the construction of the social, this chapter draws from at least three distinct intellectual traditions: social constructivism in the tradition of Vygotsky, emphasizing the relationship between learners and culture; CSCL/CSCW models of collaboration, which emphasize the action and activities of learners working together; and the multiliteracies model of pedagogy, which emphasizes difference in learners' prior experience and background.

Roque starts the section with an exploration of constructionism with families. From a wide variety of prior work, we know that engagement from parents and other caring adults can help create positive learning experiences. Chapter 18 focuses on families participating in workshops in which families create media together. This chapter contextualizes and expands the vision of the learner as a family member to help us understand how to support engaging families in socially meaningful learning experiences. Berland talks about the value of and impediments to constructionism in social spaces in chapter 19, arguing that, much like family spaces, museums, libraries, and other voluntary community-based spaces are fundamental to the future of constructionism. This chapter argues from existing constructionist projects that we can better address learners' needs by focusing more design on the spaces that young people are already using to learn with their communities.

What we create has as much relationship to the personal and social as with whom we create. Wilkerson and Gravel in chapter 20 present projects

with a participationist perspective that highlights storytelling constructionism in ways that support collective progress. They explore storytelling
as a design framework for bringing together student artifacts in ways that
support collective progress and synthesis in constructionist activities. They
argue that explicitly leveraging a storytelling lens can encourage learners
to construct artifacts that reflect heterogeneous perspectives but are also
understood as contributions to shared activity goals. Toward that end,
Forte highlights the construction of explicitly social artifacts in chapter 21,
such as wikis, blogs, online forums, a range of social media platforms, and
games. She explores how these new environments for constructing public
texts that not only facilitate communication but also have a real impact on
others. Litts, Halverson, and Sheridan then use a multiliteracies perspective
in chapter 22 to understand how, to whom, when, and why those creative
artifacts take their forms. In their chapter, they adopt a multiliteracies analytic and interpretive lens to understand how students learned to make and
share puppets created with sewable circuits, articulating how a multiliteracies framework can help us to understand what good learning looks like.

The relationship to the physical and virtual plays a significant role in
how, when, why, and with whom we create. Danish and Enyedy shift our
view of the social to propose an understanding of one's physical body as a
constructionist process. Chapter 23 builds on theories of embodied cognition and interaction to explore several key dimensions of how the body
can serve as a public artifact, as a resource for learners to explore big ideas,
reflection, and interaction. In contrast, Fields and Grimes explore what it
means to have a social, online constructionist space in chapter 24. They
conducted a multicase study that analyzed several children's DIY media
creation and sharing websites, and their analysis focuses on how these
adult-designed spaces promote, support, and limit children's opportunities
to engage in making, sharing, and understanding their rights and responsibilities in what they publish online.

The section concludes with an analysis of a large deployment of social,
collaborative constructionist curricula. Sipitakiat shows how even thoughtfully created learning interventions often progress through an initial phase
of excitement followed by a decline when real-world expectations and constraints push back. Chapter 25 presents two case studies that highlight the
important factors that influence the progression through the phases resulting in both success and failure.

18 BUILDING RELATIONSHIPS AND BUILDING PROJECTS: DESIGNING FOR FAMILY LEARNING

Ricarose Roque

In 1996 Papert wrote a book called *The Connected Family: Bridging the Digital Generation Gap*. When he was putting the book together, parents shared numerous questions with him that ranged from what kinds of computers to buy for their kids to what they should encourage their kids to do (pp. 6–8). Parents continue to ask similar questions more than 25 years later. What has changed is the proliferation of computing devices in mediating many aspects of family life, including how they connect, how they play, and how they learn. Numerous debates about "screen time" continue to shape parenting practices and anxieties.

While Papert sympathized with parents' concerns, he did not feel that this was the right direction for his book. He then consulted with some young people, who expressed a desire for wanting their parents to learn, to open up, and to try new things. Inspired by their stories, he made an important realization: "What parents most need to know about computers is not really about computers but about learning," (Papert, 1996, p. 8). This realization is not too far from what Papert had been discussing in his other writing and books: that the computer is challenging not only what we can learn but also how we learn.

In this chapter, I describe how to engage kids and their parents in constructionist learning experiences with computing by positioning parents as co-learners with their kids. I discuss how we adapted the different aspects and principles of constructionism to support family learning—especially to support families who have limited social support and resources around computing. I ground this discussion in a family program called Family Creative Learning (Roque, 2016). I reflect on the past eight years of designing and studying this program, which includes qualitative research on the design process and families' learning experiences.

When I started designing this program with community partners, we also started by talking to parents and asking what they wanted to know and do with their children in a family program. They asked questions similar to those asked of Papert in the 1990s and expressed additional anxieties. A dad shared a story of a son that preferred to read with an iPad rather than his dad. A mom wondered if her child would grow up to be a moral person if she were constantly on their phone. In my conversations with parents, I found other desires: to connect, to understand, and to be involved as a meaningful participant. In designing Family Creative Learning, my community partners and I learned that designing constructionist experiences for families was as much about building relationships as it was building projects.

ACCESS AND PARTICIPATION IN COMPUTING FOR FAMILIES

Since Seymour Papert described the image of a child exploring powerful ideas when programming a computer, there have been growing efforts to engage all children as creators with computing. Despite this increased attention, there are troubling gaps in participation, particularly among women and ethnic minorities. To understand how we can support broader participation in creative activities with computing, many argue that we need to move beyond thinking about access to technology and consider the broader ecology of social support and opportunities that surround a young person (Ito et al., 2009).

Parents can play essential roles in children's experiences with computing, taking on roles such as collaborators, resource providers, and co-learners (Barron, Martin, Takeuchi, & Fithian, 2009). However, for parents with limited backgrounds in computing, figuring out the roles they can play to support their kids and negotiating the mixed messages about the benefits or pitfalls of technology can be challenging. In studies of parents navigating new technologies, parents and families need and want access to opportunities that allow them understand the kinds of roles they can play to support one another (Livingstone, Mascheroni, Dreier, Chaudron, & Lagae, 2015; Takeuchi & Stevens, 2011). However, access to quality computing resources and opportunities remains a challenge for children and families, especially from low-income households who remain "under-connected" despite the growing adoption of Internet-enabled devices (Rideout & Katz, 2016). When we look at technology-related opportunities for families, programs are often focused on helping families to use or learn about technology rather than learning with or through technology. In imagining a family program, my community partners wanted to explore ways to engage children and parents as co-creators and co-learners with computing while building on families' existing learning dynamics and cultural backgrounds. We see family engagement as an important strategy to break perpetuating cycles of inequality as the computational landscape continues to change.

FAMILY CREATIVE LEARNING

From 2012 to 2015 I collaboratively worked with staff at community-based organizations such as Boys and Girls Clubs and community centers in housing developments to iteratively design Family Creative Learning (FCL). Over eight iterations, we developed a model that consisted of five workshops, held once a week for two hours and hosted at the community site. Families created projects using the Scratch programming language and the Makey invention kit. The workshops culminated in a community showcase where families invited other friends and family.

Each workshop had a four-part structure called Eat, Meet, Make, and Share. During Eat, families and facilitators ate dinner together from a local restaurant. During Meet, kids and parents met separately and facilitators checked in with family members. During Make, kids and parents worked on projects. During Share, families shared projects with one another. We wrote a detailed description of the model in a facilitator guide that has since been adapted in other community settings around the world (see Roque & Leggett, 2014).

DESIGNING CONSTRUCTIONIST EXPERIENCES FOR FAMILIES

What can constructionist experiences look like for families? Constructionism argues that we learn best when we are building artifacts that are personally and socially meaningful (Papert, 1980). In designing FCL, we had to adapt these ideas to support families. In particular, we needed to expand our visions of the learner as well as what "personally and socially meaningful" looked like in the context of family learning. Our study of families' experiences in these workshops included more than 40 interviews with family members and facilitators, field notes of workshops and design meetings, and photo, video, and project documentation.

EXPANDING THE IMAGE OF THE LEARNER

When we began designing FCL, we had to consider what families looked like, what they needed to participate, and how they could work together with computers. At the start of the project, my community partners and I had extensive experience working with young people, but we were new to engaging parents and whole families. We used focus groups with parents at the community sites and feedback from families participating in workshops to help inform how we may engage families in these learning experiences.

First, we needed to expand what we meant by "family." We learned to use "parents" loosely to capture the variety of adult caretakers in a child's life, which could include grandparents, extended relatives, older siblings, and family friends. Families came in a wide range of ages from two years old to eighty-eight years old. They came in different configurations, ranging from dyads to large groups that spanned multiple generations. Many families were immigrants from all over Latin America, while others had been in the United States for generations. In one FCL program, every participating parent immigrated from a different country. Every family had its own microcosm of individual dynamics and personalities. Some worked so well together, while others needed a little assistance getting started in collaborative work.

To support family participation, we had to address the different needs of families. For example, families needed childcare for younger children. Some families had varying levels of fluency and literacy across family members and needed additional support and resources, such as an interpreter, to participate. Because families had to coordinate multiple schedules and transportation, for most sites, we held the workshops after school and in the evenings. We also provided dinner to alleviate one less task on busy parents. To attract families that typically did not attend technology-related opportunities at the community-based organization, we had to rely on trusted relationships between families, staff, and other community leaders to actively recruit families.

When it came time for families to participate in the workshops, we wanted to position parents and kids alike as creators and learners in the experience. Through our design iterations, we found it was as important to create time and space for parents and children to be apart and to be together. In early iterations of FCL, when families immediately worked on projects together, parents would often step back and either watch their kids or disengage into other activities such as looking at their phones. In order to give everyone time with the tools, we separated kids and parents during Make in Workshop 1 and 2 but brought families back together during Share to describe what they each accomplished. Additionally, we had kids and parents meet separately during Meet sessions to check in with facilitators. These separate Meet sessions were especially valuable to parents who shared experiences, questions, and strategies to support their kids. Parents could see that they were not alone and they could share strategies with each other.

PERSONALLY MEANINGFUL: BUILDING ON FAMILIES' CULTURAL BACKGROUNDS

To design a personally meaningful experience, we wanted to find ways to respect and invite kids and parents to share what was personally meaningful to them as individuals and as part of a family. An important principle in engaging families was inviting them to share their "funds of knowledge," or the skills, knowledge, and stories accumulated across generations and embedded in families' networks, geography, and cultural backgrounds (Moll, Amanti, Nef, & Gonzalez, 1992). Additionally, we wanted to consider what would feel meaningful to the larger collective of families and facilitators brought together by the workshops.

We supported these multiple spheres in the ways we structured activities, giving space for individuals, peers, and families to express themselves. For example, in the very first activity in Workshop 1, we engaged families in an off-computer activity called About Me, About Us. On a small sheet of paper, each family member added his or her name, a drawing of him- or herself, something that he or she was interested in, and something he or she liked about him- or herself. Afterward, families combined their cards into a larger card called About Us, in which they wrote their family name, something they liked to do as a family, and something they liked about their family. Some families created cards for family members who were not present, such as family pets or a parent who had to work during the workshops. Then we asked each family to use their About Me, About Us cards to introduce themselves to the whole group. We concluded by asking families to put their cards up on a shared wall to create a collage of families in the room. Families could see the ways they were similar as well as learn about new interests and stories about other families.

We mimicked this overall structure in the rest of the workshops. During Make in Workshop 1, we asked each family member to create a Scratch project that featured the letters of his or her name in whichever way he or she imagined. Creating individual projects allowed kids and parents to express and connect across their individual and shared interests. For example, one kid embedded his name in a Minecraft background, which impressed his mom because he had just been talking to her about it before the workshop. Another mother created a project in which the letters of her name danced to her daughter's favorite Korean pop song. During Make in

Workshop 2, parents worked with other parents and kids worked with other kids, allowing them to negotiate what "personally meaningful" meant with a peer. For example, two parents both enjoyed music and dancing and created a Scratch and Makey Makey project that featured drums and dancing characters.

When families transitioned to working together during Make sessions in Workshop 3 and 4, we encouraged families to share their interests and "funds of knowledge." To provide a creative constraint, we asked families to agree on a shared theme. For example, one theme families explored was Carnival, an annual festival celebrated in many of the countries participating parents had immigrated from. Families created dance-themed projects, musical instruments, and games using Scratch and Makey Makey. In more recent iterations of the FCL model, we have focused on the shared practice of storytelling. We asked families to share their favorite stories, a recent memory, or a dream vacation they might take together. Finally, in Workshop 5, all families share their projects with visiting friends and family during the showcase.

SOCIALLY MEANINGFUL: LEARNING TOGETHER AND EXPLORING NEW ROLES

To design a socially meaningful experience, we were inspired by sociocultural learning frameworks (Rogoff, 1994) that emphasize the social aspects of learning. As families take up new technologies, traditional roles of who is the expert and who is the novice are continually shifting (Correa, Straubhaar, Chen, & Spence, 2013). As families worked on projects together, different, and sometimes new, dynamics and roles emerged. In designing FCL, we found that it was important to create a space where parents and kids could figure out what roles made sense to them (Roque, Lin, & Liuzzi, 2016).

For some family members, the workshop series was an opportunity to apply existing roles in this context. Some kids and parents had experience working on projects together either for school-related homework or craft projects at home. One mom was used to stepping in and out to help her kids—balancing careful observation and more explicit intervention. Some parents were surprised at how practices they had already developed to support their kids in other contexts were relevant in the workshops. For example, another mom appreciated how her interests in crafts and self-expression were needed to work on a project with her son. She especially connected with Makey Makey because she could connect conductive and craft materials to the project. She could be a collaborator with her son, whom she felt was more tech-savvy than she, rather than a passive observer.

Other families explored new roles and developed new strategies. One mother described how she and her daughter were both used to being "bosses." "Both got to have it our way," she said. As they started working together, both tried to drive the project direction. Eventually, they started to "give and take" by building on each other's ideas rather than trying to advocate for their own. Some parents tried to act as a project managers, while their child took on a creative lead role. As their kids developed ideas, parents helped them break down their ideas into smaller tasks, find material resources, or ask facilitators for help.

For kids, it was an opportunity to take on a role as "teacher" as they supported their parents. One son decided to let his mom have more input in their project because she was new and excited about their project. Other kids took on similar "teacher" roles, helping their parents, siblings, and even other families in the workshops. Some parents welcomed this role from their kids as they got much needed support on something they were unfamiliar with. One dad talked about how much he needed his kids' help because he kept forgetting how to do things. He also secretly enjoyed asking for their help because he could spend time with them.

SUPPORTING COMPUTATIONAL SAMBA SCHOOLS

In the chapter "Images of a Learning Society" in his book *Mindstorms*, Papert shared an image of samba schools as a model of community support for constructionist learning. The range of members included children to grandparents, learning side by side and teaching one another no matter their expertise. The schools inspired an image of a computational samba school that welcomed all ages, backgrounds, and levels of expertise. However, he wondered where computational samba schools might emerge:

> I am sure that a computational samba school will catch on somewhere. But the first one will almost certainly happen in a community of a particular kind, probably one with a high density of middle-income engineers.... But as an educational utopian I want something else. I want to know what kind of computer culture can grow in communities where there is not already a rich technophilic soil. I want to know and I want to help make it happen (p. 182–183).

While some might interpret FCL as a family engagement program, we see it as a *community* engagement program. When families from the same neighborhood come together, there is an opportunity to strengthen relationships, to share stories and strategies, and to build shared understanding in the context of computing. Often, when designing constructionist learning environments, we might focus on the child, but there is a broader ecology of people, places, and activities that support and interact with children across time and space.

By engaging parents in a constructionist environment with their children, parents and children had opportunities to see both themselves and each other take on more empowered roles as learning partners. Parents could see the positive and creative things that their children could do with computers—an object that was often a source of contention between family members. Children could see their parents as creative learners with computers and experience working on projects together as a family—activities that often fell in the domain of games, crafts, and homework. Through a shared experience of designing and creating their own projects, families could apply practices that they used in other activities, such as homework help, and adapt it to the context of computing. Families could build connections to this important context in their lives while building relationships within their families and connecting to other families in their community. By engaging in design-based computing activities at their own community center, parents come to understand the wider learning ecology around their children's developing interests and see the kinds of people, activities, and interactions that can support their children—and develop a variety of ways to participate in these worlds as well.

REFERENCES

Barron, B., Martin, C.K., Takeuchi, L., & Fithian, R. (2009). Parents as learning partners in the development of technological fluency. *The International Journal of Learning and Media, 1*(2), 55–77.

Correa, T., Straubhaar, J. D., Chen, W., & Spence, J. (2013). Brokering new technologies: The role of children in their parents' usage of the internet. *New Media and Society, 17*(4), 483–500. https://doi.org/10.1177/1461444813506975

Ito, M., Baumer, S., Bittanti, M., Boyd, D., Cody, R., Herr-Stephenson, B., Horst, H. A., Lange, P. G., Mahendran, D., Martínez, K. Z., Pascoe, C. J., Perkel, D., Robinson, L., Sims, C., & Tripp, L. (2009). *Hanging out, messing around, and geeking out: Kids living and learning with new media.* Cambridge, MA: MIT Press.

Livingstone, S., Mascheroni, G., Dreier, M., Chaudron, S., & Lagae, K. (2015). *How parents of young children manage digital devices at home: the role of income, education and parental style.* Retrieved from http://www.lse.ac.uk/media@lse/research/EUKidsOnline /EUKidsIV/PDF/Parentalmediation.pdf

Margolis, J., Estrella, R., Goode, J., Holme, J. J., & Nao, K. (2008). *Stuck in the shallow end: Education, race, and computing*. Cambridge, MA: MIT Press.

Moll, L. C., Amanti, C., Neff, D., & Gonzalez, N. (1992). Funds of knowledge for teaching: Using a qualitative approach to connect homes and classrooms. *Theory into Practice, 31*(2), 132–141.

Papert, S. (1980). *Mindstorms: Children, computers, and powerful ideas*. New York, NY: Basic Books.

Papert, S. (1996). *The connected family: Bridging the digital generation gap*. Atlanta, GA: Long Street Press.

Rideout, V., & Katz, V. (2016). *Opportunity for all? Technology and learning in lower-income families* (Tech. Rep.). The Joan Ganz Cooney Center at Sesame Workshop. Retrieved from http:// www.joanganzcooneycenter.org/publication/opportunity-for -all-technology-and-learning-in-lower-income-families/

Rogoff, B. (1994). Developing understanding of the idea of communities of learners. *Mind, culture, and activity, 1*(4), 209–229.

Roque, R. (2016). Family creative learning. In K. Peppler, Y. Kafai, & E. Halverson (Eds.), *Makeology in K-12, Higher, and Informal Education*. New York, NY: Routledge.

Roque, R., & Leggett, S. (2014). *Family creative learning facilitator guide. Family creative learning*. Retrieved from http://familycreativelearning.org

Roque, R., Lin, K., & Liuzzi, R. (2016). "I'm not just a mom": Parents developing multiple roles in creative computing. In C. K. Looi, J. Polman, U. Cress, & P. Reimann (Eds.), *Transforming learning, empowering learners: The International Conference of the Learning Sciences (ICLS) 2016, Volume 1* (pp. 663–670). Singapore: International Society of the Learning Sciences.

Takeuchi, L., & Stevens, R. (2011). *The new coviewing: Designing for learning through joint media engagement*. The Joan Ganz Cooney Center at Sesame Workshop. Retrieved from https://www.joanganzcooneycenter.org/wp-content/uploads/2011/12/jgc_coviewing _desktop.pdf

19 PLAYFUL CONSTRUCTIONISM IN MUSEUMS, LIBRARIES, AND OTHER VOLUNTARY SPACES: CO-CONSTRUCTION, CO-FACILITATION, AND CO-DREAD

Matthew Berland

The most equitable, just future of constructionism requires reaching out to underserved learners in *voluntary spaces*, supporting them as they learn in personally useful and meaningful endeavors. Museums, libraries, and other voluntary community-based spaces are fundamental to the future of constructionism, as these are the spaces that young people are using to connect with their communities around learning. The more we enable kids to create on their terms, the more people we can support, and the more constructionists spend time in communities, the more contextual constructionism will become. The US cultural landscape of education in which Papert was writing *Mindstorms* (1980) looks different than the current landscape. The very existence of personal computers, tablets, and smartphones means that it is now absurd to lock up teaching and learning inside of schools.[1] In 2018 we do not lack access to facts, but we still lack opportunities for connections to others' deeper understandings, communities, and values. The value of voluntary spaces is their baked-in commitment to create physical, non-age-restricted, temporary communities of learning and shared values physically located and situated in communities. That said, what this chapter calls voluntary spaces—places that learners visit as destinations, community spaces, and entertainment spaces, rather than places of consistent or required attendance, like a school or after-school club—can vary radically: Usage patterns in museums and libraries are more or less unrelated. Even so, they are united by their service to, and location in, communities and their mutual commitment to providing educational and enjoyable community experiences.

WHY BRING CONSTRUCTIONISM TO MUSEUMS AND LIBRARIES?

Constructionism is often about making games, playing games, and creative fun. A quick look at the chapters in *Constructionism* (Harel & Papert, 1991),

Constructionism in Practice (Kafai & Resnick, 1996), *Minds in Play* (Kafai, 2012), and this volume, suggests that when people want to help kids create for learning, they often phrase it in terms of games and play. This meshes well with voluntary spaces, in which people often go looking for lightness and fun.

This does not seem, at its core, surprising, but it may have surprising implications, because, while the playfulness and emphasis on games is described as motivating, enjoyable, childlike, light, and engaging, the "making" that is at the core of constructionism is enjoyable at the meta-level but frustrating at the micro-level. Writing this chapter is a creative endeavor, and it is both enjoyable and dreadful. The dread is real, because, like almost any creative act, every step makes plainer all the things that have been left out, all the problems created, and all the knowledge missing. Dread presents a conundrum for voluntary spaces, because people less frequently choose to immerse themselves in dread.

A challenge, then, for these voluntary spaces is how to manage the limited time learners have to get themselves into and then out of that dread. In schools, learners may have hours of dedicated, focused time, repeated over days, weeks, months, or years. Those timespans are necessary for deep, lasting, transformative, situated learning trajectories (Lehrer & Schauble, 2015), and often for negotiating the joy and frustrations of making. However, schooling in the United States is fundamentally, structurally inequitable: Property taxes often fund local schools, so the wealthiest simply get more schooling, more resources, and more teachers per student; content is hyperfocused on what the wealthy are already expected to know, no matter how irrelevant or archaic; and testing is designed for punitive reliability over any sense of measuring transformative understanding despite vociferous opposition to the worst instincts of reactionary policymakers on the part of teachers, parents, and administrators. Thus, we must also find more equitable contexts to do the negotiating between joy and frustration necessary for constructionist learning.

Libraries and museums, in contrast, have transformed into loci of public connections. This decade has seen a resurgence of the public library; despite radically decreased funding, they are used more than ever. Similarly, museums have become exciting, interactive, public, connected experiences that enable a breadth of knowledge and experience in a variety of content. Both are located within communities, have radically gender-, economic-, racially-, linguistically-, and ethnically diverse patrons and staff, and are structured as exploratory spaces in which regular, free learning activities for people of all ages are offered (Horrigan, 2016). This does not solve the problem of time. Even if these voluntary spaces help create contextual, communitarian learning experiences, the problems of dread and time remain: Creativity takes dread, learning takes time, and constructing artifacts takes dread and time.

Thus, the core question of this chapter is: **How can we foster equitable, meaningful, constructionist learning experiences for these voluntary spaces?**

Fostering creative, voluntary, culturally, and community-responsive experiences will never be easy (almost by definition), as it requires situating any design experience in and around each community's needs. A lesson from "Design for America" (Gerber, 2014) is that specific communities have specific needs—design can be general, but good, community-oriented design is not. This suggests the question: Is it possible to design something of meaningful worth at any meaningful scale?

This chapter presents the argument that by providing and supporting means of creating temporary communities around creative work, constructionism can be a means by which voluntary spaces can be communitarian learning spaces.

CONSTRUCTIONISM IN TEMPORARY COMMUNITIES

The most important meta-goal in any temporary community is to include people; people make communities. How do we enable people to engage other people in constructionism? Create learning environments that recognize diversity of goals, that make people's goals and processes visible to each other, that embrace creative dread together, and that engage people immediately.

Though temporary communities can be created in nonvoluntary settings—like groups in a classroom or committees at work—they are less likely in voluntary spaces. People will not be shunted into cooperation and coordination with strangers without acquiescing to the process (Cohen & Bailey, 1997). Most of the people that one will encounter at a library or museum will be strangers. This is a core question that many fields across the social sciences address: How do we get diverse groups of strangers to work together productively? This chapter does not hold the answer to that question. That said, we can sneak around it to another question just to the left: How do we design experiences such that diverse groups of strangers work together in their community on a fun learning project for a short time? This alternate question de-emphasizes goals that require people to work together with strangers to achieve a single goal for which we are explicitly designing and instead emphasizes experiences that enable people to work together across many different goals. Answering this question will, sadly, not solve the world's problems, but it may support more kids and a more diverse group of kids to create stuff that is meaningful to them.

DESIGN FOR ENGAGEMENT

When learners can engage and disengage at will, it can be hard to re-engage people. That has several implications for equity, for participation, for learning, and for any meaningful connection. If a learner does not participate in the first place, it is a failure of the (most likely aesthetic) design—this is in stark contrast to entering a more diverse school or afterschool environment, in which most students will participate and do not need to be convinced to start. If a voluntary activity is unattractive or too frustrating too early, people will stop or leave. When people have left, nobody starts creating in the first place and, as such, nobody will create temporary communities around creating. That is why it is important to design for visibility—a project needs a clear representation to those people it would like to engage (Lyons et al., 2015). This may seem simultaneously obvious and tricky. If potential learners are not attracted to an activity, they will never see it. If potential learners do not connect to some sense of why they would engage, they will not engage. As Lyons suggests, if potential learners want to start creating, they are going to need some "observational time" before they can jump right in. Visibility and clarity also enable the creation of short-term "affinity spaces" (Gee, 2005)—spaces in which learners can think with the material at hand and discuss the ways in which the material is relevant or interesting to them with other people.

DESIGN TIGHT CONSTRAINTS

This requirement of visibility dovetails with the need for a tight set of constraints; potential visitors need to be able to see only a limited number of immediate options at start. There are several reasons for this; the most salient reason is that choice paralysis is demotivating (Schwartz, 2004). However, perhaps the most manifest reason is that constructionism requires constraints and facilitation to help kids engage in creative work. Facilitation is hard to come by in museum contexts, and libraries are diffuse enough environments that facilitation is often not pedagogically matched to the content. Therefore, the design of the constraints becomes more crucial, as it requires constraints that both enable creative work and support learners in bootstrapping that creative work.

DESIGN FOR RAPID FEEDBACK

Time is so limited that strong co-facilitation scaffolds become crucial, and these constraints and scaffolds are often the most iteratively re-designed elements of our work. How do we mechanically reward learners to teach? How can we show people that they work best when they are communicating? Many constructionist projects use models of collaborative game mechanics to address these questions. As we see from Berland and Duncan (2016), once people start communicating ideas through these mechanics, they often persist. Those mechanics leverage common constructionist design practices such as rapid feedback. Though rapid feedback has been a core feature of constructionist design since the 1970s, it bears repeating and re-emphasizing in the context of library and museum spaces. In spaces in which facilitation is relatively harder to come by (Gutwill & Allen, 2012), getting feedback on what you're doing is both useful and motivating. It also supports new learners and entry-level novices in bootstrapping and scaffolding more complex creative experiences quickly, because it is likely that only by progressing to more complex creative experiences will people be able to build meaningfully. Creating environments in which failure and feedback are motivating and required to progress, rather than punitive (e.g., computer programming, games), is immensely important if any process might be learned quickly. Games, as a medium, tend toward rewarding failure rather than punishing it, like school-shaped activities tend to do. Games also suggest clearer or manifest goal structures, rewards structures, and opportunities to progress quickly, than activities that look more like school or more traditional maker activities. Thus, rapid feedback and ludic mechanisms are essential to progression that is fast enough to get learners to think about creating work that is meaningful to them and their community.

DESIGN FOR COMMUNITIES

All of the structuring and designing spaces is frankly irrelevant if this work is not situated with and for real communities, and sometimes the core of the design has to be shaped around the learners' interests, lives, and hobbies. In IPRO (Berland, Martin, Benton, Petrick Smith, & Davis, 2013), we created an iPhone game for South Texas middle- and high-school students that enabled learners to create their own "soccer player automated agent" to play against their friends. Robot soccer is not new, but by framing their work as collaboration and sharing of the customization of the learner's own individual soccer player to play against their friends, learners built their player *not* to make the ultimate soccer player but to *beat their friends at their favorite game*. While soccer may be coded as upper-middle class on TV, south Texas has a large and vibrant Latinx community, where learners are significantly more likely to be soccer fans than the average non-Texan American. That said, the game does not require the players to be soccer fans, but, rather, encourages people who are soccer fans to connect with their friends to play the game. (Therefore, simply being friends with a soccer fan is sufficient to encourage learners to play.)

DESIGN FOR WORK WITH STRANGERS

All of these suggestions notwithstanding, it all comes back to the central question: How do we get strangers to work together? One of our projects, Connected Spaces (CxS), was explicitly designed to enable people in an informal makerspace, such as library makerspaces, to connect with strangers in similar situations who might have similar interests or skills but are physically far. We structured it around the concept of "very low friction interactions"— very little energy, expertise or consideration is required to make a connection to another person in another place. The point is to enable people to feel socially, culturally, and emotionally connected with others in the context of creating something, thus staving off that creative dread. Often the things that students will create (especially in the beginning) will be useless, trivial, or broken, but they will return and improve their skills—whatever those skills may be—if they feel connected to other people.

CONCLUSIONS

It is important that we do not background the important principles of constructionism when we enter voluntary spaces: we need to prioritize liberatory, meaningful, collaborative, creative experiences for more kids by embracing the idea that kids need fun, social, creative experiences on their own terms. Constructionist design has sometimes undervalued voluntary spaces because building anything quickly in transitory spaces is unlikely (at best), but there are many benefits to improving how we approach the design of learning environments in these spaces. Perhaps most important is creating new opportunities to support people who are not in school, are scared of school, or are marginalized by school or whose classes are not particularly creative. Creating new spaces that enable people to come to constructionism (rather than creating constructionist work that comes to students) is a crucial complement to existing work.

ACKNOWLEDGMENTS

Thanks to Leilah Lyons, Taylor Martin, and the Complex Play Lab. This material was based on work funded by the National Science Foundation under Award Numbers 1713439 and 1644401. Any opinions, findings, and conclusions or recommendations expressed in this material are those of the author(s) and do not necessarily reflect the views of the National Science Foundation.

NOTE

1. When the author was young, he regularly walked to an elementary school library nearby to look something up in their encyclopedia. The process seems so arcane, it has become hard for him to remember. This is not a metaphor.

REFERENCES

Berland, M., & Duncan, S. (2016). Computational thinking in the wild: Uncovering complex collaborative thinking through gameplay. *Educational Technology, 56*(3), 29–35.

Berland, M., Martin, T., Benton, T., Petrick Smith, C., & Davis, D. (2013). Using learning analytics to understand the learning pathways of novice programmers. *Journal of the Learning Sciences, 22*(4), 564–599.

Cohen, S. G., & Bailey, D. E. (1997). What makes teams work: Group effectiveness research from the shop floor to the executive suite. *Journal of Management, 23*(3), 239–290.

Gee, J. P. (2005). Semiotic social spaces and affinity spaces: From the age of mythology to today's schools. In *Beyond Communities of Practice: Language, Power and Social Context*. Cambridge, UK: Cambridge University Press.

Gerber, E. (2014). Design for America: Organizing for civic innovation. *Interactions, 21*(2), 42–47.

Gutwill, J. P., & Allen, S. (2012). Deepening students' scientific inquiry skills during a science museum field trip. *Journal of the Learning Sciences, 21*(1), 130–181.

Harel, I., & Papert, S. (Eds.). (1991). *Constructionism*. New York, NY: Ablex Publishing.

Horrigan, J. B. (2016). *Libraries 2016*. Pew Research Center. Retrieved from https://www.pewresearch.org/internet/2016/09/09/libraries-2016/

Kafai, Y. (Ed.). (2012). *Minds in play: Computer game design as a context for children's learning*. New York, NY: Routledge.

Kafai, Y., & Resnick, M. (Eds.). (1996). *Constructionism in practice: Designing, thinking, and learning in a digital world*. New York, NY: Routledge.

Lehrer, R., & Schauble, L. (2015). Learning progressions: The whole world is NOT a stage. *Science Education, 99*(3), 432–437.

Lyons, L., Tissenbaum, M., Berland, M., Eydt, R., Wielgus, L., & Mechtley, A. (2015). Designing visible engineering: supporting tinkering performances in museums. In *Proceedings of the 14th International Conference on Interaction Design and Children*, Boston, Massachusetts (pp. 49–58). Retrieved from https://dl.acm.org/doi/10.1145/2771839.2771845

Papert, S. (1980). *Mindstorms: Children, computers, and powerful ideas*. New York, NY: Basic Books, Inc.

Schwartz, B. (2004). *The paradox of choice: Why more is less*. New York, NY: Ecco.

20 STORYTELLING AS A SUPPORT FOR COLLECTIVE CONSTRUCTIONIST ACTIVITY

Michelle Hoda Wilkerson and Brian Gravel

As new forms of expressive technologies emerge, so too do new ways for learners to build constructionist artifacts and related knowledge (Papert, 1980). But while personal meaning making is important, participationist (Kafai, 2016) and literacy-based (DiSessa, 2001) perspectives highlight that cultural status, expression, and community undergird the power of constructionism. Making and programming are central practices in constructionism in no small part because of the relative shareability and modularity of the artifacts they produce. Digital and physical constructions can be connected together, remixed, and built upon one another to create more complex ones. Thus, an important part of teaching in the constructionist paradigm is to position student-generated artifacts, which often bear different personal meanings and perspectives, as contributions that, in combination, can help accomplish collective goals.

Decades of research in education have explored how teachers can foster communities of learners that build knowledge together (Brown & Campione, 1994), including by specifically encouraging learners to engage in meaning-making by interrogating diverse, even contradictory perspectives (Rosebery, Ogonowski, DiSchino, & Warren, 2010). Within the constructionist community, studies have explored how students' ideas and code, made public through construction and sharing, can become resources for their peers (see the case of Debbie and Sherifa for just one example; Harel & Papert, 1990). More recently, constructionist designs to support sharing such as the Scratch online community or the NetLogo Modeling Commons allow learners' constructions to be accessed globally and "remixed" by others who modify, appropriate, or build upon the computer code that generates a given program.

There are still a number of open questions, however, about how the collaborative nature of constructionism can be best enacted in classroom settings. "Remixing," as it is currently conceptualized and researched, emphasizes collaboration among affinity-based communities in which students often work asynchronously, and in ways primarily driven by individual goals or interests (Hill & Monroy-Hernández, 2013). But in classrooms, students are often expected to collaborate synchronously on tightly focused projects that align with core concepts as determined by the classroom collective, curricula, or state standards. Indeed, we find that classroom teachers are often concerned that constructionist activities may lead to the generation of divergent artifacts and conclusions, rather than to consensus and shared understanding.

In this paper, we explore *storytelling* as a conceptual tool that teachers and facilitators can leverage to bring together learners' artifacts in ways that support collective progress and synthesis in constructionist activity. We argue that explicitly leveraging a storytelling lens (Ochs, Taylor, Rudolph, & Smith, 1992; Bal, 1997) highlights the potentially generative role of (1) *perspective*, (2) *material*, and (3) *problem solving* for organizing student construction and synthesis around a collective conceptual theme. To illustrate, we describe two projects that engage learners in solving locally relevant problems through digital fabrication and making and data analysis and visualization construction, respectively. First, we more deeply explore theories of narrative and storytelling to illustrate what they can add to conceptualizations of collaborative constructionist activity in a classroom context.

WHAT A STORYTELLING FRAMEWORK ADDS TO COLLABORATIVE CONSTRUCTIONIST ACTIVITY

Narrative is often cited as an overarching cognitive and communicative structure that helps humans organize their experiences. By most accounts, narrative temporally organizes the retelling of critical events that happen to some protagonist in order to present a resolution to some problem or inconsistency. While several such theories of narrative have been leveraged in the educational research literature, in this chapter we draw from two in particular that emphasize its more social and collaborative features; these are Bal's (1997) narratology and Ochs' and colleagues' (1992) notion of storytelling as theory-building activity.

Bal (1997) emphasizes that analysts should attend not to what is or is not a narrative, but rather on how storytelling and shared understandings are accomplished through the construction and consumption of artifacts. She proposes that narratives comprise multiple stories and texts written and shared within a given community. Each story is told from a specific perspective and offers an incomplete pathway through the underlying narrative system. Each text is a particular (written, visual, filmic, or other) artifact that communicates and edifies a given story. The stories, as collections, reflect shared cultural constructs that provide insight into the actors and relations that make up the underlying narrative system. A narrative is built through different artifacts that communicate those stories, and the modality/materiality of these artifacts (text, visual, spoken word) can dramatically affect what aspects of the story are emphasized. In this way, the narrative becomes a shared, multiperspectival construction that is preserved in artifacts and reflects the values and customs of the community that produced it.

Like Bal, Ochs' and colleagues' (1992) treatment of narrative focuses on its co-constructed, perspectival, and cultural nature. But whereas Bal focuses on how narratives are edified through a diversity of stories and artifacts, Ochs and colleagues describe how narratives can be co-constructed and revised in the moment verbally, by multiple interlocutors with different perspectives on the same event. Here, as in Bal's account, different perspectives may be presented as stories that together, and in interaction, make up a narrative. With a focus on synchronous co-narration, Ochs and colleagues highlight that narratives can also explain and solve problems in this way. The act of co-narrating provides people with different perspectives to iteratively correct and enrich one another's accounts of often surprising or unexpected events. This, in turn, offers opportunities to engage in complex causal reasoning and problem solving—in which an anomalous event is understood and possibly resolved through multivoiced storytelling and repair.

Drawing from Bal and Ochs' accounts of narrative highlights three major points that are especially important for collaborative work. These are that: (1) narratives are composed of multiple perspectives, (2) the layering of these perspectives allows narratives to offer complex explanations and problem solutions, and (3) that narratives can be preserved and shared through the construction of multimodal artifacts. We see a number of parallels between these features of narrative as a collective enterprise, and commitments underlying constructionist activity:

Perspective. An oft-cited benefit of constructionism is that learners are able to generate and share different solutions, procedures, or perspectives on problems (Abrahamson, Berland, Shapiro, Unterman, & Wilensky, 2006; Harel & Papert, 1990). When put in conversation with one another, these stories highlight invariances in disciplines while also bringing multiple epistemologies into contact with each other. The stories encourage reflection on different ways of thinking, allowing the learner to observe points of connection and difference between aspects of a domain.

Materiality. Constructionism's emphasis on the production of physical and digital artifacts draws attention to material in construction and learning. Indeed, constructionist activities often make use of specialized toolkits (Blikstein, 2015) intended to highlight particular construction principles, practices, or disciplinary concepts. As people imagine, create, and refine objects in the world, they are expected to enter into a reflective conversation with these objects, learning from the ways they interact with and engage them.

Problem Solving and Explanation. Finally, a major focus of constructionist theory is that it allows for explication, connection, and debugging (Papert, 1996) of the building blocks and relationships that underlie complex events, products, or problems. In this way, constructionist environments, through materials and representations, are expected to serve as sources of feedback in themselves—encouraging the learner to identify and repair misunderstandings, solve problems, and develop explanations of complex events.

EXPLORING COLLABORATIVE CONSTRUCTIONIST ACTIVITIES THROUGH A STORYTELLING LENS

Below, we present two examples of activities in which collaborative stories— and their perspectival, material, and problem-solving nature—play a central role. Both focus on investigating core scientific phenomena, energy transfer, and earth systems, respectively. Both also used storytelling as a design support to organize how learners engaged in, and reflected on, collaborative constructionist activity. In the first example, participants were in-service educators enrolled in a summer workshop focused on introducing digital data analysis and visualization to middle-school science classrooms. That case leveraged the structure of collaborative storytelling, with participants each focusing on different parts of an investigation and later assembling their findings to make inferences about the same shared world. In the second, participants were students in a design and engineering class housed in a large makerspace at a public comprehensive high school. In this case, collaborative storytelling served as a tool for two focal students to reflect on their learning after the activity and highlight ways in which their own contributions were positioned relative to, and informed by, the work of the rest of the class.

YELLOWSTONE CASCADES

Our first example is drawn from a professional development workshop for middle-school educators. The workshop focused on the use of storytelling approaches to introduce students to data analysis and visualization, especially student construction of data visualizations, in science instruction. During the second day of the workshop, participants completed an activity that involved analyzing a large, multiparameter dataset to address a driving prompt. The prompt was: "In 1995, grey wolves were reintroduced to Yellowstone National Park after nearly 70 years of absence. In the decades since there have been a number of changes within the park ecosystem, including that the rivers have gradually changed their course to form a more meandering pathway. Can this be explained by the reintroduction of just a single species? If so, how? If not, what happened?"

The story of Yellowstone wolves is well known. Most accounts assert that the paths of rivers changed through a trophic cascade, whereby wolves reduced the elk population, thus increasing the amount and size of vegetation around the river, allowing beavers to build dams in some places and stabilizing the riverbanks in others. About half of the participants in the workshop were aware of this popularized version of events. However, it has been challenged within the scientific community, and factors such as weather and human impact have also been implicated. We provided participants with a large data set about animal populations, vegetation, weather and precipitation, and other key factors. We asked them to use digital analysis tools and any other representational conventions they saw fit (e.g., pictures, graphs, flow charts) to create a visual explanation for the changing rivers and their potential relationship to wolf reintroduction, using the data as evidence.

Below, we share excerpts from one participant group's work and reflections on this project as they created a narrative to explain the potential relationship between wolves and rivers in Yellowstone. We focus on this group because they began by presenting a number of hypotheses for the change in rivers, some related to wolves and others not. These hypotheses, and participants' various areas of expertise, let different subgroups explore different aspects of the data set—coming together at the end of the activity to create a collective story artifact that was then populated by various findings and material representations created by different actors in the group.

"Does anyone think that immediately it's definitely wolves?" At the beginning of the activity, the group began by brainstorming possible explanations for the change in river paths. They were provided with a series of four photographs of the same riverbed taken in 1924, 1949, 1961, and 2003 to ground their discussion. Many participants posited mechanisms for the change to the ecosystem, often drawing from perspectives and experiences outside of the workshop or details others did not notice in shared resources. While these began focused on the impact of wolves, they quickly expanded to include a number of factors.

Daryn: I would only go so far as to say that there's some animal or plant that's prey to a different animal that is now hunted by the wolves.

Anabel: I see in these pictures those rivers changing at several points, so there must be something upstream that maybe humans are doing.

Ted: There was a huge fire in Yellowstone. Like in 94, 95.

Phil: Where there's not wolves, in 1949 and 61, there's less vegetation, so maybe there's erosion factors, or the elk walking across or eating and then in 2003, 1924 where there had been wolves, there's the same vegetation buildup along the riverbank.

Perspective, then, in this case led the group to consider a variety of potential causes very early in the activity. These perspectives then led the group to identify specific areas of expertise or interest for which participants then became responsible. The group broke the problem into smaller sub-areas to be explored (animal population trends, vegetation trends, climate/weather), making it more tractable and allowing for more in-depth exploration.

"You looked at just animals." When coming back together after conducting investigations on various categories, different pairs within the large group reported their findings and revisited whether they supported any of the many theories posited at the beginning of the activity.

Ben: Yea, we were hoping to learn just mammals, not what was happening with the whole thing, we were just hoping to understand which animals where the ones to pay attention to for our part.

Marisa: But it wasn't like, you were, you saying okay, I need to look at conifers and beavers so I can make this connection.

Ben: No.

Marisa: Okay. So we divided it by, we were looking for trends even before we starting to look for, we were looking for trends within categories or groups.

Ben: Yea. But the goal was always to eventually track those back.

Because the pair focused on their own subset of the investigation, they had to work together to develop a skeletal flowchart of causal events (figure 20.1, left). This skeleton then provided an infrastructure to link each group's claims and findings (figure 20.1, bottom and right).

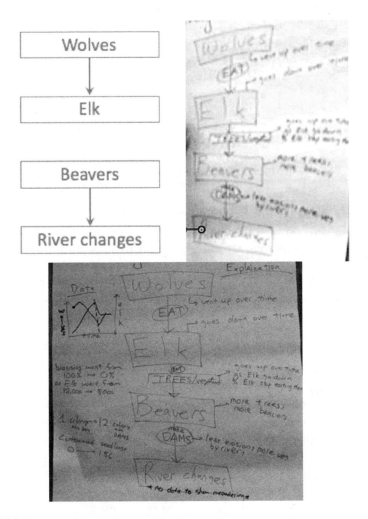

FIGURE 20.1
The group's skeletal theory of causation (left, recreated) was populated
by explanations from different members of the group (right), then linked to
specific findings from data (bottom).

"**Are there any areas that feel really iffy to you?**" Upon inspecting
the flowchart, one member of the group explicitly asked peers if they felt
unsure about any connections articulated within. This led several members
of the group to question the last link, between beavers and the changes to
rivers. One participant proposed groups add specific evidence in the form
of data or relationships for each connection on to the shared poster (see
above).

Yoel: [*gestures to Beavers connection on flowchart*]

Ted: Yea, this feels kind of loose to me.

Marisa: Could it be something, like the elk trampling it [*vegetation near the river*]?

Yoel: I didn't feel like there was a lot of evidence for this.

Marisa: I mean, we saw a reduction in I think they called it browsing.

Yoel: Yea.

Phil: It went from 100% down to 20. So, uh, should we include our empirical data?

Ted's final re-problematization of links in the group's final explanation led subgroups to revisit their data, explain it in more detail to their peers, and in some cases conduct new analyses better suited to the group's overall narrative. In this way, the shared product, as a text of the narrative the group had created, introduced, externalized, and offered infrastructure for the group to solve new problems made evident within aggregated work.

BUS STOP 2.0

Creative Design and Engineering is an experimental course taught in a making space, designed specifically for high-school students from nondominant communities. Together with the teacher, Ms. Freewoman, researchers co-designed the course to introduce students to engineering inquiry, design, and making, through problems they identified in their communities. For the culminating activity after a semester of developing facility with tools and approaches to engineering and design, students were asked about "pressure points" in their lives—places where life could be more equitable or hospitable.

The class converged on the issue of the public bus stop—"*They're cold, there's no place to charge your phone, and they smell like pee.*" Collectively, the class scoped this large problem by identifying specific features of an improved, "fancier" bus stop that they wanted to design and build. This project happened in late winter in New England and Luis and Taddeo, with memories of winter storms and cold temperatures fresh in their minds, chose the problem of heating the bus stop. They searched online for radiant floor heating systems; found them to be complicated, expensive, and described using technical language intended for contractors. Luis and Taddeo were motivated by their idea, but they were stalled in their process.

To provide Luis and Taddeo with footholds into this design problem, the researchers and teacher presented two interventions. The students were encouraged to design a wooden platform using a computer numerical control (CNC) mill, to explore the configuration of underground tubing needed for heating. They were also introduced to low-cost material resources such as "heat tape" that could be used to explore possible heating solutions, and the scientific and engineering principles that underlie them, in the context of the prototype platform. These designed interventions led Taddeo and Luis to begin constructing problem solutions across a variety of material forms. They sketched ideas, borrowed images from Google, manipulated those images to become design files in Easel, and eventually fabricated their prototype using the mill (figure 20.2). At the same time, the story of their design evolved and became interwoven with the materials through the activities they were encouraged to try.

To understand this interplay among perspective, material, and problem solving, we turn to Luis and Taddeo's own recounting of their process of design and construction. On the final day of the class, the students presented their work to an outside audience: teachers, administrators, and community members. Below are excerpts from our focal pair's description of their work, highlighting its development as it related to the work of other peer groups, different material forms, and concrete problems to be solved.

"It's like a map." Luis and Taddeo described the wooden platform they had created as a map that allowed them to try different solutions to the heating problem they had defined as the focus of their work. The platform was based on designs that other groups in the class were developing simultaneously; that would define the constraints by which their own solutions would need to operate in order to be true contributions to the class' shared construction.

Taddeo: At the time, we didn't know how big the bus stop was going to be. Depending on the structure team. We took the floor, and traced it, to start to get an idea.

FIGURE 20.2
Artifacts created by Luis and Taddeo as they prototyped their design.

Luis: We wanted to be more flexible. Our first idea was just to trace something. This gave us more freedom to put like this, or this [*gestures to different configurations of heat tubing*]."

In this way, the wooden platform served not only as a literal platform for Luis and Taddeo's potential engineering solutions, but also an instantiation of their solution that could be situated among the broader community project.

"What's going to heat the water in the tube?" By traversing a number of representations, prototypes, and functional models (Tucker-Raymond & Gravel, 2019), Luis and Taddeo also had opportunities to explore their working understandings of the scientific underpinnings of heat generation. Below, they respond to a guest who asks questions about how the heated tubing is expected to work.

Luis: We used, we used, well, he gave us another idea, which was the heat tape, um, or heat cable. Which we wrapped it around the tubes … The actual idea was the resistor, around the pipes, but we didn't have the resistor or something like that. Because, the bus stop has the electrical system, so the resistor would be collected to the electrical system.

Guest: When you say resistor, what do you, can you explain?

Taddeo: So, it would transform the electrical … oh my god, what's the name? [*Facilitator suggests "Energy?"*] … Energy! Electrical energy to heat … heating energy.

Luis distinguishes between heat tape and the "actual idea" that he and Taddeo considered for the bus stop, which involves the use of resistance to convert the electricity available at the bus station to create heat. In this way, he draws connections between the prototype and what aspects would carry over to the actual final design while maintaining the prototype as only a partial representation of the finalized conceptualization of the bus stop.

"Because you have to make it cool." Finally, the pair shared specific episodes of applied problem solving as they worked on their prototype. Below, they describe how they initially feared that the thermostat and heating mechanism in the prototype platform was not working. They realized that they had not completely explored how to control the heating element, requiring them to examine its thermostat at very low temperatures. These problem-solving challenges, interwoven with material considerations, helped the pair maintain strong connections between their prototype and the engineering task at hand, maintaining their construction's relevance to the initial problem of practice.

Taddeo: First we thought that it [*the heating element*] wasn't working, and then three days later.

Luis: We found out.

Taddeo: I don't know, a week later …

Guest: It was working?

Taddeo: Yeah, because we tried it again. And we leave it [*the thermostat*] on a long block. We leave it, like, a very long time. And we put ice.

Luis: In the ice, in the ice cup.

Examining the story these students told of their work reveals how the interweaving of perspective, material, and problem solving moved them not only toward engineering solutions but also toward making sense of the scientific principles that explain why those solutions work. The team's challenges, manifested through their need to communicate with others in order to define a problem space and solve practical problems, were immediate and acute. However, in reflecting back on the trajectory of their work, the story Taddeo and Luis told illuminated the underlying narrative relations. For example, the prototype became a template for thinking about the problem. This "map" was a structure they populated with new ideas, materials, and problems (e.g., the heat tape failing to turn on), that made more visible the actual potential problems of building a bus stop.

STORYTELLING AS A DESIGN TOOL

Engaging learners in collective constructionist activities in classroom settings can be difficult. The variety of directions that projects can take, and the different problems and material needs that arise along the way, can be intimidating for even seasoned educators. In this chapter, we introduce *storytelling* as a design framework for managing these challenges. Drawing from conceptualizations of storytelling that emphasize its collective, material, and problem-solving nature, we conceptualize constructionist activities as the production of material artifacts or *texts* that, when brought together, tell a story from multiple perspectives in ways that contribute explanations or solutions for shared problems.

This narrative approach to collective classroom constructionism can help guide the design and organization of classroom activities in a number of ways. First, it highlights the organizational and infrastructural benefits of having an explicit shared goal or common problem. In both of the cases presented above, learners were addressing very specific problems—the redesign of public bus stops, and an unknown ecosystem relationship. The specificity of these problems made it such that the learners had to not only understand but also *rely* on one another's progress on the problem. Luis and Taddeo, for example, needed the constraints and material representation of the bus stop platform provided by their peers to gain traction on their own project.

Second, it highlights the critical role of materiality—both diverse, but also shared materials to express different perspectives or solutions—in supporting collective progress. In our own work, we have found that providing learners with particular material or representational forms can encourage them to focus on desired aspects of scientific systems (Wilkerson-Jerde, Gravel, & Macrander, 2015), and can facilitate the direct comparison or synthesis of explanations or solutions across groups (Wilkerson, Shareff, Gravel, Shaban, & Laina, 2017).

Finally, and most importantly for classroom instruction, a narrative approach highlights the importance of perspective taking in constructionist activity. While the philosophical and ethical components of perspective taking are often emphasized in the constructionist literature, the examples we present here highlight the pragmatic benefits of perspective taking—for helping learners to organize and distribute joint work, deepen student inquiry, and construct more robust explanations and solutions.

ACKNOWLEDGMENTS

This work would not have been possible without our partner schools, educators, and students. Thanks to Eli Tucker-Raymond, Aditi Wagh, Ada Ren, and Vasiliki Laina for their involvement in the projects that yielded data for this chapter. This research was supported by National Science Foundation grants DRL-1422532 and IIS-1350282; any conclusions or recommendations are the authors' and do not reflect the views of UC-Berkeley, Tufts University, or the National Science Foundation. Mariana Levin introduced us to Bal's work on narratology years ago.

REFERENCES

Abrahamson, D., Berland, M., Shapiro, B., Unterman, J., & Wilensky, U. (2006). Leveraging epistemological diversity through computer-based argumentation in the domain of probability. *For the Learning of Mathematics, 26*(3), 28–35.

Bal, M. (1997). *Narratology: Introduction to the theory of narrative* (2nd ed.). Toronto, ON, Canada: University of Toronto Press.

Blikstein, P. (2015). Computationally enhanced toolkits for children: Historical review and a framework for future design. *Foundations and Trends® in Human–Computer Interaction, 9*(1), 1–68.

Brown, A. L., & Campione, J. (1994). Guided discovery in a community of learners. In *Classroom lessons: integrating cognitive theory and classroom practice* (pp. 229–270). Cambridge, MA: MIT Press.

DiSessa, A. (2001). *Changing minds: Computers, learning, and literacy*. Cambridge, MA: MIT Press.

Harel, I., & Papert, S. (1990). Software design as a learning environment. *Interactive Learning Environments, 1*(1).

Hill, B. M., & Monroy-Hernández, A. (2013). The remixing dilemma: The trade-off between generativity and originality. *American Behavioral Scientist, 57*(5), 643–663.

Kafai, Y. B. (2016). From computational thinking to computational participation in K-12 education. *Communications of the ACM, 59*(8), 26–27.

Ochs, E., Taylor, C., Rudolph, D., & Smith, R. (1992). Storytelling as a theory-building activity. *Discourse Processes, 15*(1), 37–72.

Papert, S. (1980). *Mindstorms: Computers, children, and powerful ideas*. New York, NY: Basic Books, Inc.

Papert, S. (1996). An exploration in the space of mathematics educations. *International Journal of Computers for Mathematical Learning, 1*(1):95–123.

Rosebery, A. S., Ogonowski, M., DiSchino, M., & Warren, B. (2010). "The coat traps all your body heat": Heterogeneity as fundamental to learning. *Journal of the Learning Sciences, 19*(3), 322–357.

Tucker-Raymond, E., Gravel, B.E. (2019). *STEM literacies in makerspaces: Implications for learning, teaching, and research*. New York: Routledge.

Wilkerson, M. H., Shareff, R. L., Gravel, B. E., Shaban, Y., & Laina, V. (2017). Exploring computational modeling environments as tools to structure classroom-level knowledge building. In *Proceedings of the 12th International Conference for Computer Supported Collaborative Learning (CSCL 2017)* (Vol. 1, pp. 447–454). *ISLS:* Philadelphia, Pennsylvania.

Wilkerson-Jerde, M. H., Gravel, B. E., & Macrander, C. A. (2015). Exploring shifts in middle school learners' modeling activity while generating drawings, animations, and computational simulations of molecular diffusion. *Journal of Science Education and Technology, 24*(2–3), 396–415.

21 CONSTRUCTING SHARABLE TEXT: CONSTRUCTIONIST EXPERIENCES OF ONLINE WRITING

Andrea Forte

The experience of writing has changed dramatically in the past 20 years: people are using text in new ways, they are writing collaboratively, and they are more often writing publicly for large audiences. Young people in particular are writing more and writing differently with new forms of media (Lenhart, Arafeh, & Smith, 2008). Beyond the move to text-based social interaction, toolkits such as wikis, blogs, online forums, a range of social media platforms, and even games have created new environments for constructing public texts that can facilitate communication and have a real impact on others. Writing as a learning experience has never been a more powerful proposition both in formal and informal learning contexts.

This chapter emphasizes research with construction kits that support the production of online texts as persistent, public artifacts. Text-based games, blogs and journals, discussion forums, wikis, and bespoke versions of these platforms that support collaborative practices around genres like fanfiction, encyclopedia writing, and citizen journalism stand out as online toolkits that introduced new possibilities for informal, collaborative learning through text production. These environments can be distinguished from platforms that mainly support ephemeral message passing such as texting and messaging, although these too have contributed to the transformation of text in recent decades.

WRITING AS A CONSTRUCTIONIST EXPERIENCE

Writing-to-learn has long been a feature of formal education and is associated with a rich research literature but is not often associated with constructionist learning. To understand why, one need only consider the affordances of traditional writing tools and constraints of traditional educational writing activities.

The defining feature of a constructionist learning environment is the *construction kit*, or the materials that learners use to construct public artifacts (Resnick, Bruckman, Martin, & Druin, 1998). Everyday toolkits for writing remained relatively unchanged for millennia; in the absence of a coordinated publishing system, the affordances of using paper in the classroom limited the creation of "public" written artifacts for educational purposes. Moreover, writing assignments are often designed for the teacher's eyes only and rarely for the consumption of peers or other audiences. Once graded, it may spend a proud week on a refrigerator door or resurface years later for a nostalgic perusal by the author, but often the life of a traditional school paper or essay ends with a single reader. Although such writing assignments can be powerful learning opportunities, they hardly align with constructionist goals and ideals.

In the second half of the twentieth century, word processing and networked technologies began to disrupt publishing, and it became easier to imagine learners engaging real audiences with their texts, but a few more developments were necessary to set the conditions for a radical democratization of text production. First, in many economically advantaged countries, Internet access became the norm in the late 1990s (although it wasn't until 2017 that 50% of the global population was estimated to be online[1]). Second, participatory sites began providing discussion and writing tools that made it easy for amateur writers to command broad audiences. For many, the public sphere shifted and began to occupy largely text-based online spaces. Online texts began to supplant physical books and periodicals. Suddenly, constructing essays, arguments, and explanations became an authentic opportunity for reflective and reflexive exploration and learning with a real audience. The stage was set and the barriers were low for millions of would-be authors, including children in schools, to publish written works.

The question remains, what kinds of online writing can be expected to lead to learning? Research on writing-to-learn has identified cognitive aspects of writing that result in students learning about the topic at hand as they become better authors. In her foundational work, "Writing as a Mode of Learning," Emig (1977) observed that writing "requires the establishment of systematic connections and relationships. Clear writing by definition is that writing which signals without ambiguity the nature of conceptual relationships, whether they be coordinate, subordinate, superordinate, causal, or something other," (p. 126). In other words, through writing one understands. Bereiter and Scardamalia (1987) explored that process in their *Psychology of Written Composition*, in which they described the progression from novice writing strategies that simply recount information to more sophisticated, expert strategies that result in a transformation of knowledge. Of course, the term "writing" refers to an extensive array of online activities: taking notes in a shared document during a lecture, posting on Tumblr, writing a product review, tweeting a poem, or instant messaging a friend about dinner plans. These experiences are not equivalent in terms of learning. What kinds of writing do different online environment support well? Are they aligned with the kinds of text construction that we expect to lead to learning? The following sections examine several prominent types of textual construction kits.

MUDS AND TEXT-BASED WORLDS

Some of the earliest work on text-based construction kits revolved around virtual worlds. Text-based games variously referred to as multi-user dungeons (MUDs), MUD object oriented (MOOs), or multi-user simulation environments (MUSEs), became popular in the 1980s and 1990s. These multiplayer text-based fantasy worlds offered a blended environment in which creative writing could be coupled with basic programming to craft shared interactive experiences. Bruckman (1998) pioneered constructionist research on learning in MUDs through design and deployment of virtual worlds: one for media researchers called *MedioMOO* and another for children called *MOOSE Crossing,* which included a bespoke scripting language called *Moose.* In *MOOSE Crossing,* young people wrote texts that described fanciful identities, spaces, and objects as well as scripts that imbued these objects with behaviors. Research examined creative experiences that led to learning and the supportive communities that developed within these virtual worlds as young people built text-based places and objects, interacted, and learned together. Although such online worlds still exist today, the popularity of MUDs waned in the late 1990s, while other types of text-based online environments became increasingly commonplace features of online life.

ONLINE FORUMS

Another early form of shared online texts was forums and bulletin board systems. Online forums have played an important role in transforming people's use of text, offering opportunities to exchange long-form messages with a group and create discussion spaces where people forge community norms, play, argue, and construct shared understandings. In early writings about online forums, a microcosm of the contemporary Internet can be seen: forums have been used for all manner of creative writing and playful encounters with text (Rafaeli, 1984). However, most research that situates discussion forums as learning environments has viewed them through a narrower lens. In education literature they are generally cast much like the shorter-form Internet relay chat (IRC) and later social media, as places where learners could exchange messages and engage in discussion to advance their own knowledge and that of a group (Scardamalia, 2002), rather than as sites of constructionist learning where text-based artifacts themselves are constructed as public works to share, use, reuse, admire, and critique.

BLOGS AND ONLINE JOURNALS

Blogs and online journaling tools became increasingly popular throughout the 1990s and 2000s. As a construction kit, they support (usually) single-authored, long-form public posts that are typically expressive and reflective and are used for diverse purposes that can contribute to learning, particularly when authors begin to interact with their readership and borrow from one another. Jenkins (1992) identified such opportunities for interaction as examples of de Certeau's "textual poaching," in which consumers not only actively interpret and reinterpret a cultural canon but also, importantly, reproduce and reform it in online productions. The public nature of blogs coupled with commenting features enabled writers and audiences to engage with each other in ways that had not been possible before.

In addition to supporting journaling, blogs were taken up by hobbyists writing about everything from political analysis, to parenting, to fiction. Of particular interest, fanfiction communities, which had been active in online forums and mailing lists, became increasingly visible on blogging sites (Black, 2008). Eventually, large groups of writers migrated to their own platforms with affordances to support publishing, review, critique, and, importantly, a supportive community.

Blogs were viewed by progressive educators as natural focal points for informal learning on the Internet and were also adapted to formal learning environments. Resnick and colleagues suggested that construction kits ideally connect learners to their work in both personal and epistemological dimensions; that is, construction kits should connect to learners' passions and interests as well as to ways of thinking in and about the domains they are learning (Resnick, Bruckman, & Martin, 1996). O'Donnell (2006) similarly observed that blogging has three modes—personal, knowledge building, and social—and suggested that a "constructionist approach would encourage us to ensure that each of these modes are developed in an integrated way in educational blogging projects and would discourage approaches which highlight blogs as merely communicative devices." Although collaborative blogging or tweeting is possible, blogs generally provide toolkits in which people construct single-authored texts that can attract wide audiences and provide a means for interacting with others.

WIKIS

The appearance of the wiki as a radically open collaborative space set the conditions for widespread collaborative construction of public online texts. The first wiki, WikiWikiWeb, was created by Ward Cunningham in the mid-1990s to enable the collective creation of a repository for software design patterns (Leuf & Cunningham, 2001); today, wikis are still frequently used to produce reference materials, most famously Wikipedia. Although wikis have now been adapted with a variety of permissions structures to control editing, the first wikis were radically open and allowed anyone to click an "edit" button and change the content. Wikis as toolkits for producing text represented a shift from centralized control structures, where a few gate-keepers created web content for others to read, to a decentralized model where people can not only learn by reading what others have written, but also participate in the production of texts about things that interest them. This was critical for realizing their potential to support constructionist learning. Because their openness and publicness aligned with progressive views of education, wikis were quickly adapted to support collaborative writing in educational contexts and a rich research literature about wikis as learning tools developed in education and the learning sciences.

The earliest documented uses of wiki in educational contexts were radically open and happened at the college level. In the late 1990s researchers at Georgia Institute of Technology built the initial version of CoWeb, a variation of Ward Cunningham's original WikiWikiWeb, but implemented in Squeak Smalltalk (Leuf & Cunningham, 2001). CoWeb was actively refined for over a decade and used to support hundreds of courses at Georgia Tech. Rather than designing instructional activities, researchers simply made the toolkit available to university instructors and responded to their needs. By observing the wiki activity that followed, researchers were able to study patterns of and barriers to adoption among instructors and students (Rick & Guzdial, 2006). In some cases, classes that emphasized individual accomplishment and competition erected barriers to adopting a radically open and collaborative toolkit; yet, the flexibility and lightweight nature of the technology also led to inventive and successful new uses of the wiki among many instructors.

Soon researchers and instructors at other institutions also began experimenting with CoWeb and other flavors of wiki. The variety of activities that were supported with wikis was dramatic, from documentation and deliverables for open-source programming projects, to developing reference materials in different learning domains, to supporting game design activities, instructors found that the flexibility of the wiki construction kits offered a low barrier to adoption with many possibilities. Studies found that writing on a public wiki transformed the ways students thought about their work, not only at the college level but also in high school. College students were found to consider the perspectives of potential readers when constructing arguments, while high school students reconstructed the genre of "research paper" when asked to publish it online and felt a responsibility to their audience for the quality of their work (Forte & Bruckman, 2009). Peters and Slotta (2010) worked with high school teachers to develop a specialized wiki toolkit and accompanying activities for wiki-based science learning; they observed that students enjoyed the public nature of the work and some even viewed it as a continuing work-in-progress after the project was graded and "done."

Outside of the classroom, the use of wikis expanded dramatically with large and small groups of writers forging collaborative, interest-driven communities of authorship. It is important to note that not all implementations of wikis support the same kinds of constructionist experiences. As with blogs, many major educational products like course management systems now include wikis as tools for classroom use. In such cases, viewing and editing wiki pages and blog posts is restricted to members of a particular class at a particular time. Once the class is over, learners' text productions on the wiki remain locked in the tool and even the creators themselves lose access to it, effectively reproducing the traditional limitations of paper-based classroom writing assignments.

OTHER SOCIAL MEDIA AND POSSIBLE FUTURES

Many of the text-based construction kits described above could easily be categorized as forms of social media. The potential for social media to support new conceptualizations of education has been widely explored (Greenhow & Lewin, 2016), although not all of these are immediately recognizable as constructionist learning experiences.

An outgrowth of blogs, "microblogs" such as Twitter, and other platforms designed to share images and video creations such as Instagram or Facebook have made it possible to create lightweight ephemeral messages that have the potential to reach broad audiences. It could be argued that most use of such platforms support "mere" message passing; yet, in the examples of Twitter and Facebook, the combination of brevity and features for liking, resharing, and quoting creates an environment in which texts are often celebrated not only for their message but for their composition. As these short, public compositions are amplified, recontextualized, and repurposed across a number of actors, the sometimes extremely public performances of "textual poaching" on Twitter could be reimagined as opportunities for constructionist learning.

One of the challenges for constructionist online writing experiences on the open Internet is to balance learners' need for safety as they explore ideas and identities with the advantages of interacting with a broad audience and potential collaborators. Toolkits described in this chapter have addressed these tradeoffs in different ways. For example, some wikis for use in classrooms aimed to allow for privacy as well as publicness by showing editors' real names only to class members while showing pseudonyms to all other users.

There are many new and prolific forms of shared writing, often in the context of dyadic or small group communication, that have not been investigated in this chapter as potential constructionist learning experiences. When people use texts to pass messages that allow them to coordinate plans, exchange information, provide support to one another, or initiate a friendship, these are not typically constructionist learning experiences. Yet, the potential for existing social media platforms to be reimagined as construction kits opens a wide door for educational technology designers and theorists to imagine possible futures for text.

NOTE

1. https://www.itu.int/en/ITU-D/Statistics/Documents/facts/ICTFactsFigures2017.pdf

REFERENCES

Bereiter, C., & Scardamalia, M. (1987). *The psychology of written composition*. Hillsdale, NJ: Lawrence Erlbaum Associates.

Black, R. W. (2008). *Adolescents and online fan fiction* (Vol. 23). New York, NY: Peter Lang.

Bruckman, A. (1998). Community support for constructionist learning. *Computer Supported Collaborative Work: The Journal of Collaborative Computing, 7*, 47.

Emig, J. (1977). Writing as a mode of learning. *College Composition and Communication, 28*, 122.

Forte, A., & Bruckman, A. (2009). Citing, writing and participatory media: wikis as learning environments in the high school classroom. *International Journal of Learning and Media, 1*(4).

Greenhow, C., & Lewin, C. (2016). Social media and education: reconceptualizing the boundaries of formal and informal learning. *Learning, Media and Technology, 41*(1).

Jenkins, H. (1992). *Textual poachers: Television fans and participatory culture.* New York, NY: Routledge.

Lenhart, A., Arafeh, S., & Smith, A. (2008). *Writing, technology and teens.* Washington, DC: Pew Internet & American Life Project.

Leuf, B., & Cunningham, W. (2001). *The Wiki way.* Boston, MA: Addison-Wesley.

O'Donnell, M. (2006). Blogging as pedagogic practice: Artefact and ecology. *Asia Pacific Media Educator, 1*(17), 3.

Peters, V. L., & Slotta, J. D. (2010). Scaffolding knowledge communities in the classroom: New opportunities in the Web 2.0 era. In M. J. Jacobson & P. Reimann (Eds.), *Designs for learning environments of the future.* New York, NY: Springer-Verlag.

Rafaeli, S. (1984). The electronic bulletin board: A computer-driven mass medium. *Social Science Micro Review, 2*(3).

Resnick, M., Bruckman, A., & Martin, F. (1996). Pianos, not stereos: Creating computational construction kits. *Interactions, 3*(6), 41.

Resnick, M., Bruckman, A., Martin, F., & Druin, A. (1998). *Constructional design: Creating new construction kits for kids.* San Francisco, CA: Morgan Kaufmann.

Rick, J., & Guzdial, M. (2006). Situating CoWeb: A Scholarship of Application. *International Journal of Computer-Supported Collaborative Learning, 1*(1).

Scardamalia, M. (2002). Collective cognitive responsibility for the advancement of knowledge. In B. Smith (Ed.)., *Liberal education in a knowledge society* (pp. 67–98). Peru, IL: Open Court Publishing.

22 TAKING UP MULTILITERACIES IN A CONSTRUCTIONIST DESIGN CONTEXT

Breanne K. Litts, Erica R. Halverson, and Kimberly M. Sheridan

In the fall of 2015 a team of researchers, designers, and educators across two universities, a makerspace located in a children's museum, and an environmental science–based charter school embarked on a collaborative design project to engage fifth graders in learning through making. We chose a fairly "standard" maker project: making puppets using sewable circuit technologies. Sewable circuits are made by connecting sewable components (LED lights and coin cell batteries) together with conductive thread. This kind of maker project has been shown to on-ramp disengaged youth into computing concepts (Kafai, Searle, Martinez, & Brayboy, 2014) and support interdisciplinary learning outcomes including circuitry, coding, and crafting knowledge and practices (Litts, Kafai, Lui, Walker, & Widman, 2017; Peppler & Glosson, 2013). But as our students were working on their puppets, we found that they were not particularly inspired by the project, nor were they able to articulate *why* this form of making was compelling for them. So the project shifted from making puppets to making a puppet show for younger children to learn something about environmental science. The shift was essential in engaging our fifth-grade learners by giving their work purpose, depth, and a reason for making.

This observation led us to reflect on the kinds of theories of learning that guided our design and, subsequently, what has shaped our understanding of what students get out of their participation in maker projects. In this chapter, we describe how a multiliteracies framework is useful for understanding how we shifted our design framework from a constructionist perspective to a multiliteracies perspective and how this resulted in the beginnings of a framework that highlights how these two (often disconnected) perspectives can be merged to capture how students learn through making.

Constructionism and multiliteracies are both commonly used in the learning sciences to describe what learning is and how learning happens. Specifically, work in STEM fields often takes a constructionist perspective on how people learn (e.g., Martinez & Stager, 2013), whereas literacy-focused disciplines rely on a multiliteracies perspective to describe learning and knowing (e.g., Stornaiuolo & Nichols, 2018). Constructionism is predominantly concerned with the learning that happens in a creation process (Papert, 1980) and multiliteracies is largely concerned with learning that happens through communicating or sharing a creation process (New London Group, 1996).

The maker movement challenges the traditional divisions in our understandings and theorizing of learning and presenting a type of learning best understood through a lens of convergence, especially of constructionism and multiliteracies (Halverson & Sheridan, 2014). To date, though, the majority of work in the maker movement adopts Papert's (1980) constructionist perspective to understanding learning through making, which does not capture the entire scope of learning through making. As a result, work in maker education is expanding to include additional literacies-focused perspectives. Making itself can be defined by a specific set of literacies (Santo, 2011) such that new literacies are built through a constructionist design process. In Holbert's (2016) work engaging youth in a constructionist design process of making toys, he required that youth make the toys for younger children, establishing an authentic audience for making as a design feature of the making process (Halverson, 2013). We build on this work by adopting a multiliteracies analytic and interpretive lens to understand how students engaged in a constructionist design process. Specifically, we examine how components of a multiliteracies framework—representation and audience—help us understand what students learned through making and sharing puppets created with sewable circuits.

MULTILITERACIES FRAMEWORK

The New London Group (1996) coined the term "multiliteracies" to recognize a wave of new media and the new literacy skills necessary to interact with them. Multiliteracies materialized from the understanding that, as "makers of meaning," we are constantly "negotiating a multiplicity of discourse" (New London Group, 1996) in our lives. The New London Group identifies two separate but complementary features of multiplicity: (1) the modes of meaning-making literacies available to individuals on a local level and (2) new forms of communication that more tightly connect local and global worlds, resulting in a drastic increase of cultural and linguistic diversity in our daily lives. Accordingly, the purpose of learning is to engage learners as active participants in designing (their) *social futures* (New

London Group, 1996; Cope & Kalantzis, 2000). A pedagogy of multiliteracies is built on the belief that knowledge is inextricably "embedded in social, cultural, and material contexts" (New London Group, 1996, p. 82) and that learning happens through immersive and contextualized hands-on experience (Cope & Kalantzis, 2000).

From this perspective, learning is a representational process through which learners communicate meaning to specific audiences (De Vries, 2006; Halverson, 2013; New London Group, 1996). A multiliteracies framework, therefore, conceptualizes learning as having two critical components: representation and audience. Through the design process, learners create representations of self and knowledge in ways that illustrate and communicate their learning. Moreover, as part of this representational process, audience functions as a design feature of support defined by the avenues of making *for*. Inspired by our observations of youth making puppets through a constructionist design process, we adopt this multiliteracies framework to understand the emergent features (e.g., discourse of representation and audience) of the making activity that facilitate youth's meaning-making process.

CONSTRUCTIONIST DESIGN PROJECT: MAKING PUPPETS

We adopted Papert's (1980) constructionist approach to develop a design project motivated by the idea that we produce knowledge through constructing external artifacts, and, in our case, students made fabric puppets that light up with sewable circuits. As a team of researchers, museum educators, and classroom teachers, we conducted a design experiment—six sessions stretched across two settings: classroom and museum. Three sessions were in the students' classroom, and the other three were in the makerspace of the nearby children's museum. All sessions were facilitated by the museum's lead teaching artist, assisted by museum staff and researchers. A class of twenty-five fifth graders participated in six sessions, in which they designed and built puppets using sewable circuit materials including lights, batteries, and conductive thread. Students then came together in groups of two or three to create puppet shows focused on environmental issues to teach kindergarten and first-grade students at the museum. Participant students attended an environmental science charter school, so the classroom teacher selected the theme for the puppet shows to align the project with internal instructional goals. Each week, students documented their work by taking photos and writing reflections in a closed, online platform, where they could get feedback from their peers and from adult maker mentors, who were researchers working on the project with expertise in making. At the end of the project, eleven teams of two and three presented two-minute puppet shows that were recorded and shared at the museum space for younger students. We gathered data on all steps of their puppet design, puppet making, and puppet show process, including sketches, photos, written reflections responding to the prompt "What was I doing?", recordings of their pitch and final presentation of their puppet show, and weekly progress interviews. Table 22.1 summarizes the project milestones and corresponding data collected.

Using bidirectional artifact analysis, a method we have developed for analyzing extended, creative production processes (Halverson & Magnifico, 2013), we traced participants' puppet making and puppet show processes. Here we present one student's process from initial puppet design to final partner presentation to demonstrate how students participated in this puppet-making activity, the core features of their production processes, and how students made sense of their making process in situ. We chose this

Table 22.1 Summary of maker project timeline

Week & location	Project milestones	Data collected
Week 1: School	Introduction to project: focus on *sewing* and *puppets* Introduction to documentation: focus on *brainstorming* and *keeping track of your work*	Audio of classroom discussion
Week 2: Museum	Sketch of puppet 1 Hand-sewn puppets using embroidery hoops	Artifacts: Initial puppet sketches Written reflections Progress interviews Teaching artist audio
Week 3: Museum	Sketch of puppet 2 Hand-sewn puppets including sewable circuits	Artifacts: Revised puppet sketches Written reflections Progress interviews Teaching artist audio
Week 4: School	Finished puppet with sewable circuit	Progress interviews
Week 5: School	Puppet show pitch	Puppet show pitches Progress interviews
Week 6: Museum	Puppet show performance	Puppet shows Artifacts: Final puppets, scripts Focus group interviews

example because it illustrates how the students engaged with representation and audience through their design process.

THE RENEWABLE ENERGY PROJECT AND ANNE'S "PERSON PUPPET"

Anne and Sam, two fifth graders, created the "renewable energy project" to describe renewable energy and to explain the benefits of renewable energy over coal in a way that was accessible to kindergarteners and first graders in their school. In sessions one through three, Anne and Sam worked separately to build their individual puppets, and in sessions four through six they collaborated to write, pitch, and perform a puppet show. To illustrate the full scope of students' design process, we share Anne's process and how she reimagined her design when she paired up with Sam to make a puppet show (see figure 22.1 for Anne and Sam's puppets).

Teaching artists, who are the museum's makerspace facilitators, described the puppets as sewing projects with a "bonus: your puppets will have the ability to light up" (Teaching Artist Audio, Session 1). Teaching artists

FIGURE 22.1
Puppet characters from left to right: Anne and Sam's narrator, Sam's shark, and Anne's "Sheila."

promised to teach students how to sew, how to make circuits, and to provide a space to "brainstorm what puppet idea you might want to have ... [and] consider how you want to build your [idea]" (Teaching Artist Audio, Session 1). Anne persisted throughout her making process to create a person puppet named Sheila. In Session 2, she piloted a "person hand puppet" as her first iteration but ended up with a "person mitten puppet" for her second iteration and carried this into her eventual design and build. Aesthetic features—buttons for eyes, a red fabric mouth, and string for hair—remained the same across her two iterations. In her first iteration, though, she discovered a design flaw: when sewing the front and back together, she sewed the pieces too close to the bottom. She described this prototype: "The only problem is my hand can't really get in it, which is a problem," (Interview, Session 2). In response to this, Anne shifted from a hand puppet to a mitten puppet, which would give more space for her hand to operate her puppet. During Session 5, she reflected, "Since I couldn't fit my hand through the sleeve [of the hand puppet], I decided to make something [bigger] that was also a human," (Interview, Session 5). She "traced [her] thumb a bit bigger so the thumb [has space]" for her "surprise feature," an LED light in the thumb of the puppet (Interview, Session 3).

By the end of Session 4, Anne had completed her puppet. Throughout Sessions four through six she worked with Sam to create a puppet show about renewable energy. Anne made Sheila the puppet, and Sam made a dwarf shark puppet. As Anne was finishing her puppet, she referenced this impending partnership and her struggle to integrate her design with the content:

Interviewer: So how is your puppet going to be incorporated into your puppet show with other people?

Anne: I'm working with [Sam] ... And, we're doing solar power. And I guess ... well to be truthful not really solar power but the pollution of coal and I'm not really sure how I'm going to incorporate this in.

Interviewer: Incorporate the puppet?

Anne: Yeah ... but I gotta ... hopefully it will work out. (Interview, Session 4)

In fact, the connection between her puppet and their show never came together. There is no discernable connection between her "person puppet" and the team's puppet show. Sam described their idea: "Hello, people. Today I'm pitching about my show to teach you about renewable energy and how it is better than using coal to make energy" (Pitch, Session 5). While they had each created one puppet prior to developing their puppet show and used these two puppets to pitch their idea, the final show had three puppets. They added a generic narrator puppet, who served as an audience to their two main characters by asking questions to prompt explanations. Their design decision was in direct response to feedback from their adult maker mentor, who wrote, "I wonder, for your final puppet show, if you can explain that big term—'renewable energy'—for the little kids. For instance, maybe the shark and the purple-haired person could just focus on wind energy and how a windmill works. Or maybe just focus on some of the bad things coal does to the environment," (Feedback, Session 4). The third narrator puppet served as the audience for Anne and Sam's puppets by asking questions that lead their puppet characters to explain the basic facts of renewable energy in a way that would suit their real-world audience of younger students.

MULTILITERACIES IN CONSTRUCTIONIST DESIGN

Anne and Sam's renewable energy project is a representative example of the design process through which students engaged in our puppet maker program. To illustrate the role a multiliteracies perspective plays in enriching a constructionist approach to teaching, learning, and design, we highlight two core components of multiliteracies—representation and audience—that were key characteristics of the youths' design process.

Design as Representation

By adopting a multiliteracies framework toward our puppet-maker project, representation becomes an outcome. Our earlier work on digital artmaking (e.g., Halverson, 2013) has demonstrated that creating digital art over time affords the development of metarepresentational competence, the marriage of narrative and tools such that learners come to understand when to use which tools for which narrative purposes. We find similar representational trajectories are made possible through making, particularly when the making process is oriented toward the production of narrative and/or explanation. We identified a spectrum of the role representation through narrativization played in students' puppet show–making process. During Session 4 of our maker program, students began collaborating with partners to produce a puppet show using the puppets they designed.

On the one hand, Anne was inspired by her love of fantasy novels and stories of "regular people with extraordinary powers" in designing her human puppet with an LED light. She imagined the light would be her puppet's power, and that it turned on and off because "if you had a power would you always want it to be on?" (Interview, Session 5). The narrativizing and identity of her puppet shaped the design decisions she made, specifically where to put her LED light and the use of a switch. When it came time to merge her puppet in the renewable energy show, she did not re-narrativize her initial puppet identity and maintained the representation of Sheila, the purple-haired human with the light super power, even though it wasn't connected to the renewable energy message of her puppet show.

On the other hand, other students approached the puppet show production by reconsidering their own puppet as a component of a larger narrative. For example, Sarah described to an adult facilitator how she reconceptualized her "Mr. Potato puppet" transition:

> I am making Mr. Potato ... and me and Jennifer and me and Makeda, we're all in a group and we're going to be doing something about litter. And I'm pretending that someone littered me on the ground ... cuz he's a potato ... and I'm like a rotten potato. And they leave without me. (Teaching Artist Audio, Session 4)

In this case, Sarah (re)purposed her puppet to meet the needs of the narrative she and her partners were building. She made no changes to the puppet itself but fitted its already existing design into an emergent narrative structure. In the final puppet show, "Mike P. Potato" instructs viewers that "one step to not litter is to keep track of where you are throwing your garbage," and works with the other puppet characters to pick up pieces of litter and put them in the trash can.

Audience as Design Feature

From a multiliteracies perspective, audience emerged as a critical design feature in the students' puppet-making process. All of the fifth-grade puppet makers crafted puppets and designed a show that communicates environmental issues to an audience of younger students. The significance of integrating an external audience, specifically an audience of younger kids, is a well-established design feature of production and making processes (Holbert, 2016; Magnifico, 2010). Moreover, many students employed a strategy of integrating narrator characters into their puppet shows to explain concepts and use language geared toward their younger audience. These design decisions are directly related to the fifth graders' understanding of what kind of puppet show would be both appealing and understandable to five- and six-year-olds. For example, Anne and Sam responded to the feedback of making renewable energy more accessible by creating a third puppet as a narrative trope to whom their other puppets could explain more complex constructs. As another strategy of appealing to their younger audience, Jake, Devon, and Kendall, who created a puppet show about pollution, anthropomorphized their three object characters (a factory, pollution, and the sun) to introduce them with accessible language:

Factory: I am a factory, I make things

Pollution: I am pollution, I make things cloudy and bad

Sun: I am the sun, I make the days sunny

In these ways, students designed for the real-world audience by embedding an audience character or anthropomorphizing object characters in their plays. As a result, audience became a design feature of both the overarching making activity as well as within the writing and performance of the puppet shows.

BRIDGING WORLDS TO FRAME LEARNING THROUGH MAKING

The maker movement has prompted interdisciplinary investigations of learning by offering constructionist design processes at the intersection of traditional disciplinary boundaries. For example, in this project youth sewed and constructed puppets with sewable circuit technologies, which include crafting, coding, circuitry, and design. As maker education shifts our understanding of learning, more work crosses the STEM-Literacies chasm and sits at disciplinary intersections. In the same way, we argue that these constructionist design processes sit at theoretical intersections and, thus, by leveraging the convergence of theories of learning, we are able to better understand what is happening in learning through making.

ACKNOWLEDGMENTS

We would like to thank Abby Konopasky, Beau Johnson, Lisa Brahms, Molly Dickerson, and the MAKESHOP team. This material was based on work funded by the National Science Foundation under Grant No. 1216994.

REFERENCES

Cope, B., & Kalantzis, M. (2000). *Multiliteracies: Literacy learning and the design of social futures*. London, UK: Routledge.

De Vries, E. (2006). Students' construction of external representations in design-based learning situations. *Learning and Instruction, 16*(3), 213–227.

Halverson, E. R. (2013). Digital art making as a representational process. *Journal of the Learning Sciences, 22*(1), 121–162.

Halverson, E. R., & Magnifico, A. (2013). Bidirectional artifact analysis: A method for analyzing digitally-mediated creative processes. In R. Luckin, S. Puntambekar, P. Goodyear, B. L. Grabowski, J. Underwood, & N. Winters (Eds.), *Handbook of Design in Educational Technology* (Chapter 37). London, UK: Taylor & Francis.

Halverson, E. R., & Sheridan, K. (2014). The maker movement in education. *Harvard Educational Review, 84*(4), 495–504.

Holbert, N. (2016, June). Bots for Tots: Building inclusive makerspaces by leveraging ways of knowing. In *Proceedings of the 15th International Conference on Interaction Design and Children,* Manchester, United Kingdom (pp. 79–88).

Kafai, Y. B., Searle, K., Martinez, C., & Brayboy, B. (2014). Ethnocomputing with electronic textiles: Culturally responsive open design to broaden participation in computing in American Indian youth and communities. In *Proceedings of the 45th ACM technical symposium on computer science education,* Atlanta, GA (pp. 241–246).

Litts, B. K., Kafai, Y. B., Lui, D. A., Walker, J. T., & Widman, S. A. (2017). Stitching codeable circuits: High school students' learning about circuitry and coding with electronic textiles. *Journal of Science Education and Technology, 26*(5), 494–507.

Magnifico, A. M. (2010). Writing for whom? Cognition, motivation, and a writer's audience. *Educational Psychologist, 45*(3), 167–184.

Martinez, S. L., & Stager, G. (2013). *Invent to learn: Making, tinkering, and engineering in the classroom.* Torrance, CA: Constructing Modern Knowledge Press.

New London Group. (1996). A pedagogy of multiliteracies: Designing social futures. *Harvard Educational Review, 66*(1), 60–92.

Papert, S. (1980). *Mindstorms: Children, computers, and powerful ideas.* New York, NY: Basic Books, Inc.

Peppler, K., & Glosson, D. (2013). Stitching circuits: Learning about circuitry through e-textile materials. *Journal of Science Education and Technology, 22*(5), 751–763.

Santo, R. (2011). Hacker literacies: Synthesizing critical and participatory media literacy frameworks. *International Journal of Learning and Media, 3*(3), 1–5.

Stornaiuolo, A., & Nichols, T. P. (2018). Making publics: Mobilizing audiences in high school makerspaces. *Teachers College Record, 120*(8), 1–38.

23 CONSTRUCTING WITH AND THROUGH THE BODY

Joshua A. Danish and Noel Enyedy

Theories of learning and cognition have long overlooked the role of the body, either ignoring it completely or treating it simply as an extension of the mind. However, embodied cognition has seen a renaissance of sorts in the last decade with increasing value placed upon the role of the body in supporting unique aspects of cognition (Barsalou, 2016; Shapiro, 2014). As in so many other cases, Seymour Papert (1980) was ahead of his time in recognizing the important role of the body as a concrete and important resource for learning. To illustrate the role of the body, Papert provided the example of a child attempting to draw a house in Logo as a simple triangle on top of a square. The child had programmed Logo to draw both objects individually, but when she combined her programs—draw square, then draw triangle—the triangle was inscribed inside the square instead of on top of it as intended. The child was intrigued by this unexpected result. She got up and physically enacted the role of the turtle, carrying out the instructions she had programmed and, in doing so, realized that, upon ending the first program, she was facing the wrong direction, and that is why program did not produce what she had intended. Her embodiment was crucial to resolving her programming dilemma!

In this one example, Papert (1980) was able to illustrate three ways in which the body was used as a fundamental resource for learning. First, Papert coined the term *syntonic* learning to refer to how the sense of one's own body can be used to reason about ideas and activities that do not directly involve the body—in this case, the act of physically walking draws your attention to the direction you are facing to help you reason about the importance of the turtle's orientation. Second, Papert specified *ego syntonic* learning, which draws upon children's sense of themselves as agents with intentions, goals, and desires. In this case, not only did the child follow the program's instruction but she also became the turtle and experienced drawing by walking from that perspective instead of from the top-down view of the monitor. Third, Papert talked about *cultural syntonic* learning, which referred to how the activity of becoming and acting as the turtle connected cultural constructs together. In this case, the cultural abstraction of a triangle and its formal properties was connected to a different and possibly more familiar cultural activity of navigation and wayfinding.

As constructionism has grown into new realms and encompassed new technologies, this emphasis on the value of the body has been overshadowed to some degree by other ideas favored by constructionists, such as the connections between debugging and reflection, a focus on the "big ideas" that students can engage with, and attention to the role of "public artifacts" in supporting constructionist learning. The result is that while the body remains a powerful resource, it is often overlooked in newer theoretical and analytic accounts. This chapter is intended to shine the light back on syntonic learning and the value of the body to current and future flavors of constructionism. Additionally, we wish to extend our evaluation of the body for constructionism by incorporating current research into how the body supports individual cognition and how it also plays an important role in social and collective activity.

This second point is particularly important because the body is often seen primarily as an individual resource, which it certainly is. However, the body can also play a key role in cooperative action and collective knowledge building. In the remainder of this chapter, we begin by exploring how the body can support individual thinking and learning. We then explore how learners' use of their bodies also provides an opportunity for their peers to see and respond to their ideas, treating them as a public artifact. From there we note the unique opportunities for collaboration, where multiple learners move their bodies in conjunction to explore collective ideas. Finally, we examine how the role of the body in human communication has relevance beyond the way it directly supports cognition, and how the role of the body can shed light on how learners participate in constructing both physical and virtual artifacts. We close with suggestions for next steps as the field continues to build on the successful history of constructionism into new and exciting domains.

THE BODY AS INDIVIDUAL RESOURCE

When Papert noted the power of a child taking on the role of a "turtle," he introduced a whole new way of thinking about programming and about the world. Central to this account is the way that the individual body provides a unique perspective or viewpoint upon the world. Work in agent-based modeling and participatory simulations has been particularly powerful in leveraging this notion. In participatory simulations students have to physically take on the role of an agent, which can give them new insights into the way that the agent moves through the environment and responds to it (Wilensky & Stroup, 1999). Colella (2000) also demonstrated with a participatory simulation of disease spread that the physical embodiment of the first-person experience of an agent accentuates what Papert called ego syntonic learning by making the personally meaningful and affective aspects of problem solving more salient. Students don't want to catch the virtual disease, so they are fully engaged in how to socialize without socializing too much! Simply put, embodied roles engender or build upon emotional engagement in powerful ways while also providing a unique insight into how agents interact through movement.

Encouraging students to take a first-person perspective and/or physically acting out what they are investigating has clearly been fruitful to constructionist scholars and designers. Where we see an opportunity for continued expansion is in the inclusion of more recent work on embodied cognition. In addition to perspective taking, cognitive scientists and learning scientists have shown that the body plays a unique role in reasoning and helps students connect to concepts in which the physical actions of the body can mirror the actions of the system under study (Lindgren & Johnson-Glenberg, 2013). That is, focusing on the ways that embodiment is a physical analog to a phenomenon provides syntonic resources for students to simultaneously build an embodied external model and a conceptual or mental model. In our recent STEP project, for example (Danish, Enyedy, Saleh, Lee, & Andrade, 2015), students took on the role of being water particles and they moved around a physical space, enacting the different states of matter, moving slowly for ice, and more quickly for liquid and gas. This certainly built on the individual perspective that taking on these roles gave students: students had to run to make gas, and their speed was a physical analog to the speed of gas particles. In addition to the physical analog/syntonic resources, the students made a clear mapping between the energy they felt while running and the energy required to move particles in a gas. When asked what it felt like to be a gas, students immediately pointed to how it tired them out, and thus being a gas takes more energy! Here again is a case of body syntonic resources working hand-in-hand with ego syntonic resources as embodied experiences help students to connect to conceptual notions.

BODY AS PUBLIC DISPLAY AND AN OBJECT OF REFLECTION

Constructionism implies the construction of a material object that can be the object for reflection; Papert noted the importance of this kind of public artifact for helping to support and drive reflection. In the examples above, the body—where it moved and what it was intended to represent—was that object. We argue that the body is also a unique form of public artifact because people spend their entire lives learning how to represent ideas with their bodies, and how to interpret other people's body positioning, movement, and gesture. In the example above, students take barely a moment to plan how to simply move across the room as a particle, and their peers immediately interpret this as demonstrating motion in a straight line. Furthermore, this kind of motion is easily adapted or debugged—a teacher calling out that the temperature is cold can lead students to immediately slow their bodies down to demonstrate how they feel this would affect them.

More important, advances in motion-tracking technology allow designers to augment this kind of participatory model or simulation with additional features and visualizations, further enhancing the public artifact and the information that it can convey. This kind of augmented reality is a new form of public artifact that can blend cultural syntonic resources with body syntonic resources. For example, in the case of STEP a live video feed of the room was projected on one wall and students' bodies were overlaid with a simple visualization that showed the state of matter they were currently producing, even if the students did not yet understand how they were controlling the visualization (See figure 23.1, also Enyedy et al., 2016). In addition to demonstrating the states of matter, our simulation color-coded the bonds between particles (white for ice, blue for liquid, and red for gas) and encoded the strength of those bonds via the thickness of the line. These familiar visual tropes provide the culturally syntonic ability for students to "read" their motion and as helping to create specific kinds of bonds, and ultimately helped them to identify patterns in how their motion, and thus the motion of particles, contributes to different states of matter.

Constructionists have long focused on the kinds of permanent or semi-permanent public artifacts that students can create and interrogate, such as code or, more recently, electronics. However, our work, and a great deal of work in embodiment and gesture has shown that the body is also treated as a powerful public artifact for analysis both on its own and when supported by augmented or mixed reality (Lindgren & Johnson-Glenberg, 2013). We see real value for constructionist learning environments in continuing to explore the potential of the body as a form of public artifact and in

FIGURE 23.1
Students creating a participatory model (left) with a close-up view of what each state looks like (right).

unpacking how it is similar to and different from other forms of public artifacts both in terms of expressive power and for how it supports reflection.

BODIES AS COLLECTIVE-SYNTONIC RESOURCES

If one broadens the focus from one body to many bodies, we can see new types of syntonic resources develop—ones that capitalize on the relationships between bodies and aggregate phenomena. Another unique characteristic of the body for constructing public artifacts that we see leveraged in work on participatory simulations and models is that when participants embody phenomena together, they can gain unique insights into collective phenomena or complex systems (Danish, 2014). That is, they can explore phenomena ranging from disease spread to traffic patterns to honeybees collecting nectar because understanding those systems requires learners to understand how their behavior as a whole is driven by the many individual behaviors of the agents within them.

The difference between a focus on one body and a focus on many bodies is that because multiple others are participating, their actions may invite response from their peers and their peers' actions invite response from them in a continual matter. For example, when students in the STEP environment pretend to be water particles moving slowly around a space, they soon realize by viewing the simulation that their proximity to each other influences the state of matter as much as their speed. Just as in the real world, states of matter are determined by the aggregate relationship between particles—one particle acting alone cannot be a state of matter. Thus, two very slow-moving learners-as-particles that are far apart do not make a block of ice; they are simply two slow particles. And two fast-moving learners-as-particles that move in tandem are not a gas but a solid that is moving quickly in space. An important aspect of this kind of embodied construction of public artifacts is that the public artifact *requires* the participants to align their movement with each other for their movement to make sense and to achieve their shared goals. If they operate individually, they are unlikely to see the underlying phenomena. While there are certainly examples of purely virtual simulations of this nature, the unique affordances of the body allow participants to begin creating models or simulations immediately, to understand each other quickly, and to adapt in ways that are not always as easily visible in purely virtual environments. We believe there is also opportunity for synergy across levels of body syntonic connections here, as students might simultaneously reflect on both their individual experience in motion and the impact of that upon the model. That is, they might explore how they feel moving quickly as a gas particle that requires energy to maintain that speed, while reflecting on the fact that their peers' relative positions mean that they are producing a gas together. Recognizing the benefits and possible pitfalls of this kind of synergy across ways that the body can serve as a resource will be an important area of future study for constructionist researchers and designers.

BODIES AS INTERACTIONAL-SYNTONIC RESOURCES

As we saw above, the body holds a unique role in supporting individuals in exploring new phenomena because they are used to moving, perceiving, and responding fluidly in interaction, and the body is a central component of this (Hall & Stevens, 2015). Bodies, however, are more than just a resource for cognition. Humans read and respond to both overt and implicit social cues that are displayed through the body, and social interaction affects how people interpret and relate to each other as they work on public artifacts both embodied and not. We are not just saying that social interaction is as important in constructionist learning environments as they are elsewhere. Rather, we think this goes one step further and are saying that constructionism's particular focus on doing and tinkering means that the body—one's own and others—is continually informing how participants understand their rights, roles, and position in the tinkering process. Thus, these embodied cues are continually shaping how learners in constructionist environments view themselves as tinkerers or not. Vossoughi, Escudé, Kitundu, & Espinoza (2020) provide a particularly compelling example when they explore the role of participants' hands in a makerspace. They show how a mentor's seemingly small choice of answering questions about how to resolve a physical computing challenge by either pointing out a next-step or simply taking the project to fix it, positions participants as either capable of making their own fixes, or positions them as incapable. Their work further shows how this simple action of taking physical control or not has implications for who these students become, with participants who become more competent taking control of the physical space more often, and in turn being offered more and more opportunities to retain control of the physical objects they are working with. In other words, this interpretation of embodiment goes one step beyond traditional analyses of how interactional roles and rights are tied to social cues to recognizing that the role of constructionist learners as fundamentally tinkering and exploring is dependent on how they are allowed to physically engage in these acts over time.

CONCLUSION

Our read is that while constructionism has, since the beginning, given a privileged role to the body, we can go deeper and further. We can do this in four key ways:

1. Recognize that many findings from the field of embodied cognition can help us think more deeply about how specific kinds of body movements are syntonic, ego syntonic, and cultural syntonic resources that are productive for understanding deep nuances or practices. Understanding the range of syntonic resources that are available in today's technology-mediated spaces will help us answer the question: Once a student embodies an agent role, what kind of physical exploration highlights the "big ideas" that we hope they will explore?

2. Recognize that the body is a unique form of shared, public artifact that can be productively augmented to create new types of artifacts for reflection. This stems in large part from the facility with which we use our

bodies to communicate through motion, position, and gesture. Explic-
·itly attending to the value of these embodied social resources can help us
to both design new learning opportunities and to analyze existing ones
in new ways.

3. Explore how collective phenomena, which are important but often hard
to understand, can be a new type of syntonic resource and a unique way
of engaging in constructionist learning.

4. Finally, recognizing that the body is playing an active role in constructionist learning even when the individuals are not currently using their
body to reason about the phenomena under study. Our bodies tell us a
great deal about what it means to be a learner in a social space. We must
attend to this dimension of embodiment to truly appreciate all of the
other dimensions of what students may take away about themselves and
their role as learners.

Technology, including technologies that can read embodied action or
gesture and use this to support computer simulations and visualizations,
can build on and enhance all of these dimensions of embodiment for constructionist learning. However, our view is that these new technologies will
only be as productive as the underlying thinking about how the body is a
unique resource. Thus, our focus in this chapter has been on the role of the
body as a unique resource for learning in the hopes that future designers
will begin by asking what role learners' bodies may play in learning before
asking how technology can support that role.

Papert's initial and groundbreaking focus on syntonic behavior brought
attention to the body as a key part of learning. Our hope is that as we move
forward, we will see more explicit, theoretical, nuanced incorporation of
the body into our designs and analyses so that we can truly live up to this
potential as a field.

ACKNOWLEDGMENTS

Portions of this work were funded by the National Science Foundation.

REFERENCES

Barsalou, L. W. (2016). Situated conceptualization: Theory and applications. In
Y. Coello & M. H. Fischer (Eds.), *Foundations of embodied cognition: Perceptual and emotional embodiment* (pp. 11–37). New York, NY: Routledge.

Colella, V. (2000). Participatory simulations: Building collaborative understanding through immersive dynamic modeling. *Journal of the Learning Sciences, 9*(4), 471–500.

Danish, J. A. (2014). Applying an activity theory lens to designing instruction for learning about the structure, behavior, and function of a honeybee system. *Journal of the Learning Sciences, 23*(2), 1–49.

Danish, J. A., Enyedy, N., Saleh, A., Lee, C., & Andrade, A. (2015). *Science through technology enhanced play: Designing to support reflection through play and embodiment.* Paper presented at the Exploring the Material Conditions of Learning: The Computer Supported Collaborative Learning (CSCL) Conference, Gothenburg, Sweden.

Enyedy, N., Danish, J. A., Lee, C. D., DeLiema, D., Saleh, A., Dahn, M., & Illum, R. (2016). *Learning about states of matter through multiple correspondences among the body, abstractions, and reality.* Paper presented at the Annual Meeting of the American Educational Research Association, Washington, DC.

Hall, R., & Stevens, R. (2015). Developing approaches to interaction analysis of knowledge in use. In A. A. diSessa, M. Levin, & N. J. S. Brown (Eds.), *Knowledge and interaction: A synthetic agenda for the learning sciences.* New York, NY: Routledge.

Lindgren, R., & Johnson-Glenberg, M. (2013). Emboldened by embodiment: Six precepts for research on embodied learning and mixed reality. *Educational Researcher, 42*(8), 445–452.

Papert, S. (1980). *Mindstorms: children, computers, and powerful ideas.* New York, NY: Basic Books.

Shapiro, L. (2014). *The Routledge handbook of embodied cognition.* London, UK: Routledge.

Vossoughi, S., Jackson, A., Chen, S., Roldan, W., & Escudé, M. (2020). Embodied pathways and ethical trails: Studying learning in and through relational histories. *Journal of the Learning Sciences*, 1-41. https://doi.org/10.1080/10508406.2019.1693380

Wilensky, U., & Stroup, W. (1999). *Learning through Participatory Simulations: Network-based Design for Systems Learning in Classrooms.* Paper presented at the Computer Support for Collaborative Learning (CSCL) 1999 Conference, Stanford University, Palo Alto, CA.

24 SHAPING LEARNING ONLINE FOR MAKING AND SHARING CHILDREN'S DIY MEDIA

Deborah A. Fields and Sara M. Grimes

A supportive community, or "learning culture" (Kafai, 2006), has always been a key part of constructionism. Papert's (1980) descriptions of "samba schools" as learning cultures highlight in our view of constructionism that a supportive culture is not only about creating but also about sharing. Many of these learning cultures are situated in physical communities such as classrooms, computer clubs, or maker spaces. Increasingly, however, much constructionist work takes place in *virtual* communities, where people with shared interests create things together. One of the first online constructionist spaces was MOOSE Crossing, a text-based virtual world where children enjoyed sharing and receiving assistance and feedback on their projects within the environment, often logging on multiple times a day to update and provide help and encouragement to other members (Bruckman, 2000). Today, many virtual environments for making and sharing one's own do-it-yourself (DIY) media have sprung up, leading to discussions about the necessity of competencies of participation, not just creation, as key attributes of twenty-first century media skills (Kafai & Peppler, 2011).

Although many websites, apps, and digital games now contain tools for users to create and share their own content, few efforts have attended to the design of these sites. This is especially the case with publicly accessible sites where children can participate (Grimes & Fields, 2012). How can virtual spaces support children's creating, sharing, and giving constructive feedback on DIY media they have made? Moreover, how do these spaces contribute to a supportive constructionist culture online? In this chapter we share some of the findings from our multiyear work investigating a broad swath of online kids' DIY media sites as contexts of constructionism, raising key issues about the design of constructionist contexts more broadly. We argue that in studying online contexts of constructionism, we deepen our understanding of best practices and design features that are applicable to all contexts of constructionism.

REVIEWING THE LANDSCAPE OF CHILDREN'S DIY MEDIA

Our work is framed under the *Kids DIY Media Partnership*, which seeks to identify the types of support systems—regulatory, infrastructural, and technical—that most effectively and sustainably foster a rights-based, inclusive, child-centric approach to addressing children's participation online. The partnership includes academics, designers, media producers, child advocates, educators, and non-governmental organizations (NGOs), based in Canada and the United States, with a shared interest in collaborating and sharing knowledge that will contribute to a more nuanced understanding of the opportunities *and* challenges associated with online children's DIY media. As part of this collaboration, multiple phases of research were conducted over a five-year period (2013–2018). Now entering its sixth and final year, the *Kids DIY Media Partnership* is currently finalizing data collection and analysis.

The Importance of Sharing: Media Scan

In the first phase of our project, we sought to understand the landscape of websites available for children to share their DIY media. Through our "media scan" we sought to uncover all publicly accessible websites where children could share media they made, whether it be fanfiction, computer programs, physical media, videos, photos, or others. We looked only at English language sites where children under the age of 13 years were formally allowed to share DIY media. Although we found hundreds of sites for creating DIY media, the majority were eliminated because they failed to provide tools or mechanisms for *sharing* content. A small number of the eliminated sites allowed parents to share their children's work (instead of the children themselves); of those several problematically allowed parents to publish and sell their child's media creations for a profit. Despite the depth and breadth of the search process employed, only 140 websites were identified as meeting the criteria for inclusion in our study. This scarcity of sites raises the issue of the importance of sharing in constructionist spaces. What would it mean if one could create something but never see what others made, never share what one made, or receive feedback on it? Our media scan brings the issue of sharing and audience to the forefront of designing constructionist learning spaces (Grimes & Fields, 2015).

Freedom of Expression: Content Analysis

In the second phase, we conducted a rigorous content analysis of 120 of the sites identified in the media scan (Fields & Grimes, 2018). From the outset, our analysis revealed that children's freedom of expression was not always supported by the design features and user management policies present within children's DIY media websites. For instance, one of our most notable preliminary findings included the discovery that while a significant majority of sites provided tools for on-site sharing (96 percent, n=115)—which made sense given that this was a main criteria for inclusion in our study—68 percent (n=82) directed users to third-party sites such as Facebook as the preferred, and sometimes only, mechanism for sharing content. This was notable since social networking forums such as Facebook do not (officially) allow users under the age of 13 years to join or post content. This has implications for younger children. Even if a site itself appears to allow users to share their DIY content, it may not do so in a way that is actually available to children under 13.

Another aspect of freedom of expression is the ability to network and develop community. Within the sites reviewed, tools that allowed users to comment on others' projects was a common but not universal feature (80 percent, n=95), while rating, "liking," or "favoriting" others' creations was a slightly less common feature (68 percent, n=81). Of course, whenever self-expression is allowed, the issue of moderation comes up. Interestingly, only a fifth of sites (n=23) moderated user content before it was posted. Less than one-third of the sites monitored users' contributions to comment sections, on-site forums, and other communication channels. Peer moderation was more common, with 65 percent of the sites (n=78) asking users to "report" offensive or unacceptable content.

While we found some excellent examples of websites that promoted both making and sharing, provided means for social networking around shared interests, and had thoughtful policies for *children's* participation (i.e., privacy, data collection, and moderation), overall, we found a landscape characterized by spotty and inconsistent technical and social supports for children's DIY media. Tools for socializing, networking, and providing peer support were sparse and limited. There was a distinct lack of identifiable moderation policies found on many sites, raising serious questions about compliance with the US Children's Online Privacy Protection Act (COPPA) and the status of children's privacy, safety and well-being within the DIY media realm.

EXCEPTIONAL(LY GOOD) APPROACHES: CASE STUDIES

To better understand a range of thoughtful design practices, we present seven exceptional DIY media websites that were *different* in their designs and genres. The sites we chose included Scratch, Storybird, Tate Kids, DIY .org, Roblox, Algodoo, and Gamestar Mechanic. These sites were designed and managed for different types of media (coding, picture book writing, fine arts, physical DIY crafts, game design, physics-based simulations, and game development) and for different audiences (young children, older children and teens, intergenerational). First, we studied the background of the sites, reviewing popular and academic writings about the sites, applicable policy regulations (i.e., United States, European government regulations), and their business models (such as nonprofit, for profit, advertising, and purchases). Second, we analyzed the sites themselves, studying the tools and texts included the registration process, guidance for learning (tutorials, help forums), creation tools, sharing and display tools, role of remixing, moderation models, and intellectual property (i.e., who owned user creations, how creators were credited for their work).

Although the selected sites were markedly distinct from one another, several shared attributes or "issues" emerged out of the analysis. Here we will focus on underlying patterns and design trends, narrowing in on those that pertain most to the "user," or "creator,"[1] envisioned here as an abstract category or configuration, not to the specific individuals who use the sites. The themes below highlight some questions to consider and provide specific examples to illustrate some approaches identified as exemplary.

Creator Rights[2]

A key issue within DIY media sites is the rights and responsibilities designers will grant the creator regarding authorship and intellectual property. Who has ownership over the content that creators post? What responsibilities are there over copyright issues (i.e., using popular images, songs, and others in one's creation)? How do these rights and responsibilities change when the creator in question is a minor? What is the role, if any, of the parent or guardian in this process? How will the site inform creators about these rights and regulations?

The websites we studied contained a range of models for managing creator rights and addressing children's unique needs and status when it comes to legal issues such as authorship. One of the most interesting examples in this regard is Scratch.mit.edu because of the explicitly open approach taken on the site. The site uses Creative Commons Share Alike licensing, and explains in lay language to creators that anything they post on the site is under this licensing—in other words, anyone can remix what other creators post. Further, the site explains to creators that they should be careful to credit others and to use Creative Commons licensed work in their projects.

The choice of using lay language is important. Many sites in the larger (phase two) content analysis used highly technical language throughout their terms of service and privacy policies—language that is generally difficult for adults, much more for children to comprehend. Similarly, the choice of making everything available with Creative Commons provisionally resolves some of the deeper issues associated with children's intellectual property rights (or lack thereof). Admittedly, however, this may not be an approach that is available to for-profit sites using proprietary tools.

Creator Leadership

Another design question was what role(s) creators will have on the site. In DIY media sites included in our study, participants obviously share what they create. In most cases creators can comment on and like/favorite/rank others' media. However, other roles are available to creators in some sites, including leadership roles involving participating in the moderation of creator communications and content, providing help and support to other creators, and contributing to content curation.

Moderation is a key challenge in designing social networking forums for or inclusive of children under the age of 13 years. Not only written communication, but shared media (i.e., videos, stories, games) may require moderation, both to ensure COPPA compliance as well as to prevent inappropriate content from appearing on the site. Many sites take on the role of moderation themselves, using chat filters and having specific employees dedicated to screening content and responding to content deemed inappropriate. In some instances this means that user-generated content and comments are not immediately available after they are submitted but must go through a prescreening process, as is the case in Storybird, a site at least partially directed toward young children. To ameliorate the inevitable lag in review of stories and comments, Storybird allows creators to email their illustrated stories to personal contacts, thereby making the DIY creations immediately available to select known others while the creator waits for approval for public sharing. Most of our case studies also provided creators with the opportunity to play a role in content moderation, through the inclusion of designed features such as flagging or reporting "forbidden" content. This provides some ethics instruction to creators, along with the shared responsibility for community management.

Another role creators can play is in providing help to others. Surprisingly, enabling creators to "help" each other is not a universal characteristic of DIY media sites, even among the case studies we chose. Many sites, instead, simply provide their own, official instructions or FAQs, or provide tutorials on tool use. Some sites allow creators to provide help to each other in indirect ways, for instance through forums where creators can post and answer questions on threads (e.g., Algodoo, Scratch). Rarely do the sites go further than this in allowing creators to help each other. The Scratch community is a notable exception. It has a user-created wiki, wherein creators have written articles on anything from information on site management (e.g., how to report problematic content) to more advanced tutorials on tool features (i.e., how to code). Encouraging or even training creators to supply help to each other can make a DIY community more robust, though it also may involve some training for creators with stronger leadership roles.

As sites become popular, and populated by user-made content, the question of curation becomes crucial. How and where is user-generated content visible on a site? Who organizes or highlights content to help others find what they are looking for? In general, the task of curating content is assumed by the site designers themselves and largely manifests through a lens of "most viewed," "popular," or "recent." Sometimes the sites curate projects more carefully, for instance, to stimulate ideas or feature certain types of projects. Other sites actually provide creators with the ability to curate galleries or showcase projects. For instance, Storybird allows creators to repost favorite stories displaying these on the creator's profile. Although very few sites enabled creators to selectively highlight others' content in this way, the examples we found represent an important way of involving creators in meaning-making activities that contribute to fostering a shared cultural experience and sense of community.

Creator Learning

How do new creators learn the tools of media creation in a website? In other words, how do sites help creators learn about making and sharing their DIY media? We identified several models to support learning in our case study sites. One of the simplest models was to instantly allow creators access to creation tools with optional tutorials made available upon registration (e.g., Algodoo, Scratch). Scratch also allows creators to manipulate existing projects without having to join, although no saves are allowed without registering. As mentioned above, creators can also access help in the form of forums. However, several sites provided additional scaffolds or motivations for going deeper.

Two sites used a badge system to encourage creators to learn specific skills. For example, DIY.org provides patches in a range of specific skills such as art, citizenship, app development, even backyard farming. To earn a patch, one must complete three challenges in the same category, submitting proof (picture, video, instructions) of completion. The site provides ample challenges in each category so that creators can pick and choose how to fulfill the requirements of a patch. GameStar Mechanic (GSM) uses a different approach with a built-in curriculum, in which the creators of new games "earn" new elements for game design and community participation (e.g., commenting privileges) by playing the games designed by GSM itself (aka completing an extensive series of quests). The quests introduce creators to different tool features and supply creators with ideas on how particular features can be used before applying them in their own designs. On the other hand, while GSM has a model for clearly introducing features to creators in authentic (game design) ways, it provides a linear path with less room for creative divergence than some other sites. It is a challenge for website designers to develop learning for creators who may not interact with people directly. Developing learning models for DIY use in interest-driven online communities is a key area for continued work.

CONCLUSION

We identified several important areas to consider when building a virtual learning community for children to make and share their own DIY media (or other content), including the role of sharing, the ability to network and interact with others, the necessity of designing for and communicating users' rights over their creations, the relevance of enabling creators to contribute to and lead within a constructionist community, and the need to develop means to support learning. Although these issues arose in the context of online communities, they are just as relevant (if often taken for granted) in physical contexts of constructionism as well. In a class, club, makerspace or similar context, what are the rights, roles, and responsibilities of creators? How is sharing enabled? How can leader support freedom of expression?

Our *Kids DIY Media Partnership* is continuing into the next steps of studying sites for shared constructionist endeavors. One of the avenues we wish to explore is building a better understanding of the implications of legal policies on website design choices; for instance, the specific ways in which website developers work to enable third-party advertisers to access their creators or creators' data, while complying to the Children's Online Privacy Protection Act (COPPA). This is a quickly changing area with regulatory shifts in European Union as well as in the United States affecting website designs. We also have noted that apps on mobile devices are developing greater prominence in promoting sharing and designing creative media. As new technologies shift and develop, we must continue to raise awareness of issues promoting learners' abilities and rights in the contemporary children's media landscape.

ACKNOWLEDGMENTS

This work was supported by a partnership development grant from the Social Sciences and Humanities Research Council of Canada with additional support from the University of Toronto and Utah State University. Special thanks to Katarina Pantic for her participation in analysis.

NOTES

1. Here we shift from discussing website participants as "users" to "creators," since the latter term better expresses the nature of DIY media site participation and the particular rights and roles we are concerned with in the latter part of this chapter. Occasionally, we switch between the terms to provide simplicity of language (e.g., "user-made" or "user-created") or when referring to a commonly accepted term such as "user-generated content."

2. By "creators' rights" we are adopting a more expansive and inclusive variation of the common legal usage of the term "creator/creation," one that seeks to describe the rights of both those who use the tools to produce "original" and "transformative" works as well as those engaged in more mundane, anticipated uses, which may not be transformative in the traditional sense but can nonetheless be meaningful forms of self-expression to the kids who engage in them. In this definition, "creator" applies to both the kid who writes and animates an original screenplay using Scratch and to the kid using corporately controlled user-generated content (UGC) tools and content to customize a Harry Potter fan page.

REFERENCES

Bruckman, A. (2000). Situated support for learning: Storm's weekend with Rachel. *Journal of the Learning Sciences, 9*(3), 329–372.

Fields, D. A., & Grimes, S. M. (2018). Pockets of freedom, but mostly constraints: Emerging trends in children's DIY media platforms. In *Children, Media and Creativity: The International Clearinghouse on Children* (pp. 159–172). Sweden: Nordicom.

Fields, D. A., Kafai, Y. B., & Giang, M. T. (2017). Youth computational participation in the online Scratch community: Problematizing experience and equity in participation and programming. *Transactions of Computing Education, 17*(3), Article 15.

Grimes, S. M., & Fields, D. A. (2012). *Kids online: A new research agenda for understanding social networking forums.* New York: The Joan Ganz Cooney Center at Sesame Workshop. Available online at http://www.joanganzcooneycenter.org/reports-38.html

Grimes, S. M., & Fields, D. A. (2015). Children's media making, but not sharing: The potential and limitations of child-specific DIY media websites for a more inclusive media landscape. *Media International Australia,154,* 112–122.

Kafai, Y. B. (2006). Constructionism. In R. K. Sawyer (Ed.), *The Cambridge handbook of the learning sciences* (pp. 35–46). New York, NY: Cambridge University Press.

Kafai, Y. B., & Peppler, K.A. (2011). Youth, technology, and DIY: Developing participatory competencies in creative media production. *Review of Research in Education, 35,* 89–119.

Papert, S. (1980). *Mindstorms: Children, computers, and powerful ideas.* New York, NY: Basic Books, Inc.

Thornton, C. (2018). Scratch website review. *Common Sense Media.* Retrieved August 11, 2018, at https://www.commonsensemedia.org/website-reviews/scratch

25 REAL-WORLD CONSTRUCTIONISM: HOW VISION PERKS VS. HOW REALITY WORKS

Arnan Sipitakiat

This article suggests that a technology-rich educational movement or intervention tends to go through a "perk curve," consisting of three natural phases: excitement, decline, and long-term realization as shown in figure 25.1. Phase 1 is the initial excitement of an approaching new era driven by the new technological innovation. This vision usually "perks" highly enthusiastic leaders. Phase 2 is when unmet expectations raise questions about the validity of the vision. Phase 3 is the realization that the evolution process is complex and slow. This new perspective sustains subsequent progress over a longer time and at a slower pace.

Papert's vision of Logo and the future of learning have arguably gone through this process. Logo had its heydays in the 1980s when the mood had a "heady atmosphere" and "change was in the air" (Papert, 2005, p. 366). Then debates emerged questioning Papert's pedagogical visions and the possibility for systematic change in education (Pea & Kurland, 1984; Tayak & Cuban, 1995). Although the general excitement about Papert's vision never again reached the same heights as before, there is no doubt that Papert has, over the years, influenced deep changes in education even if, "the time needed is turning out to be a little longer than we imagined and the process more complex" (Papert, 2005, p. 366).

This framework emerged from my 20-year experience working with educational undertakings that have gone through a similar pattern. This paper will examine two major initiatives in Thailand: the Lighthouse project and the Thailand OLPC pilot. Furthermore, in this article, I discuss factors that can facilitate progression through these phases. Understanding this phenomenon can offer beneficial insights for those involved in other educational endeavors.

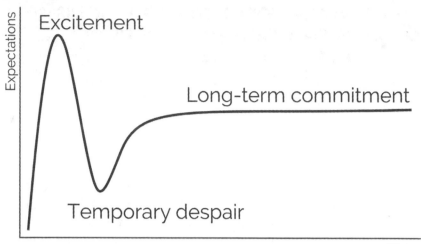

FIGURE 25.1
The perk curve describing a natural progression of technology-rich educational initiatives.

RELATED WORK AND FORMULATION

This formulation of excitement, temporary despair, and long-term commitment is quite common. Such a pattern has been used to describe progression in a large number of situations, ranging from work performance in organizational change to morale in handling a personal crisis as described in Elrod's "death valley of change" (Elrod & Tippett, 2002). Gartner's "Hype Cycle," introduced in 1995, is particularly relevant to the adoption of technology in industries (and perhaps education) (Fenn & Blosch, 2018). It identifies a pattern of relative maturity of an emerging technology entering the public, describing the progression from "overenthusiasm through a period of disillusionment to an eventual understanding of the technology's relevance and role in a market or domain" (Linden & Fenn, 2003, p. 1). They suggest that most technologies conform to the Hype Cycle as a result of people's attitude to technology (not the technology itself).

The Hype Cycle ends at the beginning of the "plateau of enlightenment," when the hype fades and the market realizes the benefits and risks of the technology. During this phase, there is significant adoption, even though the expectations are not as high as in the beginning. This is where educational change is different from the Hype Cycle. Unlike most other fields, education has resisted adoption of novel ideas or technology (at least in their initial ideal form). This work examines this lack of adoption through the lens of "evolution" rather than "reform" as suggested by Papert (1995) in "Why School Reform Is Impossible" (chapter 6 in this volume). Once the core ideas are realized and the inflated expectations are gone, "interventions take the form of influencing processes that have their own dynamic."

An important insight from the perk curve is the recognition that a dip in interest or expectation following a promising start does not necessarily indicate failure. Quite the contrary, the decline is a natural and necessary progression toward a long-term realization of an intervention. There are also cultural and institutional factors that govern the progression through these phases. The following case studies will try to highlight a few.

CASE STUDY I: THE THAILAND LIGHTHOUSE PROJECT

In 1996 a group of Thai MIT alumni started the Suksaphattana (which literally translates to "education development") Foundation with the mission to work with MIT to address fundamental educational challenges in Thailand. Papert was identified as the "educational expert" and the Lighthouse project was established. Lighthouse was a large initiative. Papert formed a working team consisting of MIT Media Lab faculty and graduate students. He also recruited a group of Thai undergraduate students from many MIT departments. In Thailand, pilot sites were established in four areas (Cavallo, 1999): informal education centers that are present in urban areas throughout the country, rural communities, formal schools, and at-risk children centers. Papert arranged workshops to introduce constructionism through projects that involved tools such as Logo programming, electronic magazines, photojournalism, and robotics.

I was first involved with the Lighthouse project when the foundation requested technical support from Chiang Mai University, where I was teaching. I ended up doing more than that. I became part of the facilitating team, helping with translation, collecting feedback, technology setup, and maintenance. Two years later, I was admitted to MIT, with Papert as a co-advisor.

The Lighthouse project's progression through the initial stage took about three years. Expectations from the Suksaphattana Foundation were high. Led by two top managers from the industry sector, the foundation moved forward aggressively and passionately. Expanding to a national scale was supposed to be just over the horizon. Papert was highly committed to this project. At least three academic staff and more than ten graduate students from MIT were involved in various five- to ten-day-long workshops conducted at the pilot sites throughout the country. The foundation offered computer labs to participating schools and learning centers, including a large and well-equipped "constructionism lab" that was established at a community center in Lampang province.

After three years, however, the reality and complexity of the project became apparent. In the late 1990s, constructionist principles such as project-based, learner-centered, computationally rich learning were still unknown in most Thai schools. All of the initial schools dropped out of the program. Management changes at community centers left few people championing and enacting the work. The constructionism lab in Lampang operated longer but eventually shut down as well. The village program shrunk with only one family continuing the practices in Buriram province. Funding for the MIT operations dried up and the flow of MIT personnel stopped, leaving only a small team. The continuation of the project relied entirely on the Thai foundation.

Although the period was clearly a steep decline, it also marked the beginning of Thailand's own interpretation and implementation of constructionism that has continued ever since. One remarkable outcome of the initial phase was that there were a number of people who "fell in love" with and became advocates of constructionism. Mr. Paron, the leader of the Lighthouse project, was one of them, and he has been a critical factor for the project's continuation. Mr. Paron, a former CEO of Thailand's largest business conglomerate, is an influential person in Thailand. He has the needed connections to raise funding, and his passion has inspired others to follow suit. Learning from direct experience how rigid schools were, Mr. Paron established Darunsikkhalai School for Innovative Learning (DSIL), a new constructionist-from-the-ground-up school in Bangkok. Since DSIL's founding in 1999, the school has experimented with and developed its own interpretation of constructionism (Isarasena, Tutiyaphuengprasert, & Sipitakiat, 2012) with little input from Papert and the MIT team.

Although the constructionism lab at the community center in Lampang was never revived, the former director, Dr. Suchin, started a new project at Ban Samkha, a rural village near Lampang. Dr. Suchin met the community leaders during one of the workshops held while the constructionism lab was still in operation. Constructionism's focus on pursuing personally meaningful projects was interpreted there as a means to identify and solve community problems. The community development work at Ban Samkha received attention from the public, and the village welcomes a constant stream of visitors curious to learn about their practices. In 2012 the foundation raised funding to build a "constructionist learning lab" next to the school open to use by students, villagers, and visitors.

Although the initial village program in Buriram had only one active villager left, that was enough to start a second round of development. Na Noi first became involved with the Lighthouse project as a farmer plagued with debt problems. She was impressed by how the Suksaphattana Foundation invested time and attention to help her community and was inspired to transform herself from farmer to community leader. Over the years, she has led community projects that have greatly improved the community's livelihood. In 2011 she received an award for her work in community water management and accepted a trophy from the king of Thailand. There is now a computer lab built next to her home, where she continues to work with adults and youth in the community.

CASE STUDY II: ONE LAPTOP PER CHILD PILOT IN THAILAND

When Thailand was introduced to the One Laptop per Child (OLPC) project in 2006, laptop computers were still a luxury item not commonly owned by school-aged learners. The idea of giving every child his or her own laptop computer was exhilarating, especially when the device was promised to cost just $100. When the Suksaphattana Foundation received almost five hundred pre-production prototypes for field-testing, it made news and the public was excited.

Ban Samkha School, located in a small rural village of northern Thailand, received 31 OLPC laptops. Students kept the laptops and took the machines home. The whole village became aware and curious about this little device. I was a primary investigator of a research project funded by Thailand's Office of the Education Council to evaluate how well OLPC worked in the pilot sites. The data collection process took place during the initial year (2008–2009). Several projects emerged that demonstrated how empowering the laptops can be (Sipitakiat, 2010). For example, there was the "OLPC band," in which students played music on the laptop keyboard together with a traditional Thai band. Students helped their parents log their income and expenses in a spreadsheet as part of the village's household accounting project.

Although these examples were exciting, upon looking back, a more complete picture emerges. Following the initial year, the Ban Samkha initiative went through a decline because of a number of concerns. For example, parents worried about students using the machines mainly for pleasure (playing games, web browsing) rather than for constructive work. There were issues with inappropriate content on the internet. Machines were stolen and parents were concerned about being accountable. Although these were isolated cases, these concerns tempered much of the initial excitement. When some machines started to wear out and required maintenance (which was difficult with OLPC), the burden fell to the teachers.

Despite the decline in enthusiasm, the project continued for at least two more years until the majority of machines broke. Since the formal research pilot had ended, the school was relieved from the requirement of creating good use cases. Thus, the use of OLPC was driven by its own merit and, in the case of Ban Samkha, was community driven. This practice served as a fertile foundation for OLPC to become part of empowering learning experiences. For example, media recording, a new ubiquitous activity, was one popular use of OLPC long before the widespread use of smartphones. When students used OLPC to take pictures of birds that migrated through the village, the goal was not only to study the birds as a class activity but also to encourage parents not to hunt the birds. Although the school had tried a similar project before with regular cameras, OLPC scaled it up to a level that had a larger impact.

Another pilot site, however, did not recover from the decline phase. Ban Sankhumpang School, a much larger pilot site located in the outskirts of the country's second largest city, received 150 OLPC laptops. The school distributed the machines to every student in six classrooms. I facilitated this pilot by bringing a team of students from Chiang Mai University to help with both the technical and pedagogical aspects of the project. I conducted workshops and also spent half a day each week offering consultation during the pilot's first four months. During that time, the overall atmosphere was filled with excitement. Selected classrooms felt privileged. Students from other classes who did not get laptops would peer through the windows to see what we were doing.

However, the project hit rock bottom during the second year when some classrooms decided that the laptops were a distraction and allowed them to be used only during break time or for projects in specific classes. In the second and third year, the laptops remained in use but the vision of transforming learning through digital fluency and computation was mostly watered down to performing simple web searches and writing reports. For the most part, what happened at Ban Sankhumpang is an example of how schools "assimilated" the new into the old without much overall change (Papert, 1995).

There was an exception to this story. One fifth-grade teacher discovered Scratch programming on the OLPC laptop. She became passionate about encouraging every student in her class to create their own Scratch programs. Her students made projects that won regional and national competitions. After three years, she was the sole active user of the OLPC laptops. She became nervous when the machines started failing over time, worrying that she would not be able to continue her one-device-per-learner approach. Because of her outstanding achievements, the school allowed her to conduct classes at the school's computer lab. The lab eventually became her exclusive classroom and was renamed the "constructionism lab." Although the excitement of the OLPC initiative had faded, the passion of one teacher kept the learning philosophy alive (although confined to only one classroom) beyond the lifetime of OLPC.

CONCLUSIONS

The two case studies presented above are representational examples from my experience. The validity of the following conclusions is based on the shared similarities with patterns observed in other fields (e.g., Gartner's Hype Cycle), despite a number of characteristics unique to education. The recognition of a perk curve offers the following insights:

- Educational interventions, especially ones that involve an emerging technology, often progress through an initial excitement phase followed by a decline. This behavior can then trigger a long-term evolutional process in which the initial vision develops in diverse and unforeseen ways.

- Educators should be cautious not to become overly excited about an emerging trend but also should not dismiss an innovation just because it is losing interest.

- The recovery and long-term realization of an intervention depends on at least three factors: the value and relevancy of the tool or approach itself, the sociocultural settings where the intervention takes place, and the institutional support received.

- Individuals can, and most often do, have a significant impact on the long-term evolution process despite the surrounding factors.

The lessons learned may not be universal, but I hope that they provide valid insights for researchers and educators who find themselves involved in educational initiatives that bear resemblance to this suggested pattern.

I will conclude by adding to Papert's vision that the eventual impact of an educational intervention on schools, communities, or other complex organizations cannot be planned. Just as curriculum can only guarantee what is taught but cannot govern what a child actually learns, one can never be certain about how an educational initiative will be taken up. It is

up to the people involved (including teachers, students, parents, administrators) to discover for themselves what works or does not work under their
circumstances and to eventually construct their own meaning of the intervention. As Papert puts it, "Complex systems are not made. They evolve"
(Papert 1995, p. 425).

REFERENCES

Cavallo, D. (1999). *Project Lighthouse in Thailand: Guiding pathways to powerful learning.* Retrieved from http://www.microworlds.com/support/logo-philosophy-thailand
.html

Elrod, P. D., & Tippett, D. D. (2002). The "death valley" of change. *Journal of Organizational Change Management, 15*(3), 273–291.

Fenn, J., &, Blosch, M. (2018, August 20). *Understanding Gartner's hype cycles.* Gartner.
Retrieved   from   https://www.gartner.com/en/documents/3887767/understanding
-gartner-s-hype-cycles

Isarasena, P., Tutiyaphuengprasert, N., & Sipitakiat, A. (2012). Growing under pressure: A Thai school learning how to prosper while being different. *Proceedings of Constructionism 2012,* Athens, Greece (pp. 610–614).

Linden, A., & Fenn, J. (2003). *Understanding Gartner's hype cycles. Strategic Analysis
Report N° R-20–1971.* Gartner, Inc.

Papert, S. (1995). Why school reform is impossible. *The Journal of the Learning Sciences, 6*(4), 417–427.

Papert, S. (2005). You can't think about thinking without thinking about thinking about something. *Contemporary Issues in Technology and Teacher Education, 5*(3),
366–367.

Pea, R. D., & Kurland, D. M. (1984). On the cognitive effects of learning computer
programming. *New Ideas in Psychology, 2*(2), 137–168.

Sipitakiat, A. (2010, June). Moving towards learning with one-to-one laptop: A longitudinal case study on tools, people, and institutions. *Proceedings of the 9th International Conference of the Learning Sciences. 2,* International Society of the Learning
Sciences, Chicago, IL (pp. 328–329).

Tayak, D., & Cuban, L. (1995). *Tinkering toward utopia: a century of public school reform.*
Cambridge, MA: Harvard University Press.

IV   DEVELOPING THE CREATIVE

Creativity has been a focus of constructionist design since its earliest days. The goal of the constructionist is often to support learners in creative expression and exploration, to make, code, or build something compelling and new (to the learner, at least). However, constructionists themselves also engage in a creative process of construction, designing and building learner environments, tools, and technologies with which learners will construct. In section IV authors examine how does this construction process support the building and refinement of knowledge structures and describe techniques to create experiences that support diverse learners in encountering and deeply exploring the wide range of ideas in which they might be interested.

Section IV opens with a reprint of Ackermann's "Experiences of Artifacts: People's Appropriations/Objects' 'Affordances.'" In chapter 26, Ackermann examines the "radical" implications of Piaget's constructivism—that we all co-construct our understanding of the world with and through objects and artifacts. As designers, we must engage in the construction process carefully and thoughtfully, aware that construction is a conversation with the object and that any future users will have their own conversations. In chapter 27, "Restructuration Theory and Agent-Based Modeling: Reformulating Knowledge Domains through Computational Representations," Wilensky examines the ways in which representations support and transform our thinking. In this chapter Wilensky encourages the learning sciences and constructionist communities to design and study restructurations—representational systems that fundamentally transform the cognitive infrastructure of conceptual domains. Such representational systems dramatically change the practice and activity of domain experts as well as democratize access to topics and domains previously thought too complex for young people and other novices.

Kafai and Jayathirtha continue this exploration in chapter 28 by examining how tangible construction objects can become "objects-to-think-with." In "Hi-Lo Tech Crafting: Tinkering with Textiles, Paper, and Everything Else," the authors describe a modern revision of Fröbel's gifts—"low-tech," making materials such as paper and textiles, enhanced with "high-tech" microcontrollers, sensors, and actuators. Chapter 29 examines the relationship between the body and representational systems. Focusing on the design of bodily and culturally syntonic representations in embodiment theory, in "Syntonicity and Emergence: A Design-Based Research Reflection on the Piagetian Roots of Constructionism," Abrahamson and Chase model learning in a middle-school mathematics model-based activity as an emerging cluster of inter-constraining schemes, proposing "reverse scaffolding" as a mechanism to support this embodied construction process.

But representations have a role to play beyond the cognitive. Chapter 30, Sheridan's "Constructionism in Art Studios," highlights the centrality of representations in both the visual and media arts and constructionist experiences. This alignment suggests constructionist designers can learn a lot from arts education and the studio model. Providing an overview of theories on creativity in chapter 31, "Creativity as Sustained Social Practices: Four Pillars for Creative Learning Design," Zhang situates creativity as sustained social practice. He argues that learning designs to support creative practices need to approach these elements in a way that enhances student epistemic agency for co-organizing their journey of creative inquiry.

Section IV closes with two chapters focused on how educators can design learner environments to support the creative exploration of a host of curricular topics. In chapter 32, "Sailing in Open Waters: Choosing, Charting, and Navigating Constructionist Learning Experiences," Svihla and Kubik describe the importance of including teachers as constructionist learners. The authors argue that as teachers may only have past instructionist experiences to draw from, it's important to provide them with their own constructionist experience so that they will be better prepared to design and support such experiences in their classrooms. Finally, while many constructionists have proposed inviting young people to build games, in chapter 33, "Constructionist Learning Games in School," Klopfer, Anderson, and Perry propose that under the right classroom conditions the playing of some games may offer equally interesting constructionist experiences.

26 EXPERIENCES OF ARTIFACTS: PEOPLE'S APPROPRIATIONS/OBJECTS' "AFFORDANCES"

Edith K. Ackermann

To a constructivist, knowledge is not a mere commodity to be transmitted—emitted at one end, encoded, stored, and reapplied at the other—nor is it information, sitting "out there" and waiting to be uncovered. Instead, knowledge is (derived from) experience, and actively constructed and reconstructed by subjects in interaction with their worlds. In Piaget's words (1937), "Intelligence organizes the world by organizing itself" (p. 311). In Ernst von Glasersfeld's terms: "The world we live in … is always and necessarily the world as we conceptualize it" (2007, p. 7).

One of the implications of adopting a constructivist stance is the idea, dear to radical constructivists, that "reality" as we know it "lies forever beyond our experiential field" (von Glasersfeld, 2007, p. 5) and that "knowledge does not [and cannot] represent a [true] picture of the 'real' world but provides structure and organization to experience" (ibid., p. 6). In other words, "What determines the value of conceptual structures is their experiential adequacy, their goodness of fit with experience, their viability as means for the solving of problems—among which is, of course, the never-ending problem of consistent organization that we call understanding" (ibid., pp. 6–7).

A second implication is a strong call to abandon the *conduit metaphor* of human communication for what Reddy refers to as the *tool-maker's paradigm* (Reddy, 1993). At the core of the *conduit metaphor* lays the deeply rooted notion that meaning resides in words, and that words are carriers of meaning (containers), to be conveyed (like on a conveyer belt) between speakers and listeners. The *tool-maker's paradigm*, by contrast, emphasizes that meaning does not reside in words, texts, or artifacts. Instead, "it is subjective in origin and resides in a subject's head, not in the word which, because of an association, has the power to call up, in each of us, our own subjective representation" (von Glasersfeld, 2007, p. 8).[1]

In my tribute to Ernst von Glasersfeld, I wish to address some of the paradoxes that arise if one adopts a non-critical radical constructivist stance to account for creative people's interactions with—and through—(hu)man-made artifacts, in particular as they engage in the process of "world-making," to use Goodman's expression (1978), or designing in a broad sense.

CONSTRUCTIVISM AND THE PRACTICE OF DESIGN

Designing (*projettare* in Italian) can be seen as the flipside of reflective abstraction: an iterative process of mindful concretization, or materialization of ideas (*concrétisation réfléchie* in French).[2] To design is to give form, or expression, to inner feelings and ideas, thus projecting them outwards, making them tangible.

In the practice of design, the purpose is not to represent what is out there (or model how things are) but to imagine what is not (or envision how things could be) and to bring into existence what is imagined. Creators are fabricators of possibilities embodied: They both make and make up things! Important here is the notion that a designer's projections emerge through a conversation with—and through—their own and other people's externalizations. The nature and quality of this conversation are a key to all forms of learning, and paramount to intelligence itself. In Schön's terms, learning is designing, and designing is a conversation with—and through—artifacts (Schön, 1983, p. 76).

In what follows, I explore why treating our own externalizations *as-if* they had an existence, beyond our immediate rapports with them, is a viable mental attribution—even if we know that we cannot know their whereabouts. In substance, expecting our creations to have integrity (lending them autonomy, permanence, identity) while remaining mindful of their qualities (letting them "speak" and celebrating them for what they are, at the risk of overinterpreting) are two facets of cognitive adaptation, as defined by Piaget.[3] Their function is to elevate human transactions (between me/not me) beyond blind projections, or assimilation pure, with its unfortunate consequence: reducing anything that is other to a mirror-of-me (over assimilation).

As Ernst von Glasersfeld remarks, Vico saw long ago that

> facts are made by us and our way of experiencing, rather than given by an independently existing objective world. But that does not mean that we can make them as we like. They are viable facts as long they do not clash with experience, as long as they remain tenable in the sense that they continue to do what we expect them to do (2007, p. 7).

Along with Piaget, I think that attributing, or projecting, meaning in the objects of our experience is a pillar of cognitive adaptation.[4] In contrast to Piaget, I put more emphasis on the accommodative pole of human adaptation—which does not come without complications within a constructivist framework.[5]

I explore some of the pragmatic, ecological, and epistemological consequences that arise if one opens this Pandora box. I wonder in particular: (1) How can designers take responsibility for the qualities of their creations if they assume—I caricature the constructivist stance—that people will use them as Rorschach stains anyway? (2) Beyond setting limits to our actions and/or clash with our expectations, what qualities does it take for an artifact be able to call up, in each of us, our own subjective representation?

PEOPLE AS WORLD-MAKERS AND WORLD READERS

People Are "World-Makers"
People spend a great deal of their time carving out their niches—virtual and physical—so that they fit their needs, support their purposes, and augment their potential. They build cities, homes, and furniture, they invent computers and airplanes, and they create alphabets, geometries, and musical scores. Young and old, they give form or expression to their ideas. People are also busy keeping track of their experience and leaving traces behind. They mark their grounds to find their ways, and they use the marks they leave behind as anchors to orient themselves. Newcomers to a culture are left to live with the marks traced by others.

Early on, children learn to set the stages and to build the props, which enable them to best explore, enact, and ultimately work through many intriguing or captivating events. As they reach their second birthday (with the apparition of the symbolic function), most children engage in pretend or fantasy play. As they recast their experience on a make believe-ground (do as if), young pretenders bring their feelings and ideas to life and, by the same token, make their dreams come true. This act of projection enables them to revisit personal experience *as if* it was not theirs, and, through this act of distancing, engage in a dialogue that brings about greater intimacy and deeper understanding.

People Are "World-Readers"
People "read" meaning into existing forms, be they their own or those produced by others, and they do so in creative ways. Readers, in other words,

are in no way passive consumers. Instead, they engage designed artifacts by reconstructing them through the lens of their interests and experience.

In the same way that designers are readers (they constantly re-edit their drafts), readers are constructors. As Bordwell mentions about film audiences, "The artwork sets limits on what the spectator does. But within these limits, the viewer literally *recasts the play*" (Bordwell, 1985, p. 30). Viewers impose their order upon things by rearranging or replacing clues, by filling in blanks or "creating phantoms," by ignoring clues, and by forcing causal-temporal connections. In Piaget's words, world-readers assimilate incoming signals (in this case, a narrative unfolding) to feed their views (they interpret them through the lens of previously reconstructed experience), and they accommodate their views only in so far as some unexpected puzzlements or surprises are called upon by the materials.

ARTIFACTS AS INTERLOCUTORS

Artifacts Set Limits to People's Reconstructions

They do so by opening up greater or lesser mental elbowroom (*spielraum* in German) for personal interpretation. Indeed, to suggest that readers *recast the plot* does not entail that they do so from scratch. Instead, people compose with what is offered by the materials—one may say with what the materials evoke—to improvise their part.

For a text, like any other artifact, to capture our imagination, it has to embark us in a journey filled with wonders and surprises. At the same time, it needs to provide the right balance of freedom and structure to allow for personal reconstruction. A setting that gives out all its secrets before you even start wondering is disengaging because it excludes you as a partner. A setting that offers no resistance at all is disengaging because it is predictable (too malleable, it mirrors). Both will not have much evocative, or holding power. Objects (*gegenstände* in German) stand against our tendency to blindly assimilate them.

Learning as a Conversation with Artifacts

People learn by switching roles from being producers to being critics, from being actors to being audiences, from holding the stage to moving into the background. People also zone in and out of situations to change their stance. In other words, no matter how embedded we are in a situation, there comes a time when we distance ourselves to look at things from afar. Putting on a critic's hat and shifting perspectives enable us to engage our own creations *as if* they had been produced by "another" or existed independently, and then, re-engage them again (Ackermann, 1996).

As designers converse with their externalizations, they usually start a dialogue with a whole range of interlocutors, imaginary or "real," to whom they address their work and from whom they borrow, or draw inspiration (Valéry, 1940). As soon as an idea takes shape, or form, it gains both a physical and a social existence (Habraken, 1985). It is not exaggerated to say that while interacting with the world, a creator's mind moves both in and out of its own expressions (from production to critic), and back and forth from itself (to include viewpoints of others).

MINDS ENGAGE FORMS AND FORMS ENGAGE MINDS: RADICAL CONSTRUCTIVISM IN QUESTION

Strengths

Radical constructivism offers a solid framework to discuss how meaning is constructed and interpreted through form.

Based on the assumption that any organism, to be viable, needs to carve a niche within a world too big to ensure anyone's survival, radical constructivists remind us that if the world appears to us as we see it, it is not because it is made that way, but because we are made the way we are (Watzlawick, 1984)! In other words, reality takes on unrecognizable facets when captured through the prisms of different creatures. Conversely, what we think of as "shared realities" feels shared because they are produced and recognized by minds of a similar kind.

Ernst von Glasersfeld makes a compelling case for why taken-for-shared stabilities are not true to reality but akin to the organism's survival and growth. Early on, human infants make sense of their experience by building *stabilities* in the world. These stabilities, or cognitive invariants, as Piaget refers to them, are constructs of the mind. Object permanency, conservation of object-size, and the creation of a coordinate system to situate objects and movements in space are examples of cognitive invariants built by humans in interaction with their world. Creating invariants is a needed self-orienting device invented by intelligent organisms to find their ways or survive (Ackermann, 2004).

Limitations

While offering a solid framework to discuss how meaning is constructed and interpreted through form, radical constructivism leaves partially unanswered the question of how forms engage minds. At the cost of caricaturing, let me put it this way: fellow constructivists seem to ignore that, once launched, an artifact takes on a life of its own, thus transcending both the author's intentions and any singular act of interpretation.

As fellow humans, we share (or think we share) enough common ground that we sometimes forget that "what we know depends on how we came to know it!" (Watzlawick, 1984, p. 9). We then act *as if* our invented realities had always been there and we rely on them—and refer to them—as tangible and shareable entities (objects to think with, and relate through).

In other words, as they interact with people and things, intelligent beings tend to exaggerate both what they have in common and how stable our world is. While this amnesia is a problem to constructivists, it is also a viable strategy when it comes to designing artifacts for others to live or learn in: Lending autonomy and existence, we posit, sharpens our sensitivity to—and respect of—their qualities, independent of their author's intentions and our immediate relation with them.

EVOCATIVE POWER OF (HU)MAN-MADE ARTIFACTS

Objects' Affordances

Don Norman (1988) introduced the term "affordance" to refer to an object's ability to signal its potential uses. Borrowing from Gibson, he used the word to gauge the qualities of everyday object. To Norman, a poorly designed object is one that fails to signal its built-in affordances. As an example, a lamp that does not tell you how to switch it on, a doorknob that remains ambiguous as to whether it wants to be pushed or pulled, or a panhandle that confuses you: "hold me/do not hold me" (i.e., I burn you if you do, I let you down if you do not).

The concept of affordance, while limited to uses, provides a first step toward understanding how forms engage minds. It highlights that indeed human-made artifacts signal potential usages through their built-in features, or embedded qualities.

Genius Loci!

In *Poetics of Space*, the French philosopher Gaston Bachelard further explores why humans can be deeply moved by what he calls *felicitous* objects or places, and why felicitous objects and places can, in turn, be said to *reverberate* atmospheres, or ambiances, in ways that capture human imagination (Bachelard, 1964). To Bachelard, felicitous objects and spaces (things able to transport us) cannot and should not be characterized by functionality alone. Instead, they attract us because they have become topographies of our intimate being. As such, they "speak a language" that enters in resonance with felt human aspirations.

Even a doorknob, to take a previous example, could become a felicitous object if it did not just call up our urge to "push or pull to enter." It too could retain our attention, suspend our breath and, why not, slow down our steps, by conveying something that speaks to, or evokes, our experience of passage between places. Everyday objects could speak a language much more intangible and rich, in resonance with our being and aspirations. Ideally, designers could endow objects with the ability to speak such language.

To take a less trivial example, think of the differences between different types of shutters, such as a persienne, a vénitienne, and a jalousie. All are shutters, yet each calls upon different feelings along the continuums of seeing being/seen, privacy/public, light and darkness. My European friends usually prefer French windows to American guillotines not just because windows can be cleaned and shutters keep light and thieves out, but because the opening of both windows and shutters are along a vertical axe (left and right from the center), allowing arm movements that enter in syntony with breathing in and out, which procures a sense of delight as one opens or closes, letting light and air in.

Bachelard offers important insights into what it takes for (hu)man-made artifacts to enter in syntony with our needs as sensory-motor creatures (smooth to our senses), to tackle our expectations as rational beings (functional), and to "speak to" our aspirations as artists and poets (poetics). He explores the phenomenological touchpoints between people's experiences of intimate things, and the thing's capacity to inspire and "transport" people.

TO CONCLUDE

Constructivism, especially in its radical form, emerges from the growing awareness that any so-called reality is—in the most immediate and concrete sense—the construction of those who believe they have discovered and investigated it. What is supposedly found is an invention whose inventor is unaware of his act of invention, who considers it as something that exists independently of him; the invention then becomes the basis of his world view and actions. (Watzlawick, 1984, p. 10)

This being said, not all "constructed realities" are equally engaging, as partners or habitats. Some feel delightful while others leave us cold. Some please most of us, while others attract only a few.

Like a good conversationalist, a well-designed object is one that "knows" how many surprises and wonders contribute to capture people's imagination. Like a narrative text, it offers "a dynamic system of competing and mutually blocking retardatory pattern" (Sternberg, 1978, p. 177). In Shklovsky's words, "a narrative text is less like an elevator than a spiral staircase which, littered with toys, dog leashes, and open umbrellas, impedes our progress" (quoted by Bordwell, 1985, p. 38).

From a pragmatic-ecological standpoint, it seems essential for designers of human-made artifacts (from educational software to playgrounds and books) to take responsibility for their products by not assuming—I caricature the constructivist's stance—that learners will use them as Rorschach stains anyway (projective test). Designers need to acknowledge that their products will survive after them, and that it is ultimately the built artifact, rather than the builder's intentions, that becomes part of other people's cultural heritage. It is "its" qualities that will persist to evoke or signal potential uses to newcomers who encounter them for the first time. Denying the power of places and things to impact people can bread a culture of "not caring."

Surely, designers cannot predict how their creations will be appropriated. What designers can, however, do is be attentive to the idea that, once conceived, their creations are no longer a mere extension of themselves. Instead, they come to exist as separate entities. They gain both autonomy and an identity as "invented realities," an integral part of the cultural landscape in which other newcomers will live and grow.

People read into artifacts because of who they are, and because artifacts offer clues. Like archeological sites or eroded landscapes, they are marked by their history, and they embody the knowledge or collective experience that went into their being (both reflecting and transcending builders' and readers' intents and aspirations). The constructivist's nightmare may well come true! Yes, human-made artifacts can call upon certain experiences and uses, and discourage others. And they sometime impose their logic, or constraints, beyond the builder's intents and any particular act of interpretation.

From an epistemological standpoint, it seems equally important for learning researchers and educators to rethink the role of accommodation in cognitive adaptation. To Piaget, we have seen, intelligence is adaptation, and adaptation is the ability to maintain the maximum of what is acquired while opening up to the maximum of novelty. Adaptation, in other words, calls for a balance between openness and closure, assimilation and accommodation.

In Piaget's own words, "Assimilation is by its very nature conservative, in the sense that its primary function is to make the unfamiliar familiar, to reduce the new to the old" (Piaget, 1954, pp. 352–353). Accommodation, by contrast, shakes and decrystallizes existing schemes so that they fit to the demands of the environment. Its primary function is to make what is familiar unfamiliar again, and to question the old by listening to the new.

Circular reaction was a term introduced by Baldwin, and used by Piaget, to refer to infants' ability to modify their activity in relation to an unexpected effect and actively reproduce some interesting events, which were at first discovered by chance. The concept of circular reaction is a concept of major importance to psychologists. According to Flavell, the principle's value "lies in the fact that it is the device *par excellence* for making new adaptations, and of course new adaptations are the heart and soul of intellectual development at any stage" (Flavell, 1963, p. 93).

Radical constructivism, I suggest, gives more weight to the assimilatory role of human adaptation. While this is an important contribution, especially in an intellectual climate mostly dominated by inneist or empiricist views, it is useful to remember that an organism that solely assimilates is not viable. Such an organism fails because it is insensitive to variations in the environment that may help it adjust its conceptual structures. Such an organism closes up to surface perturbations for "blindness" to others and inconsideration for odds. Conversely, an organism that solely accommodates is at risk of disrupting its own momentary equilibrium, for an excess of openness to external solicitations. An act in which assimilation and accommodation are in balance constitutes a truly adapted act!

ACKNOWLEDGMENTS

I thank Ernst von Glasersfeld for having given me an opportunity to write this essay, in response to his forthcoming book. Ernst has always been a mentor to me, and over the years, he has become a colleague and dear friend. I also wish to thank Marie Larochelle for her insightful comments on my draft and for the work she put into finalizing the text. It would be wonderful to have a conversation with both Marie and Ernst over a cup of tea!

NOTES

1. The tool-maker's paradigm, according to Reddy (1993), is a far better candidate than the "conduit" metaphor to understand how meaning is built and read into form. Words are not like little wagons, which transport meaning back and forth between a sender and a receiver (who load and unload them at each end). They are more like a misty landscape, or an obscure blueprint, the contents and textures of which are filled in by the interlocutors. The tool-maker's paradigm further suggests that people's minds are like secret gardens surrounded by big walls. In each garden,

the terrain and resources available are partially shared and partly unique. Inhabitants communicate among themselves by exchanging notes (blueprints, questions, suggestions), which they annotate and reedit to come to closer understanding.

2 The term "concrétisation réfléchie" was coined by G. Céllerier (1992), who noted that Piaget had given it less thought than to "abstraction réfléchissante."

3. To Piaget, human cognition derives from biological adaptation, yet biological adaptation is not sufficient to define human cognition. Psychological adaptation allows infants to modify their own internal states, to enlarge their field of experience, and to construct an increasingly sophisticated set of strategies to deal with ever more complex situations. Psychological adaptation implies the organism's ability to expand its activity over greater and greater distance—in space and time—and over more and more complex detours.

4. Piaget broke down the biological notion of assimilation into 3 distinct forms. (1) *Reproductive assimilation* asserts that when an organism has a structure available, there is a tendency to exercise it. Its adaptive advantage is to consolidate activity through repetition. The need that triggers the behaviour is the very consolidation of the scheme itself, rather than any external stimuli. (2) *Generalizing assimilation* asserts that when an organism has a structure available, there is a tendency to exercise it in all sorts of different situations. Its adaptive advantage is to expand the experiential field. And (3) *Recognitory assimilation* asserts that when an organism has a structure available, there is a tendency to incorporate the objects acted upon into the structure of the scheme. In other words, an object that has been sucked and/or touched and/ or seen is recognized as a "thing" to suck and/or to touch and/or to see. The adaptive advantage of recognitory assimilation is attribution of meaning in a very primitive sense: objects can be "tagged" by use, and "gauged" according to how they fit or resist usages. The "thing to" gains both permanency and identifying features as a result of its consistent answers to given interventions.

5. Accommodation is the adaptive principle complementary to assimilation. It accounts for the adjustments of a scheme necessary to ensure effectively the success of an action. A baby who sees the bottle and wants to reach it has to learn how to do so if the bottle is presented in a slightly different position. The adjustments necessary to succeed, despite variations in the context, are referred to as accommodation. The overall function of accommodation is to provide the baby with the possibility to adjust her/his pre-existing schemes so that they fit to the demands of the environment.

REFERENCES

Ackermann, E. (1996). Perspective-taking and object construction: Two keys to learning. In J. Kafai & M. Resnick (Eds.), *Constructionism in practice: Designing, thinking, and learning in a digital world* (pp. 25–37). Mahwah, NJ: Lawrence Erlbaum.

Ackermann, E. (2004). Constructing knowledge and transforming the world. In M. Tokoro & L. Steels (Eds.), *A learning zone of one's own: Sharing representations and flow in collaborative learning* (pp. 15–37). Amsterdam, The Netherlands: IOS Press.

Céllerier, G. (1992). Organisation et fonctionnement des schèmes. In B. Inhelder, G. Céllerier, E. Ackermann, A. Blanchet, A. Boder, D. Caprona, J.-J. Ducret, & M. Saada-Robert (Eds.), *Le cheminement des découvertes chez l'enfant* (pp. 255–319). Neuchatel: Delachaux et Niestlé.

Bachelard, G. (1964/1994). *The poetics of space. The classic look at how we experience intimate places* (M. Jolas, Trans.) (2nd ed.). Boston, MA: Beacon Press.

Bordwell, D. (1985). The viewer's activity. In *Narration in the fiction film* (pp. 29–62). Madison, WI: University of Wisconsin Press.

Flavell, J. (1963). *The developmental psychology of Jean Piaget.* Princeton, NJ: D. Van Nostrand.

Goodman, N. (1978). *Ways of worldmaking.* Indianapolis, IN: Hackett.

Habraken, J. (1985). *The appearance of form.* Cambridge, MA: Awater Press.

Norman, D. (1988). *The design of everyday things.* New York, NY: Doubleday Currency Editions.

Piaget, J. (1937/1973). *La construction du réel chez l'enfant* (5th ed.). Neuchâtel: Delachaux et Niestlé.

Piaget, J. (1954). *The origins of intelligence in children* (M. Cook, Trans.). New York, NY: International Universities Press.

Reddy, M. (1993). The conduit metaphor. A case of frame conflict in our language about language. In A. Ortony (Ed.), *Metaphor and thought* (pp. 284–324). Cambridge, MA: Cambridge University.

Schön, D. (1983). *The Reflective practitioner: How professionals think in action.* New York, NY: Basic Books.

Sternberg, M. (1978). *Expositional modes and temporary ordering in fiction.* Baltimore, MD: John Hopkins University Press.

Valéry, P. (1940). The course in poetics: First lesson. *Southern Review, 5*(3), pp. 92–107.

von Glasersfeld, E. (2007). *Key works in radical constructivism* (M. Larochelle, Ed.) (pp. 249–259). Rotterdam, The Netherlands: Sense Publishers.

Watzlawick, P. (1984). The invented reality. New York, NY: Norton.

27 RESTRUCTURATION THEORY AND AGENT-BASED MODELING: REFORMULATING KNOWLEDGE DOMAINS THROUGH COMPUTATIONAL REPRESENTATIONS

Uri Wilensky

The theory of restructurations, how knowledge domains can be transformed by using different representational infrastructure, was developed by Papert and myself, in the 1990s, and further emerged in conversation with a number of scholars (including DiSessa, Hoyles, Noss, Turkle, Sherin, and Kay) engaged with thinking about how computational representations can affect knowledge and learning. While Papert and I worked on a paper introducing the theory of restructurations to the learning sciences, Papert suffered a tragic traffic accident. With Papert unable to continue working on the paper, I wrote an abbreviated version, which was shared at the Constructionism 2010 conference (Wilensky & Papert, 2010). Herein, I wish to reprise and extend the ideas in that paper and illustrate how they have been embodied in the work of students and colleagues in Northwestern's Center for Connected Learning and Computer-Based Modeling (CCL).

In the 2010 paper, we opened by noting that, although the advent of powerful computation has had a dramatic impact on science practice, it has not resulted in significant change in the world of science education. The authors of that paper worked for many years on projects directed at bringing the benefits of these changes to students. Our aim then was to develop a conceptualization of this enterprise in historical and epistemological terms to suggest broad new directions for the sciences of learning.

To present this idea, we examined the shift from Roman to Hindu-Arabic numerals in arithmetic. While this was not done with an "educational intent," it had profound consequences for education. Restructuration theory's purpose is to more systematically study changes of this kind, to examine the practices of science in search of cases that could have had similar educational consequences, and to consider the possibility of deliberately making such changes in thinking about scientific (and, indeed, other) topics with an educational intent.

Papert and I began by looking more closely at the Roman to Hindu-Arabic transition through the lens of a thought experiment.

A THOUGHT EXPERIMENT

Imagine a country, FOO, where people represented numbers as the Romans did, using symbols such as MCMXLVIII. Learning science researchers in this imaginary country were very concerned with the difficulty of learning to handle such numbers, and they worked hard to make these skills accessible to more citizens. They engaged in a number of different approaches. Some researchers collected the misconceptions and typical mistakes made by children. Others constructed and studied computer programs that allowed students to practice numerical operations. Still others constructed specially developed manipulatives—wooden blocks marked with the symbols C, X, V, and I—to help students learn. It is not hard to imagine, in our thought experiment, that many of these approaches brought about substantial improvement in learning. But let us now imagine that, at some point, Hindu-Arabic numerals were invented by the educators of this country. This invention then opened up a new way to handle and think about numbers. Resulting gains in functional numeracy would likely far outstrip any of the benefits that would have accrued from any of the improved techniques for teaching with the Roman numeral system. Before: the learning gap in arithmetic was immense, only a small number of trained people could do multiplication. After: multiplication became part of what we can expect everyone to learn.

This parable is not intended to show that the other approaches were wrong. The point is that the most dramatic improvements did not come from what we usually think of as the main part of the science of learning.

In fact, Hindu-Arabic numerals were not invented with an educational intent. But they could have been, and that allows us to show the need for a new branch of the learning sciences with the mission of understanding, facilitating, and even designing shifts similar to the shift from Roman to Hindu-Arabic numerals.

A first step is to name the sort of innovation associated with the shift from Roman to Hindu-Arabic representations of number. This sort of transformation has no name in the standard educational discourse. In terminology Papert and I developed, we say that we have a new *structuration* of a discipline. Structuration refers to the encoding of the knowledge in a domain as a function of the representational infrastructure used to express the knowledge. A change from one structuration of a domain to another (by using a new representational infrastructure) is called a *restructuration*.

Of course, this parable has a historical counterpart. In the decade and a half since we first presented this parable, I continued to delve into the spread of Hindu-Arabic numerals. Hindu-Arabic numerals arrived in Europe around the turn of the second millennium. At that time, the general population used Roman numerals and could not multiply and divide. They took their multiplication and division problems to special *"caluclatores"* who would take in their problems and give them answers several days later. Many European scientists recognized the advantages of the Hindu-Arabic representation, in particular that the inscription of a number grows logarithmically with its magnitude as opposed to linearly. A few hundred years into the millennium, Italian shopkeepers kept two sets of books: one where they did their actual calculations in Hindu-Arabic and a second set of books laboriously copied into Roman numerals, to satisfy the state officials. It took about 500 years for the population at large to take up Hindu-Arabic numerals. When this transition was over, there was a huge gain in arithmetic facility that democratized access to the calculations that were previously considered too hard for most people. This property of restructurations, that they take a long time to become infrastructural, is a key component. We call it *"restructurational inertia."*

Max Planck (1949) has observed that a new scientific truth does not triumph by convincing its opponents and making them see the light, but rather because its opponents eventually die, and a new generation grows up that is familiar with the new way of thinking. Restructurations spread even more slowly than scientific concepts as an entire representational infrastructure must be introduced and incorporated, and the older one often replaced. As we will discuss, acceptance of a proposed restructuration requires evaluation of the potential gains it can bring.

The Roman-to-Arabic example is just one of many historical examples. diSessa, in his book *Changing Minds* (2000), describes Galileo's historical restructuration of simple kinematics from a text-based to an algebraic representation. He describes Galileo struggling to handle a problem involving the relationship between distance, time, and velocity without being able to appeal to algebraic notations such as d = vt. Algebraic representation transformed what was hard for Galileo into a form that is within the intellectual grasp of every competent high school student. The vista opened to the imagination is dramatic: if the problems with which we struggle today could be so transformed, think of the new domains we could enter and conquer! Or as educators, we might take the prospect in a different slant: if algebra could make accessible to students what was hard for Galileo, our holy grail should be whatever can similarly transform what is hard for them today.

What prompts the creation of a restructuration? Most often, there is a practical problem that the current structuration does not address. In the Roman historical example, the economic world was getting more complex, science was advancing. Both of these necessitated working with large numbers, and the Roman structuration did not scale well. Second, a functioning society in this increasingly complex world required a more numerate citizenry. This created an atmosphere conducive to incubation of possible restructurations. Some innovations may have been minor improvements, some just-misses, but with Hindu-Arabic numerals, the answers to both of these challenges were addressed.

Herein, we argue that computation-based restructurations are making significant impact on knowledge domains and are poised **to have an infrastructural impact**. The advent of ubiquitous computation is again complexifying our world. It requires the ability to work with and understand complex systems to keep both the world and the experience of the individual in balance. Yet, like multiplication and division were then, research has shown that understanding complexity is difficult (Chi, 2005; Wilensky & Resnick, 1999). It is a propitious time for a restructuration to appear and transform our society from one in which only a few "calculatores" can reason about complex systems to one in which there is universal facility.

WAYS TO EVALUATE RESTRUCTURATIONS

From our current perspective, it is obvious that the Hindu-Arabic restructuration leads to better results in being able to handle numerical relationships than the Roman structuration. However, to the people of FOO and to FOO's evaluators and test-makers, it was not obvious. In our thought experiment, students who learned the new Hindu-Arabic system would likely not be able to pass the standardized tests developed using the old Roman system. Suppose they were asked: Which is the largest, CIX, XCI, or CXI? A student of the Hindu-Arabic system might not even understand this question yet still be much better prepared to deal with real-world arithmetical problems. The same set of difficulties may be anticipated today. To overcome this difficulty the learning sciences must strive to create evaluation measures that go beyond the specifics of a representation, which is a means to an end, and instead devise measures for the ends themselves. In order to study and evaluate restructurations, we found it useful to focus on five core properties of structurations (Wilensky & Papert, 2010): power, cognitive, affective, social, and diversity properties.[1] The challenge to the learning sciences is to invent and to assess other possible restructurations and their impacts on learning using properties such as the ones outlined here.

TURTLE GEOMETRY AND BEYOND

I now turn to concrete examples of restructurations. The examples given make use of computational objects as their representational infrastructure. In these examples, the computational object replaces a more traditional mathematical representation. As we will see in the examples, the computational object (a.k.a. agent) has power properties that make it attractive to scientists and has cognitive, affective, social, and diversity properties that make what we currently think of as advanced topics learnable by a much wider and younger population.

I introduce the first restructuration by looking at a number of ways to think about a circle. For Euclid, a circle is defined by the fact that all its points are at the same distance from a certain point called its center. In this definition, determining if a point is on the circle requires access to a point that is not on the circle: an ant crawling on a path could not use this definition to decide whether the path is circular.

The second view of the circle is its definition by an equation such as $x^2 + y^2 = K$. This was made possible by a major restructuration of geometry, due to Descartes, by representing geometric entities in algebraic form.

The third view will be presented anachronistically in terms of a computational object known as "the turtle" or "the Logo turtle" (Papert, 1980). The turtle is much like Euclid's point (which has position *and no other properties)* except that it has position and *one* other property, its heading. A turtle in motion has two velocities: its linear velocity is the rate of change of its position; its angular velocity is the rate of change of its heading.

With these preliminaries, we can state our third view of the circle. If a turtle moves with both velocities constant, it will draw a circle! What is remarkable about this is that the turtle draws the circle without reference to any external entity such as Euclid's "center" or Descartes' "coordinate axes."

Another way of saying this is that with this definition, an ant walking on the circle can know that it is a circle. Yet another is that even with a tiny field of view one can tell whether a figure is a circle by looking at all parts of it confined at each instant to the tiny field of view—and this is true no matter how tiny the field.

Using a computational object to define a circle in this way also enables us to explain the concept at the core of "calculus," although most contemporary students who are required to undergo school courses with this name would probably not recognize any connection. Newton's great achievement in the invention of calculus was to deduce a global property (such as being a circle) from local properties (such as having constant curvature at each point). This achievement gave rapid rise to a restructuring of large areas of science. But—and one might say that this is the main theme of this chapter—this restructuration could be appreciated and used only by a highly skilled and knowledgeable few. That is, until the computer enables us to restructurate the restructuration and so make it accessible to many more people—particularly, children considered too young to "learn calculus" in its pre-computational form.

This last assertion will be elaborated shortly, but first we introduce our fourth way of thinking about a circle. Place a large number of turtles at the same place. Give each one a random heading. Make them all move forward by the same amount. They will form a circle. In some ways this goes back to Euclid's definition, but it has a new slant: the circle *emerged* from the behaviors of a large number of agents. Although this case is obvious, we shall see how the interaction of large numbers of agents each following a very simple rule can give rise to complex, scientifically interesting, and by no means obvious emergent effects.

It did not take long after Newton's mechanics before scientists tried to apply mechanics to large populations of entities, especially the molecules of a gas. But it was not until the nineteenth century that the mathematical methods were developed to create statistical mechanics, which led to a deep restructuring of the understanding of states of matter as the aggregate behavior of large numbers of molecules. Here again, representing these phenomena as collections of computational agents has allowed us to make accessible to young students a level of understanding that in the past has been very difficult even for much older students (Wilensky, 1999b).

The centrality of emergence in a wide variety of phenomena is core to our claim that computational agents form a new computational infrastructure that is already restructurating scientific disciplines, and that careful thought is needed in order to both understand the impact of these restructurations on learning of the knowledge domains and to design restructurated curriculum that takes advantage of the properties of the restructuration. We take a brief digression to introduce agent-based modeling.

EMERGENCE

Complex systems are characterized by "emergence." An emergent phenomenon is a global characteristic or pattern that arises out of the uncoordinated interaction of many individual elements. Emergent phenomena are everywhere, though we may not notice their emergence, often noticing only the aggregate patterns or noticing the element behaviors but not connecting them to the aggregate pattern. Examples include how a flock of birds emerges from the interactions of individual birds, or how the price of a commodity emerges from the interactions of many buyers and sellers. To understand an emergent phenomenon, you need to understand it at least two levels—the macro-aggregate level and the micro-element level. So, to have an understanding of, say, our flock of birds, at the aggregate level, we'd need to be able to recognize the pattern easily when we see it, and we might need to formalize that understanding in some mathematics. To understand it on the element levels, we would need to understand what the birds are doing. Further, it is through connecting the behavior of the birds with the aggregate flock that we come to more deeply understand that system.

So, like Europeans entering the second millennium, the world of the third millennium is rapidly complexifying. This complexity requires new understandings and skills from the citizens. Those understandings and skills are in very short supply in the current society, so the time is ripe for a restructuration that transforms emergence from an obscure topic that only few people understand to one that we can expect all members of our society to understand and master.

AGENT-BASED MODELING

One powerful methodology that has emerged from complex systems theory is agent-based modeling (ABM). In contrast to more traditional mathematical modeling, which is typically done with equations, ABM makes use of simple computational rules as the fundamental modeling elements. The equational modeling game is to observe a phenomenon and try to fashion an equation that fits the observed data. In contrast, in ABM, the core elements are computational objects or "agents" in the system—for example, lynxes or hares in a predator-prey model. Each of these agents has state variables that describe its particular state, such as age, energy level, and hunger. The behavior of the agents is determined by the computational rules that tell each agent what to do at each "tick" of a clock. The rules are framed from the agent's point of view. For example, if the agent is a lynx, the rules might say: Move a step in the direction you are headed, reduce your energy variable by a fixed amount, look for prey in the vicinity, if found where you are, try to eat it, if not turn to face closest prey you can see ... To determine the state of the system at future time T, rather than solve the equation for T as you would in equation modeling, in ABM you run the system for T clock ticks. The ABM modeling game consists of formulating the agent rules that will generate the aggregate phenomena to be modeled.

Scientists across a wide variety of domains are increasingly making use of ABMs as both explanatory and predictive tools. In the natural sciences, ABMs have several advantages over equational approaches. Chief among these are (a) the epistemological match—rules for individual predators or molecules are closer to our intuitive notions of these "objects" as distinct individuals rather than as aggregate populations; (b) the greater adjustability—equational representations tend to be brittle, that is, for some small change in environmental conditions, the algebraic forms themselves do not typically change only a little; and (c) visualization—related to the epistemological match is the greater realism afforded by visualization of individual lynx and hare and their dynamic behaviors rather than just dynamic graphs of their populations.

All three of these advantages are magnified in the educational context. Students can reason about and visualize individual animals in an ecology far better than they can population levels. They can draw on their own body and sensory experience to assess and/or design sensible rules for the behavior of individuals. They can therefore make much greater sense and meaning from the agent-based representations. Furthermore, the extensibility/adjustability of the models enables students to engage in real inquiry by asking what-if questions of the models and adjusting rules in order to get answers to their questions. The alternate representation, in effect, enables students to think more like scientists (Wilensky & Reisman, 2006).

In the educational context, there is one more advantage that is greatest of all: the greater ease of mastering the representations themselves. Learning to master the differential equations that describe a predator-prey system requires the prior mastering of an extensive algebraic and calculus-based infrastructure that is out of reach for large numbers of our students. And even those students who do eventually master algebra and calculus do so late in their student "careers." Agent-based representations, in contrast, require significantly less effort to master. Research we have conducted shows that middle school students can profitably employ these representations with only a small amount of prior instruction (Wagh et al., 2017).

Widespread adoption of agent-based representations has the potential then to lead to tremendous democratization of scientific knowledge. Over the past two decades, the CCL Lab has created a large set of agent-based restructurations of natural and social science content using the NetLogo agent-based modeling environment (Wilensky, 1999a). The content domains and the target age groups vary widely. Examples from natural science include restructurated curriculum in molecular and evolutionary biology, probability and statistics, electricity and material science. Examples from social science include units in economics, psychology, and wealth inequality. Our next example employs ABM to restructurate advanced biology content, making it more learnable as well as accessible to young learners.

EXAMPLE: GENEVO—GENES, PROTEINS, AND BEYOND

The nature of biological research has changed significantly with the incorporation of newer technological tools, the use of computational modeling methods, and an increasing focus on complex systems thinking. For example, understanding of gene regulatory networks and how stochastic chemical interactions between biomolecules such as proteins and DNA lead to complex cellular and organismic behaviors is fundamental to understanding advances in modern biology—such as finding targets for cancer treatment, to using CRISPR to create genetically adapted plants more suited to face climate uncertainty. In schools and universities, student exposure to the deep explanatory ideas of molecular biology continue to rely on static models that depict molecular interactions as deterministic processes (figure 27.1a and 27.1b) or differential equation–based representations that require mathematical sophistication to understand the core ideas (figure 27.1c). None of these existing structurations explain how simple biochemical interactions between these molecules allows a cell to make emergent complex decisions and perform complex functions. As a result, students don't gain access to the cutting-edge ideas of molecular biology that allow them to reason about biological processes. Our restructuration of these ideas in modern biology involves representing biomolecules as visualized agents with agent interactions forming system-level behavior of an organism.

In our work on this restructuration, we have created a curriculum, GenEvo (Dabholkar & Wilensky, 2016). We have implemented this curriculum with both high school and middle school students in several different settings. We briefly describe below how power, cognitive, and social properties of the restructuration play out in the classroom setting.

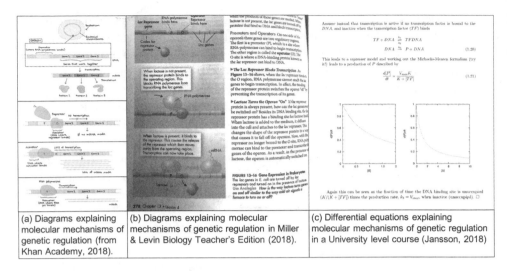

(a) Diagrams explaining molecular mechanisms of genetic regulation (from Khan Academy, 2018).	(b) Diagrams explaining molecular mechanisms of genetic regulation in Miller & Levin Biology Teacher's Edition (2018).	(c) Differential equations explaining molecular mechanisms of genetic regulation in a University level course (Jansson, 2018)

FIGURE 27.1

Describing molecular mechanisms of genetic regulation through existing structurations of molecular biology.

Power properties. The GenEvo restructuration represents a genetic network of bacterial cells as a population of bacterial cell agents competing for a resource. In each model, the agents and their behaviors at the micro-level are computationally coded, and students observe and explore agent-level interactions and system level patterns represented in spatial structures or graphs. In contrast to commonly taught models, the agent-based representation is of stochastic interactions, which enables reasoning about molecular dynamics. For example, an RNA polymerase, a potato-shaped brown protein, moves around randomly in the model; however, when it happens to be near a promoter, a green part of DNA, it latches on and moves when the operator, orange region, of DNA is unoccupied.

Cognitive and affective properties. Our restructuration of mechanisms of genetic regulation and microevolution increases "learnability" of these advanced ideas. Simple representations of biomolecules and their interactions in these computational models do not require students to have sophisticated mathematical understanding in order to make predictions and reason about aggregate emergent cellular behaviors. They only need to reason about the cells as "objects to think with." We have taught this curricular unit twice in the United States and twice in India and, in each case, have seen significant increase in middle school students' understanding of advanced ideas in genetics and evolution (Dabholkar, Anton, & Wilensky,

2018). Vidya, a rising eighth-grade student in India, described her learning in GenEvo from the cell's point of view: *"I was observing (potato-shaped things). So first I observed that it was just random movement. Then I saw that it was going on a straight line (on DNA), so I saw that it was rolling along the DNA. And then suddenly, when it went off pink triangles and rectangles were produced. I did this experiment 2 or 3 times and then I figured out that the RNAP produced LacZ and LacY and when one RNAP rolls it produced 5 LacZs."* Note the nonchalant passing from simple agent properties such as shapes and colors to the more technical vocabulary.

We have also seen how students' collaborative construction of knowledge is mediated by engaging with the computational model as a mediating artifact that provides cognitive and epistemic scaffolds. From even a cursory view of our classroom video, it's apparent that the students are deeply and excitedly engaged (figure 27.2). Without prompting, they described in their post-interviews that learning in these courses was highly enjoyable.

Social properties. The simplicity of behavioral representations in these models enables students to share their ideas easily and build off of each other's ideas. Pairs of students are asked to explore a model and identify an aspect that they find interesting to investigate. Their findings collectively

FIGURE 27.2
Middle school students using an agent-based model to reason about emergent properties of molecular mechanisms of genetic regulation.

build toward ideas about the emergent properties of genetic regulation and evolution.

GenEvo students were learning advanced molecular biology, usually reserved for graduate students. Using a traditional differential equation–based structuration, pre-college students are left out as they don't have the mathematical sophistication. Instead, to the extent this content is covered, pre-collegiate students are told about these ideas authoritatively by their teachers using static models or animated videos. Whereas, in the GenEvo course, students learned these powerful ideas by collaboratively constructing knowledge through scientific investigations in the context of an ABM.

One rising direction ripe for computational restructuration is the social sciences. Whereas early examples of ABM-based restructurations primarily pertained to the natural sciences, there is increasing recognition of social science as a powerful context for restructuration. Mathematics has worked amazingly to describe physical sciences, but its successes in the social sciences have been less impressive. Because of the wide variation of human behaviors, it is not usually effective to represent system behavior as aggregated from mostly similar agents. Behavioral economics describes individual differences and irrationalities as essential elements of economic modeling. But traditional differential equations do not adequately address such variant models. In contrast, because ABMs start with properties of individuals they easily accommodate these human variations. For a long time, an assumption of "rationality" was imposed on economic agents. These assumptions made the mathematics of solving them tractable. But agent-based restructuration enables us to relax rationality assumptions.

A special form of ABM—participatory simulation—is especially promising for helping students understand complex social issues because it allows students to bring human beliefs and emotions into the simulation while experiencing the macro-micro interactions. As opposed to regular ABMs, in which all agents' behavior is pre-programmed, some agents in agent-based participatory simulations are controlled directly by students, who project themselves into the models by taking on the roles of the agents and acting out their behaviors (Colella, 2000; Wilensky & Stroup, 1999, 2000). Such tools immediately engage the social properties of restructurations. The CCL has developed several restructurated units using participatory simulations. A promising restructurated curriculum entitled Mind the Gap (MTG) uses participatory simulation to address the topic of wealth inequality (Guo & Wilensky, 2018) and has been successfully implemented in secondary classrooms.

CONCLUSION

In this chapter, I have briefly laid out the theory of restructurations and called for careful consideration of, in particular, agent-based restructurations of science content and instruction. While I have presented a few brief examples of restructurated curricula, in the CCL Lab, my students, colleagues, and I have engaged in a long-term effort to design and study restructuration across a wide variety of domains. Many of these have been widely used in classrooms. The properties of restructurations described here can serve as guidelines for evaluating candidate restructurations, and further development of the properties and evaluation measures is an important direction for research.

NOTE

1. See Wilensky & Papert, 2010, for further elaboration of these properties.

REFERENCES

Chi, M. T. H. (2005). Commonsense conceptions of emergent processes: Why some misconceptions are robust. *Journal of the Learning Sciences, 14*(2), 161–199.

Colella, V. (2000). Participatory simulations: Building collaborative understanding through immersive dynamic modeling. *Journal of the Learning Sciences, 9*(4), 471–500.

Dabholkar, S., Anton, G., & Wilensky, U. (2018, June). GenEvo—An emergent systems microworld for model-based scientific inquiry in the context of genetics and evolution. *Proceedings of the International Conference for the Learning Sciences (ICLS 2018)*. London, UK.

Dabholkar, S., & Wilensky, U. (2016). GenEvo Systems Biology curriculum. Center for Connected Learning and Computer-Based Modeling, Northwestern University, Evanston, IL. Retrieved from http://ccl.northwestern.edu/curriculum/genevo/

diSessa, A. A. (2000). *Changing minds: Computers, learning, and literacy*. Cambridge, MA: MIT Press.

Guo, Y., & Wilensky, U. (2018). Mind the gap: Teaching high school students about wealth inequality through agent-based participatory simulations. *In Proceedings of the Constructionism 2018 Conference*. Vilnius, Lithuania.

Papert, S. (1980). *Mindstorms: Children, computers, and powerful ideas*. New York, NY: Basic Books.

Planck, M. (1949). *Scientific autobiography and other papers*. New York, NY: Philosophical Library.

Wagh, A., Levy, S. T., Horn, M. S., Guo, Y., Brady, C., & Wilensky, U. (2017, June). Anchor code: Modularity as evidence of conceptual learning & computational practices of students using a code-first environment. In *Proceedings of the 12th International Conference on Computer Supported Collaborative Learning (CSCL 2017)*. Philadelphia, PA.

Wilensky, U. (1999a). *NetLogo*. Center for Connected Learning and Computer-Based Modeling, Northwestern University, Evanston, IL. Retrieved from http://ccl .northwestern.edu/netlogo/

Wilensky, U. (1999b). GasLab: An extensible modeling toolkit for exploring micro-and-macro-views of gases. In N. Roberts, W. Feurzeig, & B. Hunter (Eds.), *Computer modeling and simulation in science education* (pp. 151–178). Berlin: Springer Verlag.

Wilensky, U., & Papert, S. (2010, August). Restructurations: Reformulations of knowledge disciplines through new representational forms. In J. Clayson & I. Kalas (Eds.), *Proceedings of the Constructionism 2010 Conference*. Paris, France (p. 97).

Wilensky, U., & Reisman, K. (2006). Thinking like a wolf, a sheep or a firefly: Learning biology through constructing and testing computational theories. *Cognition & Instruction, 24*(2), 171–209.

Wilensky, U., & Resnick, M. (1999). Thinking in levels: A dynamic systems perspective to making sense of the world. *Journal of Science Education and Technology, 8*(1).

Wilensky, U., & Stroup, W. (1999). *HubNet*. Evanston, IL: Center for Connected Learning and Computer-Based Modeling, Northwestern University. Retrieved from http://ccl.northwestern.edu/netlogo/docs/#HubNet.

Wilensky, U., & Stroup, W. (2000). Networked gridlock: Students enacting complex dynamic phenomena with the HubNet architecture. In B. Fishman & S. O'Connor-Divelbiss (Eds.), *Proceedings of the Fourth Annual International Conference for the Learning Sciences* (pp. 282–289). Mahwah, NJ: Erlbaum.

28 HI-LO TECH CRAFTING: TINKERING WITH TEXTILES, PAPER, AND EVERYTHING ELSE

Yasmin B. Kafai and Gayithri Jayathirtha

Papert (1980) opened his book *Mindstorms* with a preface titled "The Gears of My Childhood," in which he reflected on the pivotal role observing and playing with gears had on his early intellectual and emotional understanding of differentials and other mathematical ideas. He wanted computers to become the very same "objects-to-think-with" (Papert, 1980) that would allow learners to engage with the world of computing and mathematics in not only intellectual but also tangible ways. Indeed, the first Logo floor turtle was a dome-shaped robot with an attached pen at its base that had learners write programs to draw geometric patterns on paper on the floor. But Papert (1980) also realized that what playing with gears did for his understanding of mathematical ideas was not necessarily true of other learners and thus searched out opportunities to make connections to everyday objects, materials, and activities.

Papert was not the first to think about construction kits and various materials for learning. In the early 1800s, the German pedagogue Friedrich Fröbel—perhaps best known for coining the term "kindergarten"—developed a series of twenty toys and activities, which he called "gifts," for hands-on learning (Brosterman, 1997). These gifts were designed to help young children recognize and appreciate the common forms and patterns found in nature. The Fröbelian gifts ranged from woolen balls for toddlers to touch and bounce in their cribs, to various wooden building blocks that allowed young children to practice hand-eye coordination and work with different geometric shapes when building structures, to paper and textile-based materials that involved intricate stitching and folding and, finally, clay that let children learn from their own building materials.

Many of today's popular construction kits, such as Lincoln Logs and LEGO blocks, have been inspired by Fröbel's gifts and, more important, are still found and played with by millions of young children. Early development efforts have focused on computational expansions facilitating either screen-based constructions such as video games, graphics, and stories or physical constructions such as building robots, cars, or houses. Among the most well-known is LEGO Mindstorms that originated from LEGO/Logo, which was one of the first computational construction kits that connected motors and sensors with wires to the familiar branded plastic building blocks, which millions of kids had played with before. A review of five generations of these physical computing devices illustrates how the development of new microcontrollers and inclusion of various functionalities opened up computing to different ideas and groups of learners (Blikstein, 2015). The emergence of the Maker Movement has made construction activities popular again, connecting crafting, traditionally low-tech materials, with high-tech domains such as computing and engineering. With hardware becoming more affordable and accessible, numerous physical computational construction kits have been developed that move beyond bricks and motors to use everyday low-cost materials such as paper and textiles and involve crafting activities such as sewing and folding.

We present examples of various construction kits for designing interfaces and greeting cards using paper materials and pencil drawings and kits for designing wearables using textiles and conductive thread. We discuss how these construction kits provide learners with objects-to-think-with that are situated in the physical world—just like Papert's gears—and elevate the often neglected material side of learning. In our view of Constructionism, objects-to-think-with are constructed in the mind as much as in the physical world, and it is through realizing their ideas, exploring different options, and making adaptions—in short: tinkering—that learners make connections with the histories and cultures in which everyday materials and artifacts are situated.

DESIGNING INTERFACES WITH EVERYDAY MATERIALS

Fröbel's gifts not only introduced children to various forms and practices but also used everyday materials available during his time such as wool, paper, thread, wood, and clay. This inspired Millner's early design (2005) of the Hook-Ups construction kit that enabled youth to become creators of interactive, tangible experiences by providing lower-cost access and minimizing programming. His work illustrated how youth can learn about electricity, design, and programming while crafting tangible interfaces from everyday materials and objects, such as cardboard boxes, plastic balls, and scissors. Construction kits such as Makey Makey (Silver, Rosenbaum, &

Shaw, 2012) took this a step further by opening up design opportunities for physical computing which require programming. Unlike LEGO Mindstorms and other computational construction kits, Makey Makey requires neither extensive setup nor deep technical knowledge and thus has widened opportunities to tinker, particularly among younger children.

Essentially, Makey Makey can turn anything conductive into a tangible user interface, simply by using alligator clips as the connective tissue (figure 28.1, *top row*). The Makey Makey plugs into the computer using a simple mini-USB to USB cord. Another cord is a connection to earth, which grounds the circuit. The third connection is a set of wires that connect to conductive objects. Exploring the range of attachable conductive objects is where much of the fun lies, as children often start by connecting aluminum foil or quarters, dimes, or other conductive materials. But they soon find conductivity in the unexpected, including pieces of Play-Doh clay and even fruits such as bananas and apples. When a user holds earth in one hand and touches the Play-Doh, the circuit is complete, running electricity from the computer, through the Makey Makey to the everyday object (Play-Doh in figure 28.1), and then back. With the circuit complete, the computer interprets touching the Play-Doh as akin to touching the space bar, or another designated pre-programmed key on the Makey Makey board.

Other projects have used Makey Makey to design music devices by making stairs into musical keys that generate sounds as the steps are touched. Makey Makey also allows beginning game designers to move beyond the screen to create their own touchpad interfaces for their online Scratch games using clay, feathers, textiles, and more. Even traditional board games can be augmented with Makey Makey to bring the computer as a dice or recording device into play (Kafai & Burke, 2016). Makey Makey thus gives beginning designers the ability to use conductive objects to replace the typical input (e.g., the up and down, right and left keys) and in the process learn not only about conductivity but also about the interactional nature of input and output. Along with the pre-programmed keys, makers can remap the pins to new keys using the resources on the Makey Makey website (www.makeymakey.com). In the process, learners get opportunities to explore the conductivity of different materials around them and learn basic circuitry principles such as polarity and the need for grounding. Further, integrating new materials such as a pencil sketch or even water expands the playground for learners to explore computational ideas in the context of visual arts and music.

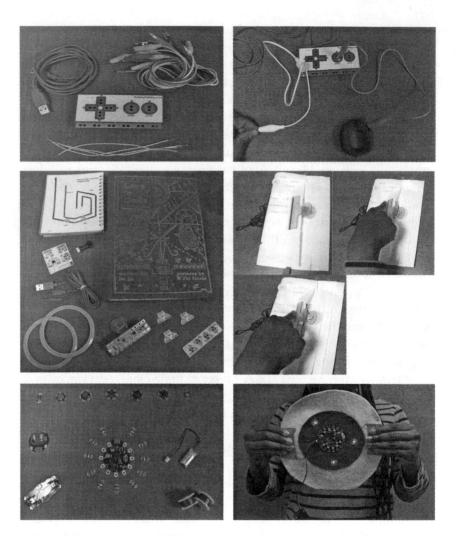

FIGURE 28.1
Various computational physical construction kits: Top row: (left) Makey
Makey construction kit, (right) interface with Play-Doh; Middle row: (left)
Paper construction kit and (right) a sketchbook integrated with circuit to
highlight chosen page numbers; Bottom row: (left) e-textile construction kit
with LilyPad Arduino microcontroller (center) with battery holder, buzzer,
vibe board, accelerometer, light sensor, and tricolor LED and a Captain
America shield (right).

ILLUMINATING AND AUGMENTING PAPER

Several of Fröbel's more advanced gifts, #13, #14, and #18, involved cutting, weaving, and folding colorful paper stripes into paper cut with long slits. Even to this day, all grade school students are familiar with paper. Students already interact with paper as they read, write, draw, paint, and craft. These features—familiarity among young learners, easy availability, and durability—make paper a great candidate to be augmented with electronics and promote computation. An early example of connecting the worlds of paper-based crafting with computing was Eisenberg's development of hypergami (1998), allowing learners to design or program foldable shapes and figures on the screen that could then be printed out to be realized in actual 3D origami designs. A more recent example is paper mechatronics (Oh, Hsi, Eisenberg, & Gross, 2018), which provides young makers opportunities to test out their ideas by making paper-based prototypes of engineering models. This effort usually entails learners using regular microcontrollers such as Arduino boards and using hard cardboard sheets to bring their ideas to life before making a more permanent structure using 3D printed or laser-cut materials. Connecting back to Fröbel's paper-based activities, scissors, tape, and cardboard provide an easy entry point for learners to realize their ideas.

Yet another approach to using paper in computation includes redesigning interfaces of regular electronic components such as microcontrollers and LED lights to make them compatible with paper. Drawing or painting connections using graphite pens, conductive ink, or sticking copper tapes brings circuits to life on paper and can turn them into computational objects. For instance, *Love to Code* provides Chibi Chip, a paper-based microcontroller with LED lights that can be connected to copper-tape circuits added to paper (figure 28.1, *middle row*). This microcontroller can be programmed using either a graphical or text-based programming language, very similar to the Arduino. In addition, a web-based interface allows the microcontroller to be programmed using an Internet-enabled smartphone. Additional sensors for light and color, and other actuators, such as the recently added servo sweeper motor, give more options for programmers to make artifacts with capabilities beyond blinking lights.

Extending computing with paper, *Code Collage* is yet another unique approach in which learners control circuits by manipulating the very circuit elements on paper-based electronic modules called "code stickers" (Qi, Demir, & Paradiso, 2017). For example, one can turn a knob in the circuit to control voltage sent to lights instead of passing numerical values to a function in a program; one can press a button to manually record actions that must be repeated instead of typing the actions within a loop statement in a computer program; or one can move conductive elements on the "code sticker" to make logical gates and realize if-else conditionals. Qi and colleagues made an interactive city skyline collage that lights up when the sky is covered using LEDs, a light sensor, and if-else conditional "code stickers." This new modality makes transparent the electronics behind computational constructs. These early explorations with the medium afford learners to explore basic, event-based computational ideas without any on-screen programming. The collection of "code stickers" includes moving components that also allow for 3D projects.

The familiarity with paper materials, pencil drawings, and copper tape can encourage makers to test new ideas in less time, thereby supporting easy iterations of designs. Circuits on paper not only introduce a new degree of transparency but also allow learners to annotate and make sense of the circuit on the same medium. Further, abundant availability of paper both lowers the barrier of entry among novice learners and raises the bar for expert makers to design and develop sophisticated artifacts that demand advanced conceptual understanding. At the end, all of these efforts do not go to waste. Unlike the conventional electronic prototyping tools that involve making circuits on breadboards, circuits built on paper with copper tape or pencil drawings are durable. These artifacts can be stored and even remixed by simply unsticking the copper tape connections.

MAKING WEARABLE INTERACTIVE ARTIFACTS

Unlike the popular wooden blocks or paper activities, Fröbel's twelfth gift is often overlooked: It uses needle, colorful thread, and fabric pieces to engage young children in sewing and embroidery to produce samplers with various stitch patterns. However, more than a decade ago, Buechley (2006) initially prototyped building electronic components such as microcontrollers, lights, and sensors using fabric. As seen in the bottom row of figure 28.1, these electronic components have modified interfaces consisting of metal-coated holes, making them readily sewable and compatible with soft materials, such as fabric. Augmenting daily-use objects and materials with electronics and programming the microcontroller to produce certain behaviors turns these objects into interactive computational artifacts, such as light-sensitive hats and musical jackets (Buechley, Peppler, Eisenberg, & Kafai, 2013). Electronic textile artifacts such as these are made of soft and flexible material and can be augmented with fabric-based daily-use accessories, unlike other artifacts such as robotic arms or 3D printed parts made using other computational kits.

Buechley's initial research efforts soon led to the commercial production of an expanded range of sewable microcontrollers such as SparkFun LilyTiny, Flora and Gemma, Adafruit Circuit Playground, and BBC micro:bit, increasing access to electronic textiles. Boards such as SparkFun LilyTiny come with preprogrammed pins that help learners realize certain ideas, such as blinking and fading lights, without programming, thereby lowering the barriers of entry for young makers and learners. In addition to preprogrammed boards, block-based programming interfaces such as Modkit also contribute to lowering the barriers of entry for young learners. Furthermore, newer microcontrollers, such as Adafruit Circuit Playground, come with enhanced features such as multiple on-board sensors and increased input/output pins that provide opportunities for makers to try out advanced ideas and projects.

During the last decade, thousands of students across formal and informal learning settings have realized a wide variety of electronic textiles artifacts, such as temperature-sensitive lunch bags and interactive wall murals (Jayathirtha & Kafai, 2019). Making these computational artifacts involves designing circuits, stitching the microcontroller and other required components using conductive thread, and programming the controller to achieve the desired outcome. For example, making a touch-sensitive Captain America shield (figure 28.1, *bottom right*) entails designing the artifact along with the circuit specification, making the shield and augmenting it with the microcontroller, touch sensors and lights, and programming such that the lights behave in relation to the data from the sensor.

Research has shown that students in these spaces develop a positive attitude toward circuitry and computing, learn circuitry concepts such as connections and polarity, and learn computational concepts such as variables and control flow as they make these artifacts (Kafai, Fields, & Searle, 2014). However, as our recent synthesis of the field points out, a majority of the projects using these e-textiles construction kits have been limited to introducing novices to basic computational ideas involving either only lights or single set of inputs and outputs, with very few studies exploring complex engineering and programming ideas in their projects. More advanced e-textiles projects were mostly realized by undergraduate and graduate students who created weather-sensing heating/cooling jackets. Realizing these advanced projects also required learners to draw expertise from a wide range of domains such as programming, engineering, and arts, something that is almost out of reach for grade school students. While students can realize more complex e-textile projects, there is a need for an expansion of technical and pedagogical scaffolds in order to make this more accessible to younger learners.

CONCLUSIONS

These high- and low-tech construction kits introduce new learners to computing by using everyday materials, objects, and practices. They also engage learners with what Papert and Harel (1990) called "tinkering"—an approach that involves messing around with various concrete materials, trying out different things before finding a solution in making an artifact. Papert saw tinkering as a much-needed complement for engaging with computing, in addition to the planning or analytical approaches often promoted in schools. More importantly, these high-tech kits with low-tech materials also open doors for diverse groups of participants within the field of computer science. A recent survey of the users of textile and paper-based construction kits revealed that significantly more female users than male users purchase these kits when compared to traditional Arduino users (Buechley, Peppler, Eisenberg, & Kafai, 2013). Moreover, they also afford design of a more diverse range of artifacts, compared to robots and drones featured in many Arduino projects. These findings illustrate that connecting everyday materials with computational construction kits have moved constructionist learning beyond the traditional STEM activities with games and robotics. Crafting with paper, textiles, and everything else brings new objects-to-think-with into learning that builds connections with familial (see chapter 18) and cultural traditions (see chapter 16) often ignored in school. These construction kits are the "gifts" for learners in the twenty-first century.

REFERENCES

Blikstein, P. (2015). Computationally-enhanced toolkits for children: Historical review and a framework for Future designs. *Foundations and Trends in Human-Computer Interaction, 9*(1), 1–68.

Brosterman, N. (1997). *Inventing kindergarten.* New York, NY: Abrams.

Buechley, L. (2006). A construction kit for electronic textiles. In *2006 10th IEEE international symposium on wearable computers* (pp. 83–90). Montreux, Switzerland: IEEE.

Buechley, L., Peppler, K., Eisenberg, M., & Kafai, Y. B. (2013). *Textile messages: Dispatches from the world of e-textiles and education. New literacies and digital epistemologies.* New York, NY: Peter Lang.

Eisenberg, M., & Eisenberg, N. (1998). Shop class for the next millennium: Education through computer-enriched handicrafts. *Journal of Interactive Media in Education, 98*(8), 1–30.

Jayathirtha, G., & Kafai, Y. (2019). Electronic textiles in computer science education: A synthesis of efforts to broaden participation, increase interest, and deepen learning. In *SIGCSE'19: Proceedings of the SIGCSE Conference*, Minneapolis, MN.

Kafai, Y. B., & Burke, Q. (2016). *Connected gaming*. Cambridge, MA: MIT Press.

Kafai, Y., Fields, D., & Searle, K. (2014). Electronic textiles as disruptive designs: Supporting and challenging maker activities in schools. *Harvard Educational Review, 84*(4), 532–556.

Love to Code. (2018). Retrieved on October 29 from https://chibitronics.com /lovetocode/

Makey Makey. (2018). Retrieved on October 29 from https://makeymakey.com

Millner, A. (2005). *Hook ups: How youth learn through creating physical computer interfaces*. (Unpublished master's thesis). MIT, Cambridge, MA.

Oh, H., Hsi, S., Eisenberg, M., & Gross, M. (2018, June). Paper mechatronics: Present and future. In *IDC '18: Proceedings of the 17th ACM Conference on Interaction Design and Children*, Trondheim, Norway (pp. 389–395).

Papert, S. (1980). *Mindstorms*. New York, NY: Basic Books.

Papert, S., & Harel, I. (1990). Situating constructionism. In I. Harel & S. Papert (Eds.), *Constructionism* (pp. 1–18). Norwood, NJ: Ablex.

Qi, J., Demir, A., & Paradiso, J. A. (2017, May). Code Collage: Tangible programming on paper with circuit stickers. In *Proceedings of the 2017 CHI Conference Extended Abstracts on Human Factors in Computing Systems*, Denver, Colorado (pp. 1970–1977).

Silver, J., Rosenbaum, E., & Shaw, D. (2012). Makey Makey improvising tangible and nature-based user interfaces. In *Proceedings of the ACM Tangible Embedded and Embodied Interaction*, Kingston, Ontario, Canada (pp. 367–370).

29 SYNTONICITY AND EMERGENCE: A DESIGN-BASED RESEARCH REFLECTION ON THE PIAGETIAN ROOTS OF CONSTRUCTIONISM

Dor Abrahamson and Kiera Chase

When thirty-year-old Papert arrived in Geneva in 1958, Jean Piaget's International Center for Genetic Epistemology was already well established. Nicknamed "Piaget's Factory," this industrious institute thrived as a global font for groundbreaking theories of children's cognitive development. These powerful theories shaped Papert's pedagogical vision.

Per Piaget, children arrive in the world with a capacity for learning about the world but little knowledge about it. Coming to know the world is a process neither of direct apprehension and emulation (a "rationalist" view) nor an accumulation of stimulus-response associations (an "empirical–behaviorist" view). Rather, infants' knowledge of the world as they find it is constituted through their own active exploration of the environment: performing motor actions, experiencing their sensory outcomes, and iteratively selecting and refining sensorimotor couplings that promote the attainment of their local humble goals. In so doing, the infants unwittingly become better prepared for subsequent encounters with other situations perceived as similar. Critically, children's perception of what is out there and how they may act on it is bound by, or filtered through, the residue of their prior activity and reflection. Perceiving and therefore knowing are constructed through action. As Piaget (1971) famously stated, "Knowing does not really imply making a copy of reality but, rather, reacting to it and transforming it (either apparently or effectively) in such a way as to include it functionally in the transformation systems with which these acts are linked" (p. 6).

Infant knowledge is thus constituted not as subject–object dualism, that is, what *I* know about *something*, but as an intrinsically relational scheme, where perception and action co-adjust adaptively, iteratively assimilating the world to achieve enhanced capacity for effecting change benefitting the organism. Knowledge, or rather *knowing*, is foremost prereflective, presemantic, presemiotic, presymbolic, situated modal capacity: an ad-hoc cognitive construction that is inherently subjective, contextual, and relational. Knowing is constituted and reconstituted in its enaction, and the world comes forth for us only inasmuch as we have formed capacity to engage it in ways pertaining to our individual needs and interests.

The child's early operative structures, the schemes, enable, regulate, and constrain the child's anticipation, interpretation, and response to events. At the same time, these structures are permeable, flexible, and modular. They may become either generalized or differentiated as necessity occasions the child in natural and sociocultural environments, and they may be mixed and matched to form more complex superstructures when coordinating two or more such schemes proves vital for overcoming an impasse to attaining a goal. When concerted cognitive effort is required to resolve a puzzling situation—when we *stop to think*—hitherto ineffable structural qualities of our cognitive schemes may rise to conscious reflection as meanings that lend themselves to discursive reference. Therewith these schemes become amenable to signification, elaboration, and evocation in the sociocultural linguistic context.

What might it mean, given this provocative theory of mind, for a child to learn cultural notions traditionally considered as transcending the material world, such as mathematical concepts? How might a sensorimotor organism come to know the would-be abstract idea of algebra? What might be the primitive transformational systems undergirding a child's conception of formal disciplinary knowledge that is normatively encoded in arbitrary symbolic notation? In turn, to the extent that endorsing these cultural forms requires a child to negotiate epistemic rupture from their naïve knowing of situations to techno-scientific structurations of these same situations, what pedagogical intervention might prove useful for mending this rupture? In particular, what technological artifacts, activities, and environments might foster epistemic continuities between a child's sensorimotor schemes and the formal routines of mathematics (what Papert called "civilization's crowning jewel of achievement")? These enduring theoretical and practical questions have shaped the careers of numerous educators informed by Piaget's theory. For Papert, it was questions such as these that drove the pedagogical vision of constructionism.

In this chapter, we wish to highlight two big philosophical-cum-educational ideas—intellectual veins—that, we argue, run from Piaget's epistemological cosmos through Papert's pedagogical universe to current design-based research on STEM learning and into the future. Both ideas are about the nature of human learning. Yet, as design-based researchers, we will paint one idea, *syntonicity*, as more about informing a general design rationale guiding the process of envisioning technological environments for learning, in particular via the framework of *embodied design*. The other idea, *emergence*, is more about the analytic work of modeling empirical data collected in these studies in terms of the cognitive growth they implicate, in particular through paradigms and methods of coordination dynamics. Following a section, below, that presents these two powerful ideas, we will exemplify them in the context of a technological design for early algebra, Giant Steps (Chase & Abrahamson, 2018). The chapter will then end with a conjecture on the future of educational research informed by syntonicity and emergence.

TWO POWERFUL IDEAS: SYNTONICITY AND EMERGENCE

By coining the phrase "powerful ideas," Papert signaled both that young minds are prepared for complex intellectual encounters and that designers should facilitate these encounters. One big idea about learning is an insistence on designing environments that maximize potential for concordance with a child's tacit enactive capacity in natural and cultural ecologies, an idea Papert (1980) called *syntonicity* (i.e., body syntonic, culture syntonic). As a pedagogical heuristic vying with Piaget's genetic epistemology (Piaget, 1968), *body syntonicity* calls for learning activities that draw on the child's intuitive facility in simple situations—what a child knows by virtue of being an experienced, sentient, multisensory, mobile, corporeal, and agentive terrestrial organism. These include the manifold of informal know-how, such as the embodied sensations of somatics, proprioception, orientation, rhythmic movement and coordination, perceptual judgments, the recognition and manipulation of generic objects, rudimentary quantitative reasoning, heuristic inferential routines and biases, and basic navigation and action in the peri-personal space and beyond. *Cultural syntonicity* encompasses facility with facets of familiar individual and social practices involving artifacts and joint action, such as sailing, juggling, hiding and chasing, singing a tune, decorating a house, telling a story, dancing together, preparing food, planning a hike, or engaging in a basic commercial transaction.

For educators, syntonicity specifies that formal representational structures, such as hierarchical systems of computational procedures for information technology, be couched and introduced to a child such that they pertain not to immaterial forms serving obscure functions. Rather, these complex structures should be couched such that they pertain foremost to familiar objects and meaningful situations—to things that can be perceived and handled toward some ends that are coherent, meaningful, and engaging. Learning to program could thus initially be not about figuring out the most efficient algorithm for sorting a list of numerical values but about using stuff to build a thing that does something, such as writing a Logo program that gets the turtle to paint a rainbow. The same would go for mathematics.

Another powerful idea we see Papert offering educational scholars and designers is that of *emergence* as an intellectual paradigm for investigating the evolution of adaptive, stable, and self-regulating complex dynamic systems, be these natural, social, or cognitive phenomena. Piaget's genetic epistemology is inherently systemic (Piaget, 1970), in that he formulates a theoretical model accounting for the process by which simple knowing evolves into sophisticated knowing, where each construction either modifies or coordinates existing structures vis-à-vis shifting situated goals. These adapted cognitive structures thus self-accommodate to assimilate variation in environmental encounters, where difference is perceived as either similarity or novelty. As such, the child's world is a goal-oriented systemic construction, where haphazard contingencies ever constrain the pruning, specialization, and assembly of better-adapted coping mechanisms. Learning in the natural and cultural–historical social ecology is nondeterministic, nonlinear, nonteleological genetic evolution, in which stable environments nurture and regulate individuals' inherent capacity into fully adapted wherewithal, complete with linguistic, quantitative, technological, and moral aptitudes.

Papert sought to further refine Piaget's model of cognitive development by proposing a principle for the organization of schemes into hierarchical clusters ("Papert's principle," see Minsky, 1985). This structuralist epistemological model strove to characterize cognitive development, such as the conservation of volume, as an iterative optimization search process, in which primitive judgment aptitudes (e.g., "taller-than," "wider-than") are exploratively grouped by family resemblance to make salient within-situation critical conditions for inferring properties in question ("more-than" or "same"). Emergent superstructures, such as the idea that material quantity is conserved when no substance was added or removed, consolidate iteratively through empirical proof of their replicability, validity, and utility.

An epistemological theory that acknowledges the essentially emergent quality of cognitive development appears to imply a pedagogical approach that recognizes a need to provide for each child's idiosyncratic path, even as it guides all students toward common-enough knowledge and skills. Such a pedagogical approach might lead to *restructuring* curricular subject matter content (see Wilensky & Papert, 2010), such as rudimentary algebra, not only to render it body/culture-syntonic but also to cater for the emergence of content knowledge as a cluster of simple cognitive structures self-assembled to serve greater conceptual objectives. This multischeme assembly process would be mutually interadaptive, where a set of relevant schemes evokes, interconstrains, and prunes each other, as gauged vis-à-vis its global replicability, validity, and utility, into a functional transformation system. This evolving cognitive system would be manifest for external observation in the child's adaptive behavior, culminating in the fluent enactment of solutions for a class of situations presented in educational activities, such as algebra problems bearing unknown quantities.

What might all of this theorizing look like in the form of actual learning resources? True to this volume's orientation on constructionism in context, the remainder of this chapter will attempt to support the argument for the dual legacy of syntonicity and emergence, from Piaget through Papert and beyond, by discussing a more recent educational design-based research project that was nurtured by these big ideas. The project in question may not be a paradigmatic exemplar of constructionist pedagogy, in that it was not conceived to permit children full sway in pursuing and manufacturing their own worlds. Rather, the educational design in question is far narrower in its pallet of actions and building choices offered to the child than, say, a Logo microworld. Yet it does aspire to constitute a body- and culture-syntonic environment, and students' experiences therein lend themselves auspiciously to systemic modeling of learning as the emergence of a cluster of interconstraining schemes. Following a section on the project, below, we will offer some observations on the future of educational technology inspired by constructivist/constructionist principles and, perhaps, taking them one tiny step farther.

GIANT STEPS FOR ALGEBRA AS A MODEST EXAMPLE OF CONSTRUCTIONIST PEDAGOGY: A CASE FOR SYNTONICITY AND EMERGENCE AS POWERFUL IDEAS FOR DESIGN-BASED RESEARCH

Giant Steps for Algebra (GS4A, Chase & Abrahamson, 2018) was a design-based research doctoral dissertation project conceived as a response to the problem of US students' underachievement in mathematics, particularly in algebra. Viewing this enduring national problem as a challenge to educational practice, many researchers have implicated students' cognitive difficulty in transitioning from arithmetic to algebra: whereas arithmetic curriculum typically fosters the conceptualization of equivalence ("=") as *operational*, that is, an action "on the left" with a result "on the right," algebra requires a *relational* conceptualization of equivalence between two quantities. As design-based researchers of mathematical cognition, teaching, and learning, we chose to explore pedagogical solutions with the potential to better pave the arithmetic-to-algebra learning transition.

Our first task was to investigate existing algebra curricula so as better to understand current pedagogical approaches and perhaps glean their underlying epistemological assumptions and conceptual structuration. This initial analytical process revealed to us the *balance metaphor* as the most common educational introduction to the relational structure and logic of algebraic equations. The balance metaphor is typically presented to students by invoking interactions with relevant cultural artifacts, such as the twin-pan balance scale. Yet whereas balance scales per se appear to be *body* syntonic, in that they draw on an embodied sense of equivalence, it is not clear whether this particular sense enables students to build from their robust arithmetic skills toward the relational conceptualization of algebraic equations. Moreover, twin-pan scales are increasingly substituted with electronic scales so that their alleged *cultural* syntonicity may be lost to the target audience of algebra learners.

Further search of the literature revealed that Dickinson and Eade (2004) had tackled a similar design problem by using the double number line as a diagrammatic form for modeling linear equations. Figure 29.1 shows a fragment from our GS4A adaptation of their model into a dedicated microworld (later in this section we explain additional elements in this figure). The GS4A problem narrative depicts a quasi-realistic situation, in which a giant performs two consecutive journeys along a path. The narrative for the figure 29.1 example reads as follows:

> A giant has stolen the elves' treasure. Help the elves find their treasure! Here is what we know. On the first day, the giant walked 3 steps and then another 2 meters, where she buried treasure. On the next day, she began at the same point and wanted to bury more treasure in exactly the same place, but she was not sure where that place was. She walked 4 steps and then, feeling she'd gone too far, she walked back one meter. Yes! She found the treasure!

Thus, these two journeys—Day 1 journey and Day 2 journey—begin at the same point of departure (the Start flag on the left) and end at the same destination (the Treasure flag on the right). However, the journeys differ in terms of the agent's process. The two journeys correspond to two equivalent algebraic expressions: here the algebraic proposition "$3x + 2 = 4x - 1$" is rendered into the progressions "$3x + 2$" (Day 1 above the line) and "$4x - 1$" (Day 2 below the line).

Our evaluations of the activity with pre-algebra study participants suggested the syntonic design quality of students diagrammatically modeling

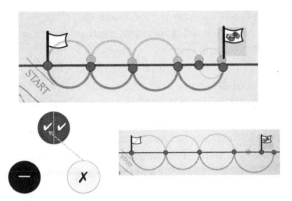

FIGURE 29.1

Giant Steps for Algebra: example of diagrammatic activity and its cognitive modeling. *Above:* A student's first attempt at solving a narrative instantiation of the algebraic proposition of $3x + 2 = 4x - 1$. On both Day 1 ($3x + 2$, above the horizontal path line) and Day 2 ($4x - 1$, below the line) the giant traveled from the Start flag on the left to the Treasure flag on the right. Dark grey arcs represent giant steps (the variable x), and light grey arcs represent meters (the fixed integer units). In building this diagram the student has apparently attempted to maintain consistent measures (SILO 1) of giant steps and meters, respectively, but has not achieved equivalent expressions (SILO 2) above and below the line (note different end points of Day 1 and Day 2 journeys), consequently failing to create a shared frame of reference (SILO 3). *Bottom-left:* The student's current conceptual knowledge state, as evident in their diagram, is modeled as an emergent system composed of these three interconstraining schemes. The arrow depicts the student's consequent inference, as evident in their subsequent modification of the diagram (bottom right) that repaired the violated equivalent expressions by readdressing the consistent measures, thus achieving a shared frame of reference that led to calculating the size of a giant step in this particular narrative as 3 meters.

an algebraic text narrative. First, the pilot study corroborated prior findings from psycholinguistics research that text-comprehension processes are enactive–imagistic (e.g., Zwaan, 2004) as witnessed in the participants' multimodal utterances and construction actions. Engaging with the narrative brings forth body-syntonic know-how. This tacit knowing becomes reified, conscious, modified, and combined by virtue of depicting the narrative as a perceptually durable and shareable display upon the interactive virtual canvas. Second, the study suggested that students can develop new forms of mathematical reasoning capacity through constructing and adjusting given resources into a depictive diagram (Martin & Schwartz,

2005). Students act on features in the GS4A interface, interpret products of these actions, and then act again, a design process that Bamberger and Schön (1991) call "see–move–see."

What types of body- and culture-syntonic know-how did the participants bring to bear in depicting the text narrative? What were their situated abstractions (Noss & Hoyle, 1996)? What cognitive models emerge through this process? As researchers who develop instructional resources with well-defined curricular goals in mind, we chose to name children's proto-conceptual know-how *situated intermediary learning objectives*, or *SILOs*. Our micro-analyses of the video and screen data suggested the following three SILOs.

1. *Consistent measures.* All variable units (giant steps) and all fixed units (meters) are respectively uniform in size both within and between expressions (days).

2. *Equivalent expressions.* The two expressions (Day 1 and Day 2) are of identical magnitude—they share the "start" and the "end" points, so that they subtend precisely the same linear displacement (even though the total distance traveled may differ between days, such as when a giant oversteps and then goes back).

3. *Shared frame of reference.* The variable quantity (giant steps) can be described in terms of the unit quantity (meters).

As cognitive constructs, the SILOs thus hover in an epistemic space between the locally pragmatic and the conceptually generative. SILOs are thus expressed both as embodied experience and cognitive constructs—both contextual and universal—grounded both in body-syntonic know-how, such as assuming that by default the giant struts along in equally sized strides, and culture-syntonic methods, for example using conventional arbitrary units, such as meters, to measure linear extension. The SILOs render cognitively *transparent* the operational logic of procedural actions in an otherwise opaque activity structure such as algebra. The construct of *transparency* (see Meira, 1998) captures the psychological relation between an individual and the artifact they are using toward the accomplishment of some goal. We say that the artifact is transparent to an individual when he or she has developed an understanding for how its embedded features function to promote the accomplishment of its systemic objective. The SILOs distil and render transparent the operational logic of GS4A algebraic problem-solving mechanics. By engaging conscientiously with the GS4A activity, students achieve the design's SILO system, thus mentally constructing procedures for creating and maintaining equivalence, even as they literally construct and debug a solution model for a problem narrative (see figure 29.1 and Chase & Abrahamson, 2018, for results from analyses of empirical data gathered in experimental design interventions).

Let us now turn to emergence as a principle for modeling the evolution of students' cognitive growth through working in the GS4A environment. Above, we have described each of the three SILOs as logically independent. And yet our analyses revealed that the process of constructing each SILO is ontogenetically interdependent upon the process of constructing the other two SILOs. In particular, the SILOs niche ecology coalesces iteratively, through the ongoing reflective practice of iterating on the depictive model, with each SILO constraining the emergence and calibration of the other SILOs (Chase & Abrahamson, 2018).

By design, users build algebra as a transparent practice. This design consisted of a task, resources, and a specific activity flow that scaffolded for the emergence of mathematical cognition. In Chase and Abrahamson (2018), we coined the phrase *reverse scaffolding* to capture our pedagogical methodology for guided emergence of mathematical concepts in technological environments, where instructional-interaction decisions are implemented in software procedures. The *reverse scaffolding* design architecture works as follows. Once students' diagrammatic construction makes evident that they have successfully generated and managed a mathematically appropriate structural property of their model (i.e., they have achieved one of the SILOs), the software "takes over" by automatically enacting and maintaining this property for them. When students initially encounter the GS4A interface, they must manually construct and monitor all structural aspects of their diagrams, such as ensuring that all giant steps are equivalent. Yet once a student articulates a SILO—perhaps commenting that giant steps are uniform—the interface responds by entering a new "game level," in which the giant step is automatically produced for the user and changing one giant step uniformly changes all other giant steps on the screen. Crucially, *reverse-scaffolding designs perform for users only what they already know to do, not what they are not able to do, as in mainstream applications of the scaffolding metaphor.* Reverse-scaffolding interface actions are thus designed to promote student agency in the emergent construction of their conceptual systems.

The *reverse scaffolding* design was conceived as a pedagogical approach that could straddle the divide between purist constructivist learning approaches and automated educational technologies. We want students to discover, invent, and engage an emergent network of interconnected schema, and, yet, we acknowledge that continuing to reinvent from scratch can become tedious. Conversely, if educational technologies automate and scaffold users' production and process from the start, these functions are liable to remain opaque to the user, effectively robbing users of the opportunity to construct their own understanding. The reverse-scaffolding activity architecture enables the emergence of the cognitive superstructure for early algebra, through the iterative consolidation and systemic interconstraining of each SILO.

To our evaluation, the GS4A project made both practical and theoretical contributions aligned with principles of syntonicity and emergence carried down by Papert from Piaget. Both theoretically informed and developmentally appropriate, educational designs based on the interactive diagrammatic modeling of narratives create opportunities for students to elicit and build their situated knowing into transparent, functional conceptual structures that expand their capacity to engage in the cultural practices of mathematics. Furthermore, the design-architecture heuristic principle of *reverse scaffolding* creates for educators a template to plan for the sequential emergence of students' conceptual knowledge. Finally, students' learning process as well as researchers' analysis process are organized around the cognitive construct of SILOs, situated intermediary learning objectives, thus making for coherent design-based research studies of mathematical cognition, teaching, and learning.

MOVING FORWARD: COORDINATION-DYNAMICS RESEARCH ON THE EMERGENCE OF KNOWLEDGE FROM SYNTONIC DESIGN

Plus ça change, plus c'est la même chose
(Jean-Baptiste Alphonse Karr, 1849, *Les Guêpes*)

Papert did not like education. At least, he disliked how this word connotes that somebody is doing something to a child, whereas in fact it is the child who is learning. And so rather than "pedagogy," Papert (1980) spoke of *mathetics*, "the set of guiding principles that govern learning" (p. 52). An "applied mathetician," Papert is mostly known as a learning futurist, a diviner of all things to come in learning technology, one who sedulously practiced the adage, "The best way to predict the future is to invent it" (attributed to Alan Kay). Yet while Papert was busy inventing the practice future of body/culture-syntonic learning, the theory slow coach of cognitive sciences considered resonant ideas on embodiment that, in turn, seeped into educational research as *embodied design* (Abrahamson & Lindgren, 2014).

Embodiment perspectives in educational research by and large reinstitute Piaget's post-dualist systemic theory of cognitive developmental psychology by underscoring the constitutive role of sensorimotor activity in the emergence of adaptive coping in natural and cultural ecologies. Accordingly, embodied design is a heuristic methodology for creating learning environments, including materials, tasks, and facilitation guidelines, wherein students are ushered to spontaneously appropriate legacy cultural methods as powerful means of enhancing their innate or early developed sensorimotor capacities, such as perceptual judgments or motor coordination. Indeed, laboratory evaluations of an *action-based embodied design* for proportions have corroborated empirically a central tenet from Piaget's genetic epistemology, reflective abstracting. Combining eye-tracking and clinical data, we demonstrated the emergence, and then the verbal articulation, of new dynamical perceptual structures that came forth as gestalts in the child's imagined visual display to coordinate spontaneous solutions for bimanual movement problems (Abrahamson, Shayan, Bakker, & Van der Schaaf, 2016). We view this design-based research as extending the theory of coordination dynamic (Kelso, 2014) into conceptual realms of human capacity.

Even as theories of learning change, they could be essentially more of the same thing. Piaget might call this a type of conservation that we come to appreciate through intellectual interaction. As a framework for building learning environments, embodied design attempts to implement Papert's notion of syntonicity that, we have argued, in turn realizes Piaget's insight into the emergence of knowledge through situated interaction. Notwithstanding, things do change in important ways, even as they remain the same. Constructionism has changed the way we think about designing for learning, as we believe the Giant Steps for Algebra project has demonstrated. If we build designs, the students will come. If students build artifacts, they will construct powerful ideas.

ACKNOWLEDGMENT

For their thoughtful comments on earlier drafts of this manuscript, we wish to thank Colin Foster and Dragan Trninic.

REFERENCES

Abrahamson, D., & Lindgren, R. (2014). Embodiment and embodied design. In R. K. Sawyer (Ed.), *The Cambridge handbook of the learning sciences* (2nd ed., pp. 358–376). Cambridge, UK: Cambridge University Press.

Abrahamson, D., Shayan, S., Bakker, A., & Van der Schaaf, M. F. (2016). Eye-tracking Piaget: Capturing the emergence of attentional anchors in the coordination of proportional motor action. *Human Development, 58*(4–5), 218–244.

Bamberger, J., & Schön, D. A. (1991). Learning as reflective conversation with materials. In F. Steier (Ed.), *Research and reflexivity* (pp. 186–209). London, UK: SAGE Publications.

Chase, K., & Abrahamson, D. (2018). Searching for buried treasure: Uncovering discovery in discovery-based learning. In D. Abrahamson & M. Kapur (Eds.), Practicing discovery-based learning: Evaluating new horizons [Special issue]. *Instructional Science, 46*(1), 11–33.

Dickinson, P., & Eade, F. (2004). Using the number line to investigate the solving of linear equations. *For the Learning of Mathematics, 24*(2), 41–47.

Kelso, J. A. S. (2014). The dynamic brain in action: Coordinative structures, criticality, and coordination dynamics. In D. Plenz & E. Niebur (Eds.), *Criticality in neural systems* (pp. 67–106). Mannheim, Germany: John Wiley & Sons.

Martin, T., & Schwartz, D. L. (2005). Physically distributed learning: adapting and reinterpreting physical environments in the development of fraction concepts. *Cognitive Science, 29*(4), 587–625.

Meira, L. (1998). Making sense of instructional devices: the emergence of transparency in mathematical activity. *Journal for Research in Mathematics Education, 29*(2), 129–142.

Minsky, M. (1985). *The society of mind*. London, UK: Hienemann.

Noss, R., & Hoyles, C. (1996). *Windows on mathematical meanings: Learning cultures and computers*. Dordrecht, The Netherlands: Kluwer.

Papert, S. (1980). *Mindstorms: Children, computers, and powerful ideas*. New York, NY: Basic Books.

Piaget, J. (1968). *Genetic epistemology* (E. Duckworth, Trans.). New York, NY: Columbia University Press.

Piaget, J. (1970). *Structuralism* (C. Maschler, Trans.). New York, NY: Basic Books. (Original work published 1968).

Piaget, J. (1971). *Biology and knowledge: An essay on the relations between organic regulations and cognitive processes* (B. Walsh, Trans.). Chicago, IL: University of Chicago Press.

Wilensky, U., & Papert, S. (2010). Restructurations: Reformulations of knowledge disciplines through new representational forms. In J. Clayson & I. Kallas (Eds.), *Proceedings of the Constructionism 2010 Conference (The 12th EuroLogo conference)*. Paris, France.

Zwaan, R. A. (2004). The immersed experiencer: Toward an embodied theory of language comprehension. In B. H. Ross (Ed.), *The psychology of learning and motivation* (Vol. 44, pp. 35–62). New York, NY: Academic Press.

30 CONSTRUCTIONISM IN ART STUDIOS

Kimberly M. Sheridan

One of the origin stories in constructionism is that walking by an art class, Papert watched a student carving a simple soap sculpture, and he imagined what it would mean to make the representational process as visible, evolving, and evocative for math as it is in art (Papert & Harel, 1991). In constructionism there exists an articulation of the value in giving students in all disciplines time to represent their ideas, means to make them visible to others, and flexibility so that they can connect their representations meaningfully with prior knowledge and change them through collaborative reflection. In this sense, studio art education can be thought of as a prototype of constructionist learning.

Studio arts learning is centrally about exploring form and meaning of representations (Halverson & Sheridan, 2014). In studio arts classes, students are typically engaged over extended periods of time on the construction of an artifact often in response to open-ended prompts. This construction is often informed by demonstrations of techniques and discussion of examples from art history, contemporary art, and the work of other students. Each student's work becomes a public object of conversation in varied ways: between an individual and their artwork in conjunction with a teacher, for the class community, and for exhibition to audiences beyond the class. Pedagogical strategies are used to help community make meaning of the evolving artifact and to envision possibilities for how it could develop further (Hetland, Winner, Veenema & Sheridan, 2013).

ARTISTIC REPRESENTATION

Creating and responding to art primarily involves working with representations. Though much of the research and work in cognitive and learning sciences on symbolic representation has focused on discursive symbol systems with specialized notational systems for communication (e.g., mathematics, linguistics, logic), the arts importantly involve what Langer termed presentational symbol systems (Langer, 1978). The symbol is perceived as a whole and the meaning of the representation cannot be meaningfully abstracted, translated, or reduced from its form. Thus, this raises questions about how we come to understand these presentational symbol systems in arts.

Goodman identifies *symptoms* of the *languages of art* to clarify how we make sense of how presentational symbol systems communicate, how we build our understanding of the work and the world (Goodman, 1976). In Goodman's view, art is semantically and syntactically dense—or *relatively replete*—and through complex chains of reference, we iteratively construct its meaning. Though the considerable philosophical debate on the nature of aesthetic symbolic representation is beyond the scope of this chapter, Goodman's approach has several implications for a constructionist view of arts learning.

First, arts and science are both important ways of understanding and making meaning of our worlds. However, whereas learning physics may involve seeing the common mathematical simplicity underlying the motion of both machines and planets, the work of learning arts is expanding the ways you can appreciate the particularities of replete artistic representations. The meaning and value of an artistic work—whether our own or another's—can grow with each new interpretation and shift with context. Art education engages students in this constructive representational process, both in terms of creative production and critical response.

Second, Goodman also argues that a key question is not what is art, but when is art? His argument aims to explain, for instance, why a urinal in one setting is a functional object, and yet the same object placed in an exhibit by Duchamp is a work of art that transformed history. But, for my purposes, his argument also highlights the role of context in art learning: art is not an inert object with specific fixed properties, rather it is a communicative event shaped by the intentions of the producers, the meaning-making of the viewers, and the context of its viewing. This broad perspective aligns deeply with a constructionist view of learning: students' artifacts are better understood as evolving representations that communicate understanding in specific social contexts rather than inert, abstracted products.

LEARNING IN THE ARTS

Conceptualizing and assessing learning in studio arts has proved challenging. Researchers have found it easier to identify learning when looking at art, rather than in its production. Another substantial body of research avoids delineating what is learned within the arts, focusing instead on how arts participation transfers to gains in realms outside of the arts (e.g., literacy, SAT scores, general academic achievement). Within creative production in the arts, educators often take a "we know good work when we see it" approach: expert consensus is a common technique in assessing student's art portfolios, whether in competitions or advanced placement and international baccalaureate exams. Though expert consensus can reliably assess diverse creative products, it gives little insight into learning.

However, constructionist approaches to learning may provide a lens to examine important aspects of learning in the arts, such as the following two dimensions of envisioning and meta-representational competence. To this end, Halverson (2013) draws on diSessa's construct of meta-representational competence (diSessa, Hammer, Sherin, & Kolpakowski, 1991) to examine how, in the artistic realm of video production, students develop an understanding of how narrative and aesthetic tools, conventions, and devices contribute to how ideas are represented and how they communicate to an audience. By tracking the representational trajectory of a given work, Halverson documents how the shifts produce not only higher-quality work but also broader competence in the languages of artistic representation in the specific area of video production.

Another invisible but equally important part of the artistic process is envisioning—imagining what is not there and picturing what is possible. In artistic production, envisioning is not just one phase of a design process, rather it is an embedded and ongoing part of creating an artwork. Students are continually observing their work in progress and picturing what else is possible—and are explicitly encouraged to explore varied possibilities (Sheridan, 2011). Envisioning can also be a collaborative process. For instance, in mid-process critiques, students may observe and discuss each other's works in progress. Students see the decisions others have made, imagine how their own and others' works could be changed, and try to articulate these differences (Hetland, Winner, Veenema, & Sheridan, 2013; Soep, 2006). This envisioning is seen across diverse art forms. For instance, in her analysis of varied after-school programs, Heath (2001) found that the language of students in arts programs compared to other programs reflected what she termed *imaginative actuality*, the tendency to envision and articulate possible actions and approaches and then also discuss plans on how to bring them to fruition. Similarly, aesthetic educator Greene described the arts and this envisioning capacity as central to developing our capacity to see and change our worlds, imagining the world "as if it were otherwise" (Greene, 1995).

STUDIO STRUCTURES SUPPORTING STUDENT LEARNING

Studio arts education has long been centered on supporting the thoughtful construction of public artifacts, so it is unsurprising there are close connections to constructionist approaches to learning. Constructionist approaches have already drawn from some common practices of studio arts pedagogy, such as how to use sketchbooks and portfolios to track students' evolving representations. However, a closer look at studio arts pedagogy reveals further potential connections, particularly on how to model thinking about a representation during its planning and construction and supporting meaningful critique of students' products both during and at the end of the making process. Studio arts learning environments typically feature four types of pedagogical structures: Demonstration-Lectures, Students-at-Work, Critiques, and Exhibitions (Hetland, Winner, Veenema, & Sheridan, 2013). These four studio structures act as interchangeable blocks that make up a typical studio arts class, not a particular sequence. Each plays a slightly different role in supporting students' construction of artistic representations, and each aligns with constructionist approaches to learning.

In *Demonstration-Lectures* a teacher poses a problem, demonstrates a technique or process, or provides context for a problem. This aligns with the constructionist approach of modeling ways to approach a problem and activating relevant prior knowledge. Demonstration-lectures tend to be highly visual and involve analyzing artworks and envisioning possibilities for future artworks. For instance, in a high school drawing class, the teacher asked students to analyze how the space was treated between two figures in a Richard Diebenkorn painting and the expressive impact of this treatment. Students talked about color, negative space, light, repetition, and how it created a sense of quiet tension and unease between the figures, pointing out how and why they thought that. Other students argued that they found it calm, pointing to muted color tones. This discussion around another artist's representation—analyzing its features, how it was created, and its contextual and expressive effects reflects a constructionist stance toward understanding an object as a public entity. The interpretation is based on observation of a representation in the world, students are coached to attend to it more closely and build their own representation of meaning and function; they construct an interpretive model of the referent, and so become more conversant in the "languages of art." Furthermore, in a studio class this analysis of another artists' work forms the basis for one's own creative production. In the above example, students were invited to complete a series of sketches where they, too, focused on the space between two fellow students who were posing in the room. Thus, their preliminary co-construction of an interpretation scaffolds their own creative work.

During *Students-at-Work*, students engage in constructing their responses to an often open-ended prompt that sets some guidelines around content, materials, techniques, and or processes. During this time, the teacher circles the room, watching as students work, and interacts with them individually to support their learning. These interactions often involve impromptu, brief, one-on-one demonstrations or critiques. Akin to constructionist approaches, they involve a dynamic process in which the teacher adapts the assignment goals to the individual students, based on their current work in progress, their prior work, and their future goals. In our case studies of high school art classes, we found that Students-at-Work composed the bulk of a studio arts class, and teachers had over 75 interactions with individual students per hour of Students-at-Work time. In analyzing over 4000 of these videorecorded interactions from five different teachers, we found teachers used these times to encourage students to reflect on their working process, to observe their evolving representation more closely, to identify its expressive properties, to envision alternate approaches, and to explore new ways of approaching the artistic problem (Hetland, Winner, Veenema, & Sheridan, 2013). These individual interactions reflect a central process of constructionist approaches to learning: a dialogue between the student, teacher, and evolving object. The "product" of interest is both the object the student is creating and the habits of mind the product and artistic process reflect in their ongoing development as an artist.

Through the studio structure of *critiques*, the reflection on representations becomes heightened. In mid-process critiques, the work process is paused and time is taken to review and discuss the varied student works in progress. This may involve a quick "gallery walk," in which students just stand up and walk around the room, looking at how their peers have approached the problem, or it may be a more intensive discussion in which works are analyzed in depth. Mid-process critiques often involve drawing attention to qualities in the work and collectively envisioning possibilities for directions the work can go. Diverse strategies encourage students to see the work in new ways and provide constructive feedback, such as routines where students are encouraged to note what they see and wonder about in an artwork, or imagine if it were altered in some way. Critiques vary widely in their depth: in our observations, we observed critiques that lasted just a few minutes and some that lasted two hours. Some focused on relatively simple and concrete formal aspects of the work; others explored rich and personal aspects of meaning and identity

(Hetland, Winner, Veenema, & Sheridan, 2013). Regardless of length and type, the aim in critique is to move beyond simple expression of preference or evaluation to deeper insights about how and why a particular artwork communicates using evidence in the work (Soep, 2006). As with constructionist approaches to learning, just making a visible artifact does not create its meaning: educators scaffold social construction of the meaning of works through the practice of critiques.

Last, students' artworks do not reside solely in the classroom. *Exhibitions* to a broader public are a fairly common practice—emphasizing the role of audience in arts learning. Exhibitions allow students to experience how their work may be perceived by different audiences in varying contexts. Exhibitions expand the representational possibilities of the work and align with the constructionist focus on the public and distributed meaning making of artifacts. When student works become public objects of conversation, the thinking involved in their creation becomes more varied and visible.

ARTS LEARNING AND NEW TECHNOLOGIES

Studio arts learning environments are not limited to formal classrooms; informal settings have long been important sites of arts learning. More recently, interdisciplinary and technology-focused creative production sites such as FabLabs and makerspaces have emerged (Peppler, Halverson, & Kafai, 2016; Sheridan et al., 2014). There are diverse in-person and online sites for collaborating on art, forming communities around shared affinities, and diverse art making practices (Karpati et al., 2017). The social contexts for art learning have been in rapid expansion in recent decades, often intertwining with new technologies, and transforming studio arts learning and pedagogy. New digital tools and technologies are rapidly changing the forms of art making available to youth. Novice-friendly tools for video editing, animation, 3D-modeling and fabrication, e-textiles, and other areas have transformed the representational process. Furthermore, the social contexts for arts learning have also been in expansion in recent decades.

The convergence of these new technologies for artistic production with domains more commonly associated with constructionist learning, such as computer programming, create opportunities for more comprehensive accounts of learning. Youth working in Scratch, for instance, can work directly within others' projects, transforming them into their own. Though many analyses have focused on the computational and collaborative aspects of Scratch, this ability to directly "mix" other visual art as a common social practice is transformative for what it means to be an animator, designer, and arts learner (Peppler & Kafai, 2007). As youth combine a notational, discursive symbol system like computer programming with a holistic artistic product like an animated video, they shift across symbol systems in new ways (Sheridan & Gardner, 2012).

As educators incorporate these new technologies and practices for multimedia creative production, they can also further draw on the pedagogical practices of studio arts education that support the complex representations needed. For instance, when viewing students work, art educators regularly identify contemporary and historical artists that reflect the style and interests of the student. Thus, a student is encouraged to go look up DuBuffet because he uses line and negative space in a way that is similar, or to look at the work of Carrie Mae Weems because, like the student, she also uses visual culture to examine race. Other disciplines could support similar identity connections, encouraging students to read biographies not because they are part of a standard curricula but because the educator sees an affinity with how the student thinks.

CONCLUSION

Like Papert's initial envisioning of "soap-sculpture math," studio arts education has been mined for pedagogical practices to support rich constructionist learning—the use of sketchbooks and portfolios as tools for documentation and reflection on representations comes to mind. The influence of constructionist approaches to learning are seen as students in diverse classes are increasingly called upon to create multimedia presentations, video documentaries, infographics, and other varied forms that use artistic representational forms to construct and demonstrate their understandings. Educators supporting these learnings can draw from the powerful pedagogical practices in studio arts, using modeling in interactive demonstrations, reflective practices from critiques and exhibitions, and the professionals in the field throughout history as personalized resources to help students see connections between their own work and the larger world.

REFERENCES

diSessa, A. A., Hammer, D., Sherin, B., & Kolpakowski, T. (1991). Inventing graphing: Meta-representational expertise in children. *Journal of Mathematical Behavior, 10*(2), 117–160.

Goodman, N. (1976). *Languages of art*. Indianapolis, IN: Hackett Publishing Company, Inc.

Greene, M. (1995). *Releasing the imagination: Essays on education, the arts, and social change*. San Francisco, CA: Jossey-Bass.

Halverson, E. R. (2013). Digital art making as a representational process. *Journal of the Learning Sciences*, 1–42.

Halverson, E., & Sheridan, K. (2014). Arts education and the learning sciences. In R. K. Sawyer (Ed.). *Cambridge handbook of the learning sciences* (2nd ed., pp. 626–646). Cambridge, UK: Cambridge University Press.

Heath, S. B. (2001). Three's not a crowd: Plans, roles, and focus in the arts. *Educational Researcher, 30*(7), 10–17.

Hetland, L., Winner, E., Veenema, S., & Sheridan, K. M. (2013). *Studio thinking 2: The real benefits of visual arts education* (2nd ed.). New York, NY: Teachers College Press.

Karpati, A., Freedman, K., Castro, J. C., Kallio-Tavin, M., & Heijnen, E. (2017). Collaboration in visual culture learning communities: Towards a synergy of individual and collective creative practice. *International Journal of Art & Design Education, 36*(2), 164–175.

Langer, S. K. (1978). *Philosophy in a new key: A study in the symbolism of reason, rite and art* (Vol. 3). Cambridge, MA: Harvard University Press.

Papert, S., & Harel, I. (1991). Situating constructionism. In I. Harel & S. Papert (Eds.), *Constructionism* (pp. 1–11). Norwood, NJ: Ablex Publishing Corp.

Peppler, K. A., Halverson, E., & Kafai, Y. B. (Eds.). (2016). *Makeology*. New York, NY: Routledge.

Peppler, K. A., & Kafai, Y. B. (2007). From SuperGoo to Scratch: Exploring creative digital media production in informal learning. *Learning, media and technology, 32*(2), 149–166.

Sheridan, K. M. (2011). Envision and observe: Using the studio thinking framework for learning and teaching in digital arts. *Mind, Brain, and Education, 5*(1), 19–26.

Sheridan, K. & Gardner, H. (2012). Artistic development: Three essential spheres. In A. Shimamura and S. Palmer (Eds.) *Aesthetic science: Connecting minds, brains, and experience* (pp.277–296). Oxford, UK: Oxford University Press.

Sheridan, K., Halverson, E. R., Litts, B., Brahms, L., Jacobs-Priebe, L., & Owens, T. (2014). Learning in the making: A comparative case study of three makerspaces. *Harvard Educational Review, 84*(4), 505–531.

Soep, E. (2006). Critique: Assessment and the production of learning. *Teachers College Record, 108*(4), 748–777.

31 CREATIVITY AS SUSTAINED SOCIAL PRACTICES: FOUR PILLARS FOR CREATIVE LEARNING DESIGN

Jianwei Zhang

Constructionism, since its inception, has sought to explore a new creative vision for the future of education. Driven by the notion of "child as builder" (Papert, 1980), a rich set of technological and social innovations has been developed to support students' creative work with designs and ideas (Halverson & Peppler, 2018; Resnick, 2017). The prominence of such innovations rooted in constructionism and other theories of learning for knowledge creation (e.g., Scardamalia & Bereiter, 2014) is heightened in the twenty-first-century contexts in which creativity has become the key to societal prosperity and individual growth. It is more urgent than ever for educators to explore new models of learning and education for creativity. Such efforts need to capitalize on the affordances of new technology and also tap into the new conceptual insights in creativity and learning. The purpose of this chapter is to synthesize these conceptual insights, drawing upon advances in the fields of creativity research and the learning sciences. I will first elaborate a view of creativity as sustained social practice and then identify four pillar elements of creative social practice. In light of each of the elements, I will discuss opportunities for researching and designing creative learning environments.

CREATIVITY AS SUSTAINED SOCIAL PRACTICES

Creativity is commonly defined as the process to generate creative products of various kinds, which have recognizable novelty, quality, and relevance for specific contexts. A challenge is to understand what characterizes this process. Traditional views depicted the process of creativity as unique, somewhat mysterious sparks of new thoughts in the minds of talented individuals, who attempt to break away from their prior experience. Recent research has demystified this process and re-conceptualized creativity as incremental and social (Sawyer, 2007). First, creative insights emerge from incremental development and continual improvement of ideas. Many mini-insights are gradually generated and selectively advanced and combined, leading to the emergence of complex, often unexpected insights. Second, this sustained process requires intentional and deliberate efforts, which involve active pursuit and use of knowledge, skills, and experiences (Ward & Kolomyts, 2010). Creativity is enabled by productively using accumulated knowledge, instead of being squashed by it (Weisberg, 1999). Third, the sustained process of creativity is deeply social and cultural. Even though individuals may need quiet personal time for focused thinking, their progress often involves dynamic idea contact and collaboration with peers and further builds on the knowledge of the larger fields (Sawyer, 2007). Therefore, creativity takes place in a social system that includes the individual, knowledge/cultural domain, and social field. Individuals, who often work in teams, acquire domain knowledge and skills and generate new contributions to the domain(s). The potential value of their contributions are reviewed by the "gatekeepers" of their field (Csikszentmihalyi, 1999), such as journal editors and reviewers.

In parallel to the advances in creativity research, progress in the learning sciences has expanded our notions of learning. Complementing existing frameworks of learning that focus on student knowledge acquisition or participation in social communities, recent theories offer a new expanded view of learning as knowledge creation (Paavola & Hakkarainen, 2005). Working as innovative knowledge communities, learners engage in interactive activities and conversations to create and develop shared cultural objects (theories, designs, instruments), which mediate their personal understanding and collaborative social practices. Their interactive activities and conversations lead to not only the sharing of existing ideas and practices but also continual advancement of the "state of the art" of their community's knowledge (Scardamalia & Bereiter, 2014) and transformation of shared practice. As two strong learning programs that encourage knowledge creation, Knowledge Building theory and pedagogy have a primary focus on transforming learning in classrooms (Chan & van Aalst, 2018; Scardamalia & Bereiter, 2014), while constructionism-based programs such as makerspaces often center on advancing learning outside schools (Halverson & Peppler, 2018). Future research could benefit from efforts to delineate core principles of creative learning that rise above the different programs and contexts.

FOUR PILLARS OF CREATIVE LEARNING

This section delineates a set of four pillars of creative learning practices as the focus of learning research and design.

Working with a Collective Knowledge Space

Creative knowledge work requires the participants to build on their community's knowledge and make new contributions to advance the "state of the art" (Scardamalia & Bereiter, 2014). The community may be defined at different levels, ranging from a small team, a local organization such as a classroom or school, to a larger intellectual field or cross-disciplinary area. The knowledge essential to this context is collective knowledge as a social product with an out-in-the-world existence, such as theories, designs, and narratives represented in various public spaces. To do creative work in a field, participants need to assimilate and build on the community's knowledge and appropriate the inquiry practices to bring about valuable novelty (Csikszentmihalyi, 1999). To ease knowledge assimilation and innovation, ideas in a public domain need to have permanent and accurate representation that is easily accessible. As Csikszentmihalyi (1999) put it, "The more accessible the information, the wider range of individuals who can participate in creative processes" (p. 318). Sustained creativity can be further advanced through supporting cross-fertilization of ideas from different domains and cultures that leverage dynamic contact of diverse ideas. Through monitoring the knowledge in their domain(s) and concerting with the ideas of others, creative contributors selectively pick up ideas that have potential and develop them into better, more advanced ideas (Sternberg, 2003).

Recent research in education drawing upon new technology informs new ways to support students' productive work with knowledge as a community, broadening opportunities for all students to access as well as to contribute to collective knowledge for public good. These include open educational resources that give students easy access to updated knowledge in various domains, social annotation and bibliography tools (e.g., Hypothesis, CiteULike) for students to collect, annotate, and share references, and authentic professional databases with which students investigate real-world challenges. Innovative inquiry-based environments further offer students public spaces where they are empowered to create and contribute knowledge artifacts. These include collaborative platforms (e.g., Knowledge Forum), where students contribute theories, designs, data, and diverse perspectives for continual knowledge-building discourse (Scardamalia & Bereiter, 2014), maker spaces for students to produce and share creative works of art, science, and engineering and explore the related ideas (Halverson & Peppler, 2018), online communities for coding, sharing, and remixing computer programs (Kaifa & Burke, 2014), and various citizen science initiatives in which students can collect and share data and contribute to scientific discovery in connection with professionals. A critical challenge is to create support for students to navigate the collective pool of knowledge and resources in a way that inform (not depress or overwhelm) their creative efforts.

Generating and Improving Creative Objects
Participants make contributions to advancing their community's knowledge and practices by generating various creative objects, which represent the output of the creative work. The specific forms of the creative objects may vary, ranging from theories, models, and evidence in science, to inventions in engineering, and stories in creative writing. Therefore, Resnick (2017) underlines the need to engage children in multiple types of making—building a house using LEGO bricks, programing an animation, or writing a story—which can give students a rich understanding of the creative processes.

To engage in creative work, students need to approach creative objects in productive ways. First, creative objects must be approached as *thinking-intensive* and *idea-centered*. Creative objects may take on various material forms, but they are creative primarily because of the thinking represented and embodied in the work. Hence, creative contributors strive not only to do and produce good work but also to stay meta-cognitively on top of their work to approach the assumptions and ideas, including what they need to achieve, why things work in certain ways, and what differences they can make so that they can continually innovate and improve.

Second, creative objects are *ever improvable*. Creative contributors are willing to take risks to work on ill-defined problems—generating initial ideas that may be rough or crazy and continually improving the ideas over time. As new progress is made, they continually identify new problems and challenges to be addressed, engaging in progressive problem solving and sustained innovation. This process involves playful tinkering (Resnick, 2017) as well as hard thinking and systematic investigation for deliberate improvement. Participants work with design-mode thinking (Scardamalia & Bereiter, 2014) to continually improve the exploratory power, coherence, and usefulness of ideas through experimentation, refinement, and incremental build-on of ideas, which may give rise to major, often unexpected advances.

Third, creativity objects take on specific *social and material forms that support deeper thinking, action, and conversation*. Idea-centered, creative objects are socially shared in various forms, such as written and visual presentations of theories, prototypes of designs and devices, or cases and stories. Despite the specific forms, creative objects are not closed boxes but open-ended and ever unfolding, signifying new possibilities of thinking, revealing unknowns, and projecting into future actions (Knorr Cetina, 2001). The objects created become part of the contexts for future practices and serve as "objects-to-think-with" (Papert, 1980) to support deeper creative thinking. In group settings, they also serve as the anchor of shared attention for collaborative discourse and practices through which members make sense of the objects, advance the ideas, and develop personal and social actions that may lead to the creation of new knowledge objects. Therefore, creative objects not only provoke ideas and thoughts but also evoke interest and passion for engagement (Turkle, 2007).

Finally, powerful creative objects take on *a social life of their own* in various communities through people's visit, appreciation, uptake, use, improvement, connection, and re-creation of the objects. The creative output of one member may be revisited, reinterpreted, or modified in an unpredicted manner and reused in new contexts in connection with other seemingly unrelated ideas, leading to new creative outcomes. In this sense, creative objects are penetrative: they offer means to cross social, spatial, and temporal boundaries to bridge the work of different members and communities, so creative work can continually evolve and transform over time in each knowledge domain and beyond.

Educational designs for creative making and inquiry give students the opportunities to produce creative objects. However, in current practices, student work tends to focus more on the presentation and display of knowledge than on advancing knowledge and ideas. Each activity tends to run for a short period of time, which does not allow students to continually improve their ideas and objects or engage in sustained thinking, action, and conversation around the objects. A few research-based programs have made major advances to address these issues. In the Lifelong Kindergarten project (Resnick, 2017), students use Scratch and programmable devices to create designs that can meet specific needs or create animations of stories. They carry out iterative design and tinkering: engaging in a personally meaningful idea, putting together something that sort-of works, looking for ways to continually improve it, and learning from mistakes. The objects created are shared with peers for them to interact with, play, and possibly create something different or new. In classrooms that use Knowledge Building pedagogy and technology (Scardamalia & Bereiter, 2014), students put forth problems of understanding and generate theories to explain how things (e.g., rainbows) work. Their theories are treated as ever-improvable artifacts instead of wrong versus right beliefs. They engage in knowledge building discourse that involves constructive criticism and examine their different ideas in light of evidence and information from authoritative sources, leading to increasingly better explanations (Zhang, Scardamalia, Reeve, & Messina, 2009). Currently, the various creative objects produced by students often live in different platforms in disconnected spaces, such as those for online discourse, video sharing, data tracking, and code hubs. Future research should create interconnected spaces and repositories for students to search, connect, build on, and reinvent creative objects drawing upon innovative cyber-infrastructures. Such cross-space connections may give student ideas an extended social life: Students may pick up a scientific theory contributed by a peer and test it with data, elaborate on it by creating a video, game, or animation, or apply it to an engineering prototype. The different forms of creative objects must be traceable across spaces to see how ideas evolve.

Dynamic Collaboration and Knowledge–Creating Discourse

Creativity is situated in and actualized through the social interactions of the individual participants. In knowledge-creating communities, members engage in sustained knowledge-building/knowledge-creating discourse by which they not only share ideas and perspectives but also continually advance their knowledge. They continually explore the unknowns, raise and solve emergent problems, and build on one another's input to develop better theories and more powerful designs (Chan & van Aalst, 2018; Scardamalia & Bereiter, 2014). For example, in productive research labs, researchers perform cognitive operations and pass the results on to peers, who then use the results as the input to further cognitive operations to create new scientific theories and experiments. A series of small operations may lead to major, sometimes unexpected discoveries, which often cannot be attributed to any individual. Such dynamic discourse and interaction require flexible forms of collaboration. The most innovative teams often restructure themselves in response to unexpected shifts in the environment (Sawyer, 2007).

Educational designs to cultivate student creativity must engage students in dynamic collaboration and knowledge-creating discourse. Existing designs give preference to prestructured collaboration in fixed small groups that work with predesigned tasks. Recent research reveals the power of dynamic, opportunistic collaboration. For example, Zhang and colleagues (2009) report a three-year design experiment conducted in a fourth-grade classroom that studied light. The collaboration evolved from fixed small groups to interacting groups and then to opportunistic collaboration. The analyses revealed the most productive processes and outcomes were achieved through opportunistic collaboration. As students restructured participatory roles over time and shifted between small-group and whole-class structures, they encountered diverse ideas, monitored gaps, and developed more coherent perspectives and deeper knowledge goals (Zhang, Scardamalia, Reeve, & Messina, 2009). The above findings coincide with Resnick's (2017) observations of student collaboration in the Scratch community, which tends to be "fluid and organic, with people coming together based on shared interests or complementary expertise" (p. 96). This high level of dynamics is necessary for supporting productive tinkering: students cannot simply follow a step-by-step procedure that leads to a tidy end product, rather, they need to work with emergent goals and make constant changes during the process to take advantage of the unexpected.

Reflective Assessment and Social Review of Creative Contributions
A critical part of the social process of creativity is the gatekeeping mechanism for reviewing and selecting creative contributions as potential additions to the collective knowledge in a domain (Csikszentmihalyi, 1999). The creative objects produced by various individuals and teams often go through various peer review and recognition before they are broadly shared. After that they are subject to further critique by peers from the broader field. While the specific criteria may vary across fields, the peer review process typically focuses on the quality, novelty, and usefulness of the work, which are aligned with the defining criteria of creativity. Working in a creative field and context, members appropriate such review criteria as social expectations to guide their own planning and self-reflection. To support creative advancement, the social criteria must meet a certain level of rigor while encouraging nontraditional experimentations. As Csikszentmihalyi (1999) points out, "both too little and too much freedom for the field are inimical to creativity ... Criteria that are too liberal for accepting novelty may end up debasing the domain" (p. 325).

Innovations in assessments are critically needed to support students' creative work. Several research teams are developing new analytics and assessments for knowledge creation, including using e-portfolios for students to document the high points of their collaborative discourse and reflect on deeper problems (Chan & van Aalst, 2018), using the Idea Thread Mapper (https://idea-thread.net) to trace collective idea progress in various problem areas and document the journey of thinking (Zhang, Scardamalia, Reeve, & Messina, 2018). Such assessments and analytics serve to provide ongoing feedback and further instill a shared habit of creativity: Inquiry is viewed an ever-unfolding journey and ideas can be continually improved, so students should not settle for a fine idea that they have found but always be ready to make it better.

CONCLUDING THOUGHTS

Understanding the four interrelated pillars of creative learning is important for rising above the existing programs of learning through making, designing, and inquiry to develop a coherent future of creative learning. These elements may serve as reflection points to guide the design of creative environments utilizing various technology platforms and spaces. For example, the designers may ask: How can students access and navigate a collective knowledge space in a way that informs their own creative contributions? What creative objects will be produced, and how the objects will be improved, represented, publicized, and used to sustain thinking-intensive interactions over time across social spaces? How will students pursue open conversations and dynamic collaborations to continually deepen their work while responding to new opportunities and possibilities? How will reflective assessment and peer review be embedded in the learning contexts to support student monitoring of shared progress as well as problems, challenges, and potential dead ends? Essential to all the pillar elements, it is important to encourage students to enact epistemic agency for making creative decisions about high-order issues, such as what they need to create, why, how to best create and learn, and in connection with whom in what areas (Zhang, Tao, Chen, Sun, Judson, & Naqvi, 2018). Doing so requires a different approach to instructional design and planning: Lesson planning in schools focuses on pre-defining learning goals and activity procedures for students to follow; similar strategies are often applied to designing after-school programs. Creative learning design must support students to co-organize their journey of inquiry as their work unfolds so that they can explore, tinker, and improvise; work on new ideas and directions emerged from their deepening work and from interactive peer input; and turn unexpected discoveries and challenges into creative opportunities.

ACKNOWLEDGMENTS

The writing of this chapter is based on work sponsored by the National Science Foundation (#1441479). Any opinions expressed in this material are those of the author and do not necessarily reflect the views of the National Science Foundation.

REFERENCES

Chan, C. K. K., & van Aalst, J. (2018). Knowledge building: Theory, design, and analysis. In F. Fischer, C. E. Hmelo-Silver, S. R. Goldman, & P. Reimann (Eds.), *International handbook of the learning sciences* (pp. 475295–475307). New York, NY: Routledge.

Csikszentmihalyi, M. (1999). Implications of a systems perspective for the study of creativity. In R. J. Sternberg (Eds.), *Handbook of creativity* (pp. 313–335). New York, NY: Cambridge University Press.

Halverson, E., & Peppler, K. (2018). The maker movement and learning. In F. Fischer, C. E. Hmelo- Silver, S. R. Goldman, & P. Reimann (Eds.), *International handbook of the learning sciences* (pp. 285–294). New York, NY: Routledge.

Kafai, Y. B., & Burke, Q. (2014). *Connected code: Why children need to learn programming.* Cambridge, MA: MIT Press.

Knorr Cetina, K. (2001). Objectual practice. In T. R. Schatzki, K. Knorr Cetina, & E. Savigny (Eds.), *The practice turn in contemporary theory* (pp.175–188). London, UK: Routledge.

Paavola, S., & Hakkarainen, K. (2005). The knowledge creation metaphor—An emergent epistemological approach to learning. *Science and Education, 14*(6), 535–557.

Papert, S. (1980). *Mindstorms: Children, computers, and powerful ideas.* New York, NY: Basic Books.

Resnick, M. (2017). *Lifelong kindergarten: Cultivating creativity through projects, passion, peers, and play.* Cambridge, MA: MIT Press.

Sawyer, R. K. (2007). *Group genius.* New York, NY: Basic Books.

Scardamalia, M., & Bereiter, C. (2014). Knowledge building and knowledge creation: Theory, pedagogy, and technology. In K. Sawyer (Ed.), *Cambridge handbook of the learning sciences* (2nd ed., pp. 397–417). New York, NY: Cambridge University Press.

Sternberg, R. J. (2003). The development of creativity as a decision-making process. In R. K. Sawyer, et al. (Eds.), *Creativity and development* (pp. 91–138). New York, NY: Oxford University Press.

Turkle, S. (Ed.) (2007). *Evocative objects: Things we think with.* Cambridge, MA: MIT Press.

Ward, T. B., & Kolomyts, Y. (2010). Cognition and creativity. In J. C. Kaufman & R. J. Sternberg (Eds.), *The Cambridge handbook of creativity* (pp. 93–112). New York, NY: Cambridge University Press.

Weisberg, R. W. (1999). Creativity and knowledge: A challenge to theories. In R. Sternberg (Ed.), *Handbook of creativity* (pp. 226–250). Cambridge, UK: Cambridge University Press.

Zhang, J., Scardamalia, M., Reeve, R., & Messina, R. (2009). Designs for collective cognitive responsibility in knowledge building communities. *Journal of the Learning Sciences, 18,* 7–44.

Zhang, J., Tao, D., Chen, M. Sun, Y., Judson, D., & Naqvi, S. (2018). Co-organizing the collective journey of inquiry with Idea Thread Mapper. *Journal of the Learning Sciences, 27,* 390–430.

32 SAILING IN OPEN WATERS: CHOOSING, CHARTING, AND NAVIGATING CONSTRUCTIONIST LEARNING EXPERIENCES

Vanessa Svihla and Tim Kubik

> Instead of us just trying to force them on a trajectory, we kind of let their engagement and—and their levels of interest sorta guide the project, and we—we, you know, we have the oars, we're at the helm, but they may be the winds that that push the sails. […] Maybe we're the wind and they're at the helm.

In this quote, Mr. F, a participating teacher at Design-Build Academy, describes the challenge of sharing ownership of constructionist learning experiences with his students while guiding them toward meaningful skills and content. In this chapter, we build on his metaphor, viewing student voice and engagement as the wind in our sails as we navigate issues related to designing and enacting constructionist learning experiences.

Shifting from the instructionist transmission model, which emphasizes that teachers cannot share what they don't have, is challenging because it means sailing into unfamiliar waters as students bring unexpected questions, interests, and experiences to the teacher's planned instruction. When asking teachers to design and support constructionist learning experiences, we may be asking them to create something they have never experienced firsthand—at least not in a classroom as a student. Providing such experiences can help teachers hold a constructionist vision for their classrooms (Svihla, Gines, & Yang, 2014), charting a course to making what could be, rather than transmitting what is—a critical shift in thinking for constructionist teachers.

We've been helping teachers navigate this shift through extended participant observation and professional coaching at Design-Build Academy, a public, not-for-profit charter that serves marginalized youth. Here, we offer observations from a project—Constructing Identity in the Workplace (hereafter, Constructing Identity)—a project that started out in the relatively safe haven of a teacher-directed learning experience but became an exemplar of how student voice can be vital to arriving at learning that is authentic and relevant for all involved. Along the way, we discuss how teachers find project ideas (choosing a destination), plan and shape those ideas (charting a course), and how they adaptively implement and share ownership with their students (navigating the course).

CHOOSING A DESTINATION

Schools provide exhaustive lists of outcomes and objectives as possible ends in mind. While instructionist approaches may feel efficient and offer the potential to cover more territory, in most cases they fail to get all students to the destination. A generative way to come up with project ideas is to shove off for destinations outside of school. Consequential problems abound in the workplace and communities, and these provide opportunities in which foundational skills and content knowledge are valued in authentic contexts.

However, authentic problems—even those with potential to engage students—are rarely packaged tours. Often, such problems are not relevant problems for students. In some cases, they may be inert, anchored firmly in the safe haven of academic project learning (Zhao, 2012). Or they may be too complicated for students. Authentic projects, driven by collaboration with community partners as clients, can also lead students to place their efforts on superficial aspects, spending inordinate amounts of time polishing and refining a deliverable for public consumption, but sacrificing opportunities for deeper learning. Swabbing the decks does not necessarily result in a better sailor.

In the Constructing Identity project, Miss H's vision came from an inspiring graduate course (Kubik, 2018). Initially, she approached the project from an instructionist stance. Having learned about critical race theory in her own studies, Miss H wanted to share this with her students so that they could apply this knowledge to their studies of diversity trainings in the construction industry. Excited and impassioned by her own learning, Miss H and her colleagues, Miss L and Miss B, chose a destination they already knew.

In itself, this was not a bad destination to choose. Yet choosing a destination in constructionist learning requires more than holding an end in mind. It requires teachers to select destinations that meet the problem, and those engaged with it, head on. No matter how authentic, a problem is not likely to be meaningful to students if teachers can't see a relevant point of connection to their students' lives. That connection might come from students' own experience with a similar problem or their sense that their actions might actually help others. Miss H and her team had only identified one possible solution to one possible problem.

When selecting a destination, our best advice is to consider what kinds of problems are worth the effort and involvement of teachers and students together, as a learning community. Some teachers start with students' questions about a shared community issue (Kubik, 2017) or a short menu of potential options from community partners that spur questions. These then lead to meetings with workplace or community members engaged with such problems. Observations of the Constructing Identity project taught us that in such meetings, successful teachers learn to shift between roles as explorers, seeking potential for engagement and learning in worldly problems, and ethnographers, seeking understanding of authentic problems and those who engage them. In this way, teachers and students are likely to feel much less alone on open waters.

CHARTING A COURSE

Journeys through authentic problems are designed rather than planned, and this requires teachers to chart a course. Early in the Constructing Identity project, the teachers planned that students would sequentially study race, class, and sexuality, to feed into the diversity training they were re-designing. Students chose a person from the list provided by the teachers to research and create a *retablo*—a common and usually religious, small framed altar depicting a saint, festival, or similar. When students make choices of this sort, they can direct what they might study, but not how they might study. Such choices leave no meaningful room for student voices. In Miss H's case, it only took a few days to realize that her well-planned tour was going nowhere. On the bus home from a field trip to visit the client and see their existing training, she recalled realizing that her "privilege was transformed to a lack of experience. [...] They already know. [...] They don't always discuss these things because they fear the response of authority, including from me as a teacher. It's not always that they don't even know the words, but that they've learned what they cannot say" (Kubik, 2018, p. 168).

Different students will like different things about a destination, and if student voice is the wind in our sails, we need to be prepared for the possibility that they may blow us off course to pursue their own learning. Therefore, before charting a course of lessons and experiences, teachers may find it extremely valuable to invest in some broad-ranging ideation about the problem. While teachers enjoy this kind of ideation, we find they sometimes feel guilty about time spent casting about for possibilities because they know they won't be able to incorporate them all. This is unfortunate. Exploring the "deep wells" that surround project destinations can help deepen the project in a way that enables teachers to navigate potentially troubling waters when students show interest in an unexpected or unplanned area (Svihla et al., 2016). Charting the course in this way shifts the focus from mapping a plan across the surface of the waters to understanding the potential depths of a project. This allows teachers to be more improvisational when navigating the kinds of experiences that engage and benefit students.

NAVIGATING THE COURSE

Once teachers have carefully chosen a destination and charted a course, they often set "essential" or "driving" questions to direct students through a series of planned experiences and assessments. However, these questions are rarely open invitations to a journey of discovery. Despite commonplace advice that projects should provide students with "voice and choice," many projects are not constructionist in terms of what it is that students will make, because the teacher has already planned the making for them. Students commonly must choose unquestioningly from the teacher's menu of topics (e.g., choose a president, country, surgical device, biome) rather than interrogate problems; likewise they commonly choose formats (present a poster, presentation, or pamphlet) rather than designing authentic solutions to problems (Zhao, 2012).

Once time and effort are invested into choosing a destination and charting a course, teachers can become blind to the fact that the plan to achieve the destination may no longer appeal to the students. Students' own interests or experiences may also lead them in directions teachers may perceive as mutinous. Concerned about the challenges of authentic assessment, many teachers tack back against the winds students blow into our sails. For many teachers, standardized assessment limits not only what we think to assess but also what we think students are capable of demonstrating. As a result, assessment often remains focused only on rote memorization or minimal application of skills and concepts rather than on actually making something. For others, alternative and more authentic forms of assessment for learning (Chappuis, Stiggins, Chappuis, & Arter, 2012)—such as demonstrations of professional competencies or student portfolios—lead to uncharted waters, where every student will need their own, uniquely tailored, personalized learning plan.

Reflecting on the Constructing Identity project, the teachers noted, "The first two weeks really were only the first two weeks … but then we changed it." They adapted the project as they saw which way the wind—students' knowledge and interest—was blowing. After that bus ride home, everyone realized the learning targets were off course, so the teachers called all hands on deck. They took away everyone's desks (including their own) and sat in a circle to re-negotiate the project in a way that would acknowledge and leverage students' prior experiences (Kubik, 2017, 2018). The students were savvy enough to know that in trainings like the one used by their client, no one was going to actually learn to value diversity. Adept at code-switching, they started to pose questions for the client, "How do you want us to talk?" and "How do you see this benefitting [your company]?"

These insights led to a re-framing (Svihla & Reeve, 2016) or re-negotiation (Kubik, 2017) of the both the course and the destination. We term this kind of shared work as *framing agency,* meaning both teachers and students con-tributed to consequential decisions about how and what they would learn. The teachers and students agreed to a course organized around students' experiences rather than academic theories, and they agreed to have "circle time" at the end of each project period. Students quickly realized this was a space where their honesty, ideas, and reframings were welcome.

The teachers responded by guiding the students to write poems about themselves; these were then laser cut into wood and displayed during a mini-exhibition. Miss L explained that the "kids that didn't complete the task were really upset, like they were—it's not shamed, more just, they wanted to be proud of it, part of it, they weren't a piece of it. Kids walking away they were feeling it, 'Wish I would have done it.' 'Can I still be part of it?'" The wind was back in their sails!

As for the destination, instead of using critical race theory to update the training to meet regulatory requirements, the students insisted they could design trainings that might actually educate companies about the real-world issues employees experienced. The companies had been open about the fact that their diversity trainings were not working, but this move was risky. The school leader was concerned about what might happen if students of color came into the workplace of a key industry partner and called out their insti-tutionalized racism. But the students knew well the dangers in these waters and brought their own life experiences—navigating people's perceptions of them—to the task (Kubik, 2018).

From experiences like Miss H's, we've learned that project launches are best understood as provocation, with uncertainly about exactly where the winds will take you. A constructionist project launch provides framings of the problem that make it interesting and accessible, inviting curiosity and questions about the problem itself, not just the solution. Incorporating student voice can be risky. Because they have framing agency, students are empowered to explore alternative courses and even alternative destinations.

SAILING IN OPEN WATERS

We see constructionism as being about embracing complexity (Byrne, 2014)—including the complex possibilities of student-centered assessment *as* learning rather than the complicated work of teacher-centered standardized assessment *of* learning for each student. If a constructionist classroom is a sailboat, an instructionist classroom is more like a galley ship, where rowers engage to the teacher's drumbeat as fast as they can. It is an exercise in standardization that does not tolerate those who cannot keep up, and so the focus shifts to the "grit" or "perseverance" of the individual rower, rather than the effort of the team. Endless rowing may build some mental muscles, but it does little to teach students how to pilot once they graduate to open waters.

Like constructionist classrooms, sailboats are piloted not just by a captain, but by a team. But who is the team? Who, other than the teachers, is ready to sail? Students' expectations—derived from past instructionist schooling—may make them reluctant to engage when invited to a team effort. While a well-charted project may be more likely to succeed in catching students' interest and engaging them in challenging work, the relationships in that project are perhaps the ultimate determinant of individual success, inviting students to share responsibility for navigating, whether they are on course, or off.

Teachers at Design-Build Academy meet daily, year after year, with students as advisees. Over the years, they've come to realize that in addition to building and sharing physical things, sharing and building three specific relationships is critical to the adaptability necessary for success in constructionist learning experiences: relationships with oneself, relationships with co-learners (including teachers), and relationships with outside experts who may offer answers to questions, or whose answers they may question (Kubik, 2013). Relating to oneself means understanding one's own assets and being open to learning more; when a project is structured around students' deficits, they are unlikely to build this relationship. To survive sailing in open waters, teachers need to know what students are bringing along and how that can sustain their interest in the journey ahead. When students have an opportunity to share and learn from one another's assets as well as those offered by their teachers, they then learn how to learn from outside subject matter experts in the community, and this learning helps them to begin to discover how to pilot their own ships once in the open waters as members of that community.

Expert sailors use the structure of the sailboat and their team to take advantage of winds they have; constructionist teachers leverage these three relationships to navigate more ambitious learning experiences. Once the wind was in the sails, students in the Constructing Identity project presented the training they developed to employees. They shared both the research they did on diversity topics and authentic examples of how they themselves had made modifications to a house to accommodate a sister's wheelchair, or how two groups of students had fought because of different cultural norms. They piloted the connections between their own, personal stories and formal, academic terms like "whiteness," many of which Miss H envisioned at the outset. These were no longer inert terms, but terms that informed their making and learning.

Our advice for constructionist teachers? Launch toward a destination with an openness to what you might learn together when the winds blow you off course. Chart a course that acknowledges the deep possibilities in the waters across which you sail. Navigate learning in a way that draws on the strengths of the whole team, not just the teachers.

ACKNOWLEDGMENTS

This material is based upon work supported by the Spencer Foundation/ National Academy of Education and the National Science Foundation under Grant No. EEC 1751369. Any opinions, findings, and conclusions or recommendations are those of the authors and do not necessarily reflect the funders' views.

REFERENCES

Byrne, D. (2014). Thoughts on a pedagogy of complexity. *Complicity: An International Journal of Complexity and Education, 11*(2).

Chappuis, J., Stiggins, R. J., Chappuis, S., & Arter, J. (2012). *Classroom assessment for student learning: Doing it right-using it well.* Upper Saddle River, NJ: Pearson.

Kubik, T. (2013). *Quality projects? Put relationships before the rigor.* Retrieved from https://www.bie.org/blog/quality_projects_put_relationships_before_the_rigor

Kubik, T. (2017). The world won't wait for graduation. *ASCD Express: Global Ready Students, 12*(9).

Kubik, T. (2018). *Unprepared for what we learned: Six action research exercises that challenge the ends we imagine for education.* New York, NY: Peter Lang.

Svihla, V., Gines, M., & Yang, Y. (2014). Teachers as learners then designers: Shifting from instructionist to constructionist approaches. *Proceedings of FabLearn.* Stanford, CA: Stanford University.

Svihla, V., & Reeve, R. (2016). Facilitating problem framing in pbl classrooms. *Interdisciplinary Journal of Problem-based Learning, 10*(2).

Svihla, V., Reeve, R., Field, J., Lane, W., Collins, J., & Stiles, A. (2016). Framing, reframing and teaching: Design decisions before, during and within a project-based unit. *International Journal of Designs for Learning, 7*(1), 19–36.

Zhao, Y. (2012). *World class learners: Educating creative and entrepreneurial students.* Thousand Oaks, CA: Corwin Press.

33 CONSTRUCTIONIST LEARNING GAMES IN SCHOOL

Eric Klopfer, Emma Anderson, and Judy Perry

Papert (1980) believed that powerful learning emerges when the learner constructs knowledge through the creation of an object that is discussed and shared with others. In this chapter, we argue that playing games can manifest this kind of rich learning within the constraints of a formal classroom. There is a rich literature documenting activities in which students *make* games within constructionist learning experiences (e.g., Kafai, 2006). These activities share many commonalities with the examples in previous chapters—project-based initiatives in which students design and build activities for use by their peers or other specific audiences. Constructionist learning experiences where students *play* games, particularly video games, is a much more recent development. There is good reason for this. From one perspective, games and constructionist learning might seem antithetical; while constructionism focuses on learner agency and construction of shareable, personally meaningful artifacts, conversely, games are built on constraints that limit choice and value quantifiable outcomes. This would indicate that designing experiences that embody constructionist learning in an environment that manifests and values the affordances of games would be not only hard, but impossible. So, perhaps this chapter will be very short.

On the other hand, an argument could be made that most, if not all, games have significant constructionist overtones. Constructionism in practice is not about starting with a blank slate but rather a set of interesting constraints that suggest particular possibility spaces for design and construction of artifacts that can be shared and discussed. This aligns well with contemporary digital games in which players frequently share artifacts from their gameplay in public ways; for example, in displaying digital farms via social media or streaming their play through online services. As out-of-game streaming, commentary, and sharing have proliferated, game designers have, in turn, capitalized on these services and designed games to specifically cater to the use of them. Many attribute the viral spread of recent games not only to the game itself but also to the distribution of game-related media that has been produced and shared by players, and subsequently seen by millions. With this in mind, it would be easy to argue that most games can be, or are, constructionist learning experiences. But this definition is likely too broad to be useful for either research or design.

We argue in this chapter that under the right conditions, digital games provide appropriate levels of structure to enable players to build interesting, sharable artifacts that can offer meaningful in-school constructionist learning experiences. For both designers and researchers, it is useful to define what we mean by constructionist game experiences, which lie at the intersection of constructionism, games, play, and school.

We begin with a straightforward definition of constructionism as a student-driven experience that focuses on learning through the making of shareable artifacts. It is also worth considering how a game does—or does not—support sharing of artifacts (see chapter 24). Some games support this process, while others require external means to capture and share artifacts, making the constructionist component more dependent upon the facilitator.

The explanation of what is a game is less well defined. Some have succinctly described games as "the overcoming of unnecessary obstacles" (Suits, 2005), while Salen, Tekinbaş, and Zimmerman (2004) call games "a system in which players engage in an artificial conflict, defined by rules, that results in a quantifiable outcome" (p. 80).

What is key is that games are defined by their limitations—the unnecessary obstacles, rules, boundaries, and constraints. It is overwhelming to be given a blank page and told to "write something." But that same blank page with the additional constraint to "write a sonnet about something you saw on your way to school today" becomes more manageable and in many ways a more productive constructionist prompt than the blank page alone. Take that structure too far (e.g., asking a student to fill in the missing words of a Shakespearean sonnet), and the constructionist context disappears entirely. Constructionist learning games find the middle ground, providing a set of interesting constraints to promote exploration, learning, and creation. However, these games ought not be too open ended. Playing *Minecraft* in creative mode with no structure is similar to the analogy of the blank page. Nor should these games be too linear and defined in their goals (the game equivalent of filling in the missing worlds from a sonnet) to truly fall within this middle ground of constructionist learning games.

DEFINING CONSTRUCTIONIST LEARNING GAMES

We have elsewhere cited five dimensions in which gameplay is bounded (Klopfer, 2015). Rather than drawing a line between games and non-games, the degree to which these factors are present in experiences define those experiences as being more or less "gamey." Below, we provide a brief description of these factors that define a game:

1. Interesting Decisions: Decisions that engage players deeply are not purely random but instead require the player to consider and apply information about various possible outcomes.

2. Consequences to Decisions: The decisions the players make ultimately have observable consequences with some predictability.

3. Clearly Defined Goals: Rather than a single goal, good games have multiple goals that players can weigh on their own to determine which goals they prioritize.

4. Visible Measurable Feedback: Feedback comes to players in many forms. This is not a single score, but many metrics such as wealth, collected gear, and accomplishments that, again, players can value based on their own perceived merit.

5. Underlying Model or Systems: Some coherent system underlies gameplay. This may be a series of interconnected simulated systems, or simply a well-defined set of rules.

The structure of games offers a lot to school learning. It provides enough constraints to focus on a topic, practice, or skill, while leaving as much room as possible for exploration and ownership. Another example beyond crafting sonnets might be around physics. Imagine a simulation in which there are thousands of parts to potentially assemble a rocket. By luck or extremely detailed knowledge, some students might successfully build their rocket, enabling them to study the relationship between thrust and mass. But there are many more ways to fail than succeed in this scenario, so the majority of students would likely be frustrated and confused. Alternatively, imagine this simulation with the addition of simple design challenges focused on a reduced set of rocket parts. Over time, the constraints (scaffolding) guiding the construction may be reduced and additional goals made available. This follows principles of good instructional design in which scaffolding is initially provided to learners and removed over time. This scenario now provides a much more productive environment for learning given the additional structures and constraints.

This describes *Kerbal Space Program*, a rocket construction game, which is part of the engineering genre of games. *Kerbal Space Program* actually has one mode in which you can build anything you want, but it also has modes that provide constraints and tasks. For most people who are not extremely knowledgeable about rockets, the constrained modes provide on-ramps into the construction process that challenge players but do not challenge them beyond their Zone of Proximal Development (Vygotsky, 1980). Instead, it keeps players in that zone, where they are challenged just beyond their current expertise and provided the scaffolding they need to move ahead.

However, the gaming structures by themselves may or may not make them playful. Here, we argue that powerful learning ought to be playful in nature, providing rich opportunities for deep, personally meaningful engagement. Osterweil's Four Freedoms of Play (Klopfer, Osterweil, & Salen, 2009) suggest design principles for playful experiences:

1. Freedom to Fail: Playful experiences provide low-stakes opportunities with a safe space to fail. Through feedback from failed attempts, the player internalizes a model in which failure is not only possible but often necessary to move toward future mastery.

2. Freedom to Experiment: With freedom to fail, the player now has latitude to explore and test ideas, selecting goals and ways in which they will test their theories, knowing that this exploration can lead to acceptable/productive failure.

3. Freedom to Try on Identities: Playful experiences allow players to take on different roles, those of both dragon and dragonslayer. In game-based experiences, this can extend to identities of game players, including teacher/learner.

4. Freedom of Effort: Playful experiences enable players to alternate between intense and relaxed modes of effort. Play experiences are self-determined rather than externally regulated, without expectation of uniform effort.

When executed well, these freedoms do not simply balance the constraints of the system, but the constraints and freedoms complement each other. For example, a well-designed system allows a player to experiment as they consider ways of obtaining goals, with a low cost to failure along the way.

Constructionist games, at their heart, offer players opportunities for the creation of personally meaningful artifacts, often through the lenses of each of these four freedoms. The latitude offered by playful experiences, in which users have agency to pursue threads of their own choosing, within the context of a structured game, can shed some light on the kinds of constructionist learning game experiences one might hope to replicate.

The social component of these playful, constructionist experiences is also key. Games in which gameplay centers around the construction of an artifact enables players to externalize their thinking, goals, and strategies. The artifact also affords others the opportunity to observe, interrogate, and interact with the ideas of its creator. When a game artifact is created via playful context, the artifact manifests the individual's decisions, enabling each artifact to differ from those created by their peers. The diversity of artifacts represents the diversity of approaches and ideas. But perhaps, even more importantly, the playful nature enables a nonthreatening context in which peers learn through conversing around their shared artifacts. *What did you create? How did you make that?* What conclusions can students draw when comparing, contrasting, and critiquing each other's artifacts?

The inverse is also true. The lack of a playful approach to constructionism, with minimal opportunities for experimentation and paralyzing aversion to failure, restricts opportunities for the creation of meaningful artifacts. The design affordances of the game, intentional or not, which enable players to explore their ideas, rather than those narrowly prescribed to them, provide the necessary kindling to spark the player's curiosity and interest.

The final point of intersection is school. While school looks different everywhere, most schools have well-defined systems (in terms of curriculum, school infrastructure, schedules, and social systems), feedback mechanisms (e.g., grades), and goals (gaining knowledge toward acquiring proof of mastery, e.g., a diploma). In these ways, similar constraints of game systems align well with schools. Interesting decisions and student agency, however, are not always central with traditional school environments.

So, where are the intersections of these spaces? While contructionist learning games can be situated in many contexts from home, to clubs, to schools, here we focus specifically on the formal school context. We think that constructionist learning games that fit well into a formal school experience, by definition, need to be intentionally designed to

1. Have players **build artifacts in the game world** as a central part of their experience, and encourage sharing, reflection, and authentic conversations about the artifacts

2. Provide agency to players as they build, allowing them to make **interesting decisions**, thus creating multiple pathways and solutions

3. Be constrained in terms of outcomes to align with the more **limited goals** of school

4. Contain ways for obtaining quantifiable **continuous feedback** on progress

5. Allow players to safely **fail** and build **identity**

There are a growing number of games that fit this definition. These games fall into two categories—(1) games that were specifically designed to be in-school constructionist learning games and (2) games that have been redesigned to be in-school constructionist learning games. The former category contains games that have been designed by academics, non-profits, and educational media organizations for the primary purpose of being learning games. The latter category contains commercial games that many have discovered to be good fits for school learning, which have either been modified digitally or supplemented by additional curriculum and support materials to fit into school.

Where do coding/programming games fit into this discussion? While there is a rich history of these games dating back at least to *Rocky's Boots,* an early PC game from the 1980s, we do not include a category related specifically to coding games for three reasons. First, more open-ended coding "games" are essentially programming environments with some constraints and goals and therefore share more in common with constructionist non-game experiences discussed elsewhere in this volume. Conversely, overly restrictive computational thinking activities don't belong in this volume at all. Second, we explore games by genre here, rather than content. Coding games may fit into some of the categories here but aren't a parallel category by themselves. Third, there are a plethora of domains in which constructionist experiences can be set, and coding represents just a small fraction of the school curriculum; we attempt to establish the most broadly applicable criteria we can.

CASE STUDIES OF CLASSROOM CONSTRUCTIONIST GAME GENRE

How do different kinds of games provide interesting decisions, define goals, and provide feedback? What types of models and rules are implemented? Is there space for identity exploration, failure, and ease of play? How do these games incorporate the creation of meaningful artifacts and provide space for conversation? Finally, in regard to school, can these games fit into the constraints and expectations of a classroom? Below we present case studies representing several genres of games to illustrate how these genres fit into these aspects of constructionist learning games.

World-Building Games

World-building games, such as *Civilization*, *SimCity*, *Age of Empires*, and *Zoo Tycoon* typically place the player in control of a complex model of a civilization, city, or similar entity and are full of interesting decisions. Which resources do you use and where do you place them? How do you prioritize your actions? And what happens based on those decisions? Feedback comes in many forms from the resources that you have accumulated, to the deals you have brokered, to the territory that you have occupied. Did your society expand, or were its borders reeled in? In-game feedback helps provide direction in achieving the goals of the game. Yet, players also have latitude to shape their own personally meaningful goals. There are also typically well-modeled systems in these games, from the dynamics of troop interactions to the locations of resources to the technological systems existing in these worlds. Yet these structures also enable players to be playful, by reshaping history, trying on identities such as urban planner, sociologist, military strategist (Squire, 2008), and exploring multiple pathways (are the player's goals best achieved through war? commerce? tyranny?).

In general, world-building games provide many opportunities for the player to build an authentic artifact as creation of a world is key to game-play. Yet for these to be constructionist learning games, and not just building experiences, there must be rich discussion around these created worlds. It is up to the educator to provide space for a conversation. For example, discussions around the consequences of players' choices in creating their *Civilization* empires, and how these might relate to actual historical empires and geopolitics, could easily be woven into a social studies curriculum. Their episodic nature also makes these games well suited to the constraints of a school schedule.

A sub-genre of world-building games include farming games like *Farmville*, which are typically highly constrained, agrarian-themed games in which players cultivate their territories. While there are still decisions, due to its bounded nature, the decision space, goals, feedback to player, and the artifact are more straightforward and, as such, provide a shallower game experience.

Given their content and format, pure farming games have weaker connections to school curriculum. In-game activities require a longer investment of (real) time, which runs counter to playful notions of experimentation. Unlike other genres, these "casual games" are frequently played in intermittent, short bursts of time. In controlling the pace and flow of the game, the freedom of effort lies largely with the player. However, conversely, the constrained space of the game can limit the diversity of artifacts, undermining opportunities for constructionist learning.

Stardew Valley is an interesting variation, mixing farming with construction and social interactions to provide a more diverse decision-making space. It offers more interesting decisions, owing to its multidimensional forms of interaction, and more diverse artifacts to create through both farming and crafting. As such, *Stardew Valley* has potential for discussions around equitable use of land in a community. This could align well with a social studies class or an economics course exploring land rights or different economic systems.

ENGINEERING AND SANDBOX GAMES

Engineering games such as *Backyard Engineers*, *Bad Piggies*, and *Fantastic Contraption* provide a challenge along with a variety of tools, materials, and constraints to reach the goal. They are all about tinkering and embrace experimentation as challenges that are solved through feedback from playful failure. Sandbox games similarly provide tools and materials to build within the game world. However, their challenges are less rigid and the solutions more flexible. Both genres provide a range of play experiences, from more structured modes to more open-ended modes. In a school context, where there are specific learning goals, games that are able to find the middle ground balancing open-ended exploration and constrained possibilities can offer rich learning experiences (e.g., *Kerbal Space Program*).

It would be a disservice not to consider *Minecraft*, a quintessential sandbox game. *Minecraft* has many modes of play from Creative, where resources are unlimited, to Survival, where players need to gather resources and fend off enemies, to online hosted games, where players interacted in worlds created by others. Creative Mode is not a game experience because it lacks clearly defined goals and feedback and progress through structured playful tasks and obstacles. There are no real consequences to the decisions one makes. So, while the player can create meaningful artifacts, the experience is missing the essence of the game-like experience. In Survival Mode, the player has to find materials, build structures, and survive against enemies. While more game-like, Survival Mode is hard to link to traditional school curriculum. In the online hosted games the player interacts with experiences whose goals and rules are built by others (e.g., navigating a maze or playing capture the flag). These experiences tend to lack opportunities for players to create a meaningful personalized artifact. Because these created worlds are specifically designed, they can be made to better fit within the classroom (e.g., learning about circuits via redstone for a science curriculum), but these may or may not be playful or game-like. The different flavors of Minecraft allow the player to encounter playfulness, gamey-ness, or creation of a meaningful artifact, but it rarely weaves these into one unified experience.

MASSIVELY MULTIPLAYER ONLINE GAMES (MMOGS)

Many massively multiplayer online games (MMOGs) such as *World of Warcraft* or even explicitly educational MMOGs such as *The Radix Endeavor* (Klopfer, Haas, Osterweil, & Rosenheck, 2018) and some experiences within *Whyville* (Kafai, 2010) are deeply organized around the in-game infrastructure. In an MMOG, a large number of players who represent themselves as avatars interact with the virtual environment and one another in a shared world to solve a challenge or complete a quest. Interesting decisions are prominent at many scales, ranging from which kind of character to play (e.g., Warrior, Monk, Rogue, Priest), to which quest to pursue, to which weapon to level up, to which categories to build skills in (e.g., a better healing spell, or gaining the profession of a fisherman). These choices can drastically change gameplay (gameplay for a damage dealer is much different than that of a healer), and different quests can take the player to new worlds and influence the specializations the player has over time. The complex nature of these game worlds' underlying models enable players to build theories based upon close observation of in-game phenomena, which in turn help them and their peers build strategies to progress more successfully through the game world. These games are also playful, situating players in an imagined, often fantasy-themed world.

Typically, MMOGs offer players opportunities to build theory as part of gameplay, which can prompt discussions—a key component of constructionism. However, these theory-building experiences are challenging to map to a traditional classroom context. This is due to lengthy time requirements for gameplay and in part because content is not typically grounded intentionally in curriculum domains. However, these same features (e.g., narrative thread, character building, quests, collaboration) can be compelling opportunities for engagement with the virtual world for exploration, discovery, failure, and discussion.

Game designers have recognized these deep learning possibilities, deliberately creating in-game activities that more closely map to traditional curriculum. For example, *Whyville* (Kafai, 2010) and *The Radix Endeavor* (Klopfer, Haas, Osterweil, & Rosenheck, 2018) considered many of these constructionist goals in their design. In both of these examples, designers worked to deliberately weave STEM curriculum into the game quests. *The*

Radix Endeavor (Klopfer, Haas, Osterweil, & Rosenheck, 2018) enables players to create artifacts that embody specific principles of genetics and mathematics. A player might breed some novel plants and create an interesting variety to share or construct geometric structures for buildings that can be displayed or given to other players. As players share and discuss these artifacts, along with their understanding of the game world, they generate theories not only about gameplay but also about the content being explored.

CONCLUSION

In this chapter, we explore how games can be tools for constructionist learning in classrooms. There are wide varieties of game genres that have the potential to be constructionist learning experiences. Arguing with a classmate about which modification helps a rocket ship fly faster in *Kerbal Space Program* or sharing a strategy for breeding genetically modified plants in *The Radix Endeavor* (Klopfer, Haas, Osterweil, & Rosenheck, 2018) can enable powerful learning. Constructionist learning game experiences can allow students to be playful, fail and try again, and have meaningful discussions all around curriculum valued within schools. There is great promise for the future of constructionist games in the classroom, as they can provide the support needed to create playful, productive spaces in schools. Yet, we recognize that this is hard to do. Successful constructionist implementation of learning games requires a blend of digital experience from the game and context provided by the teacher. The educator needs to shape the classroom culture, creating space for conversation, and making links between the game experience and the larger curriculum. If teachers are able to do this, bringing constructionist games into the classroom opens up space for student agency, identity exploration, experimentation, discovery, and joy. But there is also a need for designers to create games that meet the intersection of constructionism, games, play, and school to provide opportunities for this approach to learning across more domains. Researchers need to help parse and understand in what ways these experiences enable new kinds of learning and allow a wider range of learners an entry point to construct their own knowledge.

REFERENCES

Kafai, Y. B. (2006). Playing and making games for learning: Instructionist and constructionist perspectives for game studies. *Games and Culture, 1*(1), 36–40.

Kafai, Y. B. (2010). World of whyville: An introduction to tween virtual life. *Games and Culture, 5*(1) 3–22.

Klopfer, E. (2015). *Learning games are hard fun*. Retrieved from http://onlineteachered .mit.edu/files/games-and-learning/week-1/Games-Week1-Klopfer-as-presented -compressed-pdf.pdf

Klopfer, E., Haas, J., Osterweil, S., & Rosenheck, L. (2018). *Resonant games*. Cambridge, MA: MIT Press.

Klopfer, E., Osterweil, S., & Salen, K. (2009). *Moving learning games forward*. Cambridge, MA: The Education Arcade.

Papert, S. (1980). *Mindstorms: Children, computers, and powerful ideas*. New York, NY: Basic Books.

Salen, K., Tekinbaş, K. S., & Zimmerman, E. (2004). *Rules of play: Game design fundamentals*. Cambridge, MA: MIT Press.

Squire, K. D. (2008). Video games and education: Designing learning systems for an interactive age. *Educational Technology*, 17–26.

Suits, B. (2005). *The Grasshopper: Games, life and utopia* (pp. 54–55). Peterborough, ON: Broadview Press.

Vygotsky, L. S. (1980). *Mind in society: The development of higher psychological processes*. Cambridge, MA: Harvard University Press.

V THE FUTURE OF CONSTRUCTIONISM

34 CONSTRUCTIONISM AND CREATIVE LEARNING: INTERVIEW WITH MITCHEL RESNICK

How you see yourself as a constructionist?

When I met and started working with Seymour Papert, one of the biggest influences on me was Seymour's emphasis on the interplay between constructing things in the world and constructing ideas in your mind. For me, that's always been the essence of constructionism: the back-and-forth between creating things in the world, which enables you to create new ideas, which then pushes you to create new things in the world, and on and on in a never-ending cycle of creating things and creating ideas.

Another thing that attracted me to constructionism was the attention to building on people's interests. That was a central aspect of constructionism for Seymour. I loved it when Seymour said, "Education has very little to do with explanation. It has to do with engagement, with falling in love with the material."

What do you think are defining features of what you consider constructionism or constructionist projects?

In recent years, I've been talking about constructionism through a framework that I call the "Four P's of Creative Learning": Projects, Passion, Peers, and Play. For me, those are all essential elements of constructionism. I feel that the seeds of all four Ps are in Seymour's writing and in the core constructionist community, though not always played out fully. In my own work, I see myself as trying to nurture some of the seeds that have been planted by Seymour and the constructionist community. Of the seeds that Seymour sowed, some have sprouted and flourished, some are still in the ground, some sprouted and were stomped on by systems that made it difficult for them to keep growing. So I think Seymour planted the seeds for all the things that I'm working on now with Projects, Passion, Peers, and Play, but the seeds need nurturing.

Nurturing can take on many different forms: new technological tools that enable the seeds to be expressed and grow, new ways of pedagogically supporting them, new types of activities that let them come to life, and so on. To nurture the seeds, I think about how can we support kids working on projects that are based on their passions, in collaboration with peers, in a playful spirit.

Of course, the framework itself evolves sometimes. I sometimes talk about a fifth P: Purpose. Purpose in the sense of making a meaningful difference in the world. You can be passionate about superficial things, but purpose involves something that's going to make a meaningful difference to you, your community, to those you care about, to society at large. Seymour started out as an activist. He had to run away from South Africa because of his anti-apartheid activities. Purpose was always part of what was motivating Seymour. To the extent that Seymour's motivations and missions are the underpinnings of constructionism, I think that Purpose is something that needs to be there and is something that motivates me as well.

Can you think of any particular, or particularly difficult, choice points in your trajectory or in the history of constructionism that might be instructive for how constructionism will grow and develop in the future?

What comes to mind are ways of engaging with schools. On one hand, there are many constraints of schools that make it very difficult to play out the vision and mission of constructionism. On the other hand, the desire to reach broadly and diversely means that it's very important to engage with schools. That tension has led different people to make different choices at different times. In the constructionism community, it's sometimes talked about as evolution versus revolution. Can we work within the existing system to bring about change, or do we need to come up with fundamentally new systems to play out the constructionist vision?

With most of the projects we work on in my group at the Media Lab, we usually don't start with looking at the current curriculum or standards. We usually start in a very child-centered way. What is going to be deeply engaging for kids? What do kids want to work on? What do kids want to create? We are convinced that if the tools we build support Projects, Passion, Peers, and Play, rich learning experiences will result. With this approach, it can sometimes be difficult to fit into the existing structures of schools.

On the other hand, we do want to reach broadly, so there's clearly a tension. Currently, use in schools is the fastest-growing part of the Scratch community. So we're constantly trying to figure out how we can support

Scratch in schools while also staying true to our commitment to Projects, Passion, Peers, and Play. There's some use of Scratch in schools that does not align with our values and our visions. We want to push against that and offer alternative pathways for introducing Scratch that are more aligned with constructionist values.

What are some opportunities brought about by the international movement for computer science education? What should we be cautious about?

Obviously, the growing cultural support for kids learning to code presents an opportunity. It allows us to offer more kids coding-based activities that we see as rich learning experiences, helping kids develop their creative capacities and creative thinking. There is an opportunity to ride on the back of the interest in coding to try to bring in new visions of education and learning; we sometimes call it the Trojan Cat model. As more people pay attention to coding, there's an opportunity to extend the reach of Scratch, not just as a language, but as a philosophy, which builds on Logo philosophy, building on constructionism. It provides an opportunity to bring that philosophy into schools.

But of course there are also pitfalls and dangers. In computer science education, the goals are often about teaching some core computational concepts or preparing students for careers as professional programmers. That can be a good thing to do, but it is also a narrow focus. With that narrow focus, we risk not paying enough attention to supporting the development of creative capacities.

In describing our goals with Scratch, I often say that we want to help kids learn to think creatively, reason systematically, and work collaboratively. Many efforts in computer science education focus on helping kids learn to "reason systematically"; with Scratch, we also focus on engaging kids in "thinking creatively" and "working collaboratively." We created Scratch in a way that allows kids to make all sorts of different projects— interactive stories, games, animations, simulations—so that they learn to express themselves creatively. And we integrated the Scratch programming language into an online community so that kids learn to work collaboratively.

At least initially, the constructionism community focused on individual learners and didn't pay as much attention to the social side of learning. One of the biggest differences between Logo and Scratch is that Scratch was launched with an online community. We were thinking about that social interaction right from the beginning. It's not that previously people had ignored the social side, but it wasn't as prominent and tools to support it didn't exist.

I'm not fully comfortable with the current focus on "computational thinking." I'm certainly in favor of helping kids develop as computational thinkers, but it's not enough. In addition to helping kids to develop their thinking, we want them to develop their voice and develop their identity. This is, again, something that I learned from Seymour. When you're constructing something, you're getting your ideas out to the world— you're developing your voice, your ability to express yourself, and you're developing your identity. You start to see yourself differently, to see that you can play a role in the world, that you can take charge of the technology and make things happen with it.

I prefer the phrase "computational fluency" to "computational thinking." I take seriously the analogy between learning to code and learning to write. In both cases, you learn to organize, express, and share your ideas. And as you become more fluent, with either writing or coding, you start to see more ways that you can contribute actively as a member of society.

Another phrase from Seymour that's associated with constructionism is "powerful ideas." When Seymour talked about powerful ideas, he was referring to ideas that empower you to do more things, to create more things, to learn more things. Seymour always felt that schools didn't pay enough attention to powerful ideas, and I think that's true of current efforts around computer science education, which are often focused too narrowly on learning particular computer science concepts, or somewhat more broadly on developing thinking skills. Seymour would have wanted it to be broader than that, and so do I.

Where do you see constructionism in the next ten to twenty years?

I'll answer it two different ways, one focused on tools and activities, and the other on how it might change systems and structures. I think the constructionist community has always tried to look at each new wave of technology and say, "How can we empower kids to design, create, and share with this?" As microcontrollers became smaller and less expensive, we developed LEGO Mindstorms, because we could then put the computer inside of a LEGO brick. As use of the Internet became more widespread, we made an online community for Scratch.

Sometimes it's more difficult than at other times. Mobile devices are a challenge. Of course, they're great for sharing, but there's less screen real estate for creating things. So each new technology has some ways in which it can open up new possibilities, and some ways in which there are new challenges.

It's also important to try to change spaces and systems in the world so that they're more open to constructionist approaches. When I think about changing schools, I sometimes think about it in terms of breaking down barriers or crossing boundaries. There are lots of barriers in schools today. There's the barrier between disciplines. We're trying to break those down, supporting activities that cut across disciplines. There's the barrier between ages, with kids segregated kids by grades. We know that kids can learn a lot by working with others of different ages. That's why we have initiatives like our Computer Clubhouses, where kids of many different ages work together. There's the barrier of time, with schools locked into fifty-minute class periods and one-week units. Kids need more time to work on meaningful projects. And there's the barrier between inside-of-school activities and outside-of-school activities. My hope is that schools become much more integrated into the community, that people from the community are coming into the schools, and bringing in their expertise, and that kids from the schools are going out to the communities.

When Seymour wrote *Mindstorms* in 1980, he expected that the proliferation of computers in society would naturally lead to breaking down many of these barriers in schools. He was right that computers would spread through society, but he was overly optimistic about the impact on schools. The proliferation of digital technologies has opened up the potential for dramatic change, but in most places the barriers have not changed much in the nearly forty years since Seymour wrote *Mindstorms*. Obviously, there are some good examples, in particular schools, where new technologies have been used to break down barriers, but it has not happened throughout the culture. For me, that's still the ultimate goal—to really change the nature of the spaces and structures and systems that are constraining a lot of learning experiences these days.

I sometimes say that I'm a short-term pessimist and a long-term optimist. I know how difficult it is to make serious change in educational systems. It requires shifting people's mindsets and shifting bureaucratic structures that are resistant to change. But I'm a long-term optimist, because I really believe that the constructionist learning approach is critical for helping young people thrive in today's fast-changing society—and it will be even more important in the future. Students engaging in constructionist experiences will be better prepared to thrive both in the workplace and outside of the workplace. Over time, parents, educators, and policy-makers will take notice of the value of the constructionist approach. Ultimately that's going to win out.

35 NEW AND FUTURE CODING PARADIGMS: INTERVIEW WITH R. BENJAMIN SHAPIRO

Do you see yourself as a constructionist, and, if you see yourself as a constructionist, how do you see yourself as a constructionist?

No. Being a self-identified constructionist seems to require periodic participation in conferences, panels, or other rituals of worship at the altar of Saint Seymour. I don't have any desire to do that. We'd all be better off if there were less of that and more critical, evidence-based attention to research on learning and teaching.

What are some of the key ideas that you relate to in constructionism?

The framing of constructionism as an orienting framework for design as opposed to a theory about learning *per se*, I think, is useful. One way to help people to learn well is to encourage them to make concrete instantiations of mechanistic ideas; sharing those concrete instantiations can offer opportunities for surprise, reflection, and theory testing. Theory refinement—modification of those instantiations over time—lives with refinement of one's own ideas and so on ... I buy all of that.

I do think constructionist design should attend more explicitly to sociocultural theories of learning. I think the early emphasis on epistemology in the constructionist work is in some ways about reducing what matters in educational settings to abstract ideas. That's not to say that Papert and others at the time didn't write about things like samba schools and other socially constructed spaces for learning. But, Megan Bang and others have pointed out that there are multiple valid epistemologies for understanding a space. I think an opportunity for constructionism is to support dialogue across epistemological worldviews.

Outside of the constructionist community, how do you think your work or your values take up some of those core commitments?

To take a step back, I spent the last two days co-running a workshop for forty-four new computer science assistant professors from all over the country. When we talked to them about teaching, we talked about things that are actually very similar to what happens in good constructionist learning environments, even though we never used the word "constructionism." Two of the things we talked about were peer instruction and creating activities in which students make predictions, turn to the person next to them and share why they had that prediction, and then try to understand why the other person came to a different prediction. This isn't constructionism in the typical sense, but it has a lot of things in common with it. There's (1) this epistemology of the runtime environment for your program; (2) some code that is executed within that notional machine; (3) you making some predictions about what would happen; (4) you getting a correct or incorrect answer and checking your mental model; and (5) the effort to debug it. This is very much in common with the ways that, from the very beginning, constructionist writing has talked about the value of the computer for supporting learning.

A big difference is that people today actually care about kids learning *computer science*; I don't think Papert particularly did, and I think he's right to not care given his framing. His interest was mostly about using a computerized tool as a formal expressive system to learn other epistemological systems.

I think a bigger question is, what are my beliefs about learning? I think, probably, my view is pretty similar to Leah Buechley's (and others), but perhaps distinct from classical constructionism in that I think there is value in people being able to make things that are meaningful to them, apart from any of the epistemological characteristics of those things. The lovely work Kristin Searle did with American Indian kids as part of her dissertation work with Yasmin Kafai is a good example. There are overtures to epistemology with symbology representing metaphysical beliefs about nature, but they're not really mechanistic—in fact, they're more symbolic. I don't think kids learn very much about electronics. But the work is excellent because of its other virtues, like young people making technologies through intergenerational connections with their own cultures. An epistemic frame cannot value all the ways that that work is great.

Personal and community impact was underappreciated in the early constructionist work. In a recent book chapter I wrote with Mike Tissenbaum, he calls this *computational action*. In the early Mindstorms-era writing, Papert never says everybody should know computer science. He emphasizes powerful ideas and computation as a formal system for encoding and testing ideas. In a lot of the later work, including our own, it's like, "No! You live in a fucked-up Trumpy world, and you could make things to change that world! Computation is a powerful tool to do that."

You've done some work exploring alternate computing paradigms. How does this work connect to your argument about the epistemological versus the more utilitarian value of programming?

I wrote an article in *Communications of the ACM* with Rebecca Fiebrink and Peter Norvig. The intended audience is teachers of computer science undergraduates; the core message is, "Hey, this machine learning thing, it seems very popular! What are the implications for the undergraduate CS curriculum?" In machine learning, some of the epistemological characteristics of a computer program are different. People have spent many decades trying to figure out systematized ways of unpacking natural language, and there have been some things that have worked well in that paradigm, and some that have not. In the recent past, language translation systems have gotten much better, because in many ways we took humans out of the loop and let computers teach themselves to understand human language, at least for some sense of "understanding" that is defined as the ability to make a meaningful translation of some text into some other language. But whereas, in the past, for a software engineer, writing good software was about having an epistemology of a domain that one was able to represent systematically in some program code. Machine learning has changed that. We can now create systems that do better at some kinds of work than before, sort of projecting our epistemology into computational artifacts. But this comes at the cost of no longer being able to fully understand the mechanisms of those systems! In a sense, these computational systems have an internal epistemology that, at least at the current state of the art, is not knowable to us. And that's a pretty deep change in the relationship between humans and computers and shared epistemology between them.

This seems to break the idea at the heart of classic constructionism that, by building a system, you have to understand its components and their relationships.

If what you care about is science as a process for generating mechanistic accounts of how things work in the universe and you're interested in computation as a way to construct and test those accounts, then more traditional coding paradigms (NetLogo or something like it) are fantastic. But I think we also need to recognize the limitations of those contexts. We may decide that the implications and the value of these alternate paradigms of computing are such that we can ignore "meaning" or mechanistic accounts.

It's worth noting that none of these models are new. People were doing them in the 1960s. Most of the educational programming tools that are out there now are a really great introduction to a 1970s model of computing!

That's not to say that there's not value in that—there's tons and tons of value in that—but let's be clear, this is not new.

What's new is the combination of thinking about what it can be like for kids to do this stuff, and a change in the culture where many people have networked systems running on their bodies via smartwatches or cell phones executing continuously in their homes. If we want to understand, to have literacy, about the computational systems around us, we can't stay in just a classical computing paradigm.

What are some of the big questions or issues the constructionist community should be addressing?

For those that have a strong commitment to "kinds of thinking"—computational thinking, engineering thinking, design thinking, mathematical thinking—I would love to see more transfer studies. It would be great to understand "what are the bounds on this?"—everything from cognitive bounds to the task transfer bounds. There's a lot of fine-grained classical learning sciences work to do. I think many of us don't want to do it, because we are familiar enough with the history to have the sensible default assumption that transfer ain't easy. But it would be good and healthy for the field to acknowledge this difficulty and do the basic work to demonstrate the existence or nature of these "kinds of thinking." If we do that then we can start to think about the ways in which constructionist activities can build on each other, can be jumping off points for doing work that looks more like "spiraling" in traditional schoolwork.

There's also a ton of interesting work to be done around how people might construct computational systems that are hybrids—that synthesize classical ways of writing software with other paradigms. In the 1990s, there was a lot of work done on programming by demonstration—the ToonTalk work is a great example of this. In ToonTalk you give concrete cases, and then you use the "Dustbuster Tool" to take out a bit of the concrete detail to make a more abstract version of your procedure. A more contemporary analog of that might use supervised machine learning to give some labeled examples, and then you inspect your model behavior and start to edit your data by pruning some data that you think it's overfitting to or creating additional data to have it handle corner cases. Rebecca Fiebrink's work has done this extremely well.

I think there's also tons of interesting stuff to be done around ethics and societal-level decision making: a "Weapons of Math Destruction" standpoint on the ways that we can be doing much, much more to connect computing education to civics education. I'd love to imagine what happens if you get someone like Chris Emdin paired up with somebody doing this work, and really thinking about "what would that pedagogy look like?"

We can't even understand how a lot of machine learning systems work, but now we're recommending prison sentences by machine learning. How do we, as a society, inspect and debate that? What role do computational systems play in understanding and changing those social systems. What's the education for that? I think there's a ton there that I would love to see get done.

Where's constructionism, constructionist work, or even just work influenced by constructionism in twenty years, in twenty-five years?

One of the things that I've been wanting to teach is an undergrad and a grad class on the Internet of Good and Evil Things. It's a year-long software engineering sequence where you and a team of other students build some sort of prosocial cyber-physical system to enhance the campus or the space around the campus. Then, midway through the class, I let on that Google or Facebook has just bought your startup, and they've decided they want to make some changes to the product to be able to spy on everybody, and so you're going to turn this intentionally good thing into an evil thing. Your job is to figure out how to do that conversion with the least amount of effort. Basically, the point is that we may have altruistic political values, but the world changes around us and that it's very easy to take the systems that we are constructing and to push them in directions that we wouldn't necessarily have even been willing to do up front, but now we have no choice. A third phase of the class would be that now we're giving you a time-turner, you have to go back and restart this from the standpoint of being able to accomplish all of your prosocial goals but engineer the system in such a way that somebody could not turn it evil. I would like to imagine that educational experiences like this help us to [anticipate] a future in which the broader pressures—economic, political, etc.—that are shaping the world right now are not going away; in fact, they are being magnified.

Thanks, Ben! Are there any other topics or ideas that you didn't get a chance to talk about that you feel are important here?

I'm sure the three of us could talk for a very long time, but I think one thing I would like to see more of is educational researchers developing more knowledge about computation. There's a lot of tail-wagging-the-dog happening now, where the materials themselves, like the Arduino, have started to dictate the curriculum and, in a sense, narrow aspirations for what students might learn. I would like to see a greater creative imagination about what kinds of computational things young people could create and what the computational ideas are that they're interested in as well as the kinds of impacts on the world beyond computation that they might be able to achieve.

I don't know a way around that other than somehow creating spaces where the educational researchers, who generally are pretty smart and savvy about how people learn what is hard and valuable, and what the possibilities for catalyzing social change, work more closely with creative computer scientists.

Another is that, in the history of computing education, as you look across schools serving communities of different socioeconomic status, different things are labeled as computer science. So, if you are in a school serving lower-income kids, it's PowerPoint and keyboarding. If you go to wealthier areas, it's legitimate CS. I have a real concern that the emphasis on computational thinking, and its definition being so broad as to include work that has nothing to do with computers and computer science—actually creating software systems—may actually legitimize this continued inequity. It creates a space to say, "We're doing all these things, see look we're working towards equity!" But actually, no, it's bullshit: you're literally having kids do the "Hokey Pokey" and saying that they're doing an algorithm. That's not the same as learning very concrete applicable skills for creating things that are meaningful to you, skills that may have real economic implications for your family. It's not the same. And the discourse around computational thinking legitimizes this inequity.

36 ADVANCING MAKING WITH BIOLOGY: INTERVIEW WITH ORKAN TELHAN AND YASMIN B. KAFAI

Can you each say a bit about how you see yourself as a constructionist, and tell us how your project on biological design fits into this view?

Yasmin: For me, constructionism is an approach to look at learning and teaching—interacting with the world around artifacts. I came to constructionism by engaging kids with making games, and designing with digital media when working at the MIT Media Lab in the late 1980s. Then, the artifacts that learners could make were either physical or digital. Today, these artifacts can also be living materials, and this influences how and what is being made in significant ways.

Orkan: My involvement with constructionism started with my early work at the MIT Media Lab. I then moved to University of Pennsylvania's School of Design and started working with Yasmin on a number of projects, from electronic textiles to biological design, that are bringing learning and design into new contexts. Right now, we are working together on creating new methods of learning using living organisms: first, to explain to youth how to work with living organisms so that we can really understand what does it mean to design with them—to create new kinds of applications and products; second, to understand the underlying principles of what it means to really learn with them. When we explore new models of with living organisms, we care about bringing the social, environmental, and the political aspects into the foreground to push beyond the scientific approaches. It's a multi-tiered approach to learning with an emphasis on making the invisible world of the living organisms visible for the K-12 population.

Yasmin: The idea that living organisms can become the building material was really something new and intriguing. And for me, one of the connections is also that we actually now understand what the building blocks are and what their rules are for construction. I saw an immediate analogy to coding. For this reason, I think biological design has something to contribute to our understanding of constructionism that is very much framed by the digital and physical world. Because the way we make things in biology is very different from how we are accustomed to work with computational or electronic construction kits, which are digital and tangible. You have immediate feedback on what you're doing. And, in biology, you work with liquids and there's no immediacy or feedback. Instead, you have to wait twenty-four or forty-eight hours for anything to happen. In constructionism we have very much become accustomed to a particular genre of construction. I think we should consider a much wider array! When the affordances we usually have with artifacts like games or robots don't hold true, what does this mean for learning? Can this actually help us design better learning experiences, when we don't always rely on those principles?

Are there core aspects of constructionism that you see as being extended or played with in a new way with this work?

Orkan: I think that one of the most important things that constructionism did is that it took certain domains of knowledge or expertise from the hands of engineering and sciences and make it accessible to the rest of us.

There's a certain way of treating these domains of knowledge as a form of literacy so that you can introduce them in a good capacity. So, for example, when we think about primitives or building blocks, we might imagine saying, "Okay, instead of LEGO blocks we'll use DNA as a new kind of building block."

But if you're teaching how to work with living organisms in a constructionist framework, I don't think that that's the right building block. You need a different kind of abstraction. You need to maybe work on an organism level, on a higher level where there's feedback to the learner.

I think the transformation of things from sciences to designed artifacts is a way of moving across different levels of abstraction, and those abstractions are all negotiated based on the audiences. Sometimes you go to a lower level if you're working with an older audience. Sometimes you go to a much higher level and look at color changes made from bacteria. As long as bacteria changes color in response to temperature, we may not really care if it is the natural response by the organism or if the organism is designed to do so with a new piece of DNA inserted into it artificially. We can deal with the level of detail that we need and blackbox the rest.

Yasmin: This is a really great analogy because I think in constructionism, where we look at coding languages, we also have to realize these are designed interfaces which operate on different levels of abstraction. Nobody asks kindergartners to code in machine language! And so, what are the appropriate levels of abstraction in bio design?

Orkan: Technology responds to the immediate needs of its times, whether it's the web, the mobile app, virtual reality, or other venues. As technologies change, constructionist methodologies also need to change. But when we think about biology, that doesn't really happen so often. The underlying vocabulary, methods, and approaches are pretty much the same since 1950s. We are still speaking the language of DNA, nuclear bases ... If we still operate on that level, we cannot really adapt them to today's language, or today's tools and today's metaphors. Can you imagine everyone talking about transistors while sending an email or ordering from a website?

When we design with biology, it seems that some of the kinds of things that we might think of as being good educational design—like feedback or tinkering—look very different. How have you adapted to this difference?

Orkan: There are fundamental differences when we work with biology. First of all, there's nothing solid. We design with liquids. Everything else in the constructionist world, whether soft or hard, are solid objects ... You can touch them, manipulate them, put together and break apart ... they remain the same. But in the biology world things leak, perish, get contaminated. Nothing stays the same over time. So, when you think about tinkering or abstraction you have to think differently.

With regard to tinkering ... There is always an undo in the tinkering process when you're working with electronics or programming. But biology happens in the time domain; you cannot reverse most processes in the time. I mean, if you mix two liquids, you cannot separate them because they underwent a chemical change. Or, if there is a physical transformation, it may not easily go away.

A third difference is the agency of the organism. You instruct them to do something, but they have an agency of their own. They respond to their environment: they change or mutate. They do not carry on the tasks that are a burden for them.

So, these three things: the materiality; the temporal, physical, and spatial scale; and the agency, require us to really think about what we used to know, in terms of good methods of constructionism, in a totally different way.

I'm not saying it's impossible to tinker. It is just a different kind of tinkering. For instance, instead of working with one version of something, you work with three different versions, you work with multiples at the same time. You try something here, you try something there. It's bringing experimentation into the game. Then whatever works, you just pick that path and continue with that version as opposed to relying on an undo. So, we may work in parallels as opposed to in a seriality when we talk about tinkering in biology.

Scale—or visibility— is also a big deal. Even if you have the best microscope, you won't be able to see the DNA or a single bacterium, so you have to see what the organisms do, you have to look at the outcome, you have to look at how they change or what they change. One organism doesn't really matter; you have to see millions of them to be able to see a small change. Instead of working with one, we focus on how to make many of them. Abstraction, tinkering … what would be another one that we would think about, Yasmin?

Yasmin: Well, the products that are created. When you do the transformations, you end up with other liquids, which have to be put in a context. In trying to make bio design accessible to high school students, we have to think about how to make these transformations visible. We have worked on designing applications in which you create color pigments—where bacteria fluoresce in the presence of another element. Many of these have already been developed by others, but I think using a constructionist lens that thinks about the embodiment of knowledge—not unlike how Papert thought of the turtle—what are ways we can make embodiment of an object possible?

Orkan: I think the keyword is *embodiment*. I'm glad that you touched on that. When living things are in liquid form, obviously, there's really no easy way to experience them. But you can encapsulate them into solid forms. We often capture them into little beads or drip the liquid into filter paper so that the paper traps the liquid. During the design process, we create visible, tangible, physical representations of the organisms. So just like the way information needs some embodiment in computation, biology needs a different kind of embodiment to turn into design. We not only need organisms to be visible and tangible but also use these embodiments to able to keep them alive. Living cells need to be able to constantly get fed, they need to be kept humid, otherwise they die.

What are you most excited about in this space of bio design? Where do you see this going in the future?

Yasmin: I would like us to develop a whole array of activities and figure out what are promising applications. In constructionism we went through a similar phase of determining what are great construction kits, activities, and contexts that would make computation accessible to children. People thought dirty little hands should never touch those expensive keyboards. We have similar barrier to break through.

But we would also like to think about socio-scientific issues. We don't often do that in constructionism with the kind of artifacts we create. Who are they for? What are they good for? So, when designing with biology, it's not just about understanding science but also engaging in design activities. What else do you have to consider?

Orkan: Yeah. There's an inherent advantage in biology ... When you're dealing with programming, it's not so easy to make the students think about environmental pollution, climate change, food insecurity, or risks involved in manipulating nature. These are big issues! But when you're working with living organisms, activities can immediately tie to real world problems in which the student can actually be encouraged to think through these social, culture, and political issues. Biology is so well aligned with important and current environmental issues we are having.

As Yasmin said, I want to also design more activities that will touch on those kinds of issues in meaningful ways. But I also want to develop this framework in a more systematic way so that we can take it beyond the language of bioengineering and life sciences and give it its own legs—to figure out the right amount of abstraction for different design processes.

Where will biological design be in ten or twenty years?

Yasmin: Well, in the future we're not just going to be making, we're going to be growing things. My expectation is we are, right now, at the very beginning. That's ten to twenty years down the line, what we are talking about will actually be a reality and we will have a new vocabulary. We will create tools and media that will make bio design much more accessible and that will become part of the larger constructionist repertoire.

Orkan: Yeah. I think it will not even take twenty years. I think in ten years biological design will be as influential as programming. Just like everyone knows that algorithms are running our world, they will be like, "Oh, yeast is used in producing everything from food to medicine to our clothing." Fermentation, as a fabrication process, will be acknowledged as important as programming. We all would have to be fermentation-literate same way we are aspiring to be coding-literate.

37 SELF-DIRECTED CONSTRUCTIONIST COMMUNITIES: INTERVIEW WITH LEAH BUECHLEY

How do you see yourself as a constructionist?

I'm a believer in an approach to learning that prioritizes people's engagement and interest. I am also committed to the notion that very rich learning takes place when people build and construct things.

The systems—like the LilyPad Arduino—that I have built are really oriented around those two principles. Interest and engagement through actively building and creating things.

What is the role of materials in the way you approach your work and your thinking process? How do they take part in your thinking process or your creative process?

I think that there are two aspects to the appeal of different materials. One is a cultural-social appeal, and one is aesthetic and sensual. Culturally and to some extent politically, histories of craft and making are divided by material. There are textiles, there are ceramics, there's woodworking. Each of those material traditions is also a profound cultural tradition. Each has its own cultural history that has determined who did the work and how the work was valued, seen, appreciated, and compensated. There's deep cultural meaning that you tap into when you work with different materials. That is super interesting!

It's also the case that different subcultures, like (say) hip-hop culture or skateboarding culture, will work with different materials. These cultural associations are powerful. By working with different materials, you automatically work in different cultural contexts. A good way to connect to different cultures is by deliberately working with different materials.

The second appeal of materials is more sensual. In my own work as a designer the first place I usually start a new project is being infatuated with a new material. That's the germ of a new project for me. The infatuation is personal and very much affective and aesthetic. Then a project will grow from there. How do I connect some of the material's historical traditions to my expertise in technology and computation? Then, there's another great delight, which is more of an engineering delight, in integrating the material and the technology in a practical way. This is usually a strange and awkward process, but one that presents a lot of technical challenges that are fun to figure out and solve. The engineering challenges are usually intertwined in interesting ways with design and aesthetic challenges. The intersection of technical challenges with design or aesthetic challenges is another theme that is of great interest to me.

What are new developments in that area that excite you? Where do you see this going?

I think there continues to be beautiful new work happening in the area of e-textiles. I've found efforts to make output devices out of textile materials especially intriguing and interesting. One body of work is making electromagnetic constructions out of textiles. Making little motors out of soft parts. So you can, for example, get a magnet to jump around on the surface of a textile, which I find totally enchanting and delightful. Cindy Harnett's work in this area is fantastic (http://harnettlab.org/), as is Irene Posch's. Also, there are a range of wonderful sensors that you can build out of purely textile materials. My former student Hannah Perner-Wilson has done such beautiful work in that space.

More recently, I'm increasingly interested in using computation to generate art and design artifacts. Artifacts are designed with computation and then there's a process that is part fabrication and part handcraft that goes into creating the final object. One of the reasons that this space is especially exciting is that you can make objects that play a rich role in your day-to-day life. You can make clothes and jewelry and, most recently, I've been doing a lot of work in ceramics. These objects don't have embedded electronics, which gives them the freedom to play more obvious roles in your day to day life. They can also be gorgeous and algorithmically rich and complex. There are just lots of elements of that space that are really exciting and compelling. It also seems underexplored in the context of education and learning.

What are some new materials or emerging ways of connecting materials and technology together? Or new ways materials might become part of our thinking processes that you find interesting or exciting for this or the future?

A place to start that is super worthwhile—particularly from the engineering and science side—is to acknowledge the aesthetics of the materials that are worked with—just to acknowledge them as a part of the landscape. This is actually a deep and important thing. Often engineering constraints are tied up in aesthetics, and so thinking about aesthetics can be a great way to come up with new engineering approaches. Conversely, appreciating the aesthetics of engineered things can lead to interesting new design and art. So there's a lot of richness in deliberately acknowledging and thinking about the aesthetics of the domains that you're working in, recognizing them as a really meaningful part of the artifacts you're building, and the larger culture that you're creating as you build a community around electrical engineering or computer science or whatever.

Where do you see possibilities for constructionism to embrace or extend the arts?

The possibilities that I've been thinking about most lately, in computational design, connect really directly back to Logo. So, of course, Logo is a computational design environment. You can certainly think of it that way. One of the things that's really interesting in looking at different communities and practices around computational design is that the tools profoundly impact the aesthetics. What you see now is that there's a community of educators who still do a lot of work with Logo or Logo-inspired languages, such as TurtleArt and Beetle Blocks. What I've seen is that this work usually has a very specific aesthetic. Designs tend to look more or less like designs from the first chapter of the beautiful *Turtle Geometry* book. They are geometric constructions that have a lot of radial symmetry. They're beautiful. But, computational design and computational art coming from other communities have a completely different aesthetic.

In the professional design field right now, computational work is dominated by these lattice-like structures. Most of the work of the wonderful design firm Nervous System, for example, is based around Voronoi diagrams, these mathematical meshes in space. That kind of work is basically totally absent in educator communities, but it needn't be. Actually, tools such as, for example, NetLogo or Star Logo, could be used to create designs that would be more in sync with what's happening in professional art and design worlds. But then there's all sorts of other approaches that we can envision. Machine learning tools can generate completely different kinds of effects!

Another example is of a young woman, Sabine Weiluch (a.k.a. "bleep-track"), who has a wonderful algorithmic project online. She generates and tweets a new drawing of an insect every day. Each unique insect has wings, antennae, a body, and legs. It's a lovely little computational system, but an example that's totally different than the mesh or the geometrical symmetry thing. These are all different flavors of computational design, and only a very small subset of them have been explored in our educational landscapes. You can imagine how different tools could emphasize different aspects of these.

You have been very critical of a lot of things that happen around *Make Magazine* **and the maker movement with respect to the lack of diversity. How do you think the community as a whole responded? Where do you see some new directions that address these concerns? Who is participating in making, and what is being made?**

Let me tackle the first question of how the community has responded. It does feel like there are positive things that are happening that were perhaps somewhat helped along by my critiques. In many quarters, explicit attention is being paid to issues around diversity, and that is a really positive development. Here I wouldn't really take credit for this because other leaders in the computer science education community, like Jan Cuny for instance, have really focused on diversity and equity, which is so important and powerful and wonderful. These are things within the community that really give me hope that we're moving forward in positive ways. I guess I think perhaps the central thing that's so important for everyone to realize is that diversity doesn't happen easily. It doesn't happen automatically, or when it's treated as an afterthought. It really requires deliberate effort. To the extent that that is present in, for example, the CSforALL community, that is awesome. That is something that gives me a lot of hope for progress in these spaces.

One thing that I feel has been a harder sell—because it's harder to grapple with in all sorts of ways—is changing how we think about cultures, materials, and domains. People are really stuck in thinking about STEM in a pretty narrow way. Broadening societal perceptions of practices involving different materials is really powerful and important, but a much harder thing to get any traction on. But there are some positive signs in those directions, too. More people are thinking about culturally responsive or culturally relevant pedagogies. That's a really important path forward that begins to more meaningfully address larger cultural issues that feed into some of these dynamics.

Also, to achieve equity and diversity, I think it's essential that we engage with public schools. This can be a challenge for constructionists—it's a challenge I struggle with myself—but, public school is where truly diverse kids are. We have to engage in that messy, often difficult space.

What do you see as the direction of constructionism in the next ten to twenty years?

I'm worried about the direction computer science education is headed. I'm worried we're likely to make computer science a pretty dreary school subject. We may be missing the opportunity to do something much more interesting and exciting! I feel like it's not that we're lacking for good ideas or good practices. It's that we're lacking a charismatic, well-connected, well-funded advocate. I have a pessimistic view that in ten years we're likely to have pretty boring, entrenched computer science in schools—like drilling kids on "for loops." That's kind of sad. The brilliant, exciting, creative work will continue to happen. I just wish there were better vectors to get it into schools.

On an entirely different front, constructionism wants to be a universal educational philosophy, but it's deeply anchored in mathematics education and computing education. The community should acknowledge that more and grapple with it. For at least the last fifteen years, our society has really emphasized STEM, particularly in the context of education, and that emphasis is profoundly misguided and corrosive. An educational imperative, I think, is to restore honor and status and weight to the humanities. Constructionism can and should play a larger role in education, but it needs to grapple with its own legacy of elevating mathematics and computation and being mostly oblivious to other disciplines.

Finally, I also have some optimism that we're beginning to recover from STEM mania. As we are confronted with the horrific unintended consequences of trying to algorithmitize everything, we're hitting the point where many people, I think, are recognizing that many big problems are social, political, human problems, not really mathematical or computational problems. I think as a society we're just starting to understand that in an important way. Restoring rich engagement with and appreciation for the humanities is maybe the most important thing that needs to happen in education right now.

38 EXAMINING CONSTRUCTIONIST BODIES: INTERVIEW WITH MICHAEL EISENBERG

How do you see yourself as a constructionist?

My wife, Ann, and I together run a lab called the Craft Technology Lab at University of Colorado, Boulder. Our abiding interests have been in mathematics, science, and engineering education, and our way of working is to try and weave together—to integrate—what we see as the best traditions of children's crafts and construction with the affordances and opportunities of new technologies. I'm always very careful to use "technologies" in the plural because, in addition to computers, these new technologies include things like fabrication tools, which include 3D printers, laser cutters, computer-controlled sewing machines, and so forth. However, more generally, I think that all of these technologies operate together in an ecosystem where they support each other. In other words, focusing on what the 3D printer or the microprocessor can do for education is not as helpful, not as fertile, as considering how the microprocessor or 3D printer fit into a larger landscape of technology and considering how these things interact to enable children's activities.

For you, what are the core features or ideas at the heart of constructionism?

There are a lot of lenses through which you can look at constructionism and education more generally, and constructionism in particular. There is a technological lens, which I just touched upon. One of the themes about constructionism, for me, is that it's not reflexively but fundamentally optimistic about the possibilities of technology for children's lives. A recurring theme in my own work is to keep an eye on new technological developments to see whether some of these technologies could, themselves, be put to use as part of this larger landscape to afford kids opportunity for creative activities.

I also think that there's an extremely important anthropological or sociological lens through which to look at this, which is to view children's

construction in the light of what it means to them in the growth of identity. The nature of children's construction is part of this longer process of
autobiography construction. Thinking in those terms guides one to think
about what kinds of things he might want to design or build. How does this
fit into a certain kind of life story for a kid? Not just any old life story, but
a life story that you and they might regard as rich or dignified or creative.

This is all related to the reason that in general I don't talk in terms of
skill acquisition. I don't use that language when I'm talking about education. Rather, I talk in terms of autobiography construction or construction
of a life narrative. It's not that skills are unimportant in that process, they're
just not primary. They're things that emerge simultaneously as part of the
larger process of building a portrait of who you are. A lot of the emphasis
of standard educational rhetoric is we have to provide kids with these skills
so that they will be able to do things they want to do. I don't think that's
true to people's lives.

**In your own work you have focused a lot on crafts and interface design
in the context of technologies. What are things that get you excited
right now? Where do you see this heading?**

I'm really quite interested in technological developments around human
augmentation, sensory extension. I regard this as part of this larger technological landscape of empowering kids to be interesting people and to be creative and expressive. One of the recurring themes of constructionism, from
the earliest days, is the public display of the things that you build—it's making things that will then be shared or displayed. Part of this autobiography
construction for young people (perhaps more so for teenagers and young
adults) is actually constructing one's look. It's not just cosmetic or clothing,
it's also what are my hands able to do? What are my eyes able to do? There
are internal changes that one hones as part of constructing one's narrative.
I think that the technologies that allow people to physically expand their
bodies and senses with new kinds of extensions or prosthetics are going
to increasingly be part of kids' self-definition as time goes on. Our bodies
will be the canvases on which to practice crafts, just as other media are the
canvases for those expressions now.

What do you think are some big issues for constructionism?

I think the advent of the maker movement has been very interesting and
instructive for us in a lot of different ways. Let me circle around to the
answer to your question through a couple of themes that I feel are very
important to the maker movement and questions of what we do in the
future. There are two paradoxes at the heart of science education, I think,

in particular, but also math, engineering education, and education in general.

First, those interested in science education and in design for science education share with me the belief that a growth of interest in science, and in rational thought more generally, is a positive thing in human history. That reason is an extraordinarily powerful and generally benign human tool. However, from the standpoint of design, rational ends do not imply rational means. That is to say, most of the educational rhetoric imagines that there are totally rational reasons for becoming interested in science. We have all these discussions about teaching skills or telling kids that the world needs scientists, that there are all these jobs available for scientists and technologists. We imagine that this will motivate kids to learn science.

That's insane! People become interested in science and math and engineering for the same wonderfully irrational idiosyncratic nutso reasons that they become interested in anything! They become interested in science because they want to impress their boyfriend or girlfriend, or because they want to spend time with an older sibling, or because they admire an uncle or a teacher, or because they're just struck by how awe-inspiring the night sky is, or because they can't take their eyes off of a spider building a web, or ... In other words, they become interested in science out of irrational, personal, idiosyncratic passion. Design has to speak to that. Design has to be done with that in mind. It has to be friendly toward and encouraging of lunatic passion.

The upshot of that is that the vast majority of educational design is, in my view, tangential to most of this outlook. Designs for education often focus on making tools for skill building. But the real crucial things about design are why does somebody become crazy about physics? What can you build to help them answer to themselves and to their friends and relatives who it is they are as they're interested in physics?

The second, and even larger, paradox—one that applies to this political day and age—is that real science education in twenty-first-century America (and maybe in the West more generally) is of necessity a kind of subversive activity. I think the maker movement has, from time to time, realized this and incorporated it into their own rhetoric and style. You see it in phrases like "void your warranty," "open up the machine," and "use screws not nails." There's a certain strain of "don't trust the power structure, make for yourself" in the maker movement. I think that's consistent with the things that I'm trying to say here. In a way I'm touching on a still kind of broader issue, which is that, for the most part, when you hear people talking about the need for science education, ask yourself, what is the image being purveyed of the scientist? Who do they have in mind? You'll find that there are huge discrepancies between historically the kind of people that scientists are and the kind of lives that scientists lead, and the things that the educational rhetoric is promoting.

When people say, "We want children to be scientists," do they really want kids to spend all day in the woods gathering leaves? Do they want them to spend all night looking at the night sky? I think the closest thing to what they have in mind is a sort of scientific entrepreneurialism. They want kids to be like Bill Gates or Mark Zuckerberg. Those aren't scientists, they're businesspeople! People say, "We want programming." In this context programming usually means, "We want people to work for Google, Microsoft, Twitter, Facebook, or maybe found their own business involving computers."

If money is the metric for success, then the vast majority of scientists are failures—because they're not after money. Gregor Mendel, he was a monk! He crossbred peas, he wasn't interested in being a billionaire, he wasn't interested in founding a business, he was just really interested in this stuff. Maybe there's a way to make big money looking at far away galaxies or gathering seashells, but it's not really the narrative reason that people go into these things!

The upshot of all this is that design—what we do as constructionists— has to acknowledge, at least to ourselves, a certain kind of subversive quality to what we do. I want kids to be able to be scientists with all that means. They'll have time; they'll have resources for reflection and meditation; they won't regard themselves as wasting time if they spend all night looking at the stars; and they won't judge themselves according to the metrics that we've come to associate with late-stage capitalism. Real science is mostly incompatible with that value system.

If you're really interested in science education and math education, you're running against the grain. If you don't acknowledge that in your designs, then you're lying to somebody, to your sponsors, to yourself, to your students. I think that the maker movement has unconsciously tapped into this understanding. In much of the maker movement there is this feeling that we're living off the grid. We're not obeying the powers that be. We're a counterculture. There are elements of all those things! It's a technologically optimistic counterculture, which I find lovely.

Where do you see constructionism going in ten or twenty years?

I believe it will start to incorporate a wider range of technologies. I believe it will start to incorporate some of these biological technologies or technologies for extending senses and actuation. I think there are growths of certain technologies that will become beautifully incorporated into the constructionist community as long as the constructionist community does not remain technologically hide-bound. That's the technological answer. Part of the answer to your question, which I can't answer, depends on cultural and political developments. Will constructionism and the maker movement fizzle out? Will it be assimilated into the larger skills building rhetoric of the late-stage capitalism power structure? Will it remain true to a kind of subversive style?

On the other end maybe there will be institutions or structures that will start growing up, which will empower this kind of constructionist narrative. That is, many more independent maker spaces that can grant degrees, new ways of earning academic credit—even PhDs or their equivalent—that are founded more on patient, reflective construction and that aren't terribly expensive, ways of circumventing student debt that allow young people to become scientists and makers. Student debt itself can't be dissociated from this question because students who go into large debt then have their choices constrained after school. They have to go after money because otherwise they'll die or they'll be in ruin. Therefore, they're forced to adopt the value structure of the world around them. They don't have the choice.

Things like ways of circumventing student debt are not irrelevant to your question. The future of constructionism depends on social and cultural structures, infrastructure, institutions, and communities that allow people to move away from the current set of tracks. It might be called living off the grid except that maybe over time the grid will become less all-encompassing and there will be many more ways in which people can do this. That's my hope. The technological side of the question is hard enough to answer, but it's still relatively easier to answer that than the question of how the world is going to allow for a constructionist life to emerge.

CONTRIBUTORS

Konstantin Aal, University of Siegen

Dor Abrahamson, University of California, Berkeley

Edith K. Ackermann, Massachusetts Institute of Technology

Michael Ahmadi, University of Siegen

Emma Anderson, Massachusetts Institute of Technology

Edward Baafi, Modkit

Stephanie Benson, University of Minnesota

Laura Benton, University College London

Matthew Berland, University of Wisconsin, Madison

Marina Umaschi Bers, Tufts University

Paulo Blikstein, Teachers College, Columbia University

Bryan McKinley Jones Brayboy, Arizona State University

Karen Brennan, Harvard University

Leah Buechley, University of New Mexico

Angela Calabrese Barton, Michigan State University

Teresa Casort, Utah State University

David Cavallo, Universidade Federal do Sul da Bahia

Kiera Chase, ConnectEd and University of California, Berkeley

Alison Clark-Wilson, University College London

Sequoia L. Dance, Arizona State University

Joshua A. Danish, Indiana University

Sayamindu Dasgupta, University of Washington

Michael Eisenberg, University of Colorado, Boulder

Noel Enyedy, Vanderbilt University

Deborah A. Fields, Utah State University

Andrea Forte, Drexel University

Brian Gravel, Tufts University

Sara M. Grimes, University of Toronto

Erica R. Halverson, University of Wisconsin, Madison

Idit Harel, Gazelle Consulting Inc.

Nathan Holbert, Teachers College, Columbia University

Celia Hoyles, University College London

Gayithri Jayathirtha, University of Pennsylvania

Raquel Jimenez, Harvard University

Yasmin B. Kafai, University of Pennsylvania

Ivan Kalas, Comenius University in Bratislava

Alan Kay, University of California, Los Angeles

Anna Keune, Indiana University

Susan Klimczak, Learn 2 Teach, Teach 2 Learn

Eric Klopfer, Massachusetts Institute of Technology

Maximilian Krüger, University of Siegen

Tim Kubik, Project ARC

Chronis Kynigos, National and Kapodistrian University of Athens

Breanne K. Litts, Utah State University

Benjamin Mako Hill, University of Washington

Amon D. Millner, Olin College

Andrés Monroy-Hernández, University of Washington

Richard Noss, University College London

Seymour Papert, Massachusetts Institute of Technology

Kylie Peppler, University of California, Irvine

Judy Perry, Massachusetts Institute of Technology

Mitchel Resnick, Massachusetts Institute of Technology

Rebecca Reynolds, Rutgers University

Ricarose Roque, University of Colorado, Boulder

Piers Saunders, University College London

Kristin A. Searle, Utah State University

R. Benjamin Shapiro, University of Colorado, Boulder

Kimberly M. Sheridan, George Mason University

Arnan Sipitakiat, Chiang Mai University

Gary S. Stager, Constructing Modern Knowledge

Gunnar Stevens, University of Siegen

Vanessa Svihla, University of New Mexico

Edna Tan, University of North Carolina at Greensboro

Orkan Telhan, University of Pennsylvania

Naomi Thompson, Indiana University

Nalin Tutiyaphuengprasert, Darunsikkhalai School for Innovative Learning

Anne Weibert, University of Siegen

Uri Wilensky, Northwestern University

Michelle Hoda Wilkerson, University of California, Berkeley

Volker Wulf, University of Siegen

Jianwei Zhang, University at Albany, State University of New York

INDEX

Page numbers followed by *t* indicate a table on the corresponding page.